The Open Boat

www.openboat.com.au

Sydney
WOODEN BOAT
School
www.sydneywoodenboatschool.com.au

Golding's 22 footer Vigilant with everything up, late 1890's. SYDNEY FLYING SQUADRON COLLECTION

The Open Boat

The Origin, Evolution and Construction of the Australian 18-Footer

Ian Hugh Smith

Sydney
WOODEN BOAT
School

Also by the author:
The range of Sydney Wooden Boat School Manuals:
- Traditional Clinker Construction
- WEST System Strip Planking
- Plywood Clinker Construction
- Building the Whiting Skiff
- Build Your Own Stitch and Glue Dinghy

Published by Sydney Wooden Boat School
www.sydneywoodenboatschool.com.au

Second edition with revisions
Copyright Ian Hugh Smith 2017

ISBN: 978-0-6481386-0-0

Design and layout by Tricia Smith

Illustrations and photos not attributed to others are by the author.

All reasonable efforts were taken to obtain permission to use copyright material reproduced in this book, but in some cases copyright could not be traced. The author welcomes information in this regard.

Cover image of *Britannia*, HALL PHOTO, AUTHOR'S COLLECTION.

Contents

Part 1: The Origin and Evolution of the Australian Eighteen Footer 1850-1950

Chapter 1	The Early Days on Sydney Harbour	1
Chapter 2	The Coming of the Centreboarders	13
Chapter 3	The Shape Changes	25
Chapter 4	The Rise of the Eighteen Footer	41
Chapter 5	The Skiffs Win Out	53

Part 2: Construction of a Batten-Seam Eighteen Footer   61

Chapter 6	Designs and Lofting	63
Chapter 7	Moulds and Setting Up	74
Chapter 8	Lining Out	87
Chapter 9	Planking	93
Chapter 10	The Ribs	110
Chapter 11	Stringers and Other Internal Structures	117
Chapter 12	The Deck, Sponsons and Coamings etc.	127
Chapter 13	Masts and Spars	134
Chapter 14	Rigs and Sails	148
Chapter 15	Sailing	166
Bibliography		178
Glossary		179
Appendix I	Restorations (*Yendys, Britannia* and *Mele Bilo II*)	183
Appendix II	The Boatbuilders	190
Appendix III	Towards a Study of the Recording of Heritage Skills	199

Acknowledgements

Bruce Stannard started the whole revival in interest in the history of open boat sailing with his magnificent work Bluewater Bushmen *published in 1981. Margaret Molloy followed on with* Sydney's Flying Sailors, *her 1991 history of the Sydney Flying Squadron. Robin Elliott set the bar high with his book* Galloping Ghosts *in 2012, and made valuable comments on the first draft of this work, as well as providing the basic list of 18 footers incorporated into the Appendix on boatbuilders in this work in this work. Alf Beashel documented details of the boats sailed by the League in his booklet published in 1935 and largely reprinted by Robin Elliott.*

The National Library of Australia's website Trove *has been an indispensable part of my research, making access so much simpler than fiddling with microfiche.*

The staff at the Australian National Maritime Museum were helpful in access to their collections for research, in particular David Payne the Curator of the Australian Register of Historic Vessels. Bill Wright of Norman Wright and Sons generously allowed me access to the Wright family records and original model collection.

Robert Tearne is due the credit for the concept and the setting up of the Australian Historical Sailing Skiff Association and for starting the ball rolling with replica building, ably assisted by the late Graeme Ferguson whose dedication to the history of these boats was outstanding and is already missed. John Winning has been an irreplaceable patron of the historical eighteens movement and a formidable competitor. John 'Steamer' Stanley did invaluable work in collecting images and memorabilia for the Sydney Flying Squadron. Bill Bollard as an early member of the AHSSA collected many boat plans that could otherwise have disappeared, measured many models and redrew many lines plans in a professional style to which I can only aspire. Bill donated all of this to the AHSSA and made it available for this work. Bruce Kerridge supplied his great shots of the replica fleet.

Peter Cowie and Peter S.Cowie allowed me access to their family's extensive collection of photos and memorabilia, invaluable because of the family's connection to most of the important stages of open boat history. Michael and Stephen Prince allowed me to measure and draw up their family's model of Cygnet, *one of the first recognisable 18 footers. The Cross family, descendants of boatbuilder and skipper William Golding, preserved his scrapbooks by donating them at my suggestion to the ANMM. Crew member and mate Matt Balkwell supplied the Balkwell family photos covering several generations. Bob Chapman didn't ever get enough thanks for the time he spent helping build the* Britannia *replica, and for supplying photos of that process. Likewise Cliff Sutton cannot be thanked enough for help building* Britannia *and for making me the best steam generator I ever had.*

Riggers Joe Henderson, Brion Toss, Neville Leishman taught me aspects of traditional rigging. Boatbuilder Rick Wood taught me many of the finer points of traditional boatbuilding, including many things I thought I already knew. Larry Pardey provided a number of insights into wooden boat building during his stay with partner Lin in Sydney in 1991. Former business partner Simon Sadubin shared his research in the same areas I was looking into.

Bill Barnett, Len Heffernan, Ken Minter, Ron Balkwell, Jim O'Rourke, George McGoogan and Ron Robinson provided invaluable input on how it was done in the day.

Brian Gale was a time capsule with his knowledge of 18 footer sailing in the 1930's and '40's as well as being a top old gentleman.

My wife Tricia brought me into the twenty-first century with her knowledge of computers and spent long hours knocking the manuscript, images and drawings into shape. She has been my backer and partner in so many projects over the years.

The main acknowledgment should go to the sailors and boatbuilders of Australia's Open Boats, thousands of them over more than a century who developed the kind of racing we can still enjoy today, and to Mark Foy for shaping its progress in such a significant way. But if I can single out one person to which to dedicate this book it must be Wee Georgie Robinson, the designer, builder and skipper of the Britannia, *who inspired me to build the replica and set me on the path that led to this book.*

Introduction

Almost every Summer Saturday my crew and I rig the mighty Britannia, *a replica of the 1919 eighteen-footer and sail out onto Sydney Harbour to race against between 7 and 10 other replica eighteens. The hulls are wood, the spars (at least on my boat) are wood, they are gaff-rigged and difficult to handle and more difficult to sail well. We sail with no instruments, not even a compass. There's just the wind in your hair, the waves under you and the sun on the back of your neck, and there's nowhere else I'd rather be. And I'm not alone feeling that way, in our boat and other boats going back well over a hundred years. And beyond the immediate feelings there's that intangible feeling of contact with our forbears, doing something as close as we can to the way they did it. I get that feeling also when building a boat. I'll be shaping a piece of timber knowing that I'm doing it in the exact same way that boatbuilders have been doing it, sometimes for centuries. It's like an addiction. I can't stop building boats, and after each race we're already looking forward to the next one.*

For over one hundred years Sydney Harbour has been the venue for racing the class of boat always known as the eighteen footers. For most of this period the eighteens have been the dominant open boat racing class in terms of numbers of people involved and the level of public interest. Brisbane also had an active fleet until recent decades, and to a lesser extent so did Perth in the early days.

Throughout most of this period the eighteens were a relatively unrestricted class, and this has been reflected in the continual evolution of the boats raced, from the beamy wooden sail carriers needing crews of up to 15 hands of the 1900s to the foam, fibreglass and carbon fibre flyers of today crewed by three. But from their earliest emergence in the 1880's and 1890's until the early 1950's the boats were almost invariably built the same way, using batten seam carvel construction. This era was what I have referred to as the Golden Age of 18-footer sailing, the era when it grew to be a popular spectator sport and the exploits of the crews gave rise to a great body of folklore still familiar today to many even beyond the sailing community.

Since the publication of Bruce Stannard's Bluewater Bushmen *in 1981 there has been a revival in interest in the earlier years. Other publications have followed and the Australian Historical Sailing Skiff Association was formed. Everyone who enjoys the Harbour on Saturday from a boat or from any of the numerous viewing points on land is again familiar with the sight of the old-style eighteen-footers.*

But the focus has been on the sailing and on the exploits of the people involved, and not enough attention has been paid to the boats themselves. The boatbuilders were locally famous in their day, but they didn't write down anything about the way the boats were built, and they have been almost forgotten. Only several batten seam eighteen-footers had survived in any shape, mostly by being turned into launches that survived afloat into the 1970's. The story will be told below of how several boats were restored by boatbuilders who had built such boats in their youth or who had been trained by those who had. There was certainly enough knowledge and hard physical evidence around to enable boats to be restored and replicas to be built. Unfortunately many of those involved in the revival of interest began to build replicas using more modern laminated timber methods, and somewhere along the line the batten seam boat was ignored. The youngest shipwrights with any experience of this method are in their forties, and if no new ones are built soon direct experience will be close to disappearing.

Hopefully this book will help to redress this situation, and a set of skills that produced a type of boat construction that spanned more than seven decades will have been documented well enough to enable future generations to appreciate this aspect of their maritime heritage, and anyone that has the dedication and aptitude will be able to experience the thrills of both building and sailing these vessels.

Part 1 was originally intended to be a short historical introduction to the main body of the work, but once research got underway it became apparent that the origin and evolution of the 18-footer was a bigger subject that just an introduction, so it became the first five chapters.

Ian Hugh Smith, December 2016.

July 2017. This is the second edition with minor revisions.

Part 1 : The Origin and Evolution of the Australian Eighteen-Footer 1850-1950

Notes on the Title "The Open Boat"

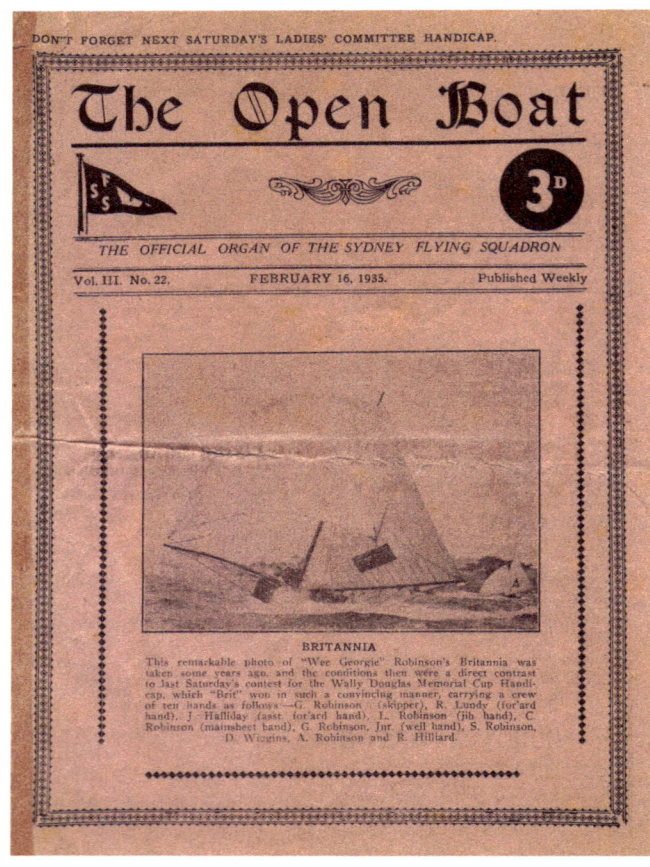

In the middle of the nineteenth century, the term "open boat" simply referred to any boat that was undecked. By the 1870's, boats that had a small deck forward of the mast and narrow side decks and sometimes a narrow stern deck were referred to as "half-deckers", but during the last thirty years of the nineteenth century the term "open boats" was often used to refer to both the completely open boats and to the half-deckers as one group, as opposed to yachts. Weekly and seasonal commentary by journalists after the 1870's used the heading "The Open Boats" to report on all the classes discussed later.

By the turn of the twentieth century, the emerging 18-footer class all had short foredecks and narrow side decks but were always referred to as "open boats". Even the sailing clubs themselves could never agree on any dividing line between "open" and "half-decked". The sixteen and twelve foot skiffs referred to themselves as "the only true open boats" because they never allowed decking.

So as a general classification to cover the types of boats described here, I think the term is fitting. It is also a nod to the title of the weekly programme sold on the ferries following the racing fleet of the Sydney Flying Squadron between 1933 and 1940.

CHAPTER 1

The Early Days on Sydney Harbour

Captain James Cook reported Sydney Harbour without entering as he sailed past in 1770 as a likely harbour, and gave more coverage to Botany Bay a few miles south where he landed, but Captain Arthur Phillip commanding the First Fleet for the establishment of a penal colony in 1788 saw that Sydney Harbour (Port Jackson) was a far superior place for settlement. The lack of suitable agricultural land (and skills!) meant that the colony of New South Wales relied on ship contact with the outside world for survival. For the first twenty-five years of the colony it was actually easier to send a ship around the world to South Africa for food than it was to cross the Blue Mountains forty miles inland. They really were reliant on ships and boats. The early spread of the colony up the Parramatta River (the drowned river valley became Port Jackson about six thousand years ago) and the Hawkesbury River further up the coast, was driven by the need for better agricultural land than could be found around Sydney Harbour. Colonial Office instructions prevented the establishment of a shipbuilding industry, and Governor Phillip was understandably nervous about convicts escaping in stolen boats and ships, but the need for transport up both rivers meant that quite a number of small vessels were built, including 22 registered private vessels by 1804 (Hardie, 1990 p30).

The vessels were naturally modelled on English craft of their day, particularly Naval vessels. Dan Hardie has thoroughly covered the types of vessels built and used (Hardie 1990) but essentially they ranged from small rowing craft through watermen's skiffs with some having provision for sail, through whaleboats which arrived with whaling vessels at a fairly early stage (see below) to ship's longboats and yawls, and on to smacks and lighters and cutters and schooners suitable for offshore work.

By the middle of the nineteenth century Sydney was an established port, with a population of about 40,000 in 1850, expanding to almost 60,000 by the early 1860's largely due to the inland Gold Rush of the 1850's. The large numbers of ships arriving with passengers and goods needed servicing in a number of ways. Wharf expansion was not keeping up with the number of ships that needed to be unloaded and so there was a great demand for lighter-type vessels to transship goods. Watermen's skiffs were numerous to cater for passenger trips between ship and shore. Both these types of vessels were needed as local transport for both people and goods as much of the settlement had expanded along Sydney's extensive waterways and roads were inadequate and sometimes impassable. The colony was exporting very little at this stage, the wool and wheat trades which developed very strongly by the 1880's were still limited in the

1.1 Detail from "East View of Sydney in NSW ca 1809" by John Eyre.   STATE LIBRARY OF NSW

1.2 "Emigrants Leaving the Ship Sydney Cove NSW 1853" by Oswald Brierly.
REX NAN KIVELL COLLECTION, NATIONAL LIBRARY OF AUSTRALIA

1850's. Most ships had to take on ballast for stability when leaving Sydney. A large fleet of registered Ballast Boats supplied the fleet with rocks cut from quarries in various places around the Harbour and up the River (like Ballast Point at Balmain). These were a disparate group of boats ranging from 5 tonners (about 20 feet long) to 25 tonners (about 35 feet long) with the majority falling into the 10-15 ton range (about 24-30 feet). (The tonnage figures are not displacement but a measure of internal capacity). There were licensed wood boats which traveled upriver to cut firewood and deliver it to the city and which were generally similar to the smaller ballast boats, and similar fruit boats for delivering from upriver orchards. A lack of mineral sources of lime for construction led to extensive use of shells, and many of the smaller types of boats (3-5 tons, 20' and under) collected and delivered shells from the nearby coastal estuaries. There were always a few whaling ships in port, some based here and some from Britain but especially the USA, so there was plenty of familiarity with whaleboats and many in use on the Harbour for general transport and official business.

A regular trade was established between Sydney and Broken Bay and the Hawkesbury River, and later with further ports, and along with the large number of working waterfront jobs meant that there was a large body of men familiar with boats and sailing.

All of these boats were rigged for sail as well as oars or sweeps. All would find themselves sometimes sailing in the same direction at the same time as a similar vessel, perhaps a business rival, and inevitably informal races happened.

Regattas

From at least the 1820's on individual skippers would challenge their rivals to a race where each would put up stake money with the winner taking all. These ranged from challenges between rival watermen in rowing skiffs, to ship's captains, local merchants and government officers challenging others to multi-oared gig races.

The news from 'Home' that the Prince Regent had organised a regatta at Cowes in August 1826 led to the first Australian regattas. The first was held on the Derwent River in Van Diemen's Land

(Tasmania) by naval officers, and the next was in Sydney, on Saturday 28 April 1827. Organised by two naval officers, the regatta had three events, two rowing races and a sailing race, with prize money put up by naval officers. Local boat owners were invited to participate. There were six entries in the first rowing race, seven in the second, and nine in the sailing race (Cheater and Debenham 2014). Setting precedents that would be followed right up to the early twentieth century local officials and worthies were invited onto the flagship, including their ladies, a brass band provided entertainment and dancing was almost continuous. Crowds gathered on vantage points at Dawes Point and Macquarie Fort, and the water was crowded with spectator boats. The regatta was favourably commented on in the newspapers.

1.3 Anniversary Regatta 1871. The timber-strewn Quay is now the cafe zone of the Sydney Opera House.   ILLUS. SYDNEY NEWS 18 FEB 1871

Other regattas followed in the 1830's, but not on a particularly regular basis. Not all were widely publicised, but a growing trade in boats, rowing and sailing equipment and bunting and colourful regatta clothing suggests there was a large number of active participants.

The regatta on 26 January 1837 was hastily organised, perhaps due to local politics (Cheater and Debenham 2014) and consisted of two sailing races, a whaleboat pulling race, a gig rowing race and three heats of a watermen's sculling match. It drew large crowds, the weather was fine and the newspapers reported it a huge success, including a mention that the gentlemen on the organising committee intended to make it an annual event. Politics again led to the regatta of 1838, the 50-year jubilee of the colony, being organised late, and comprised only three races, two sailing races for 1st and 2nd-Class boats, and a whaleboat rowing race. It was considered by all a success, and the Governor announced that henceforth Anniversary Day would become a gazetted public holiday. Each year the entries became more numerous and by 1844 ten matches were being staged including 3 sailing races (Cheater and Debenham 2014).

Gentlemen from Balmain, just west of the city across Johnstone's Bay combined to run the first Balmain Regatta in 1849, held on the Bank Holiday of Friday 30 November, St Andrew's Day. Eight matches were held: (*Sydney Morning Herald* Sat 1/12/1849 p.2).

1st. A rowing race for four-oared gigs.
2nd. Sailing Boats not exceeding 13 feet on the keel.
3rd. Sailing Boats not exceeding 16 feet on the keel.
4th. Rowing skiffs, two oars, amateurs.
5th. First class yachts. This was noted as the chief attraction of the day.
6th. Licensed watermen pulling a pair of sculls in skiffs.
7th. Yachts not exceeding 5 tons.
8th. Ballast and Wood boats.

The day was considered so successful that it also became an annual event.

The divisions into classes of sailing boats was purely arbitrary, there was no class of boats specifically built to be 13 feet on the keel, and none of the boats at this time were built specifically to race. There were no sailing clubs as we know them at the time. A short-lived Sydney Yacht Club was formed in 1856, but disappeared, or rather morphed into the Sydney Yacht Squadron and then into the Royal Sydney Yacht Squadron in 1859 which still thrives. It only catered for yachts over 5 tons. The Royal Prince Alfred Yacht Club in 1862 catered for yachts and boats under 5 tons, and the Sydney Amateur Sailing Club was set up in 1872 to cater for open boats and half-deckers. None of these clubs held more than a few races a season until well into the late 1870's and early 1880's. So anyone who wanted to race their boats held private challenges or raced in regattas. Racing every weekend was unheard of.

In addition to the Anniversary and Balmain regattas others were organised in the next decade, including, Pyrmont Regatta and Ryde Regatta in 1849 (both actually just before the Balmain Regatta, but they never became annual). Woolloomooloo Bay Regatta and North Shore Regatta in 1854 both continued for some years. Many others came and went in the 1870's and '80's but only the Anniversary Regatta and the Balmain Regatta were held every year for the rest of the century (and beyond).

Prizes in the Regattas were considerable. Some yacht races offered up to one hundred pounds for the winner in the 1850's and other popular contests such as the whaleboat (rowing) races in the same decade offered up to fifty pounds. The more common figures for the open boat races were between eight and fifteen pounds. At the time, a thirty foot gig could be built for one hundred guineas (one hundred and ten pounds), a small whaleboat-type third-class yacht (18') for twenty-six pounds. A boatbuilder could earn 6-8 shillings per day (one pound sixteen shillings to two pounds eight shillings for a six-day week), so the prizes were a definite encouragement to enter. (Imagine prizes today of 4-6 times a weekly wage!). However, entry fees were also substantial, being anything from 5-10% of the value of the first prize. There was no handicapping for open boats in the middle of the century, so you would have to consider your boat a chance to enter. This resulted in limited fleets and a fairly high turnover of boats from year to year. Boats placed in a regatta (and therefore receiving some prize money) were generally entered in other events, but boats which failed once or more did not often reappear. During a race, boats with no prospect of placing often gave up and went home.

What were these boats in the middle of the nineteenth century?

Yachts

I'm not going to say a lot about yachts because there was always a distinction between yachts and open boats, largely one of social class, even though some of the yachts were only half-decked. Mercantile men and those in the professions sailed yachts, workers sailed open boats. Not wishing to be too Marxist about it, many of these workers were clerks and administrative people who could afford a small open sailing boat or rowing skiff, but could not afford a larger yacht. This remained the case at least until the 1870's when a modified class distinction arose, that of amateurs versus professionals, but more on this later. There was a further distinction between first-class yachts and others, generally divided at the ten ton mark. Some were imported (from England), but most were built locally. There were several builders of yachts including Langford of Millers Point, Holdsworth of Pyrmont (*Eclipse*, pictured), Cuthbert in Sussex Street on Darling Harbour (from 1855), George Green of the North Shore (builder of *Friendship*) and Dan Sheehy of Woolloomooloo Bay. They were mostly carvel-planked on worked (sawn) frames, with full deep hulls and all inside ballast, mostly rigged as gaff cutters,

MR. JAMES MILSON'S OLD YACHT, FRIENDSHIP.

1.4 Friendship and Eclipse
SYDNEY MAIL, 30 JAN 1897.

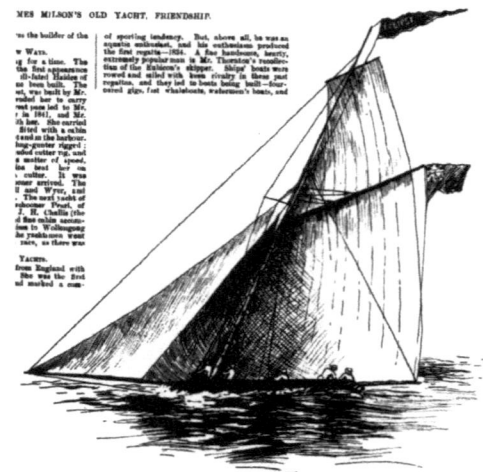

MR ALFRED FAIRFAX'S OLD YACHT, ECLIPSE.

though sliding gunter rigs were popular from about 1830 to the mid 1850's. Suffice it to say that the number of yachts in use on Sydney Harbour was small but growing, with nine first-class yachts competing in the 1837 Anniversary Regatta, seventeen in the 1839 Regatta, and nineteen owners signed the foundation document of the Australian Yacht Squadron (which became the Royal Sydney Yacht Squadron soon afterwards, and is the oldest extant yacht club in Australia) in 1859. But any detailed look at yachts is outside the scope of this work.

1.5 Small open boat of 1850

Other Sailing Boats

The sailing boats that were divided into classes according to keel length in the first regattas were a mixture of private and commercial vessels, and the greatest majority were open or at most half-decked. There was a mixture of clinker and carvel construction, the smaller craft tending to be clinker, the larger being carvel, almost invariably with worked (sawn) frames. Steam bending of frames appears to have not come into regular use in Sydney until at least the 1870's. Boats with a thirteen foot keel would be around fifteen to seventeen feet overall, and those with a sixteen foot keel would be nineteen to twenty-two feet. Rigs varied, with some rigged as gaff cutters or sloops, some lug-rigged, some with sprits'ls and some with sliding gunter rigs. Drawing 1.5 is a reconstruction of the sprit yawl on the right of Brierley's painting and Pickens' lithograph "Emigrants leaving the ship, Sydney Cove 1853" (Image 1.2). The hull shape is on the principle used at the time of the "cod's head and Mackerel tail", that is the bows are full and fairly bluff and the stern narrows, particularly under the waterline. Modern yachts are largely the reverse, with narrow waterlines forward and beamy sections well aft, leading modern commentators to sometimes denigrate the old shapes. However, Colin Mudie the naval architect who designed the Cabot replica *Matthew* pointed out that the cod's head mackerel tail shape is actually that of a hydrodynamic foil which helped in going to windward before the use of centreboards (Mudie, Colin 2001).

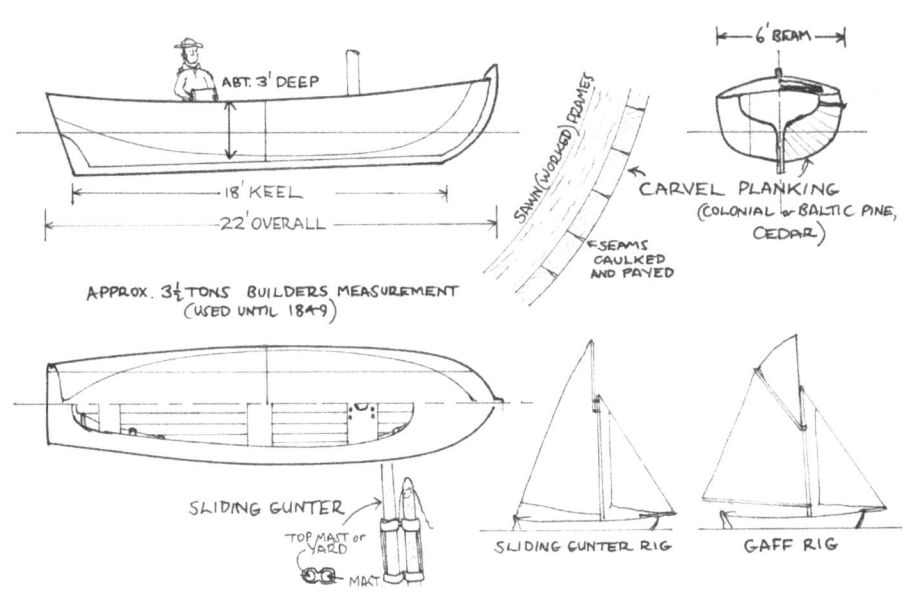

1.6 Small Ballast Boat of 1850

Gigs

Four-oared and bigger gigs were relatively common on the Harbour in the mid-nineteenth century. Most mercantile houses had one for contact with ships not yet berthed on a wharf, and many of the early rowing races on the Harbour were challenge matches between these types of vessels. Some were for private use for wealthier owners with villas around the Harbour to commute to work in the town. They were very much on the British or Royal Navy pattern and were mostly clinker-built, and either imported (most British ships had one on board for the Captain's use and would sometimes be sold in Sydney for the right price) or were built locally by builders such as Langford etc (see section on "The Boatbuilders" below).

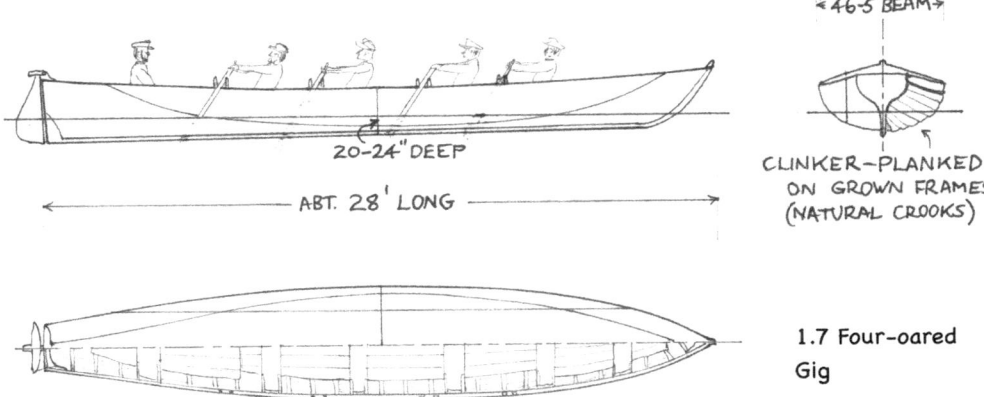

1.7 Four-oared Gig

Watermen's Skiffs

These boats evolved from British rowing wherries and Thames rowing skiffs. Many of the earliest watermen were liberated convicts who had worked as watermen in London before being transported. There was still a huge demand in the middle of the century. They were basically the water taxi of their day, rowing people across the Harbour and to and from moored ships. They were generally from 18-22' and clinker-built. Many of the larger ones were equipped with mast and sails, generally sprits'ls on unstayed masts for longer trips down Harbour or upriver. Some later boats were built batten seam carvel with the top two strakes clinker (see page 9).

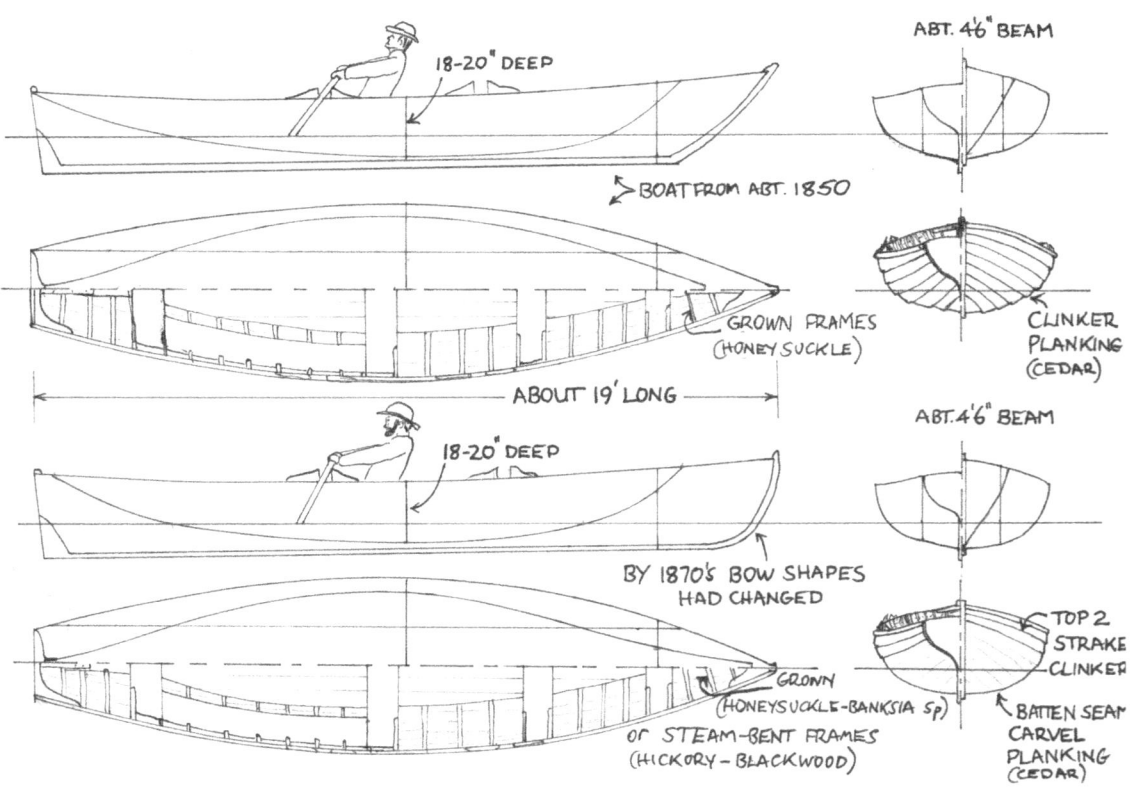

1.8 Watermen's skiffs

1.9 Watermen's skiffs drawn up opposite Customs House, Circular Quay (building still exists). POWERHOUSE MUSEUM

Whaleboats

I'm going to talk a fair bit about whaleboats because they had a huge influence on how Sydney's open boats were constructed, so firstly here's a potted history of whaling in NSW.

Sydneysiders were pretty aware of whaling, whale ships and whaleboats fairly early on in the colony. Of the fleet that brought out another load of convicts in 1791, only three years after the colony was established, 5 ships went whaling into the Pacific (including one named *Britannia*) (Dakin 1938 p8). The first locally-built whaler was the 185 ton brig *King George* by Kable and Underwood in 1805 (Dunbabin 1925 p21). The "fishery" as it was called didn't grow quickly by later standards, but by the 1820's Sydney merchants Jones and Walker had 5 whaling vessels based in Sydney. Another firm, Cooper and Levey set up a base on Bennelong Point (where the Opera House now stands), where the smell of boiling down whale carcasses managed to gather a few complaints. In 1829, a report stated that whaling "this year produced a greater net profit to the colony than have all their brethren competitors of this land" (Dakin 1938 p20). Those competitors were wool and wheat which had not developed anywhere near the level they attained later in the century.

The year 1831 was a big one: Archibald Mosman was granted waterfront land in Great Sirius Cove (which later became Mosman's Bay) and set up a considerable whaling base with facilities for servicing his own and other whaling ships. And that year another locally-built whaling ship the *Australian* was sent out for the sperm fishery and was claimed to be fitted out with all-local equipment. By 1836, there were 39 whalers registered in Sydney. Each ship had at least 5 whaleboats aboard.

Many of the earlier British whaleboats were carvel-planked, some were not even double-enders, but most were. Some were clinker-planked and these gradually supplanted the heavier carvel boats. We have the artist Oswald Brierly to thank for several paintings of clinker whaleboats of the 1840's, as he accompanied entrepreneur Ben Boyd to Twofold Bay on the South Coast of NSW where Boyd competed with Dr Imlay who had arrived

1.10 "Departure of the Whaler Britannia from Sydney Cove 1798" by Thomas Whitcombe. Britannia first visited Sydney transporting convicts in 1791. REX NAN KIVELL COLLECTION, NATIONAL LIBRARY OF AUSTRALIA

earlier in shore-based whaling (which in fact continued there until the twentieth century). There was shore-based whaling also in Hobart, and Hobart became a much bigger port for whale ships than Sydney, but we're not talking about Hobart, are we?

In 1820, Great Britain had 164 ships in the Southern fishery, but only 41 by 1841 (Dakin 1938 p115). Nantucket (US) ships had first appeared in the Pacific in 1791, and by 1844 the American whaling fleet had 675 vessels, most in the Pacific (Dakin 1938 p 69). Many of these ships would call in to Sydney. Records show that considerable business was done in whaleboats. Both British and American whaleboats were imported in the 1840's, and locally-built whaleboats were sent to New Zealand and Hobart. At least two boatbuilding firms concentrated almost exclusively on whaleboat building in the 1840's, Captain Irvine and Thomas Day, and others were built by Underwood, Redgrave, Chapman and others.

1.11 "Whalers off Twofold Bay" by Oswald Brierly 1867. (From a visit in the 1840's). ART GALLERY OF NSW

Whaleboat races were held in most of the regattas already mentioned, in fact at many events they were the prime attraction, judged by both reporters' comments and the amount of prize money offered. At most regattas they had to be bona-fide whaleboats, to the extent that they generally were required to carry their normal whaling equipment including harpoons and tubs with lines. There were generally entries from whaling ships in port including American vessels. This type of race continued into the 1870's even though whaling fleets were in decline, and they were still offering prizes of up to fifty pounds in 1873 at the Balmain Regatta. In the later years, though the boats still had to be bona-fide whaleboats, not many of them were used on whale ships if they were capable of gaining prize money. As early as 1847 one report mentions that several of the whaleboats in that year's Anniversary Regatta had been built "for the express purpose of contending in this race" (Shipping Gazette 30/1/1847). Not all the crews were bona-fide either, as crew lists in the highly contested events in the middle of the nineteenth century contain names like the Mulhalls and the Greens who were local rowing champions.

Whaleboats were used for many purposes other than whaling. They were used by Sydney Harbour pilots as well as those on other coastal estuaries and rivers, by Customs, the Police, by newspapers competing to be the first to report overseas news by intercepting arriving ships offshore, and by mercantile houses taking orders from those ships, particularly the "butcher boats" competing for meat provision orders. Numerous tenders for building whaleboats were called by government agencies and mercantile houses. Explorer Captain Sturt used one on the inland rivers in 1830. Many of these boats were modified slightly from the ones used in whaling, some were longer, up to 35' and many were smaller, down to about 18'. Whaleboats were still being built in Sydney by Luke of Balmain at 25 shillings per foot in 1883.

Batten-seam Whaleboats

Having established that there was plenty of whaleboat building going on, I'd better establish the link with Sydney's open boats. Whaleboat builder James Beetle of New Bedford built the "first combination carvel-planked and lapstrake (clinker), or 'smooth boat' with batten seams in

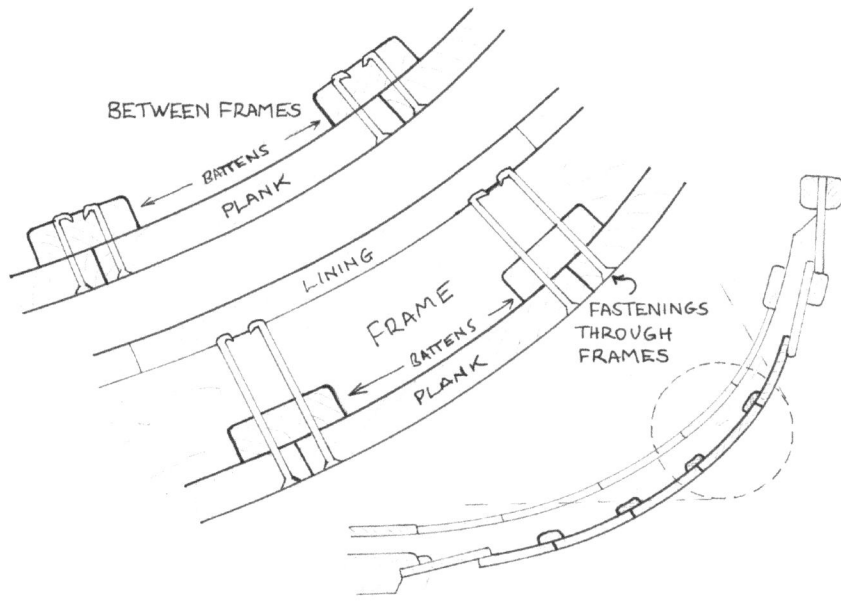

1.12 Batten-seam Whaleboat construction
(after Ansel 2014)

1833" (Ansel 2014 p41). They were seen to be quieter and therefore scared off whales less, and came into general use in American whaleboats by the 1850's. A public tender for a whaleboat for the pilot service in 1857 specifies carvel planking. Oswald Brierly describes a new whaleboat which arrived in Twofold Bay in 1847 as carvel planked and it impressed Brierly and the locals. It was built by Thomas Day in Sydney who built a lot of whaleboats. It cannot be established if this boat had seam battens, but my opinion as a boatbuilder is that it would have done. With the large number of visits from American vessels to Sydney the method would have been familiar to local builders, and I believe that by the middle of the century the requirement for lightness in whaleboats which had led to the preponderance of clinker construction would have to result in any carvel whaleboats built by then most likely having seam battens. A caulked carvel boat without battens has to be heavier than either a battened or a clinker boat, otherwise the caulking could not stay in under the conditions of use of these boats if built equally lightly. The Twofold Bay whalemen began to build their own boats not long after this, and they were batten seam carvel as the earliest photographs show.

The New Bedford method with batten-seam carvel bottom and two clinker planks on the topsides is described in a number of reports in 1877 being utilised to build watermen's skiffs and other types of open boats including a *Newcastle Morning Herald* report (13/11/1877 p.1) that two 22' watermen's skiffs built by Maitland builder J.J.Sheppard had a carvel bottom and clinker topsides in cedar with elm ribs. There are reports and several photos of fishing boats built this way, sometimes with three clinker topside planks. The first actual mention of seam battens in an open boat that I can find is in 1880 (see below). A watermen's skiff offered as first prize in a regatta in 1878 and illustrated in the Sydney Morning Herald (who sponsored it) seems to be smooth bottomed with two clinker top planks.

My considered opinion is that batten-seam carvel boats were known and used in the 1850's and 1860's in whaleboat construction and by at the latest the 1870's in light watermen's skiff construction. As we shall soon see, several classes of racing skiffs (16's, 19's and 22's) evolved out of watermen's skiffs in the 1860's and 1870's and I would suggest that many of these, perhaps the majority were built with seam battens. The heavier fishing boats that evolved into the 24' class during the 1870s (which will also soon be discussed) were quite likely caulked carvel boats as they were of heavier build, were ballasted, and were generally kept afloat. As they became a racing class and boats were built specifically for racing they changed and got lighter, and could possibly have been built with

1.13 Herald Prize skiff 1878 SYDNEY MAIL, 26 JAN 1878

1.14 Earliest photo showing battens, 18-footer Australian 1903 with the legendary Chris Webb and brothers.

seam battens (some were clinker-planked). Ellis's *Dreamland*, a 24-footer of 1880 definitely had them, and is the earliest mention I can find in a 24-footer (Sydney Mail, 6 November 1880, p.892). The new 22-footers which began to be built in the 1880's were even lighter versions of the 24 foot fishing boats and photos show the majority of these were smooth-planked, and I will venture to suggest that most of them would have been fitted with seam battens. More on these and some smaller classes later.

Several of the larger open racing boats were built with clinker planks in Brisbane, but by 1894 it was generally considered that carvel boats were faster. The 22-footer races at the Queensland Yacht Club in Brisbane in 1894 gave clinker boats an advantage in handicapping in general races, but sometimes held separate races for carvel and clinker boats.

By the eighteen-eighties the vast majority of open racing sailing boats of all sizes were carvel planked and I would bet my best lignum vitae caulking mallet that the vast majority of those had seam battens. Boatbuilders often experimented, and there are several references to double planking and diagonal planking but the general thrust is that battened seams had taken over from batten-less caulked seams. Sometimes the method was referred to as ribband carvel.

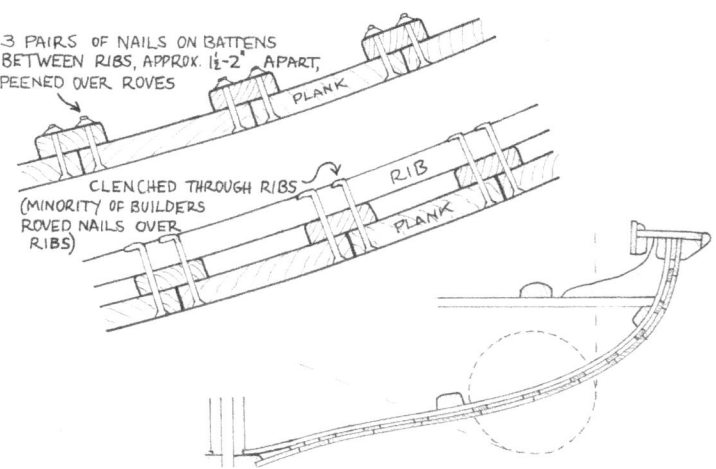

1.15 Britannia Batten-Seam Construction.

Plank Keels

Whaleboat practice also led to the use of plank keels. Early keels were set on edge with the rabbet for planking worked out of the one piece of timber or built up by adding a keel batten on top, as in Drawing 1.17. Whaleboats were built with one-piece plank keels with the sectional horizontal measurement bigger than the vertical measurement, that is, the keel plank is laid on the flat. The first use of this in Open Boats can only be guessed at, but by the time the boats' keels started to show some spring (rocker) it would have been universal. This appears to have started to happen just before the turn of the twentieth century. More on this later.

1.16 Ten-footer replica Republic, under construction 1995, shows seam battens and steam bent ribs.

1.17 Plank Keels

Steam-bent Ribs

The easy accessibility of honeysuckle timber (Banksia Species-see Box) which grew in profusion in a myriad of bent shapes perfectly suitable for small boat frames probably contributed towards the delay in Sydney boatbuilders from taking up steam bending for ribs. Worked ribs of honeysuckle are documented until at least 1874. Imported elm appears to be the first timber used for steam-bent ribs in open boats, it is commonly mentioned from 1876 with the 24-footer *Lottie* until at least 1906 when 18-footer *Scot* was built with elm timbers. The earliest mention of a local timber was hickory (Blackwood) in 1881, and it remained popular for a while until they realised that it was not particularly durable in saltwater, and is not seen after the turn of the 20th century. Ash (Silver Ash) is mentioned in a Queensland 22-footer by Monteith of Kangaroo Point in 1888, and another built by Golding in Sydney in 1891 (*Caneebie*, 22'). Spotted Gum gets its first mention as ribs for open boats in 1881, is common by the late 1890's and is almost universally used by the First World War.

Once all three of these factors were accepted as the norm by the 1890's if not earlier, batten-seam planking, steam-bent ribs and plank keels, Open Boat construction did not change other than in small modifications in boat design, scantlings and a few changes in structural timbers until the early 1950's.

Timbers

Australian Red Cedar (now Toona ciliata, var. australis, formerly just Toona australis) was discovered early on in the colony and was prized for its beauty, light weight and durability and used extensively in furniture, house construction and boat planking. Timber merchants Wilson Bros advertised 70,000 board feet of Cedar available at their Sydney establishment in 1837. By as early as 1851 commentators were noticing the price going up because of scarcity, and by 1871 there were warnings that all the accessible stands had been cut out. It was the timber of choice for boatbuilders who managed to lay their hands on enough cedar for planking right up until the middle of the twentieth century, and it is still available in limited quantities. It was ideal for open boat planking, but was considered too light and weak for yacht planking.

White Honeysuckle (Banksia integrifolia) and Red Honeysuckle (Banksia serrata) are common native trees around Sydney with a hard dense wood and both trunks and branches are crooked and bent. It is no longer used by anyone other than woodturners, but from the early days of the colony it was extensively used in worked framing of boats and small ships, utilizing its natural bends. Worked Honeysuckle was used for frames up until at least the 1870's. In 1833 land at Bexley, 9 miles southwest of Sydney (now an inner suburb) was advertised for sale with Honeysuckle for ship and boat-building as a selling point. Steam-bent rib timber didn't supplant worked timbers until the 1870's.

Tea-tree (Melaleuca quinquenervia) is a common tree in coastal areas around Sydney and like the Banksia species grows large and crooked. It appears that Banksia was the crook timber of choice because the parts used were all above ground, but suitably large trees began to get scarce and Tea-tree began to be utilized. The bigger crooks of Tea-tree need to be cut out of the buttress roots and therefore involve considerably more work.

Native Hickory (Blackwood- Acacia melanoxylon) was the first local timber used in steam-bent ribs from about the 1880's, as it bent easily. Unfortunately it is not particularly durable in the marine environment, so many boatbuilders began to use imported English and American Elm after about 1875 and by the turn of the 20th century, Spotted Gum. Silver Ash (Flindersia schottiana) is first mentioned as a rib timber in 1888, but Spotted Gum dominated as a rib timber in the early 20th century, until Ash came back as boats got lighter in the 1930's.

Sydney Blue Gum (Eucalyptus saligna) was one of the most common forest trees around Sydney and was used for keels, stringers and anywhere strength was needed. It began to be supplanted by Spotted Gum early in the twentieth century.

Spotted Gum (Corymba maculata, formerly Eucalyptus maculata). It took a while for Spotted Gum to catch on, but once it did around the turn of the century it became the rib timber of choice well into the twentieth century, as well as the first choice for longitudinal strength members such as keels and stringers.

Riga Spruce (Pinus sylvestris) was imported into Sydney for masts and spars from at least as early as 1842, when an advert appears for Danzig spars for sale at Henry Moore's wharf. No suitable local timber could be found. New Zealand Kauri (Agathis australis) was imported for spars and other uses at least as early as 1859, and Oregon Pine (Douglas Fir, Pseudotsuga menziesii) from the US and Canada from about the same time, the clearer grades of which are ideal spar timber.

Bunya Pine (Araucaria bidwillii) was used in Queensland for spars from the late 19th Century but its cutting was restricted in a rare show of concern for the indigenous peoples as they used the nuts produced by the tree. It was used quite frequently at least until the 1930's.

It is worth noting that from an early in the nineteenth century it was noticed that iron-fastened vessels deteriorated faster in the local climate, and in the middle decades of the century advertisements of boats for sale take care to mention that they are copper-fastened, and this appears to have become almost universal. They are also often advertised as coppered, that is the underwater section is covered with sheet copper for anti-fouling purposes. The latter was not universal, there is mention of most 24' fishing boats having their bottoms tarred.

CHAPTER 2

The Coming of the Centreboarders

The Centreboard Controversy

The 1850's were a period of rapid change in the colony in many ways. The Gold Rush resulted in a booming economy and rapid population growth, increasing wealth, only restricted by the difficulty of finding people to work in normal jobs. In 1851 yacht design had been revolutionised by the schooner America's win in England. The older bluff bows of ship's longboats and their derivatives, and jolly boats were considered old-fashioned and new boats were often described as clippers by which they meant narrower and finer-bowed. Even the wherries and watermen's skiffs and gigs which had always been finer forward became even more so. But the biggest event that had a huge and lasting impact on open boat racing in Sydney was the arrival of the centreboarders.

Pedants argue a lot about who invented the centreboard as it was used in different versions in many cultures around the world for centuries. Sydneysiders in the 1850's with a bit of historical knowledge would have known of the "sliding keels" developed by the British Admiralty and used in the *Lady Nelson*, a government exploration vessel in the early nineteenth century, but it is clear that the first use of the centreboard as we know it today in small open boats was developed by boatbuilders and fishermen on the east coast of the United States and was common there by the 1850's.

Discovering how the first centreboarders arrived in Sydney was a bit of a detective story. In Stephensen's history of the RSYS (Stephensen 1962) and Dan Hardie (1990) there were references to the first centreboarder *Presto* arriving from England in 1855. Hardie repeats Stephensen's claim that *Presto* was built with canvas stretched over a frame, curragh style, but I cannot find any original reference along those lines, and notes published when it was for sale later described it as planked with Larch on English Oak frames. Hardie suggests that its design was influenced by the Catboat *Una*, built by Robert Fish of Bayonne New Jersey and imported into England in 1853, which Dixon Kemp (Kemp 1895) claims spawned numerous copies in the Solent, the chief yachting area of England. I assumed that *Presto* was probably a copy of *Una*. However, *Una* was cat-rigged, that is a single mainsail on a mast stepped well forward in the bows of the boat, and all the Solent boats copied this (to this day cat-rig is referred to as Una-rig in the UK), and reports of *Presto* talked about its jib (and yard tops'l and squares'l). Further research revealed that *Presto* was imported into Sydney from Liverpool, not the Solent, and it was discovered that another boat built by Robert Fish of New Jersey, the *Truant* (2 ½ or 3 ½ tons, 20 foot waterline and 1'2" draught) was sent to Liverpool in the same

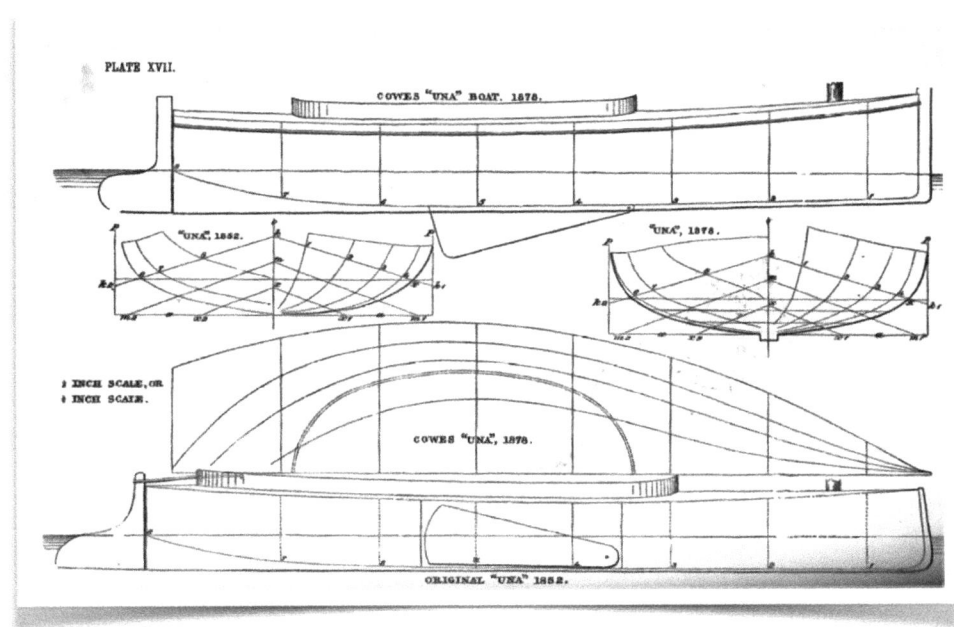

2.1 **Lines of Una.** DIXON KEMP: A MANUAL OF YACHT AND BOAT SAILING 1895 P325

2.2 Truant
DIXON KEMP: MANUAL OF YACHT AND BOAT SAILING, 1895 P265

year, 1853, or possibly in 1852, by Robert Grinnell, an American with shipping interests in Liverpool. It raced on the Mersey (Liverpool) and won most of its races. As often happens, the successful boat was copied. Phillip Kelly of Birkenhead (on the Mersey opposite Liverpool) built *Presto* (variously rated at 5 ½ to 9 tons, a bigger boat than *Truant*) for Mr A. Bower of the Birkenhead Model Yacht Club (which raced small crewed yachts, as well as models). It raced successfully on the Mersey, the Thames, Dublin, Cork and Windermere, all apparently in the northern season of 1853, beating *Truant* and another Fish and Morton boat that had arrived in Liverpool, the *Stranger*. It was purchased by Sydney businessman Sydney C. Burt, presumably while on business in Liverpool and arrived in Sydney about March 1854. Hugely chuffed about tracking this down, I discussed it with Simon Sadubin, a boatbuilding colleague and fellow researcher and he revealed that he had already found all this out! It also appears that another English centreboarder, coincidently named *Truant* of 3-4 tons was imported into Sydney by George F. Wright in April 1854 just after

Presto but came last in the Balmain Regatta of November 1854 (in which *Presto* is second) and is not heard of again.

Presto made its debut on Sydney Harbour on 3 April 1854 in a challenge match with the local yacht *Frolic* for a stake of fifty pounds a side, which *Presto* won by five minutes. In the Balmain Regatta of November 1854 *Presto* came second in the "All Yachts" race (to *Eclipse*, a much larger yacht, *Frolic* third), but capsized in the Anniversary Regatta of January 1855. Burt must have got a fright and sold *Presto* in February or March 1855 and imported a deep keel yacht in 1857. Meanwhile back in Liverpool, Mr Bower had got Kelly to build him another centreboarder, the *Challenge,* 7 ½ or 8 tons, 27'4" on the keel, 9' beam, yellow pine on oak, with bigger sails than *Presto*. It was reported to have some "extraordinary performances on the River Mersey" in the 1854 season. Bower must have liked the price he got for *Presto* because after only one season he sent *Challenge* out to Sydney to be sold on spec, and it arrived in March 1855 and was sold to T.J.Dean. *Challenge* won the All Yachts over 3 tons race at the Anniversary Regatta in 1856, beating *Presto,* which had been sold again and lengthened by ten feet at Holdsworth's yard which seemed to ruin its racing qualities.

When you're on a good thing, stick to it thought A.Bower in Liverpool and had Phillip Kelly build him another one in 1855. *Spray* was also about 8 tons, planked in yellow pine on oak. He kept this one for two seasons before sending it to Sydney where it arrived in early January 1857 and was bought by the same T.J.Dean who owned *Challenge*. Other owners commissioned local boatbuilders to copy them, and *White Squall, Scud,* and *Sylph* had appeared by 1858-9. Bower did it for a fourth time with Kelly, this time the *Charm*, also built of yellow pine on oak and about 8 tons, but with more sail area than the other three. It arrived at the end of December 1858 and was purchased by the Croft brothers for one hundred and fifty pounds.

2.3 Original Builders model of Truant. Sotheby's New York sold this in 2009 for $22,500, so provenance must have been good.

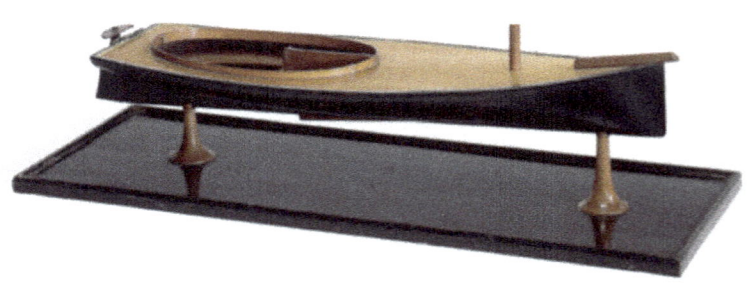

It first raced in the Anniversary Regatta a few weeks later and came second to *Challenge*. In 1859 *Charm* won the Balmain Regatta race for yachts with centreboards fixed. Wait a minute, centreboards fixed!? What's that all about?

As almost invariably happens in sailing, whenever a new boat appears that is different to most of the boats currently sailing, and it wins, the other owners get upset. That is exactly what happened with *Presto* and her sisters. They were called freaks, were deemed unseaworthy (well they did capsize and sink, didn't they?), and though they didn't actually use the term, it was hinted that they were un-British. They were accused of being only capable of racing in protected waters and not being capable of cruising and all those other things that had trained our hardy young men to be seamen who could be useful to the Empire!

So the first reaction was to ban them. It took several seasons for the resentment to build up. The recently formed Sydney Yacht Club (which soon became the Royal Sydney Yacht Squadron) was split between centreboard owners and deep keel owners. It almost broke up when the deep keelers threatened to leave in November 1857, but their tactic seems to have worked because the Club rules were changed to prohibit centreboard boats. It may have helped them that S.C. Burt, the man who imported *Presto* changed sides as he had imported *Surprise*, an English deep-keeler in 1857, and T.J. Dean who owned both *Challenge* and *Spray*, for some time simultaneously, bought *Mischief*, a deep keeler while retaining both of the others and so had a foot in each camp. The same owners kicked up when the January 1858 Anniversary Regatta committee were going to allow centreboard yachts in the first-class yacht race, so they dropped the lip and held a private race on the same day in the same waters. This did the trick, and in the 1859 Anniversary Regatta there were separate races for centreboard yachts and deep keel yachts. In the Balmain Regatta centreboards were allowed until the 1857 event where they were excluded entirely, and again in 1858. In 1859 centreboard yachts were allowed but as noted before, they had to have their centreboards fixed. Only two of each type turned up, and as it was still won by *Charm* they were banned for the next few years.

The battle raged for almost two decades, alternately swinging either way. In the Balmain Regatta, for example: 1864-67 separate races for with and without; 1869-74 fins to be fixed, and not until 1875, 21 years after the arrival of *Presto* were they allowed to lift their fins. By the late 1860's, the original centreboard yachts were not appearing very often, and the rules mostly applied to all the other classes of boats that now had centreboards. We have to remember that *Presto* and all of the others were considered as yachts: they were decked, apart from an open cockpit, were ballasted and mostly coppered and kept afloat. They were referred to as "skimming dishes" but they were only light compared to the deep keelers of the day. But the usefulness of the centreboard was not lost on owners and builders of smaller boats. They also wouldn't have missed that American whaleboats with centreboards were beginning to appear in Sydney by 1855. The first race programme to mention centreboards on smaller boats was the North Shore Regatta on the Queen's Birthday holiday on 24 May 1858. A race was held for centreboard dinghies, and three boats fronted. Mind you, the programme also had no less than four other races for open boats without centreboards so there were plainly far more boats without than with at this point. The 1859 Anniversary Regatta had four entries for a centreboard dinghy race, *Daring*, *Meteor*, *Tom Bowling* and *Surprise*. There was still some resistance from organisers: the committees of the 1858 Balmain Regatta and the Hunters Hill Amateur Regatta refused to allow races for centreboard dinghies. The owners staged a private race on the same day in the same waters.

It took a while, but eventually numbers of centreboard dinghies and skiffs reached critical mass and by 1864 most regattas had started holding separate races for open boats with centreboards and those without, but in the 1865 Balmain Regatta the race for open boats not greater than 22' with fins and centreboards excluded was still considered the feature of the day, there was a considerable amount of betting, the fleet was numerous, and at least one boat was brand new. But by 1870 there were no longer separate races, although fins and centreboards had to be fixed. By 1874-5 boats were able to lift their fins, and they just don't rate a mention after that. It is significant that this period coincided with the emerging development of distinct classes of skiffs determined by length, and the development of a class of centreboard fishing boats, both of which had a huge impact on the evolution of the open boat.

The Arrival of the Skiffs

It's not like they turned up one day with trumpets or anything but between 1870 and 1875 several different classes of skiffs started to emerge. Watermen had been sailing their skiffs for many years, most commonly under un-stayed sprits'ls, and races were held for them from at least 1853 on. They were not allowed centreboards until the mid-1860's as noted, and sprits'ls were still in use on some boats at least until 1864. The skiffs were not ballasted.

Until 1864, regatta programmes had classifications for sailing skiffs from twenty-one to twenty-three feet. Twenty-two feet, or just under must have been a common size because that was the classification that started to emerge by 1864. Regatta programmes had stopped classifying boats by keel length and substituting overall length by 1859, and this applied to boats with centreboards and without. By 1873, rules had been developed that in addition to not being over 22', skiffs had to be no more than 5' beam and no more than 20" deep. This became set, not coincidently at the same time as unrestricted use of centreboards was allowed. At some indeterminate time in the late 1860's and early 1870's the majority of skiffs began carrying gaff rigs with jibs set on bumpkins (see Chapter 13 for discussion on terminology of what many would call a bowsprit), and most carried tops'ls and squares'ls as well. Boats were built specifically for racing, not for commercial use.

2.4 19 Foot Skiff at Balmain Regatta 1878.
ILLUSTRATED SYDNEY NEWS, 30 NOV 1878, P9

Most of these were varnished inside and out rather than painted (many commercial skiffs were at least partly varnished but most were painted). There would have been both clinker and carvel-planked boats, but as discussed before, I suggest that the majority would have been batten-seam carvel planked.

Not far behind the 22's came the 19-footers which emerged as a class in 1873, with identical restrictions on beam (5') and depth (20"). The sixteen-footers were not far behind, with rules which started in 1875 as not over 16' length, 4'8" beam and 20" depth, changed only the next year to maximum 5' beam, the same as the larger skiffs, and these rules were used until the class faded by the end of the century. Both the nineteens and the sixteens carried gaff mains, jibs, tops'ls and squares'ls. All three classes had rounded hulls in section, maximum beam amidships and relatively narrow tucks, described at the time as being "peg-

2.5 Reconstruction of 19' skiff around 1880

2.6 Mr Hyam's Old 22ft Champion Skiff, Ettie.
SYDNEY MAIL, 30 JAN 1897 P230

topped" in section at the tuck. I can find no evidence of any decking at this point. The illustration 2.4 shows what appears to be a 19-footer in the Balmain Regatta of 1878 (it looks a bit big for a 16, and there were no races for 22's that year).

Owners were sometimes still men with professional watermen's businesses, rather than single boat watermen, but a number of wealthy men began to have boats built using professional crews to sail them. S.H. Hyam was one of these. He had quite a stable, with multiple boats in several classes. In 1875, Joe Donnelly, a competitive rower and builder of rowing skiffs told Hyam that he could build him the fastest 19 and 22' boats using some new ideas that he had. Hyam decided on an experiment, and ordered one of each from Donnelly, but also ordered one of each from Reynolds, one of the leading boatbuilders of the time (to whom Donnelly had been apprenticed some years before). Reynolds' boats were of the old type, with some rise in the floors and a narrow peg-top tuck, Donnelly's were flatter in the floors and carried the beam well aft to a broad tuck. Local wags termed the 19-footer *Florrie* "the flat iron". Hyam engaged four of the best professional skippers to steer them, Montgomery, Ellis, Colebrook and Fletcher. While there was not much to choose between the two nineteen-footers, Donnelly's 22-footer *Ettie* was said to be the fastest twenty-two footer in the fleet. She won the Balmain Regatta race on debut in 1875. What happened after that is a bit of a mystery. In spite of reports in later years that suggested *Ettie* was unbeatable, I can find one reference to her being beaten, and no further races in which she won after the Balmain Regatta of 1875. Perhaps there were unreported private matches. An advertisement on 12 January 1877 has the racing sails of the *Ettie* being sold, and the boat was apparently sold to Brisbane as a pleasure skiff. In fact after the Anniversary Regatta of 1876, where *Ettie* came second, no regattas appear to have programmed races for 22' skiffs! Either as a cause or result of this, S.J.Hyam lost interest in the twenty-two foot skiffs and had Donnelly build him several twenty-four foot fishing boats for racing, about which more shortly.

So the 22 foot skiffs disappeared after just a few years in the limelight. The 19 foot skiffs were considered the "boats of next season" in 1878 with several new boats in build by Donnelly and Ellis, and they continued for a few more years, fading out after 1884 when they were considered "out of fashion" by a commentator at their last appearance at the Anniversary Regatta of that year. Commentators just a few years later considered the 19's died out because of one boat getting all of the prize money, the boat being Ellis's *Desdemona*. The 16 foot skiffs however went from strength to strength, building up large fleets and only fading out in the late 1890's (although they were revived under different rules in the early 1900's, more on this later).

All of the above classes sailed under similar large gaff rigs with booms that extended well beyond the tuck, with single jibs on long bumpkins which were sprung into a curve to bring the jib tack lower, tops'ls, and extras like ballooners and squares'ls. The only ballast was a numerous crew of active hands. These rigs continued on all the open boat classes with only minor changes until the conversion to Bermudan rigs in the early 1950's.

> **Skiffs and Dingies**
>
> *Not only does spelling change over time (the modern spelling of "dinghy" only dates from the mid-20th century), but the meaning of the words does too. In the early 19th century, "skiff" referred to any light weight, generally narrow rowing boat including some that could sail. Whaleboats were occasionally referred to as skiffs. The distinction between skiffs and dingies was a grey area, there are occasional references to "skiff dingies". By the 1870's, "skiffs" clearly referred to the narrower, more shallow and lighter type, which could still be up to 22' long, and "dingies" to the beamier type of rowing craft. There were both sailing dingies and sailing skiffs also by this time. Regatta classifications for racing had skiffs of various lengths limited to 5' beam and 20" depth. The racing skiff classes retained this restriction until they died out in the last decades of the 19th century. The unrestricted classes got more and more beamy (see below). The development of the Port Jackson Skiff Club's fleet of restricted skiffs after 1901 (see below) led to a change in language, ie when one referred to the "skiffs" one was referring to the 16-footers, and all other open boat racing classes were referred to either as dingies or just boats, or just by their class length, ie 18-footers. Numerous attempts by some boatbuilders to build narrower 18-footers in the early 20th century had reporters talking about their "skiff lines" or the "skiff principle", which basically meant narrow and shallow. The language changed again in the 1920's when the 16-foot skiffs abandoned the built heel under the tuck, and the absence of a heel became one of the distinguishing concepts of a "skiff". When the eighteens at the League were built like skiffs after 1932, they were occasionally referred to as skiffs, but generally still just as 18-footers until after the 1950's. When the Australian Historical Sailing Skiff Association was set up in the early 1990's this latter meaning of "skiff" was the one understood by the older blokes who had sailed before 1950, and there was much angst and differing opinions as to whether to put the term "skiff" into the Association title. They came to the conclusion that seeing as how the eighteens had been referred to as skiffs for decades, they might as well use it. Language changes, get over it.*

The 24 Foot Fishing Boats

Regattas included races for fishing boats from as least as early as 1856 to 1880. The rules changed regularly, sometimes they were for bona-fide fishing boats, sailed by professional fishermen, sometimes without such stipulation and they raced against other open boats, and length classification varied greatly, from not greater than 18' on the keel in 1856 to 24' overall and under by the 1870's, and the majority of entrants were around 21-24' overall. They were capable of going offshore in reasonable weather. Many times fishermen were allowed to row as well as sail. Rigs were often sprits'ls but some were gaff-rigged. A number of private men began to see this type as an ideal pleasure boat, and by the early 1870's a class of boat began to emerge that were referred to as fishing boats but were owned by amateurs and used for private fishing and other pleasure pursuits such as occasional duck-shooting, as well as some racing. They were between twenty-two and twenty-four feet long, half-decked, gaff-rigged with jibs on short bumpkins (although *Sea Breeze* had a sprit-rigged main as late as 1874) fitted with centreboards, lined and fitted out with lockers, with lead or iron ballast secured beneath a sole or "ballast deck", painted (usually white with a blue gun'l stripe), with bottoms tarred and kept on moorings. They became quite numerous, with fleets of up to about a dozen in the regattas of the early 1870's, sometimes racing against the professional fishermen. There was *Kingfisher* (Gardiner), *Wyvern* (Yates), sisterships *Coryphene* and *Adelphi* (Langford), *Sea Breeze* (Geo. Barnet), *Sea Spray, Firefly, Bronte* (Reynolds 1877), *Stormy Petrel, Ripple,*(Langford 1875) *Zingara, Young Jim, Leisure Hour, Young Sam, Big Berry* (Donnelly), *Sea Belle, Young Charlie, After Dark, United Friends, Sylph, Two Brothers, Florence, Sylvia*(Gardiner 1875), *Eudora, Native Rose, Hope, Star of Hope, Constance* and *Endeavour* (at least some of these boats were used by professional fishermen at some stage). Many of these boats were the same boats of the owners that formed the Sydney Amateur Sailing Club in 1872, partly because the established clubs, the RSYS and the RPAYC catered only for larger craft, and partly because those fishermen were, well, professionals (more on the professional-amateur divide later). As

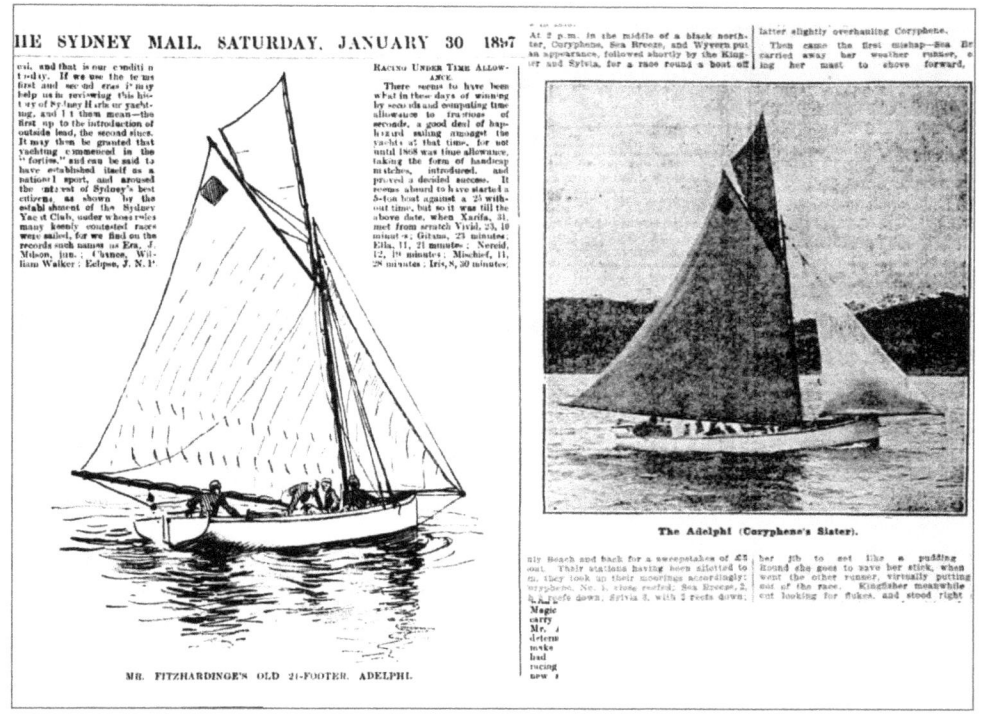

2.7 Photo and drawings of 24' Fishing Boat Adelphi

These new boats began to dominate the racing. They were lighter, with newer sails and gear, maximised for racing, and were crewed by professionals. And for all of these reasons most of the owners of the older boats such as *Kingfisher*, *Sea Breeze*, *Wyvern*, and *Sea Spray* stopped racing against them after 1877. Some boats were sold to Botany Bay just down the coast. Prejudices against purely racing boats that were not used for other pleasure pursuits were expressed, but their overriding concern was the use of professional skippers, such as George Montgomery, Tom Colebrook and others both because of the cost involved for owners and because the owners themselves wanted to steer their boats and would largely have been outclassed by the professionals. The older boats continued to race for some years with the Sydney Amateur Sailing Club, and even appeared in regattas but in separate races under SASC rules, but these races did not generate the public interest and therefore the greater prize money, as well as the gambling that stayed attached to the Open 24's with

well as the SASC holding a few races per season, there were many private challenges, several of which have gone into legend such as the race between the *Sea Breeze* and the *Kingfisher* in January 1874 in a heavy southerly offshore, and that between *Kingfisher* and *Sea Spray* in a strong westerly in 1875. There was a considerable amount of gambling on both private and regatta matches.

In 1876, S.H.Hyam had Donnelly build him a twenty-four footer, the *Lottie*. She was varnished, with a gold stripe, and clearly set up just for racing, but still carried ballast. *Lizzie* was built about the same time by Langford and was similarly varnished and intended only for racing but was lined and had lockers fitted. *Lottie* had her debut at the Balmain Regatta in late 1876 and was leading when the race was abandoned.

On 18 January 1877 *Lottie* raced *Kingfisher* over the Manly course and won. *Lottie* beat *Lizzie* in the Anniversary Regatta in January 1877, but Hyam had already sold her by then to Mr Moodie, and Donnelly was building him another called *Carlotta*.

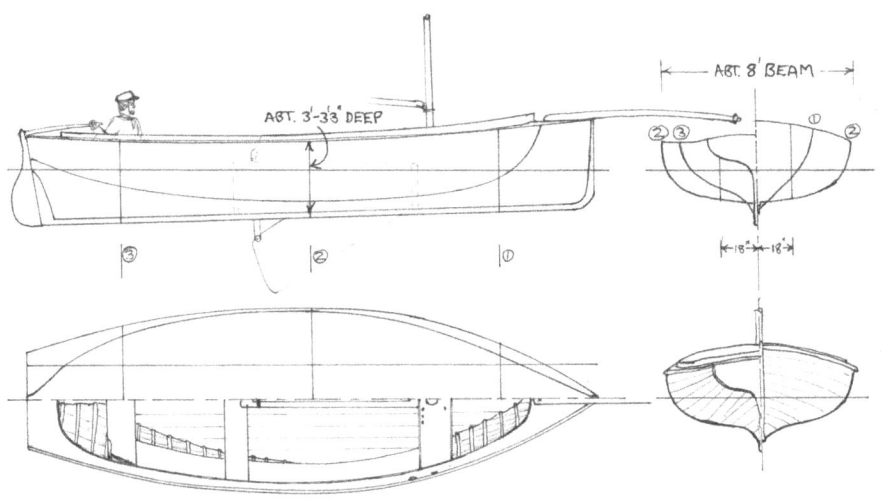

2.8 Reconstruction of 24' Fishing Boat of 1875

professional crews. At the end of the 1880-81 season the Sydney Mail's sailing columnist "Starfish" commented that "the 24' open boats always create the greatest amount of interest". Several new boats appeared, *Deronda* (Ellis 1878), *Victor* (Donnelly 1879) and *Dreamland* (Ellis 1880).

But in the mid 1880's things began to slow down. The Town and Country Journal's sailing columnist "Timon" commented in 1884 that the 24-

American Sandbaggers
Did they influence Aussie Open Boats?

The Sandbaggers were a type of boat that evolved on the waterways around New York in the 1860's and '70's. So-called because they used sandbags for ballast, shifting them to the weather deck on each tack, they were shallow and beamy centreboarders that carried huge spreads of sail in races with largely working-class crews and generally involved gambling. Sound familiar? Such similarities with Australian Open Boats make it tempting to assume there was a direct influence. However, although there are some quite close correlations between hull shapes, particularly aft of centre, forward sections of the sandbaggers are quite different. The centreboard undeniably came from American-influenced boats, but those boats were not yet sandbaggers which did not develop as a racing class until the 1860's. And as we have just seen, it took more than twenty years for centreboards to be completely accepted in Sydney, and as we shall shortly see, the boats that evolved to use centreboards here in the 1870's evolved quite clearly from pre-existing local types, the watermen's skiffs and the fishing boats. So the similarities are more due to separate evolutionary strains evolving from a common ancestor in separated geographical areas but similar evolutionary demands, i.e. all-out racing. Like humans- we didn't evolve from chimpanzees but we both evolved separately from a common ancestor.

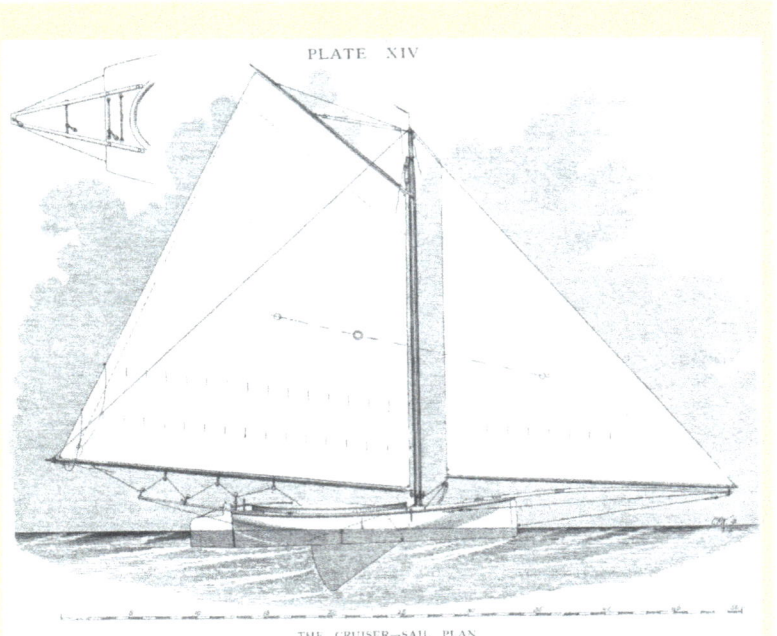

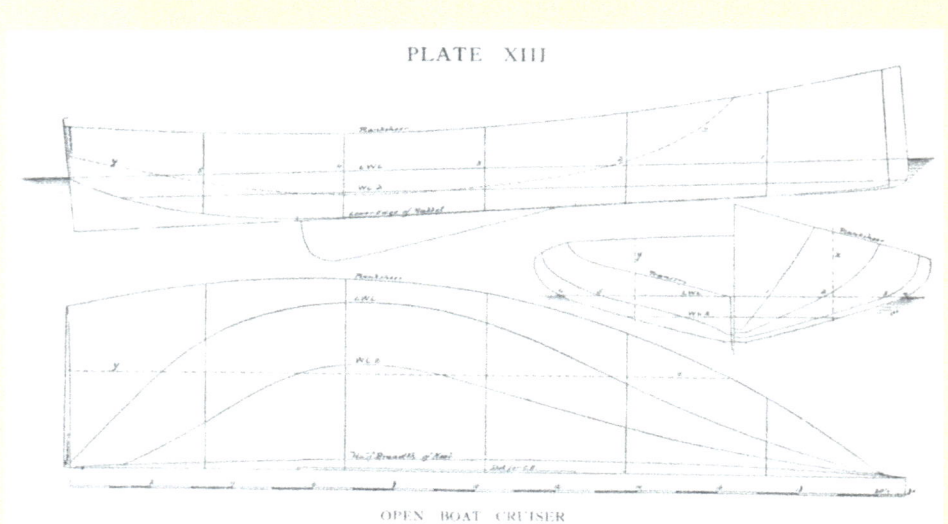

C.P KUNHARDT: SMALL YACHTS THEIR DESIGN AND CONSTRUCTION 1885

footer races "used to be the Melbourne Cup of sailing, but now there is little interest". One part of the problem commented on at the time was the retirement from sailing of S.H.Hyam through pressure of business and a political career, as Sol Hyam had campaigned and maintained a large racing fleet and was a patron to many professional skippers as well as boatbuilders. Another part of the problem was that there were relatively few races in which professionals could enter with 24-footers, so prize money declined, gambling declined and so did public interest. I can find only one 24-footer built between 1881 and 1887 when things began to pick up again. Amateurs had a brief period of supremacy in the 1880's that held back the growth of the sport for some time.

> *As mentioned, the early 24-footers had several races offshore, and when cruising often went between the Harbour and Botany Bay and Pittwater and even further. One boat was reported as having cruised to Jervis Bay about one hundred nautical miles down the coast. None appear to have got into too much trouble. But at least one, Kingfisher did capsize in the Harbour. It sank, being loaded with ballast but was raised and won its race the next day. Once the boats got beamier, shallower and with bigger rigs after the late 1880's, they generally confined themselves to the Harbour.*

Amateurs versus Professionals

The concept of who was an amateur and who a professional grew out of the British upper classes wishing to keep themselves quarantined from the lower orders. Gentlemen would follow their pursuits without being tainted with money, which they could afford to treat with disdain as they already had plenty of it. They were quite aware that those who made their living on the water would have far greater experience at boat handling and it was better to keep them out of racing rather than get beaten all the time. It applied to rowing even more than to sailing. Definitions varied a fair bit at the time, but the SASC rules were as follows in 1884:

"The word amateur shall exclude all fishermen or steermen, sailmakers, boatbuilders, or persons gaining or having gained their living on the water; any person who is or has been employed in or about yachts, boats, or ships as a means of livelihood, or who has received a monetary consideration for his professional knowledge" (Evening News, 15/3/1884 p.6). Somehow prize money in regatta and club races did not enter into the equation. George Holmes (also known as George Fletcher as his mother had remarried Mr Holmes after he had become well-known) sailed against the professionals but always claimed not to be one and continued a working life at Cockatoo Island dockyard, but a fair proportion of his income would have been his cut of the prize money.

With many more gentlemen wishing to go sailing and having the means because of business booming generally in the 1870's and early '80's a large number of new boats appeared and raced with the SASC and a few other Amateur clubs that sprang up. They were not only 24-footers but some were larger and some smaller but were generally half-decked, usually not as far back as the mast. Regatta and club programmes began to contain references to races for half-deckers, as separate from open boats, but it is hard at this distance to find any close definitions of what was an open boat and what was a half-decker, as most of the open boat classes had a small foredeck and narrow side-decks at least, and some had a narrow stern deck. These amateur boats still carried inside ballast. Regattas began to list races specifically for amateur crews from 1879, most regattas allowing separate races for professionals as well, which attracted the greatest public interest and prize money, but some regattas completely banned professional racing in some years. It went a bit the same way as the centreboard controversy, one year there would be races for both amateur and professional, the next year there would be no races for professionals, and next year they would be back again. Feelings often ran high in newspaper reports and letters to the editor. The amateur side deplored public gambling in the sport which they felt would get out of hand with professionals involved, and the supporters of the professionals felt that public interest in the racing was declining with only amateurs racing. To a certain extent they were both right.

2.9 Idothea, built by Robert Stephens for Stannard's hire fleet 1888.
HALL COLLECTION ANMM

One of the new clubs that sprang up was the Port Jackson Sailing Club, which was formed in 1888 for the sailing of hired boats. Both rowing and sailing boats had been hired on Sydney Harbour for decades, and for most boatbuilders a crucial part of their business was in hiring out boats for which most maintained a varied fleet. The gentlemen of the Port Jackson Sailing Club wanted to hire boats to race, and these hires were generally for the season. Boatbuilders built 24-footers in particular for these hirers. In 1888-9 boatshed owner William Stannard of Double Bay had R.Stephens build him two, *Isadore* and *Idothea*, H.C.Press had *Iolanthe* and another built for his fleet in Woolloomooloo Bay. Some of these boats were cedar-planked, but many were planked in New Zealand Kauri and varnished, and were referred to as the "yellow dogs". Some were carvel-built, some were clinker, and several were batten-seam carvel below with two or three clinker strakes on the topsides. The SASC and some other clubs did not allow hired boats to race as they considered they were owned by professionals, but the Port Jackson Sailing Club themselves allowed the boats but insisted on only amateur crews. Races were sometimes with limited sails and crews, sometimes with any sails but with amateur crews. Contemporary commentators noted that the boats were getting beamier and carrying bigger sails each year. The previous champion 24-footer *Lottie* joined the club late in 1890. The hired boats fleet peaked in the season of 1890-91 when at least nine new boats joined the fleet. It was one brief shining moment though, as the Port Jackson Sailing Club folded in 1894. It was clearly acknowledged in reports of the time that there was little public interest in these races, and though a few new boats were built into the early 1890's because there were gentlemen waiting to hire them, and there was a 24' Championship open to professionals as late as 1892, and regatta races for 24's with professional crews until 1897, but there was a sudden swift decline after 1897, and the 24' class quickly sank into oblivion, only appearing in mixed fleets and limited sails races by 1901 and pretty well disappearing with the First World War.

It was not only the amateur-professional debate that held back the 24's, the rise of several other classes, in particular the 16's and the 22's, and a little later the 20-footers had probably slowed the development of the 24's in the 1880's. They had the afore-mentioned revival for about a decade from the late 1880's with new boats of different shapes.

But by the mid 1890's the 24-footers were doomed by the rising popularity of the 22-footers.

The 22-Footers

Not to be confused with the twenty-two foot skiffs which disappeared after 1876, the new 22's grew out of a group of general pleasure sailing boats of this length and a little less which hadn't raced much, some appearing in an 1876 Balmain Regatta race for open boats under 23' and not less than 2'6" deep (to keep out the 22' skiffs who had their own race that day) but there were quite a few of them as the first regatta that catered for them, the North Shore Regatta of 1878 had twelve entries in the race for "open boats not over 22' under pleasure canvas". A few of the same boats plus several other ones competed in the Balmain Regatta later that year in the race for boats not over 22' and not less than 2'6" deep. Most of them appear to have been painted. A Mr Demestre had Langford build him a boat specifically to race in this class and the varnished *Syren* debuted at the Balmain Regatta of 1879 and won. Others soon followed: Donnelly built *Rosetta* and Edgar Dearing built *Uranus* for the 1880 Balmain Regatta, Donnelly had *St Crispin*

2.10 *Violet*, about 1889, also by Stephens, an early 22-footer. HALL COLLECTION ANMM

and Ellis had *Velox* ready for the 1881 Balmain Regatta. These boats were not as deep as the 24' fishing boats (at a minimum of 2'6" as opposed to 3') and were mostly quite beamy, and the sails carried were bigger with gaff rigs and long bumpkins. Crews were more numerous and I believe they were either unballasted or had only small amounts of inside ballast. From at least 1881, professionals were engaged to sail them. The same thing happened to the class as the new boats appeared and won, the older boats stopped racing or occasionally joined mixed race and limited sails and crew races, and general "Hurry-Scurry" races which were becoming popular, being for mixed fleets with limited crews on boats in cruising trim.

The 22's were built and sailed in Brisbane as well, and developed out of shallow painted and ballasted oyster boats from Moreton Bay. Without as many boats of other sizes they were the dominant class in the 1880's and 1890's. Several Sydney boats were sent to Brisbane owners, but the majority were locally built.

The best days of the 22's were still to come (more on this later), but like a lot of other classes there were to be some trials and tribulations along the way. After 1884 in Sydney they suffered in the amateur versus professional conflict. In that year only three races for professionals were held, only one of which was for 22-footers. For the next few seasons the 22's only appeared in mixed racing fleets.

Centreboards and Fins

From references in the press at the time, Presto's centreboard and that of all the earlier boats appears to have been of the pivoting type which the Americans had developed, and were made of metal, generally iron. At some stage local boats began to use loose fins of iron which dropped vertically using handles on top which also prevented the board from dropping through the case. Regatta announcements start referring to fins from 1862-3 (as in "fins and centreboards excluded") and I suggest, but can't prove that they may be referring to drop fins. In living memory our vertical drop centreboards have always been referred to as fins. A possible problem with this assumption occurs when a few writers start referring to the "dagger principle" in the 1890's. This however may refer to using fins with a small fore and aft dimension, ie a high aspect ratio. Before this time I would suggest that fins may have a considerable length fore and aft, as did rudders. But regardless, at the very latest the drop fin was used from the 1890's as they can be seen raised in some photographs.

CHAPTER 3

The Shape Changes

Another big evolutionary step was taken during the 1880's in that all of these classes began to be built beamier than the earlier boats with bigger rigs and were less rounded in section, with relatively straight sections below the waterline and a fair bit of deadrise, and a broader tuck. Sydney's leading naval architect of the time Walter Reeks drew attention to this in a newspaper article on "Yachting and Sailing" (*Illustrated Sydney News* 31/5/1888 pp 4-8), and his illustration is reproduced here. The drawing referred to as the modern half-decker shows the hull type that dominated open boat design, with only minor changes at least until the late 1940's. Reeks claimed that the changes had happened over just the previous three or four years: "to-day (1888) 9 feet are not considered too much beam for a boat of 20 feet length, whereas 7 feet or seven feet six inches were broad when the Contingent went to Egypt" (1885, see Box below). With the greater beam, and wide added sponsons or gunl's, and by carrying the beam well aft, crew weight could be further out and therefore more sail carried. Reeks commented that "straighter bottoms (in section) were found to give greater stability". Reeks designed at least two 22-footers himself, *Varuna* which raced in Sydney and *Clyanthus* which raced in Brisbane.

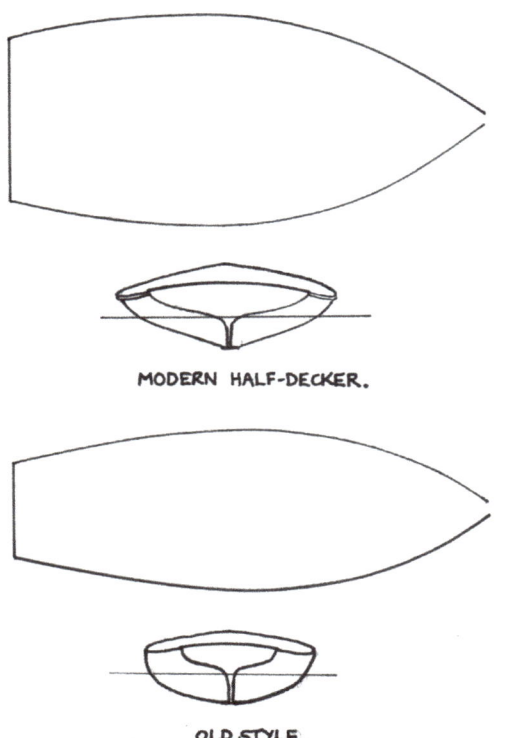

3.1 Walter Reeks drawings of changing open boat shapes. Redrawn from ILLUSTRATED NEWS 31 MAY 1888

> **Historical perspective in research**
> *Finding that article by Walter Reeks was a gem! The contingent going to Egypt in 1885 was of course the Sudan Contingent going off to fight the Mad Mahdi, and as you can see by the photo it was a big deal at the time. If you're interested in history, then finding references like this that put things into their historical context is extremely interesting and satisfying. You only have to look at a different old newspaper page or just somewhere else on that page to find stuff. Thomas Day, Cockle Bay whaleboat builder in the 1840's had assigned convict labour! Our centreboard controversy was raging at the same time as the American Civil War. And of course there are quite regular references to the British Army having trouble with the locals in Afghanistan…*
>
>
>
> POWERHOUSE MUSEUM COLLECTION

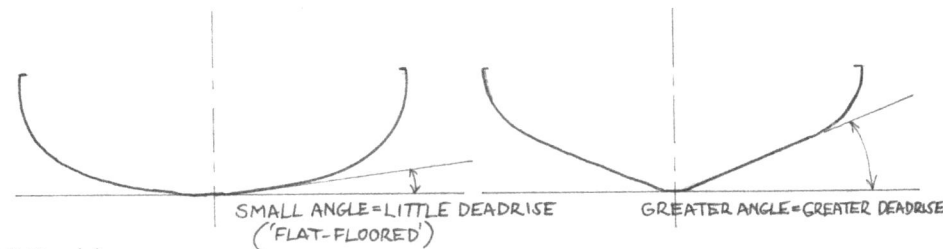

3.2 Deadrise

As Reeks was there at the time and knew what he was talking about, we have to take his word for it. But other sources suggest that even before the mid 1880's there were varying amounts of deadrise in open boats. Commentators on Donnelly's radical 22' skiff *Ettie* of 1875 referred to her as the "flat iron" due to the unusual lack of deadrise (as well as the wide tuck). A new 24-footer by Ellis in 1885 was described as beamier and deeper but with less deadrise than his 1878 and 1880 24-footers. Boatbuilders would have been well aware of the considerable deadrise on the ballasted yachts of the time, and would certainly have been aware of the shape of the *Australian*, a radical design of 1858 whose underwater sections were an exact right angle, with a straight line in section from keel to waterline. Reeks himself admitted that his designs were strongly influenced by the *Australian*. I am convinced that the 19' skiffs, the emerging 16-footers and the 14' dinghies would have followed what Reeks refers to as the "old style" as they had evolved from rowing skiffs, but I suspect that at least some of the 24' boats would have had a fair amount of deadrise and some V-shape in their sections. Nevertheless they were referred to by a contemporary chronicler as the "round-bottomed class".

Spring in the Keel

Another design feature that began about the same time and eventually became the norm was spring in the keel. Up to the 1880's all keels had been straight, sometimes horizontal and sometimes raked or deeper aft. In 1889 we see the first mention of spring in describing a new 24-footer by Harry Green for H.C. Press as having 5" of spring in the keel (as well as more rise in floor). After this there are only occasional mentions (such as Brisbane's 22' *Lady Norman* having 8" spring forward and 4" aft in 1894) until in August 1896 Donnelly's new 22-footer *Effie* is described as having "immense" spring of 9", and after this every mention of an open boat being launched refers to the amount of spring (and they all had some), at least until the First World War after which it is apparently so accepted and universal that it does not seem worth commenting on by contemporaries (except once in 1921 regarding Charlie Dunn's *Crescent III*). It obviously helped that *Effie* was an instant champion, and nothing succeeds like success.

You will have gained the impression that with all these new classes of boats and large fleets that there was a huge increase in the sport of sailing in the 1880's and '90's, and you would be right. Sailing clubs multiplied, and by the late 1880's you could race your boat almost every summer Saturday.

The new hull shapes, the increasing professionalism and as we are about to see, the active new clubs were features that steered open boat sailing towards its golden age from the 1890's to the middle of the twentieth century.

The Balmain Sailing Club

Balmain had been a centre for boatbuilding and sailing from its original development as a village in the 1830's and '40's. A large proportion of open boat sailors lived there. It is on a peninsula with the harbour on three sides, and the waterfront was a mixture of waterfront homes and waterfront industries, with the industries predominant including chemical and soap works, but also a large number of professional boatsheds for building, repair and hiring of boats. The Balmain Regatta had been organised by a committee of Balmain businessmen and professionals since 1849, but as sailing clubs began to multiply, the Balmain residents felt they needed one. The Balmain Sailing Club was formed in 1885, and held races for mixed fleets of 14's, 16's, 20's, 22's and 24's. Hired boats and amateur-only clubs were still dominant elsewhere, but Balmain took the step of allowing private boats and professionals to sail in their races. "Best and Best" was a term borrowed from the sport of rowing and began to be used in the

3.3 Lady Loch 1893 by Reid, one of the big-beam 24-footers, and one of the last ones built.
HALL COLLECTION ANMM

Balmain Club's sailing races to denote that the best crew in the best boat would win, ie no restrictions on who could sail and how much sail they could carry, the only restriction being on overall length.

The next clubs which emerged followed this pattern, and this led to a brief revival in the 24-footers, as well as stimulating the 20-footers and the 22-footers. Several new and beamier 24's were built, *Volunteer* and *Mantura* by Hubbard and others by Gardiner, Stephens, Pritchard, Donnelly, Golding and Messenger. In fact if you follow the money, in 1893 the 24-footer race at the Balmain Regatta had larger prize money (12 pounds to 10 pounds) than the 22-footer race suggesting they were narrowly the dominant class. They attracted about equal money for the next few years, but by 1896 the 22-footers had surpassed them in prize money, probably under the stimulus of the Intercolonial races (see below).

Politics seems to come into it again, as another Balmain club, the Johnstone's Bay Sailing Club was formed in late 1890 by members of the Port Jackson Sailing Club, the "hired boats" club. Their rules were not dissimilar to those of the Balmain Sailing Club, allowing professionals to race. The only club to hold out for amateurs much after this was the Sydney Amateur Sailing Club. With the advent of the Johnstone's Bay Sailing Club, the Balmain Sailing Club faded, and is last mentioned holding a smoke concert in 1892.

The Johnstone's Bay Sailing Club

Starting and finishing their races in Johnstone's Bay, on the south-east side of the Balmain peninsula opposite Pyrmont, the JBSC held races for a number of classes of open boats from the earliest. Their first event in January 1891 had two 24-footers, four 22-footers and one 20-footer, but their next race was for boats 10 foot and under, and the next for 16 foot dinghies, and in just half a season from their opening in January to late April they held twelve races for a total of 86 pounds 7 shillings in prize money, and had 32 boats on their books and 370 members (Aust Town and Country Journal 4/7/1891 p. 38). They went on as they started, holding a number of races for the bigger

3.4 Mantura by Hubbard, 1889, another big beam 24-footer skippered for its first 4 seasons by Chris Webb.
HALL COLLECTION ANMM

boats in mixed fleets as well as some individual races for each class, and championships in each class. The best boats, skippers and crews were attracted to the club and they were considered the primary open boat club in Sydney.

But……big drum roll……….

Enter Mark Foy and the Sydney Flying Squadron.

Mark Foy ran a highly successful Manchester business which grew into multiple department stores. He had been boat owner, sailor and club committee member since the 1880's,

3.5 Mark Foy
JOHN STANLEY COLLECTION

and in 1891 was on the board of several sailing clubs including the SASC, the Port Jackson Sailing Club and the Johnstone's Bay Sailing Club. In 1891, he formed the Sydney Flying Squadron Yacht Club, with some novel principles: it was set up as a private company which Foy was personally bankrolling, and the racing was to be around short triangular courses in two heats plus a final on each day. The boats were asked to carry coloured sails to be easily distinguished (Foy had envisaged alternate stripes of colours and had them on his own boats, but it appears that almost everyone else thought that was silly, and they compromised with large patches of coloured cloth in shapes such as crescents, stars and Maltese crosses sewn onto the mains'l). The handicaps in minutes were to be taken at the start, so that the first boat to cross the finish line was the winner. It was all designed to make open boat sailing more of a spectator sport. Foy even tried to lease Clark Island and charge entry fees, but the authorities were not having it. The handicap starts were not quite as novel as some commentators have made out: it had been tried by a number of clubs including the SASC on occasions over the past decade or more, and Mark Foy himself had offered a big prize for a series of such races in the Port Jackson Sailing Club in January 1891. The other clubs had always seen it just as a novelty, but it became an iconic feature of the Sydney Flying Squadron races which has lasted to the present day. The first race did not attract as many of the larger open boats as were attending the Johnstone's Bay Sailing Club races, even though he carefully avoided most calendar clashes in the programme for the first season. One clash did arise in November, and it was the JBSC which cancelled their race. Foy's promise of thirty pounds prize money probably influenced owners to sail with the SFS, but in that 1891-92 season the JBSC held more races and had more entrants than the SFS.

The committee of the Anniversary Day Regatta, (actually then called the NSW National Regatta) were not happy with the coloured sails, and announced that boats with coloured sails (or patches) would not be allowed in the regatta. They felt that the commercial nature of the SFS would lead to an increase in gambling and sully the sport. The Sydney Flying Squadron decided to hold its own regatta on the same day in roughly the same waters. Seven races were held for boats from 8' to 24' with equal or more generous prize money than offered by the official regatta. Cleverly they made coloured sails optional, and 57 entries of SFS-registered boats were joined by 26 outsiders, for a total of 83 entrants. The open boat events of the official regatta attracted only 42 entrants in 7 races.

An economic depression in the early 1890's probably affected Mark Foy's decision to liquidate the Sydney Flying Yacht Squadron Limited in July 1892. His many detractors in the yachting establishment breathed a sigh of relief. But after a hiatus of two seasons, the Sydney Flying Squadron was established as a regular club in August 1894 with the same principles of coloured sails and 2 heats plus final around a short triangular course with handicap starts. Their first race for the season was on October 13 1894 and had 10 boats. By their eighth race in March, entries were up to 21 boats, and a commentator expressed the opinion that these were the "cream of the harbour fleet". Most of the races were still for mixed fleets in General Handicaps and this continued largely for about a decade, but boats had begun to conform to set lengths, and championships and other races for boats of the same length began to appear with increasing regularity in the 1890's.

The 20-Footers

In the mixed fleets after 1884 a number of 20-foot boats began to feature. Golding's *Nereus*, Ellis's *Wingadee* and *Wonganella* and Hayes' *Maritana* were among these. They often won against bigger boats, and newer versions with more beam and depth, wider tucks and bigger rigs started to appear along with all other classes, including Ellis' *Genesta*, Golding's *Itonia* and a second *Nereus* to replace the first burnt in its shed, Hayes' *Cynthia*, Donnelly's *Angela*, *Clytie* and *Petrel* (later *Victor*). In late 1890 the *Grace Darling* was built by T. Allen of Balmain, and it was considered an extremely well-built vessel though the builder was not well-known. They still raced mainly in mixed fleets until the early 1890's, and then mostly raced as a class for the rest of the decade, until they began to be replaced by the emerging eighteen-footers (more later). In 1895 they were still contesting for slightly more prize money than the 18-footers.

The 16-Footers

Remember the skiffs, the ones limited to beam and depth? As well as the 22's and the 19's, a race for 16-footers appeared at the Balmain Regatta of 1875, a couple of years after the 19 foot skiffs, limited to 4'8"beam and 20" depth and attracted six entries. They were allowed to use and raise fins and centreboards as were all other boats from this date. Within a couple of months for the 1876 Anniversary Regatta the beam limitation had been increased to 5', the same as the longer 19's and 22's, and races for this class continued for more than twenty years, fading out in the late 1890's. The

3.6 Our Boys 16-footer, built by Donnelly, about 1886.
AUSTRALIAN TOWN AND COUNTRY JOURNAL 15 SEPT 1888 P553

16's were true skiffs, with no decking, but still carried the big gaff rigs and long bumpkins of their bigger sisters, as well as squares'ls and tops'ls. "Starfish" reported in 1881 that the 16-footers seemed to carry more sail each season. Their fleets were some of the largest through the 1880's and early 1890's. They benefited from the fact that they more often allowed professionals to sail during the period when opportunities for them were limited.

Most of the gun professional skippers of the 1890's and early 1900's spent time in the sixteens in the 1880's, including Montgomery, Colebrook, Holmes, Read, Ellis, and Golding. I can't prove it but I suspect that the sixteens began to be built with a little more deadrise in the late 1880's and perhaps with wider tucks, but this would have been limited by the fact that their overall beam and depth were always restricted to 5' and 20".

The Canvas Dinghies

Prior to the 1870's, if you were a young fellow who wanted to race sailing boats, you had to join the crew of one of the classes. This was not a problem for many young blokes as there were strong communities in most waterfront suburbs and if you were fit and keen you would be able to get a spot somewhere and asked to come back if you showed any promise. But there were no classes of smaller boats racing where teenagers and young adults could afford to have a boat built. Even the 16-footers after 1875 were not cheap to build and race. But the Anniversary Regatta of 1881 held a race for boys in canvas dinghies 12-14 feet. These boats must have been around for a little while as thirteen boats entered. They could be simply and cheaply built by teenagers, by bending 25-30 ribs over some formwork, fitting 6-8 planks of cheap pine timber each side with about an inch between each plank so there was limited skill needed in fitting, and covering the whole lot in canvas which was then stretched and waterproofed by painting, most often with wood colours so that at a distance they were difficult to detect as canvas-covered boats. Two or three stringers stiffened the inside, with three thwarts. Their beam was about 5', tuck about 4'3", depth amidships 20", depth aft 24". By 1884 a

3.7 Canvas dinghy section

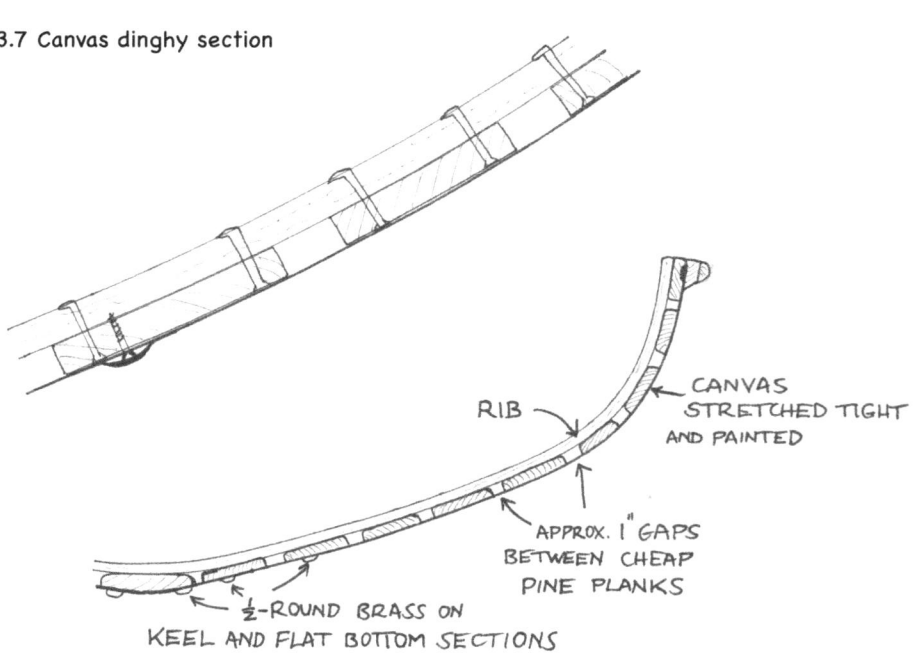

3.8 Canvas 14 Bessie by Donnelly. The 14's were unrestricted except for no decks being allowed until the 1890's. They also got beamier with bigger rigs. Donnelly's wood 14' Wanda in 1899 had Carter sails on 21' boom, 14'hoist, 12'head. An earlier boat had mast 17'6", boom 20', hoist 11', gaff 11', bumpkin projects about 8', tops'l 13' on yard, squaresails 12-14' square. They were sailed with 5 or 6 hands.
AUSTRALIAN TOWN AND COUNTRY JOURNAL 6 FEB 1892.

fashion had developed for wide gun'ls, up to 5" a side including the moulding. They also got beamier as the years went by, up to 6'8" at least.

For the first few seasons the age was limited to under sixteens or under fourteens, then to under twenty-ones, then by 1884 any crews, which lasted the rest of the life of the class at regattas other than the period during the 1880's where many races were held only for amateurs. There were no rules restricting rigs so the 14's carried every sail the bigger boats did including tops'ls and squares'ls. They were as numerous and popular as the sixteen-footers, and attracted about the same amounts of prize money at regattas.

The rules for construction of canvas dinghies were non-existent in the early years. Complaints were heard in the newspapers regarding the lack of rules, and the sub-text is that boats with closer plank spacing had an advantage, and I can only assume this was due to water leakage or fragility. It didn't take long before some boats were virtually wooden skiffs with a canvas overlay, then some deleted the canvas and built wooden dinghies with batten-seam carvel construction like most of the bigger boats. However, in most cases the canvas dinghies were faster than the wooden dinghies, and it was the wooden dinghy boys that agitated and got races for wooden boats only. The fact that the canvas dinghies were generally faster was a puzzle for commentators at the time as most of them were amateur-designed and built. I would argue that their lightness was the secret (this also was their weakness, because they did not last as long as the wooden boats, particularly as rigs got bigger). In the Anniversary Regatta of 1883, only two years after the first race for canvas dinghies there were separate races for canvas and wooden boats, which lasted until 1889, after which they raced in combined fleets until they faded in Sydney Harbour after 1905. By 1888 both canvas and wooden dinghies were being built by the leading professionals including Donnelly, and were being skippered by leading professional skippers such as George Fletcher (Holmes) and Billy Read. A youthful Chris Webb and his brother Charles sailed the 14' *Latona* and started his long career winning races.

The canvas dinghies were quite numerous and the Sydney Amateur Canvas Dingy Club was formed in April 1883, S.H.Hyam and Thomas Punch filling official roles. By 1885 they were sailing up to 8 races per season with three separate classes of boats (classed according to performance). Not all 14' canvas dinghies in Sydney were members as some raced only at regattas with professionals, but the line between amateurs and professionals appears to have been a bit blurred in this club. They held out for canvas dinghies only until 1891 when they faced reality and allowed wooden 14 footers to race. They started to hold races for the 8' and 10' canvas dinghies also about this time but the club had been struggling for several years and was not seen after 1891. The 14 footers were almost all wooden boats by this time, and they kept sailing at regattas and occasionally with other clubs (more on this later). The Sydney

Dingy Club was formed in July 1894 with many prominent members of the old canvas club but folded a few years later.

A number of the Sydney Harbour 14-footers were bought up by Botany Bay sailors and they raced with the St George Club until the First World War, but were supplanted there after the war by 16 foot skiffs. The fourteens had also spread to Brisbane, Melbourne, Adelaide and Perth, but evolved in different ways in these cities, as was noticed at several Interstate competitions where the St George boats were generally outclassed by smaller and more skiff-like boats. Somebody else can tell the story of the later fourteens.

3.9 Wood 14-footer Cutty Sark with owner Peter Cowie's daughter Ruth in 1903, clearly shows steep dead rise hulls of Sydney's open boats.
COWIE FAMILY ARCHIVES

3.10 Clio, Charlie Dunn's wood 14' dingy (mostly steered by brother Billy) in 1898.
HALL COLLECTION ANMM

3.11 Cutty Sark. The unrestricted fourteens carried all the sails the bigger boats did.
COWIE FAMILY ARCHIVES.

Other Canvas Dinghies:

The 8-Footers and 10-Footers

In 1886 the Balmain Regatta held a race for eight foot canvas dinghies, for youths under 18 (this just about coincided with the fourteens dropping their age qualification). There must have been a few of them about already because there were thirteen entries, as had happened with the 14's. And there must have been a few larger ones as well because the very next year the Balmain Regatta race was for youths in canvas dinghies ten foot and under, and in a field of twenty-one there were seven 10-footers and fourteen 8-footers! At least some of the early entrants had no half-decks and were sprit-rigged.

The following year they were also in a combined race, and of twenty entries twelve were new! After that the fleets separated. The age limit

3.12 10′ Violet (left) and 8′ Rob Roy were 2 of the earliest racing 8 and 10′ canvas dinghies in the late 1880's. Notice sprits'ls and lack of decks.   COWIE FAMILY ARCHIVES

seems to disappear about 1892, and the racing became handicapped. Decks came in and gaff rigs became dominant and sail areas grew. The stipulation that they be canvas boats disappeared

sometime in the 1890's. By 1905 they were all batten-seam carvel built. Brisbane also built up a fleet of ten footers in the 1890's and early 1900's. The tens experienced a lull in the early 1900's in Sydney, partly because many were bought by Newcastle sailors who built up quite a fleet there, but all disappeared with the coming of World War I in 1914. The 10-footers experienced a brief revival between the wars with fleets of around a dozen.

Top Left: 3.13 Zephyr 8 foot long and 8 foot wide. HALL COLLECTION ANMM

Middle Left: 3.14 Commonwealth sailing off Balmain. HALL COLLECTION ANMM

Bottom Left: 3.15 Lines of 10-footer Commonwealth. AHSSA COLLECTION

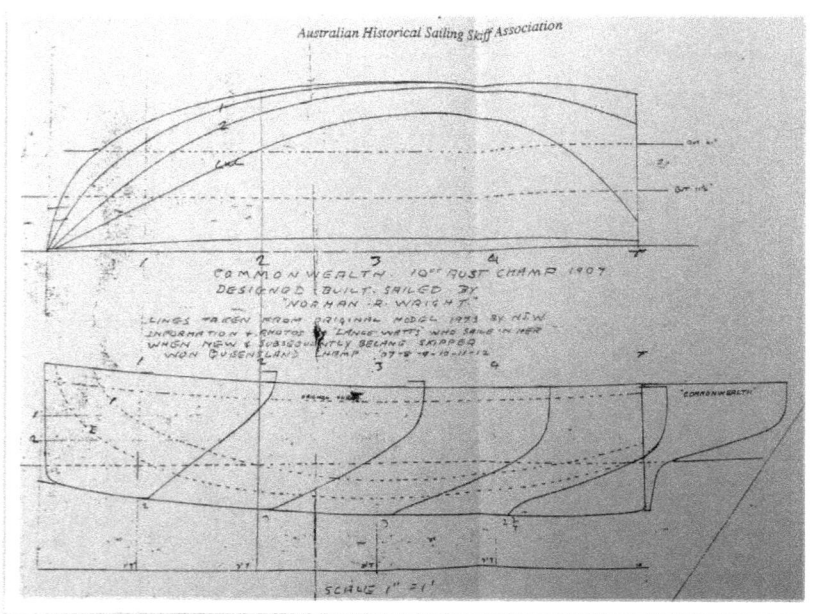

There were no restrictions other than overall length for both tens and eights. In order to carry more sail they were built beamy, just over five foot on a 10-footer being considered narrow. In 1898 the Pritchard family who ran a boatshed in Leichhardt at the shallow end of Iron Cove built an 8-footer called *Zephyr* (pictured 3.13) which famously was eight feet wide! And even more unusual, it was skippered successfully by Irene Pritchard with her two brothers as crew, with five wins out of seven starts, plus one second and one capsize. For the next season they built *Procella*, a 10-footer on similar lines (10' x 10'), which was slightly less successful. The 8-footers normally carried three, the 10-footers five crew. They had short foredecks and side-decks. Like the bigger classes they were gaff-rigged with long bumpkins and carried tops'ls and squares'ls and later spinnakers, and proportional to their size carried more sail than any other classes, eventually with three different rigs for different rig strengths. The Norman Wright-built *Commonwealth* which started racing in Brisbane in 1906 but was sold to Sydney in 1924 carried her No1 Mains'l on a boom of 19'6", with hoist of 13'9" and 11'10" on the gaff. The jib was luff 22', foot 14'10" and leech 15'5". The replica fleet built in the 1990's by the Australian Historical Sailing Skiff Association had two authentically built and rigged 10-footers, and these boats provided exciting on-the-edge sailing, the main challenge being to keep the huge rigs upright.

The 6-Footers

These were the most ridiculous of the open boats. I say this because I built a generic replica in 1994 we called *The Balmain Bug* and it still provides fun for crew and entertainment for spectators at the revived Balmain Regatta in recent years. It's not like sailing, it's more like riding a bucking bronco. If you stay upright you've

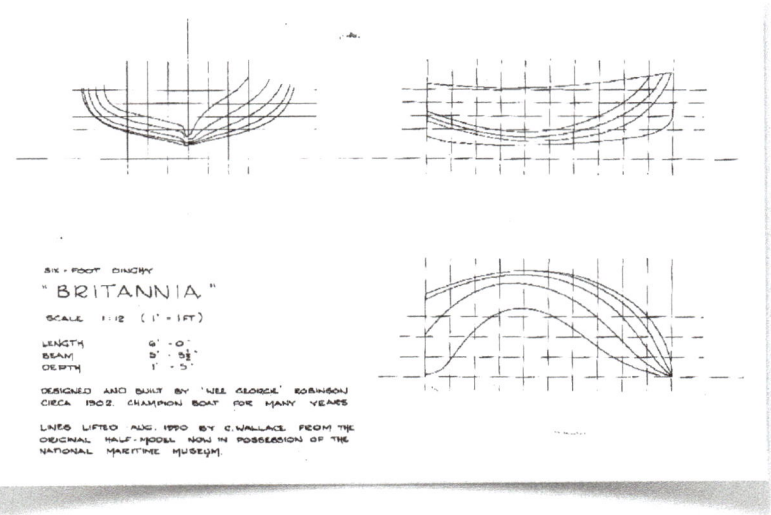

Top Right: 3.16 Ten-footer Gerard in the 1930's. Horrie Balkwell and crew collecting Championship ribbon. BALKWELL FAMILY COLLECTION.

Mid Right: 3.17 Wee Georgie Robinson and 6-footer Britannia 1915. ANMM

Bottom Right: 3.18 Lines of 6-footer Britannia. AHSSA COLLECTION

3.19 The Balmain Bug. Replica 6-footer built in 1994 by author, at Balmain Regatta. PHOTO GREG PORTEOUS BALMAIN SAILING CLUB COLLECTION

done well. Even more than the 10-footers they are as unstable fore and aft as they are side to side. They were all about as wide as they were long and were sailed by a crew of two or three very close friends. I've not seen a picture or report of them carrying tops'ls but they certainly carried masthead spinnakers and possibly peakhead spinnakers. The bumpkins were longer than the hull length.

The 6-footers first appeared at the Balmain Regatta in 1899, and lasted until 1919, with a brief revival up the Parramatta River at Concord and Abbotsford 1921-25. According to reports from the time they were mostly built by apprentices for their own use, and they were catered for by the North Sydney Dingy Club from 1899 to 1914, and the Balmain Dingy Club from 1904 to 1919 which both also held races for 10-footers. They were all batten seam carvel.

The Late 1890's

For most of the second half of the 1890's, the pattern for open boat racing on Sydney Harbour was that the two main open boat clubs, the Johnstone's Bay Sailing Club and the Sydney Flying Squadron organised races on alternate Saturdays, and a large number of boats raced in both clubs and therefore weekly. For example in the 1894-5 season, the SFS held 10 races, the JBSC held 16. The SFS kept their heats and courses, the JBSC held the more traditional longer courses. There were some races for smaller classes, generally in classifications such as 14-19' predominantly with the JBSC, but their primary racing was for the larger boats in general handicaps such as 22-24' or 18' and over.

Ferries chartered by the clubs followed the fleets, and bigger and more numerous ferries were required as the decade progressed, and both clubs were flush with money and were able to offer large prizes. Gambling did become a feature on these ferries, though it was illegal. Crooked cops would warn when a police raid was planned, so generally a blind eye was turned. Annual Championship races as well as occasional handicaps were run for the two classes which began to emerge as the biggest drawcards, the 18-footers and the 22-footers. These classes received a huge boost when a series of interstate contests were held during the 1890's.

The Intercolonial Contests

With a smaller population, Brisbane had fewer boats and fewer classes. By the 1890's their chief classes were the 22-footers and the 18-footers. As early as 1885 the twenty-twos in Brisbane were reported as growing in favour and "always the feature of our sailing regattas" (The Queenslander, 7/11/1885). The Sandgate Regatta of that year had 8 entries in the 22' race. In 1886 the local 22's were described as being about 7' broad, about 2' deep and half-decked, using ballast of railway iron. They were painted, and it seems that some of them at this stage were still working in the oyster trade in Moreton Bay. But by 1886 someone had imported *Nyoola*, a varnished 22-footer of 9' beam built by Golding in Sydney, and other boats were being built locally by builders such as Monteith and McLeer, with beam around 9' and all varnished.

3.20 Bulletin 1889 an early Queensland and Intercolonial 22' Competitor. HALL COLLECTION ANMM

Another Golding boat *Caneebie* arrived in 1891, of 9'6" beam, and a clinker planked boat *Zenobia* was built with 12' beam! By 1893 a very competitive fleet raced regularly on the Brisbane River and at regattas on Moreton Bay. Eighteen footers were the second most common class.

In 1894, the Queenslanders proposed that the Johnstone's Bay Sailing Club send up their best 22-footers to race against the Brisbane cracks. The JBSC held a test race, and three boats were selected and sent to Brisbane by ship: *Portia* (G.Holmes, skipper), *Irex* (N.Johnson) and *Latona* (Chris Webb). Two races were held on the Brisbane River over Easter 1894, and honours were divided. The local champion *Bulletin* won the first race from *Latona* (NSW) and *Zenobia* (Qld), others being *Portia* and *Irex* (NSW) and *Nyoola, Caneebie, Australian, Clyanthus* and *Turkroar* (Qld) (*Bulletin*'s design was in dispute: McLeer claimed it as his own design, Sydney's Donnelly claimed that he sold him the moulds). The second race was considered the championship, and was won by *Irex* (NSW) from *Caneebie* (Qld) and *Portia* (NSW). In January 1895 the Queenslanders sent down five boats, *Bulletin* (J.Whereat), *Waihora* (H.Prentice), *Caneebie* (T.Goodall), *Lady Norman* (F.J.Clark) and *Rose* (G.H.Clarke), the latter two being brand new, to race against a big fleet of 14 Sydney 22-footers with the cream of open boat skippers in charge: *Esmerelda* (W.Read), *Gladys* (J.Sommerville), *Irex* (N.Johnson), *Rosetta* (Tom Colebrook Snr), *Secret* (G.Fletcher Snr), *Guinevere* (H.Carpenter), *Lilian* (T.Leach), *Violet* (W.Fitzhenry), *Latona* (Chris Webb), *Elsie* (J.Robinson), *Varuna* (W.M.Paul), *Leonie* (J.Cronin), *Portia* (G.Ellis) and *Atalanta* (G.Fletcher Jnr), several of which were new. *Esmerelda* won from *Irex* and *Varuna* while the nearest Queenslander was *Lady Norman* at ninth. A NSW whitewash, but Qld saved some pride with *Bulletin* winning the 22' race in the Anniversary Regatta a few days later, and the *Lady Norman* won the second heat and final of the Sydney Flying Squadron Intercolonial Handicap the next Saturday, though skippered by NSW's Chris Webb. Third place in the final was filled by *Vera* a Queensland

3.21 Caneebie 1891 by Golding for a Queensland owner was 1896 Intercolonial Champion. GOLDING COLLECTION ANMM

18-footer, steered by Sydney's W.Holmes. We mustn't forget that there were races for 18-footers at every Intercolonial from 1895 on but they were definitely considered the junior class. In most events in both Sydney and Brisbane the local boats dominated in the 18's.

Queensland turned the tables the next season, in a series of races fought over the Christmas and New Year (1895/1896) period. *Esmerelda* and *Irex* were sent from NSW, and were beaten into second and third in the Championship race by Queensland's *Caneebie*. The Sydney boats were beaten into

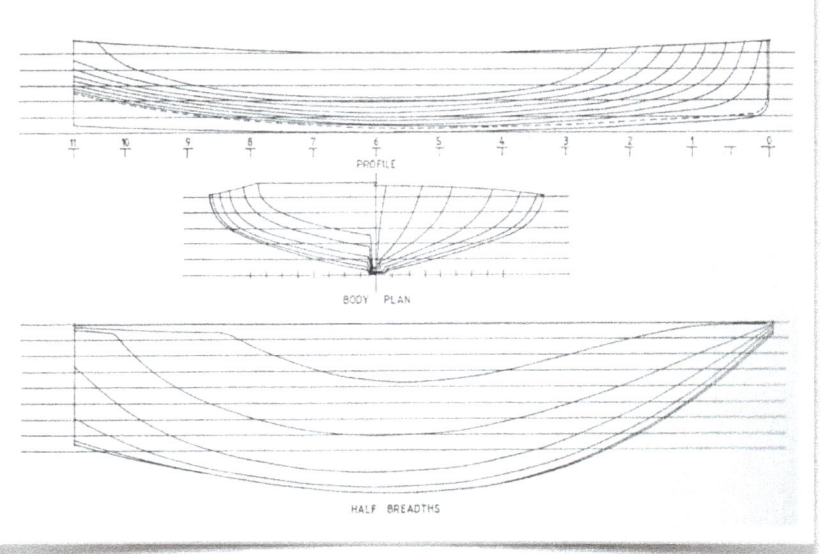

3.22 Lines of unknown Queensland 22-footer drawn by Bill Bollard from a model owned by Jack Hamilton

third and fourth at the Cleveland Regatta and second and third in a sweepstakes race.

Sydney owners and builders saw this as a challenge, so for the Sydney event in 1896-7, several new 22's were built: *Effie* by Donnelly, *Vigilant* by Golding, *Figtree* by Stephens and *Wonga* by Dearing. *Effie* was the star, and beat the others in several test races. Brisbane also built some new boats, *Hibiscus* and *Stanley*, but *Bulletin* and *Caneebie* still proved the fastest. In the January 1897 Championship race, *Effie* met with a mishap and didn't finish, and old *Irex* helmed by Fred Doran won, with the Queenslanders *Bulletin* and *Caneebie* ninth and tenth! *Bulletin* gained a little pride back by winning the Challenge race at the Anniversary Regatta a few days later.

Effie (N.Johnson) won the next Championship in Brisbane as well as two out of three of the other events contested. *Caneebie* (Goodall) and *Bulletin* (Whereat) were second and third in the Championship.

The last intercolonial event was

> *Donnelly's Effie was a bit of a design breakthrough, having what was considered an immense spring in the keel of 9". She won most of her races so convincingly that most boats after her were built with spring in the keel.*
>
> *The next design feature to turn up was hollow garboards, seen on Sam Williams' Keriki of 1898. His Australian of 1896 may also have had them.*
>
> **Hollow Garboards**
> *This expression refers to a reverse curve where the planking meets the keel, as seen in the drawing. Keriki appears to be the first boat where it is mentioned, but quite a number of boats featured hollow garboards after this. Britannia of 1919 is a prime example. The last mention I can find is of Charlie Dunn's Endeavour of 1921. It is possible that some of the later big-beamers also had hollow garboards, but after Aberdare heralded the arrival of the skiff-type 18 in 1932 they are not seen again. Len Heffernan once told me that he considered hollow garboards to be slow.*
>
>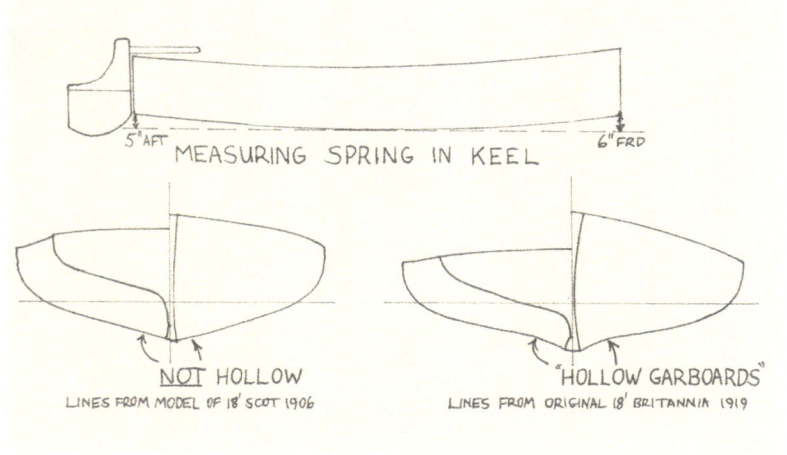

held in Sydney in January and February 1899. Queenslanders brought thirteen boats including 22's, 18's, 14's and 10's. They were resoundingly defeated in almost every event. Two new 22's had been built in Sydney, *Plover* by Donnelly and *Keriki* by Williams. *Plover* helmed by Fred Doran won the first Challenge race, but it was *Effie* that won the Championship race and cemented its position as the fastest 22-footer which ever sailed on Port Jackson. The eighteen-footer races brought out a new star, *Stella II* by Golding.

Queensland boat owners lost all interest in intercolonial contests after this, and in 22-footers as well. Brisbane events after 1900 show them only racing in general handicaps. Without the stimulus of intercolonial competition which had led to a lot of new boats in Sydney, the 22's waned in Sydney as well. The Balmain Regatta of 1901 had insufficient entries for a 22-footers race, and other than the annual 22' championships of the JBSC and the SFS and the new Sydney Sailing Club (est. Feb 1899) which kept going for a few more years, the last being the SFS 22' Championship in March 1904, the 22's only had general handicaps in which to race for the next few seasons. *Keriki* struggled on in Sydney with decreasing success against the 18's, *Plover* and *Effie* came out occasionally but the last racing appearance of the 22's in Sydney appears in the Anniversary Day Regatta of 1913, when *Keriki*, *Caneebie* and *Secret* raced in a general handicap in which the latter two were third and fourth.

But the short popularity of the 22-footers established the style of hull and rig that had evolved out of the 24' fishing boats and was continued in the class that now rose and became the longest surviving primary class, the 18-footers.

Right: 3.23 Plover 1898 by Donnelly (10' beam) was one of the last 22's built.
TYRELL COLLECTION POWERHOUSE MUSEUM

Below: 3.24 Keriki 1898 by Williams (10' beam) and Effie by Donnelly 1896 (9'7" beam) were the two fastest 22-footers of all.
HALL COLLECTION ANMM

It could have been different....

A couple of attempts were made to try out different styles of boats to the dominant open boats in the 1890's. Mark Foy himself was one of the main offenders. In 1894 he had Messenger build him a catamaran, with each hull 24' long by 2'3" beam and an overall beam of 10'6". Foy named it Flying Fish and often skippered it himself. It was capable of high speeds on a reach but was unable to win many races overall. It was believed to be uncapsizeable, but on at least one occasion it nose-dived and shed its crew. In late 1896 he had it shortened to 22' as 22's had become the dominant class, but it still didn't feature.

Flying Fish, Mark Foy's 1894 Catamaran. Detail of a painting in the collection of the Sydney Flying Squadron.

Several owners imported a new style of boat called raters in the late 1890's and heralded them as the most modern development in racing. They raced with several open boat clubs including the SASC, but did not feature particularly well against the 22's and 18's, and only survived a few seasons with the SFS. Racing with other clubs, the fleet was convincingly beaten when the Logan Brothers rater Mercia was imported from New Zealand in 1899 to the point where the class died within a few seasons.

CHAPTER 4

The Rise of the Eighteen-Footers

As mentioned, there were several eighteen foot skiffs around in the late 1870's that raced with the 19-footers, with narrow beam and shallow depth, *Alert, Bacchante, Naiad* and *Alcyone* and in just a few events dedicated to 18-footers, but these were nothing like the boats that began to emerge in the 1890's. Some of the hired boat fleet were half-decked 18-footers, like Hubbard's *Ruby* (illustrated 4.1) The credit for the first 18-footer to race that was built along similar lines to the racing 22's and 24's that were then dominant probably goes to Billy Golding, when he built *Gymea* in 1889 and sailed it with success in general handicaps with the Balmain Sailing Club (another boat *Ensign* was also built that year, but in Newcastle, and the builder is a mystery). Several other boats are listed just once each as 18-footers in Balmain races at the time, but those singular appearances suggest they were not dedicated racing boats.

In 1891, A.Pontey, an amateur builder built *Cygnet* whose lines are reproduced here. She first appeared in general handicaps with the Johnstones Bay Sailing Club in late 1891 with professional legend Thomas Colebrook at the helm, so Mr Pontey was serious about attempting to win races. About the same time *Edith* (builder unknown) and *Aztec* (Hubbard) appeared. The first two appeared in the Anniversary Regatta race for 18 and 19-footers in 1892 in which *Pandora* the old 19' skiff appeared- *Edith* won from *Cygnet*, but in the Balmain Regatta of November 1892, a race was held just for 18-footers, which Colebrook won in *Cygnet*. A few months later, the 1893 Anniversary Regatta ignored the 18's, but the Balmain Regatta later that year held an 18's race again, and from then on, every Anniversary and Balmain Regatta held a race for 18's. The Johnstones Bay Sailing Club began to hold several 18-footer races in their calendar, as well as general handicaps, and the Sydney Flying Squadron Yacht Club's first programme contained races for boats 14-18', but from its reestablishment in 1894, the SFS had 18-footers in its "all boats" races and general handicaps, and held their first 18' Championship race in 1895, as did the JBSC. *Cygnet* won the JBSC Championship but broke her bumpkin in the SFS event, won by *Ariel* (Donnelly 1894).

It has often been quoted that Mark Foy thought the 18's were "more sporting" than the 22's to suggest that it was he that led to the rise of the 18's as the chief class. He obviously felt that way, but the reasons for the emerging dominance of the 18's are more complex. The fact that Brisbane had concentrated on both the 22's and the 18's as their main racing classes in the 1890's as opposed to Sydney's multitude of classes meant that the chance of intercolonial competition stimulated the building of new examples of both of these classes. The 22's were still considered the chief class in both cities until 1901, but the decline which began to set in after the

4.1 Sketch of Ruby, Hubbard's boat slip, Glebe Point.
EVENING NEWS 4 SEPT 1900 P4

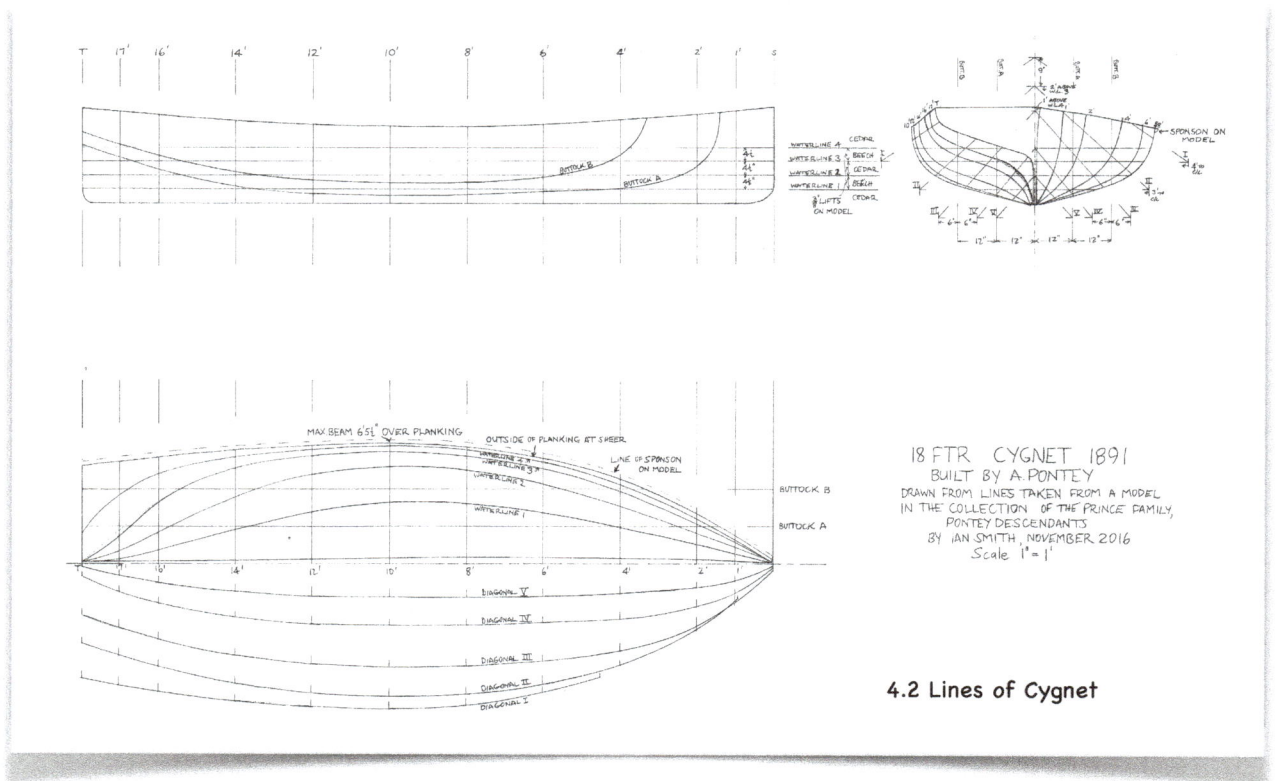

4.2 Lines of Cygnet

4.3 Cygnet model, courtesy Michael Prince.

dismal showing of the Brisbane 22's in 1899 left the 18's as the obvious choice. Several of the new Sydney 18's were beginning to beat the older 22's boat for boat in general handicaps, and the leading skippers were attracted to the class. With new boats and the best skippers, the 18's began to attract the attention of the public, and though it didn't happen overnight, the 18's were definitely the primary open boat class by 1902. I pick that year because that was the year that the prize money offered in the major regatta races for 18-footers surpassed that offered to the 22-footers. It cannot be stressed enough that Chris Webb who had been considered the top skipper since the early 1890's chose to mostly compete from the turn of the century in the 18-footers. The other top skippers such as Holmes, Ellis, Golding, and Read also concentrated on the eighteens and the competition was intense. Webb often won but he was also often beaten and the competition (and the gambling) drew huge crowds.

The numbers of 18's racing back this up. New 18's appeared every year. Including *Gymea* and *Cygnet*, thirty-one 18's were built in Sydney by 1900. A further ten were built 1901-03, then five in 1904, nine in 1905 and twelve in 1906. I can find no new racing 22-footers built after 1900. Lan Taylor's 22' *Keriki* raced with the SFS and SSC until the First World War, and he replaced her with an 18-footer of the same name in 1920. *Effie, Plover* and some of the others raced intermittently in the early 1900's but mainly in limited sails and limited crews races (for limited prize money).

Brisbane was a slightly different case. Twenty-one 18's had been built there in the 1890's, but their defeat in the Intercolonials of 1899 knocked the stuffing out of them and only four boats were built between 1900 and 1908. Many of the existing fleet however still continued local racing, and Brisbane was to rise again, quite spectacularly, after the First World War.

4.4 Launching Scot, 1906, owner Peter Cowie in white hat, Cook St Glebe. COWIE FAMILY ARCHIVES

Two or three steam ferries chartered by the clubs followed each event of the JBSC, the SSC and the SFS every Saturday. The fares were the basis of the income of those clubs and enabled them to offer large prizes. The race results and commentary appeared in the newspapers every week and the leading skippers were famous. Those who didn't want to pay gathered on Bradley's Head overlooking the Harbour, which became known as Scotchman's Hill. The Johnstone's Bay Sailing Club folded in the early 1900's (apparently due to conflict between boat owners and club officials) and the two other clubs alternated on Saturdays. This was the situation until 1925, when the SFS absorbed the Sydney Sailing Club and was the sole Sydney 18-footer club until the mid-1930's.

The few close-up photographs that exist show that the early 1900's 18's were very similar to each other (compare *Scot* 4.4 with *Australian* 1.14). There were small differences in beam (some boats getting wider and wider and carrying more spread of sail), depth and amount of spring in the keel, and probably other subtle differences in hull shape that we cannot determine, but decks and internal layouts had begun to follow the same pattern. All were built with batten seam carvel planking, almost invariably of cedar. Naturally some boats were faster than others, and though commentators at the time often thought they knew what made a fast boat, like commentators everywhere they were often wrong. *Cygnet* faded from the winning lists as newer boats came along. Dearing's *Stella* of 1894 (7'2"beam, 2'2"depth) was a winner until burnt in Dearing's shed fire of 1895. Golding's *Yvonne* (1895, 8" beam 2'1" depth) which he steered himself earned him some money and fame. The

Sam Williams-built *Australian* of 1896 (8' beam, 2'3"depth) dominated the winners' lists for some years under the helmsmanship of Chris Webb, and the builder's eponymous *Donnelly* (1898, 8'4" beam, 2'6" depth) was one of its chief rivals under George Holmes. North Shore builder Charlie Dunn's *Mascotte* of 1901 took out some prizes (Dunn's boats were generally narrower than most of the others and *Mascotte* had at least the top few strakes clinker-planked and was painted white). W. Holmes' *Arawa* under George Holmes and Billy Read ended *Australian's* dominance. Golding's *Arline* of 1903 (8'2" beam, 2'3" depth) was a winner, and became even more so when Watty Ford bought her, changed the name to *Australian* (II) and put her in the charge of Chris Webb. In fact this *Australian* under Chris Webb was the biggest winner of its time, and by itself was a drawcard and materially helped the success of the SFS and the SSC.

Lee cloths

In January 1898 we see the first mention of a boat (*Stella II*) using lee cloths, which are made of heavy canvas pinned or battened down immediately outside the coamings extending over the whole of the open part of the boat, propped up about a foot or a bit more high on the leeward side by one or more props, keeping the water out when the boat is heeling. Many felt that this was cheating, and a Johnstones Bay Sailing Club meeting in February 1898 moves were made to ban them for the next season. A similar meeting at the Sydney Flying Squadron a week later decided not to ban them, and when the issue finally was voted on at the JBSC in October they could not reach the required two-thirds majority and the issue lapsed, and from then on a majority, but not all boats carried them, but

4.5 The 18-footer fleet 1900.
THE TOWN AND COUNTRY JOURNAL 4 FEB 1900

photographs show that they were universal on 18 footers by 1914.

Revival of the Interstates

With low interest from Queenslanders, Inter-colonial or now since Federation in 1901 Interstate competition was revived between NSW and Western Australia. Elliott has covered this well, and I won't go into it much because it had little bearing on the evolution of the boats. New boats appeared every year but there were no design breakthroughs and the Interstates served mainly to provide extra interest in and publicity for the eighteens, so for the whole of the Edwardian period it was pretty much steady as she goes, except for little niggles from some of the narrow, skiff-type boats that we will go into shortly.

A number of the leading boatbuilders retired just before the First World War. Donnelly retired in 1914 aged 74 due to ill health. George Ellis moved to Vancouver, Canada in 1907. Billy Golding kept building boats until 1913. Edgar Dearing worked up until about 1914. Charlie Dunn and Charlie Hayes continued their family's boatbuilding traditions, and new builders emerged after the War.

The First World War naturally led to a slowdown in racing and building, but smaller fleets

4.6 Oweenee was only 5'6" beam with a skiff rig and gave the big beam boats a fright.
JOHN STANLEY COLLECTION

continued to race right through the war years. A new burst of activity followed, and the interwar period had the biggest fleets and biggest public interest of the entire history of open boat sailing.

Experiments in Boatbuilding – Attack of the Skiffs

Boatbuilders often had different ideas about what made a boat fast. So even though most of the boats were fairly similar, boatbuilders had different ideas about beam, deadrise, spring or rocker in the keel, bow and water entry shapes and shape of the buttocks and the run. The 16' skiffs provided a constant reminder that other shapes were possible. In 1906, Jack Robinson, a former 14' dinghy and 16' skiff sailor (and father of George Robinson the builder and skipper of *Britannia* which is the main subject of the next section of this work) built *Young Jack*, an 18-footer on more skiff-like lines, narrower than the other 18's, under seven feet. He raced it with mixed success for several seasons. The 16 foot skiffs which had started racing in 1901 (see below) were fast boats considering their limited sail area, and Jack Robinson as a former 16' skipper was not the only one to wonder if a skiff-like hull could match it with the beamier 18's. In the winter of 1906 the clubs heard that two skiff sailors were having boats built to test the theory. This caused some panic. The Sydney Sailing Club met and put a ban on any boats under 7 foot beam. The SFS declined to do so. This meant that in the 1906-7 season several boats built by Charlie Dunn plus Robinson's *Young Jack* could only sail on alternate weeks with the SFS. Only one boat that caused the panic appeared. Tom Banks had sailed his 16' (Donnelly-built) *Oweenee* with the Port Jackson Sailing Skiff Club (of which club he was a founding Vice-President) and the Sydney Amateur Sailing Club for a few seasons, with considerable success. In 1906 he had Joe Donnelly build him an 18 foot version, also called *Oweenee*. It first appeared at the January 1907 Anniversary Regatta in a race for boats 16' and over, and won from the old 20-footer *Grace Darling* and an unsuccessful 18-footer called *Blanche*. Banks appears to have been trying to find out how the boat sailed before trying it out against the cracks of the SFS, as he entered it next in the SASC Club Championship, and won. A week later he entered the SFS General Handicap amongst the other 18's. He engaged old legend Fred Doran to skipper it, but he was unplaced in his heat.

Incidentally the winner of the final was *Young Jack*. In the next week's State Championship *Oweenee* again finished amongst the tail-enders. The owners of the beamier boats breathed a sigh of relief as to them it was proved that a skiff 18 was a failure. Banks took over the helm for the next few races but could do no better. He went back to sailing his 16-footer for the rest of the season, and expressed the opinion that his "experiment" was a failure.

However in the next season, *Oweenee* entered a SFS General Handicap in December and won both the heat and the final under the care of leading 16' skiff skipper L.Rodrick. Rodrick couldn't repeat the success in the SFS 18-footers Championship in January 1908. Tom Banks took back the helm, but

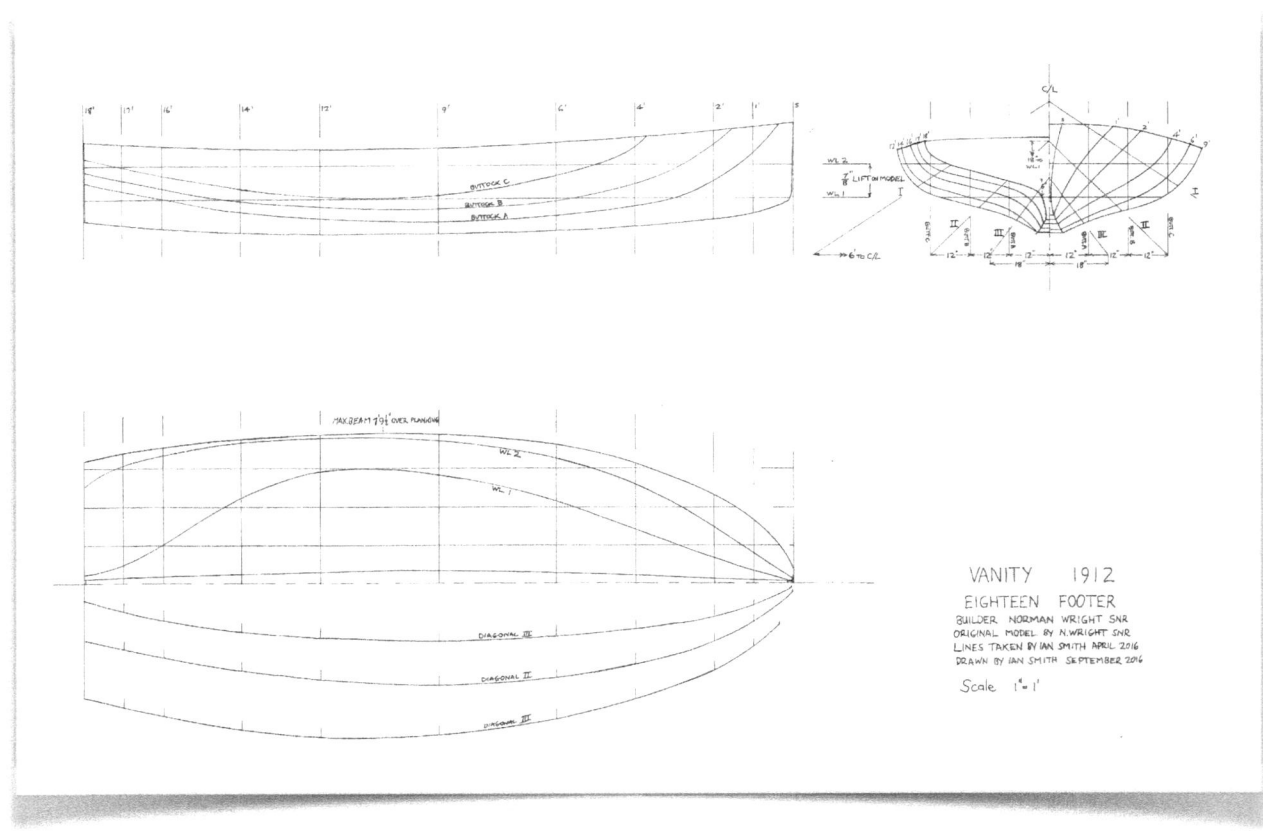

4.7 Lines of Vanity 1912 and Langham 1915, both by Norman Wright Snr in Brisbane, both typical of the big-beam boats that came to dominate 18-footer racing from before the First World War until the 1930's. Langham at 8'7" beam was one of the widest.

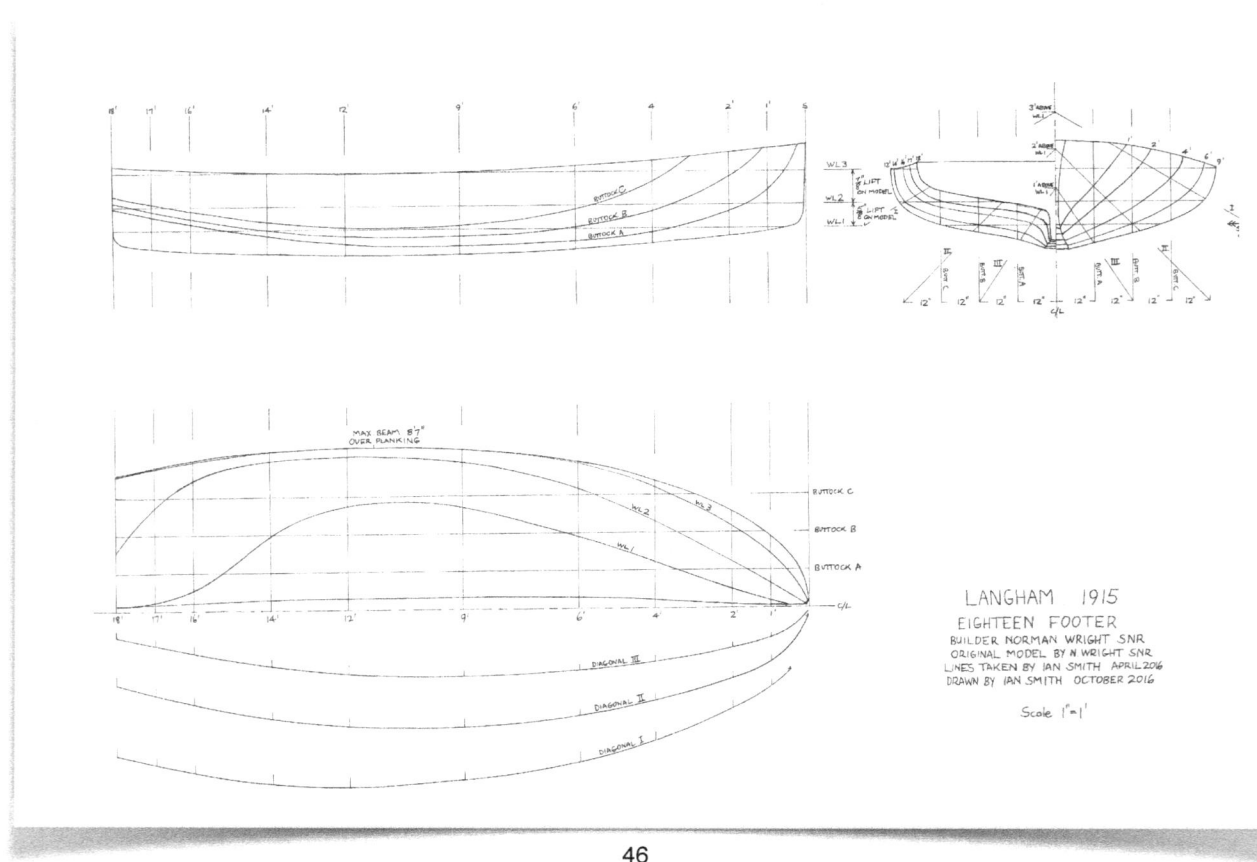

couldn't do better than a fourth in the rest of the season at the SFS, but won the Club Championship at the SASC again.

In November 1908, the SFS held a test championship as usual to see which boats would go to Perth for the Interstate contest. *Oweenee* surprised everyone by coming second to Billy Golding's *Eileen* (Billy Read) and beat Chris Webb in Golding's *Australian*. The Club Championship was the next test race and *Oweenee* won. The third test race was held by the Sydney Sailing Club, and *Oweenee* was not allowed to enter, even though Tom Banks expressed his desire not to go to Perth. He publicly questioned his banning and he had a number of supporters, arguing that best-and-best racing meant just that, and the SSC was preventing the fastest boat from representing the state. Banks put the boat up for sale, but it didn't change hands as his brother Jack Banks sailed her in a limited sails race in the Anniversary Regatta a few weeks later in January 1909. Tom Banks bought a Donnelly-built 16' skiff *Spindrift* and sailed that with the PJSSC. The following season (1909-10) Tom Banks entered *Oweenee* in a few SFS heats, winning one but being beaten in the final. He was prohibited again from being considered for the looming January Interstate carnival, but he had a moral victory by winning the SFS 18' Championship race that month. *Oweenee's* mixed success is probably the main reason for its eventual disappearance from 18-footer racing. The last race I can find which *Oweenee* entered was the 18' race at the 1911 Anniversary Regatta in which she came third. A commentator in April 1912 suggests that the boat was no longer racing and suggests that that would be the end of the experiment of the introduction of the skiff type into 18' racing. He was right up to a point, but it only took twenty years for it to happen again (see below). All new boats up to the 1930's were built to the minimum 7' beam rule. Jack Robinson retired *Young Jack* and built a beamier *Livonia* for the 1908-9 season. The beamier boats had won.

The 16 Foot Skiffs

The old 16-footers had been a big class in the 1880's and early 1890's, and best-and-best racing was the rule, with unlimited sail area and unlimited crews, with professionals contesting the major events, but they had always kept the rules on maximum beam of 5' and maximum depth of 20". They faltered and died out in the late 1890's, and the fact that this was exactly the same time as the 18-footers were beginning to become the dominant class is probably not coincidental. But in 1901 a few men gathered at the Waterview Hotel in Balmain with the object of setting up a club to race skiffs from 12 to 18', with limited sails (main and jib) and limited boom length, limited beam and limited crews, calling it the Port Jackson Sailing Skiff Club. Their expressed object was to limit the cost. Their first race in late November 1901 had seven 16' boats and one 18-footer. They were existing pleasure skiffs that were not particularly set up for racing. Many if not most were clinker-built completely open boats designed for both rowing and sailing, relatively narrow with built heels. Some were gaff-rigged, some were lug-rigged. There were eleven entries in their next race a fortnight later, again all 16-footers except for the lone, slow 18-footer. At the end of the first season the club decided to cater only for 16-footers, and rules were established that the boats had to be between 15'9" and 16' in length, no wider than 5'6" outside the planking, outside gun'ls and moulding were limited to 2" a side, there were to be no inside gun'ls and no decking whatsoever, the depth had to be between 18 and 21", and the tuck could be no wider than 3'9" outside planking. Booms were limited to 14'. Crews were limited to 3 hands, and the skipper had to be the owner or an approved substitute. They had regulation-sized coloured sail insignias and took their handicaps at the start. For the second season 1902-03, four new boats were built, one by the ageing Donnelly, one by a newcomer Tom Phillips of Balmain whose family were boatbuilders for several generations after this. The PJSSC held 18 races in this second season and had 15 registered skiffs. Another club was set up in Middle Harbour and raced mixed fleets at first, but used PJSSC rules for their 16-footers which soon became the dominant class at the club.

Commentators after this second season pointed out that the limited boom length was leading to freak rigs, including at least one lateen-rigged boat and several high aspect lugs'ls. Most of the fleet however made longer gaffs and peaked them higher than usual, almost to a gunter rig. Most of the sails were made at the same loft, Dingwall's of Balmain, and were cut with cloths square to the leech instead of parallel to the leech as was the rule

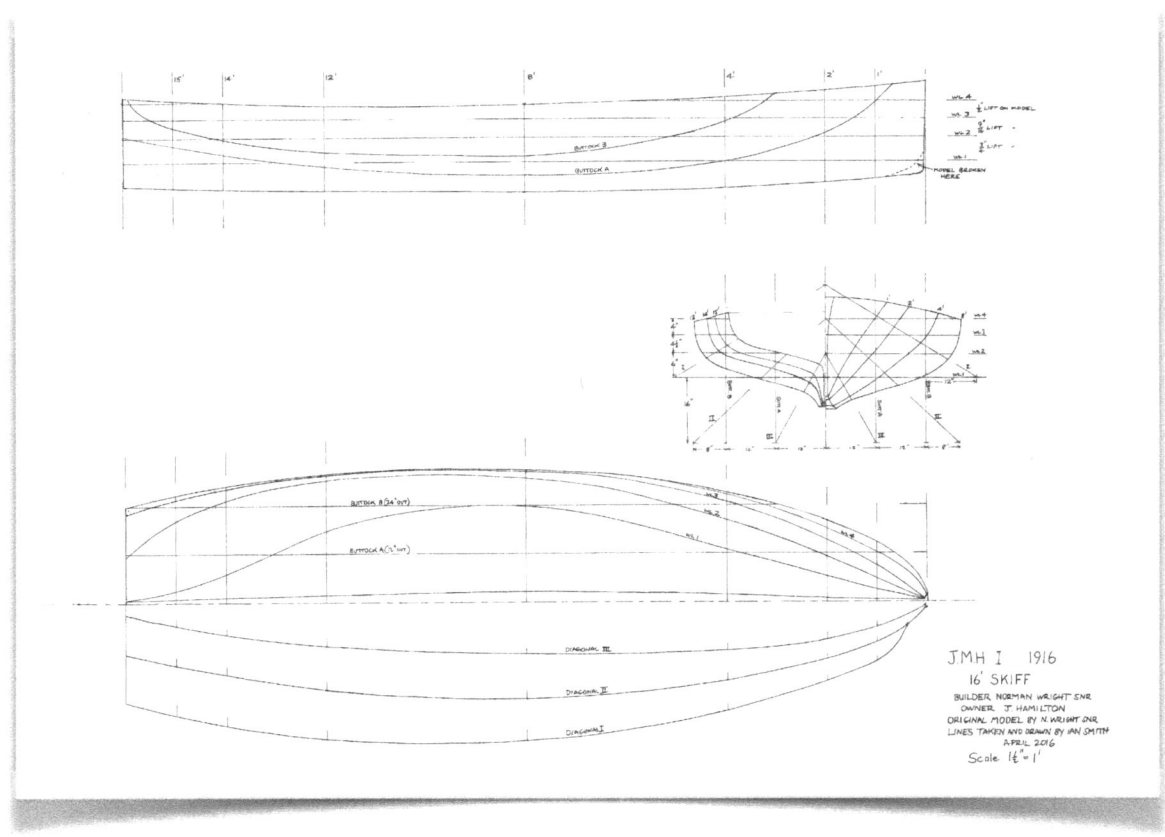

4.8 Lines of JMH 1915 and HSM (prior to 1925), Brisbane and Sydney heeled 16 foot skiffs. Note the "Brisbane Bow" on JMH, well-rounded and full on deck.

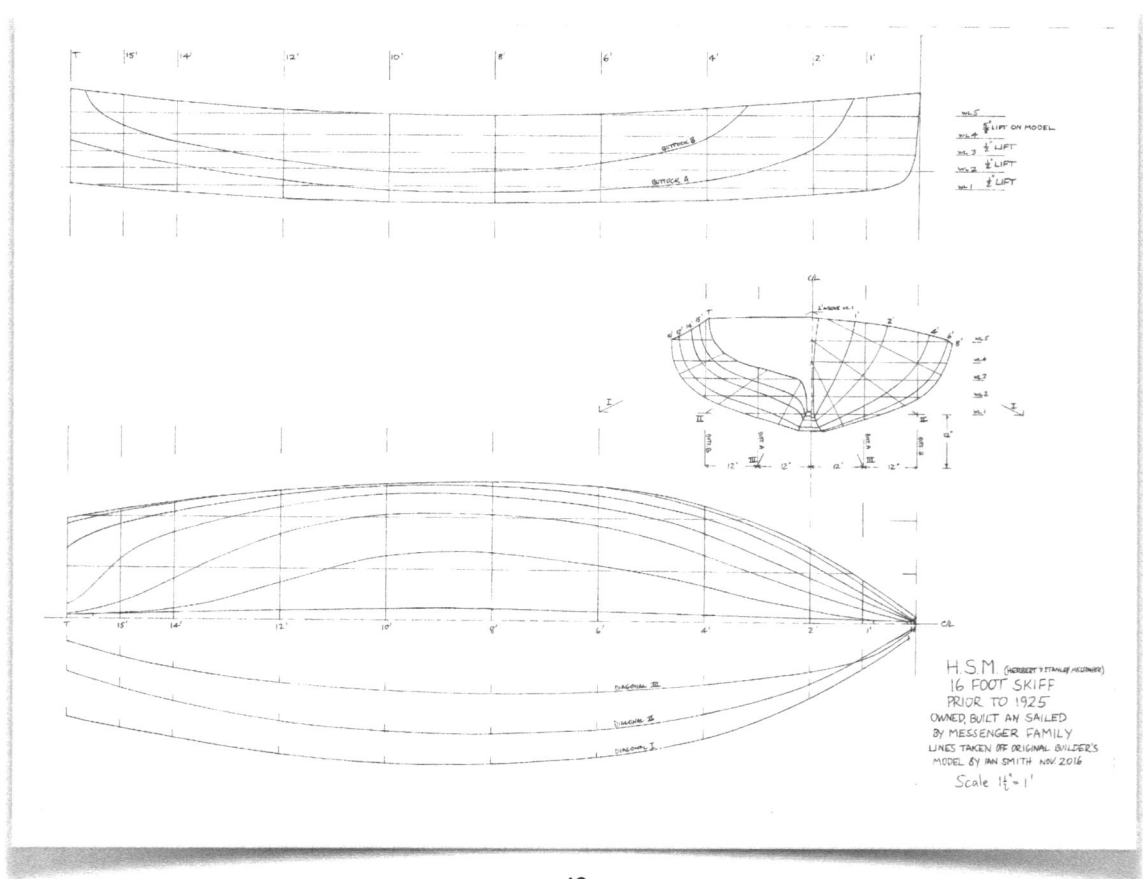

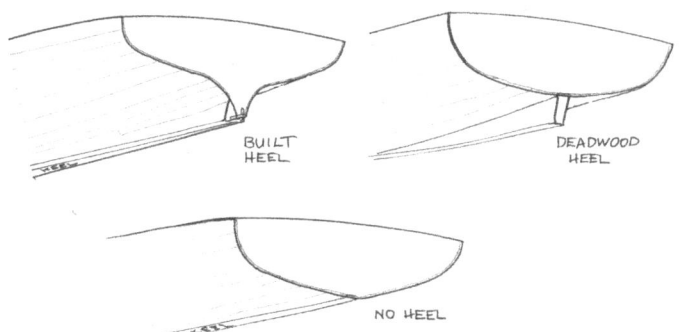

4.9 Sketch of heel and no-heel

in the 18's, and utilised full-length battens above the throat. For the third season, a limit of 220 square feet in sail area was established, and four hands were allowed, but the boom length restriction remained and the high-peaked mains of the 16-footers became very distinctive on Sydney Harbour for decades. Various other moves were made to remove the restrictions on hulls and rigs but they were always defeated, but the call for the boats to be allowed to carry extras kept appearing from about 1906 on. In April 1912 a meeting to discuss such a proposal was split 50/50, but a 2/3 majority was required. Some discussion was held about establishing a new club. Over the winter it went further, and in August the Sydney Sailing Skiff Club was established, allowing extras of up to 140 sq ft and carrying 5 hands, to race on alternate Saturdays, showing that there was some cooperation between the clubs involved. The arrangement lasted only for a season, as the PJSSC absorbed the new club in September 1913 and allowed the extras and 5 hands.

The early boats mostly dropped out after a few seasons as the newer boats built for racing were faster. Many of the original boats were clinker-planked. Because of the restrictions, 16 foot skiffs became far more standardised than the 18-footers. I can't prove it but I suspect that all boats built specifically to race with the skiffs would have been batten-seam carvel built, with fairly similar internal layouts and near-identical rigs. Some boatbuilders like Donnelly built skiffs as well as other types, but some new builders like Philips of Balmain and Douglass of Narrabeen specialised in 16 foot skiffs. Others were built by amateurs. The fleet became numerous fairly early on. By the fourth season (1904-05) there were 24 boats on the roll, and by 1910 there were 28. I've already mentioned the Middle Harbour Sailing Club (which

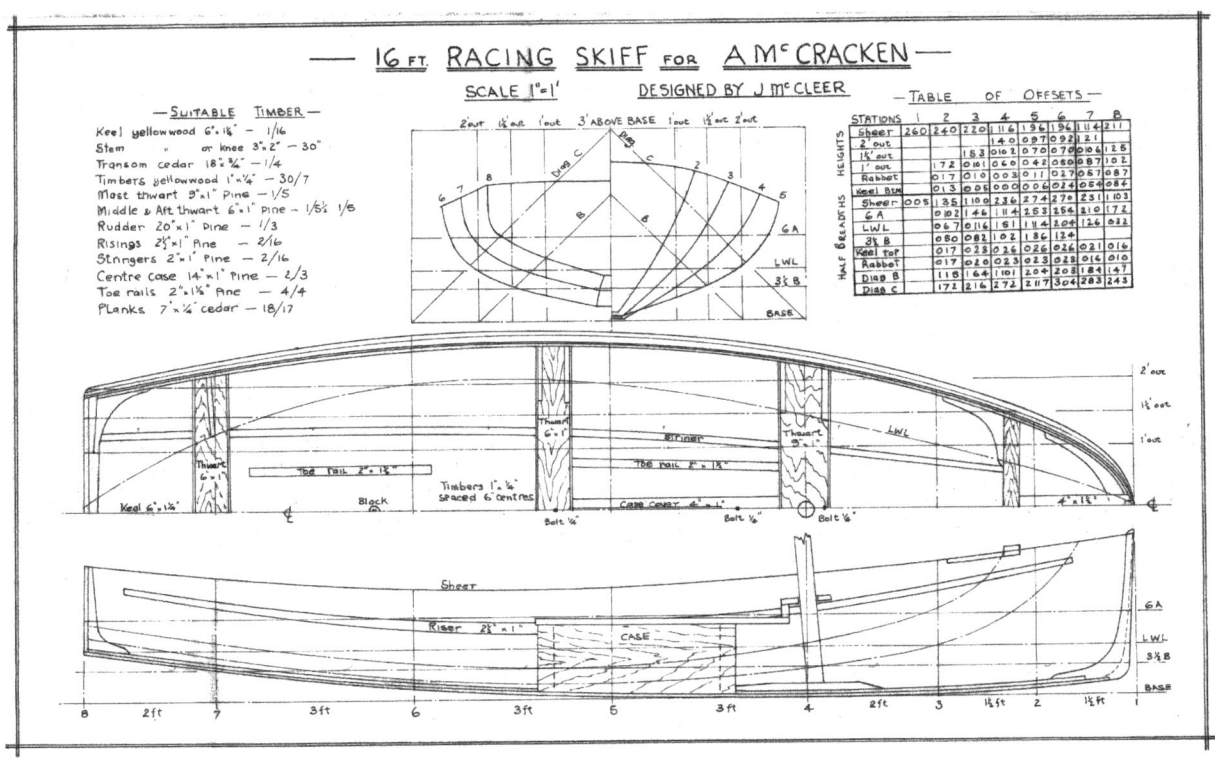

4.10 Lines of 16 foot skiff Dove IV by Jack McCleer 1935. Sixteen-footers had changed very little from the early 1920's when they dropped the heel, and Dove was competitive right up until the 1951-52 season. Traced from original blueprint by Bill Bollard 1992.

4.11 A fleet of 16-footers in the 1920's showing their distinctive almost identical rigs which showed very little change from 1904 to about 1954.   HALL COLLECTION ANMM

eventually became the MH 16-Footers Club and still exists), but other clubs started in Vaucluse, Drummoyne and in Belmont and Toronto up the coast and in Brisbane. The first Interstate races with Brisbane were in 1910. Eventually they established in Perth and to a small extent in Melbourne. The sixteens were the biggest numerical class of open boats of all during the period we are covering.

According to the late Frank Bonnitcha, sixteen foot skiff historian for both Drummoyne and Middle Harbour Clubs, at some stage in the 1920's Brisbane builders began to build their skiffs without heels, that is, the planking ran all the way to the tuck either side of the keel, with no reverse curve, and no deadwood (Bonnitcha, 2001). It has been suggested that the Brisbane builder Toby Whereat (later the builder of *Aberdare* and multiple 16' champion) was the first. These boats proved faster downwind, and Sydney and other centres began to buy boats from Brisbane builders. Sydney and particularly Lake Macquarie builders copied the fashion: Les Steel, the Chapman brothers and the Fennell brothers (all at Lake Macquarie) were building no-heel skiffs by 1924-5, and winning races with their boats. The idea for abandoning the heel was already known- Charlie Dunn had tried it in his 6' beam 18-footer *Crescent IV* as far back as 1905, and a report of the visit of St George 14' dinghies to Melbourne in 1913 had the St George boats racing against local Victorian as well as South Australian boats that were narrower, built like skiffs, with square bow transoms and "little or no heel" (many built by Charlie Peel, a Melbourne builder who had worked for J.Hayes and Sons in Sydney for a time). At least one 18-footer followed suit: in 1924 Bob Gourlay who had been Secretary of the Port Jackson Skiff Club had Balmain boatbuilder Tom Phillips built him a no-heel boat of

4.12 Sixteen-footer Rival (Harold "Darkie" Griffin, 1928) on display at Wharf 7, Sydney Heritage Fleet, was sailed until 1965.

7'3" beam he named *Furious*. It was not a particularly fast boat, and it doesn't seem like anyone copied him. But this relatively small change revolutionised the 16' skiffs and had a major effect on the 18-footers after 1932. As mentioned, narrow skiff-like hulls had been tried a number of times on 18-footers in the early 20th century with mixed success, and I suggest that the lack of a heel contributed to *Aberdare's* success after 1932, though it was not the whole story.

The 12-Foot Skiffs

Early history of the 12-foot skiffs is hard to find. According to the website of the Lane Cove 12ft Sailing Skiff Club, the original Lane Cove Sailing Club took on 12' skiffs as its main racing class in 1918, and an article in *Seacraft* magazine in January 1948 probably written by Bryce Mortlock says it was 1917 and the idea of the Club secretary Ben Roff, who insisted on unrestricted sail area. An article by JF Black in The

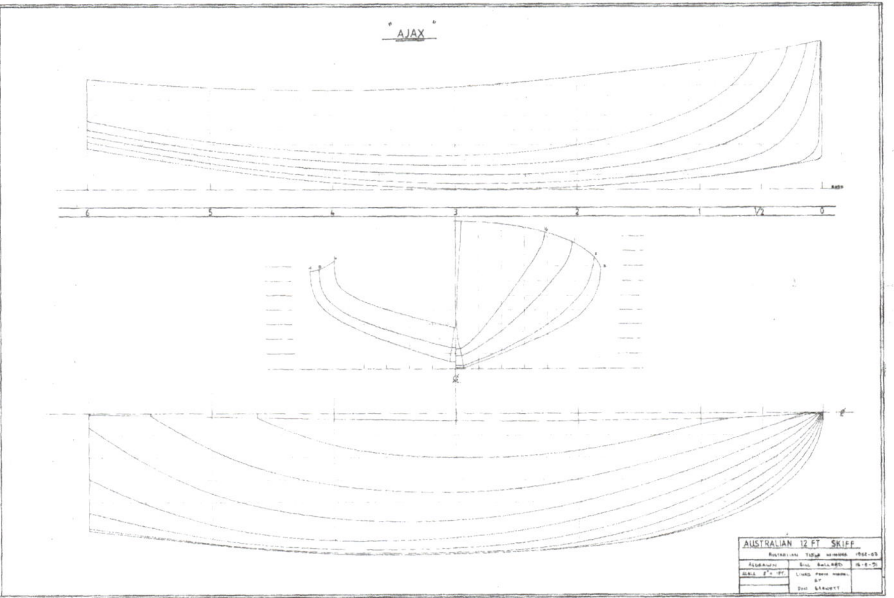

Top: 4.13 Restricted 12-footer Thunder from 1948, in 2016. Designed and built by Bryce Mortlock.

Middle: 4.14 Lines Drawing of 12-footer Ajax, late 1940's, from a model by skipper Don Barnett, drawn by Bill Bollard. Originally batten-seam carvel, Ajax was replanked with 3 skins and still exists.

Bottom: 4.15 Seacraft Magazine in 1948 had these sketches by Bryce Mortlock of the types of 12-footers then being built.

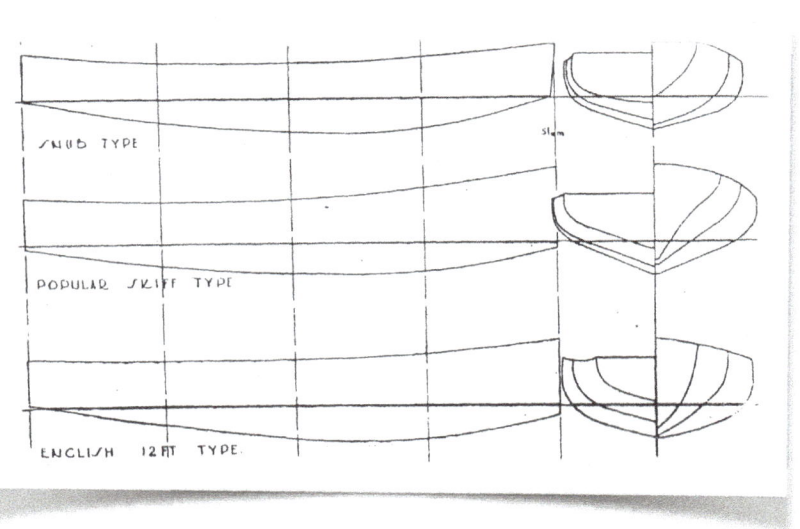

Australian Aquatic Annual in 1937 supports the 1917 date, the same year that a short-lived Cremorne Sailing Club which had introduced a restricted sail area 12 foot skiff three years earlier was wound up. Prior to the War the Lane Cove Club had been sailing mainly 10' and 6' dinghies. In January 1920 the Anniversary Regatta held a race for 12' skiffs "under the rules of the Lane Cove Sailing Club". They seemed to emulate the 16 foot skiffs, with restrictions on hull beam and depth and insistence on no decking, with the important difference of unlimited sail area. The 12's carried more sail relative to their hull length than any of the bigger classes (and still do in the 21st century). They also emulated the sixteens in hull construction and internal layouts, including I believe eliminating the built heel in the 1920's. Beam was restricted to five feet and decks were prohibited. They became quite a large class, putting a hundred boats on the water in 1948 plus 50 more in the restricted sail area class, and have survived (and evolved) as a class to the present day.

CHAPTER 5

The Skiffs Win Out

The First World War took a toll on manpower available to sail, and several boats were laid up for the duration, but fleets of up to 23 boats were seen at the SFS and SSC races during the war. Only about ten boats were built between 1915 and 1918, six in Queensland and only four in NSW, and with the end of the war the laid-up boats resumed sailing and the returned soldiers filled the boats, but building new boats took a while to get going again. In 1919 *Britannia* was the only new boat to join the Sydney fleet, and Brisbane again took the lead with nine new boats that year. Sydney builders didn't get going again until 1921 when five new boats appeared, followed by six in 1922. Between 1923 and 1932 fourteen new boats were added to Sydney's fleet, and fifteen in Brisbane and North Queensland. The most prolific builders in Sydney were Charlie Dunn, Bob Barbour and George Press, the latter two chiefly building new boats for themselves and selling the previous model, and Charlie Dunn building for both himself and customers. Jack Whereat was the most prolific in Brisbane. All of the new boats were of the beamier type with a built heel, the narrowest being Tom Phillips' *Furious* of 1924 which also had no heel but it was not a particularly successful boat. Boats built before the War were still competitive in the early 1930's. Throughout the 1920's fleets of either

5.1 Start of the SFS Club Championship November 1923. Two ferries and a crowd on Clark Island are watching from right Sydney, Life Saver, Arline beyond with diamond, possibly Avalon beyond her, Pastime (Horseshoe), Kismet, Mavis (nearest island with triangle), Britannia, Awaya, Onda. Others obscured are H.C.Press, Australia, Swastika, Endeavour and NSW. Arline (Wes West) won from Britannia (George Robinson) and Lifesaver (Trappy Duncan). Favourite H.C.Press (Chris Webb) was fourth. From a postcard, author's collection.

side of 30 boats turned up on alternate Saturdays for the SFS and the SSC, and both clubs were flush with funds from the two or three ferries that followed every race. The duplication of functions led to the two clubs combining, or rather the SFS subsuming the SSC in 1925. Newspapers wrote up every race, the boats names and skippers were famous. A regular and comforting spectacle was seen on the Harbour every Summer Saturday. All seemed right with the world.

As noted before, the sailing qualities of the skiffs did not go un-noticed by 18-footer sailors. The attempts to build more skiff-like hulls in the early 20th century had mixed success, and nothing much was attempted along those lines after the *Oweenee* controversy for over a couple of decades other than the afore-mentioned *Furious* of 1924. But in 1932, Brisbane 16-footer helmsman Vic Vaughan and owner Fred Hart commissioned builder Alf (Toby) Whereat (son of JH Whereat and a leading builder of 16' skiffs) to build a heel-less 18-footer along 16-footer lines, and the resulting boat was *Aberdare* which immediately began to beat all older boats in Brisbane. Her beam was just 7 feet, she carried a crew of only seven when the other 18's were carrying 10-15 crew, and her rig was a skiff-type high-peaked gaff with horizontal panels and full battens above the throat. Easily winning the selection trials for the 1933 Interstate Carnival, she came to Sydney with a blaze of advanced publicity, but to the immense enjoyment of the old guard she could only manage a third in the one-race Championship on a light day with only second sails.

I'll only briefly describe what happened next as it has been excellently covered in detail by Robin Elliott in *Galloping Ghosts* (2012). A number of Sydney sailors decided that the narrower type was the way they wanted to go, and rumours flew of Sydney owners commissioning skiff-types from Brisbane. They proved true when Bob Cuneo applied for registration for his boat *The Mistake*

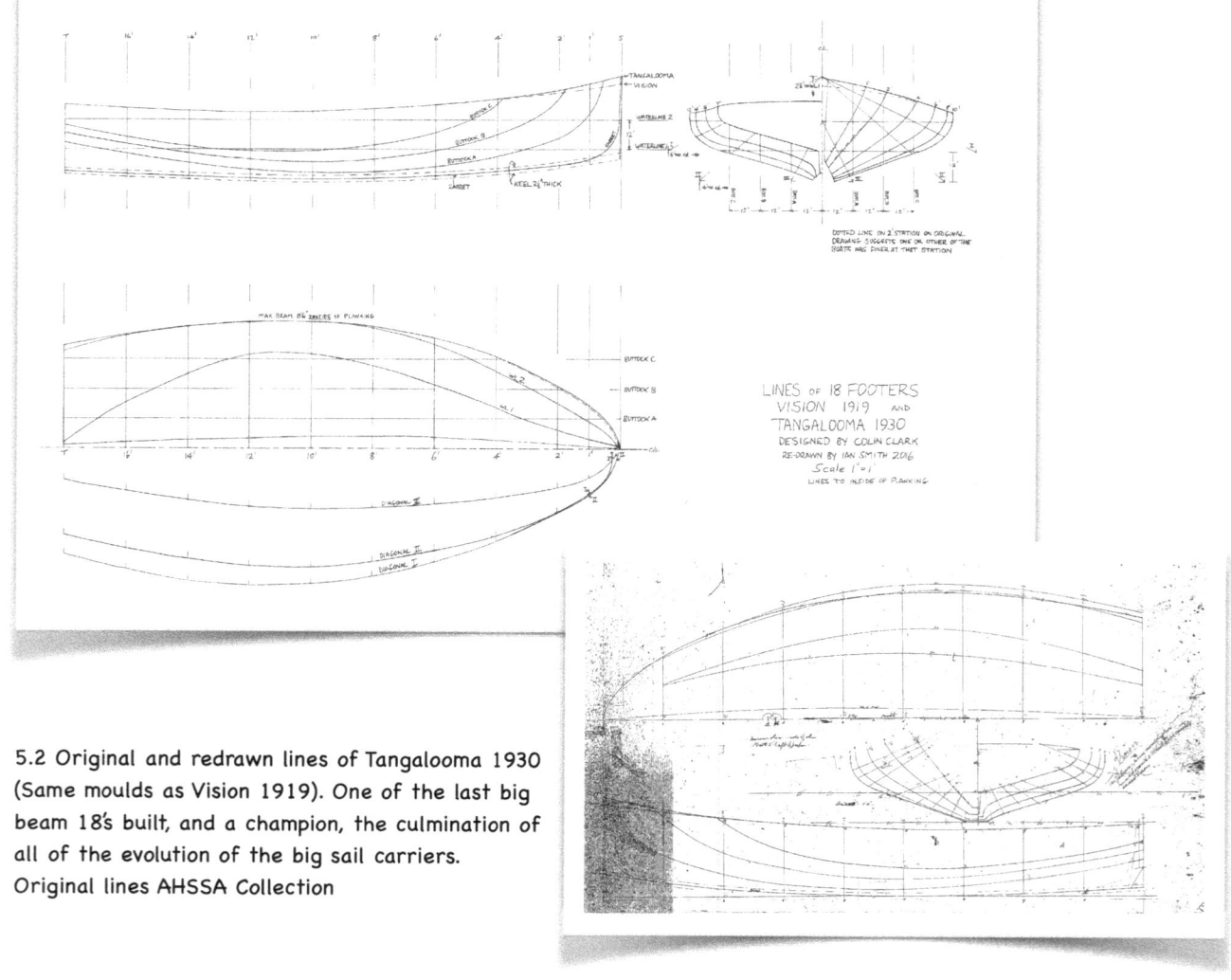

5.2 Original and redrawn lines of Tangalooma 1930 (Same moulds as Vision 1919). One of the last big beam 18's built, and a champion, the culmination of all of the evolution of the big sail carriers.
Original lines AHSSA Collection

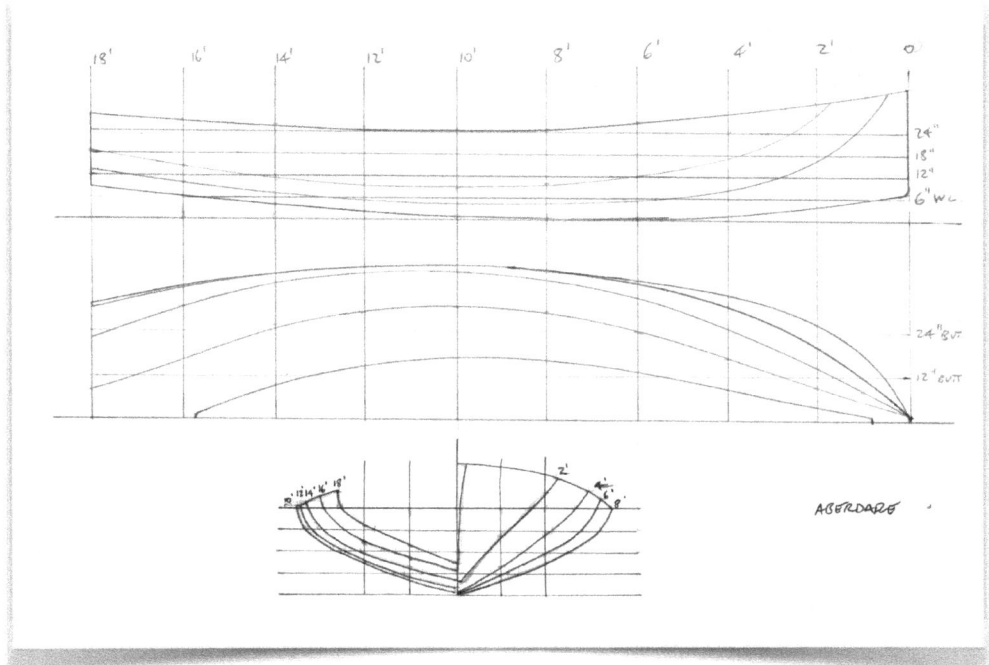

5.3 Lines of Aberdare 1932, taken from the moulds on which the 2000 replica was built by Robert Tearne, from a model taken off the original boat by Tommy Phillips in 1944. AUTHOR'S COLLECTION

1934, the big boat owners of Brisbane formed a breakaway club, and the Sydney Flying Squadron pulled out of the agreement to race the skiff boats of the Brisbane 18-Footers Club, a decision which appalled many of its own members. The movement towards the new type was growing, and it all happened very fast after that: during the Christmas/New Year break, many former members of the SFS (including Peter Cowie Snr and Jnr) formed a new club, the NSW 18-Footers Sailing League and announced on 5 January 1935 that its first event would be the Australian 18 foot Championship as they had done a deal with Brisbane. It caused quite a kerfuffle and many personal relationships were

built by Whereat (J.H. as Toby had died of pneumonia after completing *Aberdare*) as an *Aberdare* copy at the SFS in late 1933. In the absence of a rule against it, the registration was accepted, but the SFS panicked and closed its books. *The Mistake* was the third most successful boat in the SFS during the 1933-4 season and things seemed to have settled down. But the "big boat" owners in Brisbane were sick of *Aberdare* and another skiff-type *Marjorie II* beating them so consistently and led by *Tangalooma* owner Colin Clark, withdrew from the Brisbane 18-Footers Sailing Club. But this club controlled the Interstates in Queensland, and with a distinct lack of enthusiasm the SFS allowed Billy Fisher's big beam *Australia* and George Press's new 7' beamer *H.C.Press IV* to represent NSW in Brisbane, where *Aberdare* won 2 out of the 3 races. Later in

5.4 Aberdare over Tangalooma, showing the contrast in size and shape of the old big beam big sail rigs and the new skiff-type rig.
TOM CUNEO COLLECTION

damaged. The first President was James Giltinan who had been a recent President of the SFS, and had been a driving organiser behind the breakaway of Rugby League from the Rugby Union in 1908. The choice of the name League for the new club was probably his. The new League had another bombshell: all of their events were to be held on Sundays! This had never happened, and it shocked the Churches and others, but was accepted once the League promised to use some events to raise money for charity, particularly crippled children of which there were many before polio vaccination. But it was a masterstroke. Twelve and sixteen foot skiff sailors could race in their own fleets on Saturdays, and join the 18's on Sundays. The League's fleet built up quickly (many financed by bookmakers) and there were twenty or more starters in most of their races. The Squadron had similar or slightly smaller numbers. The public was quite happy to join the ferries to watch races on both days, and both clubs continued to run their races separately and with financial success for the rest of the golden age and beyond. Both clubs still exist, though the SFS stopped running a fleet of modern 18's in the early 21st century. The League runs the only modern fleet in Sydney, and the SFS has become the home of the Historical replicas.

5.5 Syd Barnett launching Lois built by F.Morrow in 1935. Syd (behind the boy holding the hat) was a brilliant hand and then skipper but died later that year.
Lois was one of the many boats built to race with the League and was owned, as many of them were by a bookie. SFS COLLECTION

The seven-foot beamers were still built with batten-seam carvel cedar planking. Planking was thinner, generally 3/8", decks were narrower, and rigs were larger versions of the 16' skiffs' high-peaked gaff, almost gunter rigs. Alf Beashel, stalwart of the League published a booklet with details of what he called the "modern type of 18-footer" with a great amount of detail of hulls and

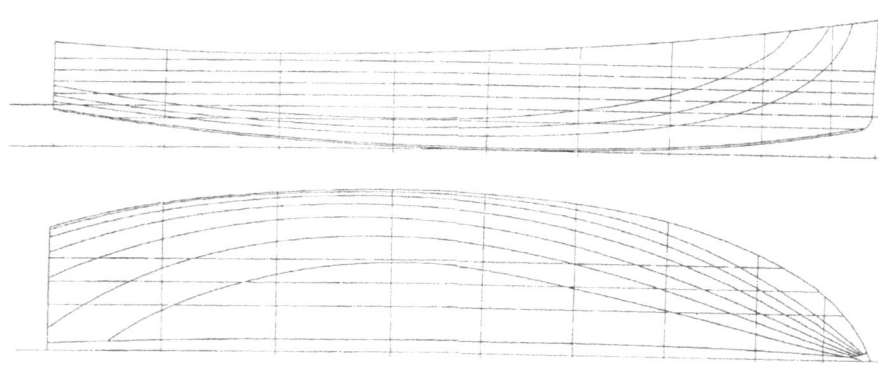
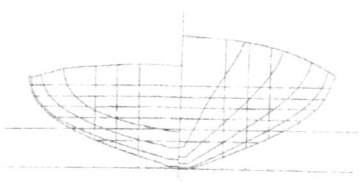

5.6 Lines of Top Weight II, Norm Wright Snr 1947, one of the last of the 7' beamers. Redrawn by Bill Bollard.
AHSSA COLLECTION

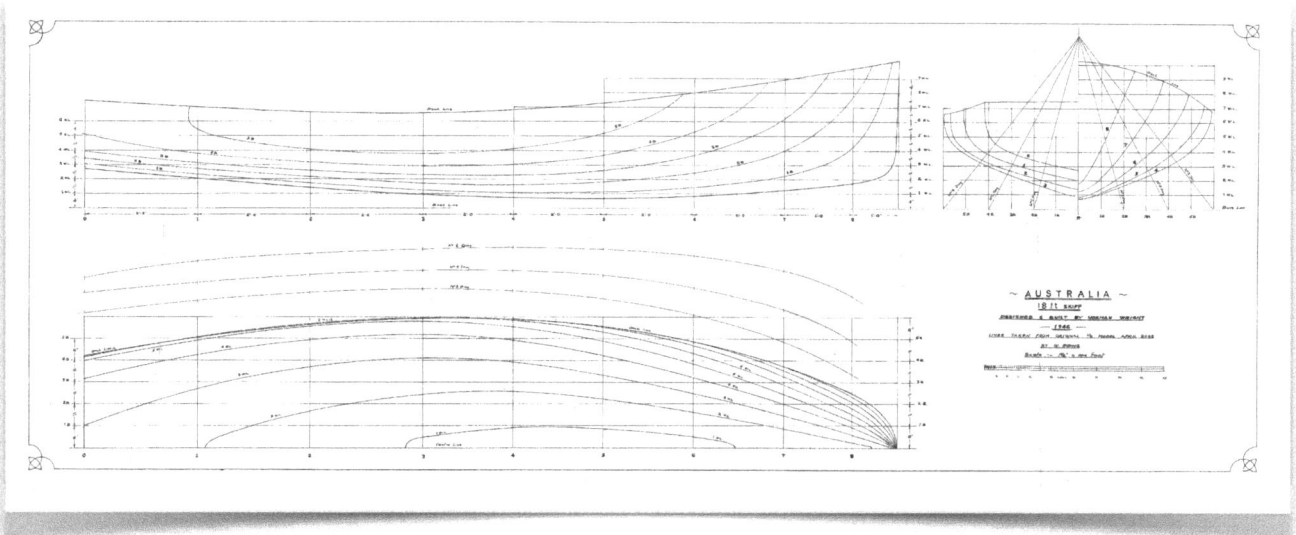

5.7 Lines of Australia 1946, one of the early 6' beamers, lifted by W Ewing from builder Norm Wright Jnr's original model, redrawn by Bill Bollard. AHSSA COLLECTION

rigs. Brisbane boatbuilders had for a long time utilised Silver Ash for steam-bent ribs, 2/3 of the weight of the Spotted Gum generally used in the Sydney boats, and Sydney builders began to follow suit. The boats were very rounded on deck and fine down at the waterline, and this became known as the "Brisbane bow" which Sydney builders found hard to build until they realised the Brisbane secret (more in Chapter 9). Many of the League boats were built in Brisbane, but within a few seasons Sydney builders were providing the bulk of new boats.

The Sydney Flying Squadron kept racing their big-beam boats, but of only 5 new boats built for the Squadron from 1934 to 1944, four were heel-less 7' beamers and one (*Zephyr* 1941) was heeled but 7'2" beam (the Squadron admitted boats of 7' beam in 1937). The vast majority of the new boats built in Sydney raced with the League, about forty of them between 1934 and 1944! About ten or eleven narrow boats were built in Brisbane in the same period. Chief among the Sydney builders were Willis Douglass who had made his name building 16-footers, Billy Fisher and Tom and Roy Phillips, and in Brisbane Norman Wright Senior and Junior and Charlie Crowley.

History has a way of repeating itself. In 1941 Brisbane builder Norm Wright tried to convince the Brisbane 18-Footers Sailing Club to do away with beam restrictions citing the lower cost as a big advantage. In 1944, George Press convinced the SFS to allow him to race a new 6'3" beam 18-footer, *H.C.Press VII*. The Squadron's fleet was ageing but it was still a surprise to many that they agreed. The Brisbane club allowed narrower boats from 1945, but found resistance from the NSW

5.8 Australia, Norman Wright Jnr 1946, one of the earliest 6' beamers.
AHSSA COLLECTION

League who still had an active fleet of 7' beamers and rejected the new boats. The Brisbane club decided to negotiate with the SFS for the next Interstates. They sent down four new 6' beamers, *Australia, Culex, Jenny Too* and *Reform* to Sydney in 1947 and resoundingly defeated the Sydney team of eight boats, only two of which were new 6' beamers, plus *H.C.Press VII* at 6'3', a three-year old boat. One of the boats was *Native* which was the Donnelly's renamed *Scot* of 1906! Wee Georgie Robinson had retired *Britannia* in 1944 and was SFS Champion with the old *Aberdare* and was the local favourite but was outclassed. The defeat spurred Squadron members to build a whole bunch of new boats for the next season when they fielded a fleet of fourteen six foot beamers plus five older boats. Several boats including *Culex, Jenny Too* and *Sea Witch* were purchased from Brisbane. Boatbuilder Bill Barnett was the new owner of the Wright's *Jenny Too* and he led the 1948 team to Brisbane. The other boats going were Horrie Balkwell's *Tiger* and two others. They were resoundingly defeated by the five new Brisbane boats. This spurred Bill Barnett to design and build his own boat *Myra* for the next season which dominated the SFS fleet of about twenty boats and easily won the 1949 Interstates in Sydney. After the win, nine new boats were built for the 1949-50 season. New Brisbane boats easily won the next series in Brisbane, so Bill Barnett built *Myra Too* and won the State, Australian and World Championships in 1951. Hang on, World Championship???

The League had conducted what they termed the 18-footers World Championship in 1938 by inviting the two classes of New Zealand boats which happened to be 18' long but with little similarity to the Sydney boats or to each other, which the League boats won easily on home waters. A return visit to Auckland in 1939 was won by a New Zealand M-Class boat in controversial circumstances involving an incident that is second only in Australia-New Zealand sporting history to the under-arm bowling incident. You can read all about it in Elliott (2012). The New Zealand connection continued after the Second World War, run by the League who shut out the SFS just as the SFS had shut them out from Interstate competition, but that story is outside the scope and time scale of this work and has also been thoroughly covered by Elliott. It had a huge influence on the evolution of 18' skiffs along with the changes in technology which led to the phasing out of boats planked in solid timber and the change to Bermudan rigs and the use of trapezes, all in the 1950's. The fact that Bill Barnett's SFS boat *Myra Too* was in the 1951 World Championship was due to a brief reconciliation between the two Sydney clubs, probably influenced by the deaths in 1950 of Mark Foy and James Giltinan. This cooperation fluctuated up until the present, with at least one more major controversy

5.9 Myra Too just after winning the World Championship pennant in 1951.
JOHN STANLEY COLLECTION

over new types of boats involving Bob Miller (later Ben Lexcen) building *Taipan* in 1959 which led to restrictions, banning, rule changes and acrimony between clubs but eventually moved the eighteen footers along with emerging technology. Some things in the organisation of sailing, as in life, never change.

  Batten-seam carvel boats were still built in the early 1950's, but change was coming. British wartime technology had led to new glues which enabled thin laminations of timber to be glued together for good strength to weight ratios. The first glues required heat to work, and the process of laminating the timber was called hot-moulding. Shortly afterwards, room-temperature glues were developed and using these was referred to as cold-moulding. Hot-moulding never made inroads in Australian boatbuilding so the first laminated boats were referred to as moulded or moulded ply boats. Batten-seam boats were simply referred to as "planked boats". British International 14's were already being moulded, and moulded yacht tenders were available in Sydney by 1950, so the idea was around. In the eighteens the first moulded boat was *Daniel Boone*, built by Dave Marks in New Zealand in 1952, closely followed by *Frolic*, built by Watts and Wright in Brisbane in 1952, but it didn't immediately catch on. Both boats were fragile and difficult to sail. Only planked boats were sent from Brisbane and Sydney to Auckland for the 1954 J.J.Giltinan Trophy contest. They were resoundingly beaten by New Zealand's *Intrigue*, a planked boat built and sailed by Peter Mander, and *Envy*, a moulded boat built in 1953 by Tom Jeffries, in a series which saw the New Zealanders using trapezes for the first time in a series. The Australian sailors had time to have a good look at the New Zealand boats and the defeat gave them a lot of food for thought. The first moulded racing boat in Sydney seems to have been a 16 footer built in the winter of 1952 by Middle Harbour skipper Jack Thom, who included normal steam-bent ribs as well. The first without ribs may have been a sixteen foot skiff *Quest IV* built by T.Denby from Greenwich (Sydney) Sailing Club, which inspired Ken Minter to build one of his *Joans* in moulded ply in late 1953, and a diagonal-planked 16-footer is mentioned as being built in Townsville in late 1953. In the winter of 1954 Bill Barnett who had at least eleven batten-seam 18's under his belt began to build Sydney's first moulded eighteen. Sailmaker George Pearce (known as "Raw Meat" for reasons which I won't go into here) made him an offer he couldn't refuse, and sailed it next season as *Sam Lands*, so Bill started another for himself which became *Myra IV*, then built another for and with the assistance of Len Heffernan called *Jantzen Girl*. In Brisbane Bill Lloyd built *Alborak* in 1954, and in 1955 Watts and Wright built *Buccaneer* and *Alstar III*, Norman Wright Jnr built *Jenny VI*, and Ron Wright built a moulded 16-footer *Joy VII*. Three other builders are mentioned at the time building moulded 16's in Brisbane, but two others continued building planked boats. I have as yet been unable to determine when the last batten-seam carvel open boat was built, but older sailors remember planked boats still being sailed in the sixteens and twelves into the late 1950's, some even with gaff rigs, but they were no longer competitive.

Robin Elliot lists approximately 370 eighteen-footers built between 1880 and 1954 that were batten seam planked. There may have been even more 16-footers built. I've tracked down fifty-four 22-footers, fifty 24-footers and twenty-two 20-footers and there are certainly more to be found. Add in the 14's, 12's, 10's, 8's and 6's plus the nineteenth century 22', 19' and 16' skiffs it adds up to a lot of boats built. Where did they all go?

Well we don't know. We can surmise from the later eighteen-footers that many were converted to other uses. Many retired eighteen-footers were converted to launches but usually didn't last too long. *Britannia*, *Yendys* and *Mississippi* all lasted into the 1980's as launches (*Britannia* was the SFS starter boat from about 1949 to about 1964). Some were given to boys' clubs like the Scouts or just given to local boys who used them for general fun and fishing until they were un-repairable. Many were sold out of Sydney, often to fishermen on the saltwater estuaries which are a feature of the NSW coast. Charlie Dunn had a connection with guess where, Crescent Head and his old *Crescent*'s all ended up with fishermen there. Boat and shipbuilder Watty Ford had business interests in the Pacific islands and sent many boats from 6-footers to 18-footers there. A large majority of boats were simply broken up or burnt for the scrap metal value of their copper fastenings. Crowley's *St George* (1938) is still afloat as a cabin yacht, one of Barnett's *Myras* was afloat at least until a few years ago as an outboard powered open skiff. The

5.10 Britannia as a launch, 1962 in this case as the starting boat for the Snail's Bay Sabot Sailing Club, Wee Georgie at the helm. GIL WAHLQUIST

National Maritime Museum has the restored *Britannia* on display. The Sydney Heritage Fleet has Charlie Hayes' 18-footer *Yendys* (1925) which was restored in the 1980's on display, Darkie Griffin's 16-footer *Rival* (1928) rigged and on display and several 12-footers as well as a fairly decrepit Douglass 18-footer *Chris Webb II* of 1949 in storage. The Brisbane Maritime Museum also has several 16's and 12-footers, and a 16-footer is still preserved in good condition at the yard of Norman Wright and Sons, Bulimba Queensland (and another has recently been found in San Francisco!). Ben Cribb's 1930 18-footer *Tangalooma* lasted into the early 1990's at the Brisbane Maritime Museum, but the original lines plan exists. Podge Newton's *Mississippi*, built as *Admiral II* in 1913 was not so lucky, surviving as a launch until the late 1980's but was cut up without being measured. Perth's *Mele Bilo II* (1922) is restored and on display at the Western Australian Maritime Museum with Jack Cassidy's 16-footer *Evelyn*. The story of the restoration of *Yendys*, *Britannia* and *Mele Bilo II* will be told below. I know of no others that have survived. I live in hope that some will be discovered in old sheds somewhere. I had a brief thrill a few years ago when I got a call from a carpenter mate who said I'd better come and look at two boats he thought were 18's he'd found in an inner city garage but they turned out to be plywood Manly Graduates (MG14's) from the 1960's. If you know where any more are, please let me know! A number of half-models exist and provided the basis for building many of the replica fleet, but the provenance and accuracy of most of these is in some doubt. We have heard awful stories about models and other records that have been thrown out over the years, and the AHSSA is compiling a database of records that still exist to avoid further loss in the future.

So we have only the museum boats and the replica fleet to show what these boats were like, and of the replicas only the 10-footer *Janis* and 18-footer *Britannia* are of true batten-seam carvel build. The skills that built these boats are only known to a handful of people and most of those are aging. Just in case a future generation wants to build more replicas, the rest of this work is a how-to guide. I can think of no better way to honour the builders of the original boats.

Part 2: Construction of a Batten-Seam Eighteen-Footer

Introduction

In 2005 there were still seven guys alive who had built batten-seam open boats in the day, Bill Barnett, Len Heffernan, Ken Minter, Ron Balkwell, Jim O'Rourke, Ron Robinson and George McGoogan. I already knew most of them, and I made it a mission to record them talking about boatbuilding.

Others know **Bill Barnett** far better than I do. I knew Bill of course by reputation as Sydney's leading boatbuilder from the 1940's to the 1970's  and as a champion skipper in many classes. He built Australia's second America's Cup challenger *Dame Pattie*, and our third challenger *Gretel II* as well as many Dragon class boats, 6 metres, 5.5's, surf boats and others. But he also built many 18-footers for himself and others, including eleven boats built batten seam carvel planked. In 2005 I recorded an interview with him in which I got him to talk about boatbuilding and batten-seam carvel boats in particular. I knocked on the door of his house perched on a cliff above Berry's Bay, and he led me down a series of flights of stairs to the boatshed far more nimbly at 90 than I could manage at 55. I needed answers to specific questions on techniques, and Bill was very forthcoming, his memory very clear. Bill's forbears were boatbuilders since at least the middle of the 19th century.

Len Heffernan had been a rival skipper to Bill but they became great friends even while competing at the top level. Len helped Bill build a few boats (for Len himself) with batten-seam carvel planking (and went on to build many more laminated boats), and having sat down with Len whom I had known through the Australian Historical Sailing Skiff Association since the early 1990's over a beer and a tape recorder, I picked his  brains also on batten-seam techniques. Len's admiration for Bill as both a boatbuilder and a skipper was clear.

Ron Balkwell and I had known each other since the early 1990's through the Wooden Boat Association and had talked boatbuilding many times, but I still sat him down with a tape recorder and asked technical questions. Ron built several 12 and 18-footers with batten-seam carvel planking before moving on, like all the others mentioned, to laminated boats. His father and grandfather  had also built and sailed open boats, and his son, the fourth generation Matt is a dab hand at boatbuilding and sailing and is regular crew on the *Britannia* replica. Ron had been apprenticed to Ken Minter, to whom he introduced me, and I also interviewed Ken.

Ken Minter was a leading builder and skipper of 16-footers in the 1940's and 50's and 60's. His boats were considered the best-built 16's around. Interestingly, some of his techniques differed from the others and he was more of a perfectionist.

Other unrecorded conversations were held over a longer period with the son of Wee Georgie Robinson, **Ron Robinson** who had built several batten-seam boats, and had sailed in the Britannia as a teenager and was invaluable in discussions in the fit-out and rigging stages of building the replica...

I also interviewed **Jimmy O'Rourke** who had worked in the 1940's for Willis Douglass a prolific builder of 16's and 18's, but a sound glitch spoiled the recording (my fault, but I took notes).

...and **George McGoogan** who built two as well as being the driving force behind the rebuilding of Yendys in the early 1980's at Cockatoo Island Dockyard where he was the Shipwright Manager.

It's just as well I recorded them when I did: Len, George, Ron Robbo, Ken and Jimmy have all passed away, and Ron Balkwell is suffering from Alzheimer's. Bill Barnett however is still bright and turned 101 in 2016.

For my own part, I have had a forty-year career in wooden boatbuilding, in which time I had a major hand in the building of upwards of 80 boats, repaired and restored several batten seam boats, and built the 10-footer Republic (a replica of Viola of 1900) and the replica of 18-footer Britannia of 1919 both with traditional batten seam carvel planking. I set up and ran the Sydney Wooden Boat School in 1990 and gained a great deal of experience in explaining boatbuilding techniques to first-timers, and began to realise that if I didn't write it down, who would?

These guys who could both build and sail their boats are my heroes. I dedicate this section of the book to them.

CHAPTER 6

Designs and Lofting

The batten-seam boat (sometimes referred to as seam-batten or batten carvel, or ribband carvel, or later just "planked" boats to distinguish them from the new "moulded" boats) is a form of carvel construction in which each seam between adjacent planks is backed up by a narrow batten to which the planks are fastened, always with roved copper nails in local boats. The method derives from whaleboat building where the boats had to be light in weight for handling off ship or shore, and be able to be stored out of the water without the seams opening too much, a requirement also for racing skiffs. From the earliest days of the settlement in Sydney Port Jackson was a whaling port, firstly when at least one of the transports in the Third Fleet (of convict transports), coincidently named *Britannia* went off whaling, and later when whales were hunted close to the NSW coast from shore-based stations. For most of the nineteenth century visiting American whalers came to Sydney Harbour, peaking in the 1850's. Up until the 1870's visiting whale ship crews raced their whaleboats in regattas.

The earlier boats were clinker-built (lapstrake), but New Bedford whaleboat builder James Beetle built the first combination batten seam carvel with top planks being lapstrake in 1833. They were referred to as "smooth" boats. "The boats with smooth bottoms were quieter, it was said, and gallied (frightened) fewer whales. Perhaps a more important consideration was that smooth boats were more easily repaired. They came into general use in the 1850's" (Ansel 2014). Batten seam whaleboats to the New Bedford design became the international standard, and huge numbers of whale boats were built and repaired by boat builders in Sydney, so there was plenty of experience in batten seam construction. Robert Towns and other merchants had fleets of whaling ships engaged in the trade out of Sydney, and the whaleboat type was used outside the whaling industry as well. Government agencies had whaleboats built for

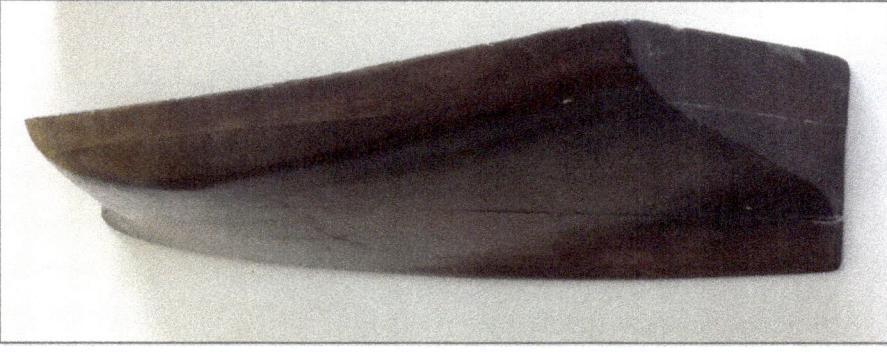

Photo 6A Original half-hull model of Norman Wright Snr's Vanity 1912

other purposes, and these were often of a smaller size (down to 20') then those engaged in whaling (up to 30' or so). Not much is recorded about how the working boats of Sydney Harbour were built, but carvel skiffs and combination carvel/clinker skiffs begin to get mentioned in the 1870's. By the 1880's this was the almost universal method of building open racing boats. A few clinker (lapstrake) boats were the exception, but racing boats built clinker style beyond the late 19th century were extremely rare (Ken Minter built a clinker semi-snub 12-footer in 1949, and always an experimenter, champion sailor-builder Ken Beashel built a 16 foot skiff in the 1960's with reverse clinker planking, starting at the sheer and overlapping each plank towards the keel).

A batten-seam boat is generally built right way up. The builder shapes a keel piece, attaches to it a transom (tuck) and stem knee and bends the keel to the required curve by tomming (shoring) it down from the shed roof. Timber moulds are built to the shape required at a number of sections through the boat and are fitted to the part of the keel representing their section. Planks are then bent around these moulds and fastened to the stem and tuck to give the shape of the boat.

The desired keel curve (spring or rocker) and the shape of the stem knee, tuck and all of the

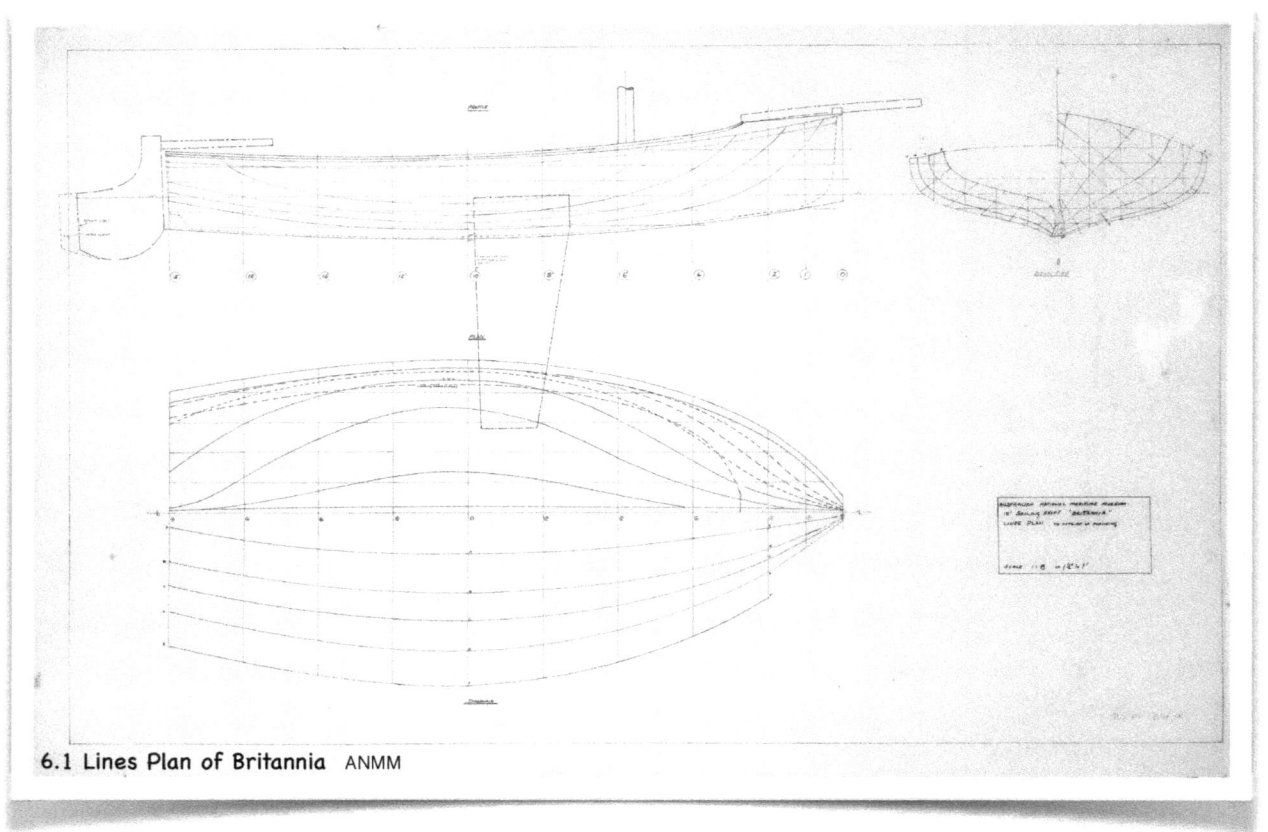

6.1 Lines Plan of Britannia ANMM

moulds is found by lofting the lines plan of the boat full size. Very few drawn lines plans for eighteen-footers exist, largely because most boats were never built from plans. A half-hull model would be carved, usually out of alternate lifts of cedar and sugar pine for contrast. It would be planed and sanded until the designer (usually the builder) was happy with the shape, then measurements were taken off the model, which were then marked out on the lofting floor, and the plans drawn out full size as described below. In many cases, moulds used for a previous boat were set up on a keel sprung to the desired curve, and modifications made to the moulds by shimming or shaving to get the desired shape.

The only yard to consistently design skiffs on paper was Norman Wright and Sons in Brisbane, but many built there were done from half-models and the still-extant company has a huge archive of both plans and models. Each of the replicas built to sail with the Australian Historical Sailing Skiff Association was based on an existing model or a set of lines either originally drawn or lifted from an existing boat. There are still lines and models available to be replicated, but as in the case of several of the AHSSA's fleet the provenance and accuracy of the model is in dispute. More care needs to be taken for future replication.

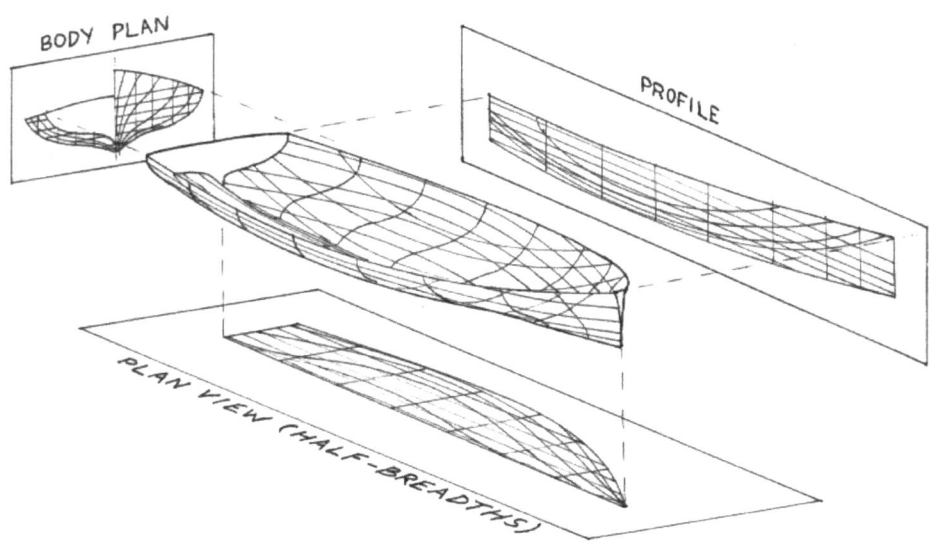

6.2 Relationship of the Lines Plan to the Hull

6.3 The Three Views Superimposed on the Loft Floor

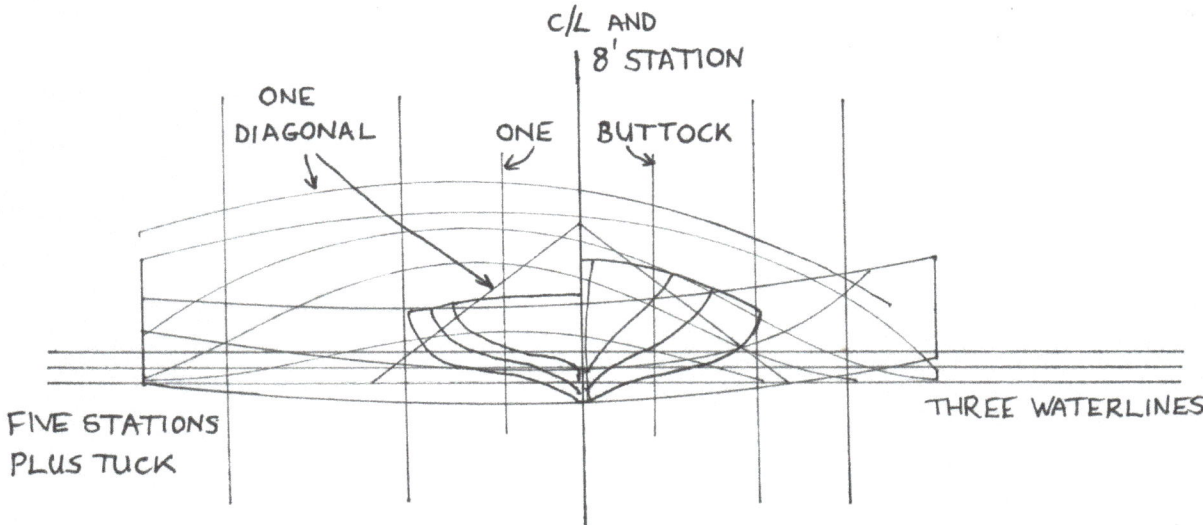

Lofting

Lofting is drawing out the lines of the boat full size so that accurate patterns can be cut for the moulds around which the planking will be bent and for the stem and transom. Drawing 6.2 shows the three views and their relationship to the hull. A table of offsets accompanies the lines plan, or is drawn up off the hull model. Each offset corresponds to an intersection of a curved hull line and a straight line on the grid. See drawing 6.3. Offsets are expressed in feet, inches and eighths of an inch. Although Australia went over to sillymetres decades ago, the original boats were all built to Imperial measurements and as part of the historical process I have used feet and inches all the way through this essay.

I have used the lines of *Britannia* as the example here. These lines were taken off and drawn up by Alan and David Payne for the Australian National Maritime Museum in the late 1980's when the original boat was acquired by the Museum. For the purposes of historical accuracy, station lines were taken at two foot intervals plus an extra one foot from the bow where the shape changes rapidly, resulting in 9 Stations. Original builders of eighteen-footers would not have used such close spacing for their moulds. Most eighteens were built using five, six or seven moulds. As explained later, to build seven moulds for the *Britannia* replica I drew in some new stations once lofting was completed and made moulds off those.

Some measurements off a scale drawing or model can be quite inaccurate when expanded to full size. At a scale of 1 to 12, a pencil line could be up to ¼"(6 mm) out. The majority of builders of open racing boats would not have drawn all three views, they would simply have drawn out the body plan and built the moulds directly off that. There would inevitably have been small discrepancies which would result in a plank having an unwanted bump or hollow in it on some mould or other, but this would be fixed by shimming or shaving the moulds until the desired effect was obtained.

> **How much lofting did the original builders do?**
>
> *Not every builder would have lofted each boat out fully. Many if not most of them would simply have taken a few measurements off the half-model and lofted out only the body plan, the hull sections where they planned to put the moulds. Taking this shortcut means that you have no guarantee that the planks fitted to these moulds will lie fairly. The original builders would simply have shimmed and shaved their moulds to get the planks to lie fair. However, seeing that my hope is that future boats will be built to known lines, lofting out all three views is the only way to be sure of the greatest accuracy in replication. I would also contend that any time spent on the loft floor actually saves time on the build.*

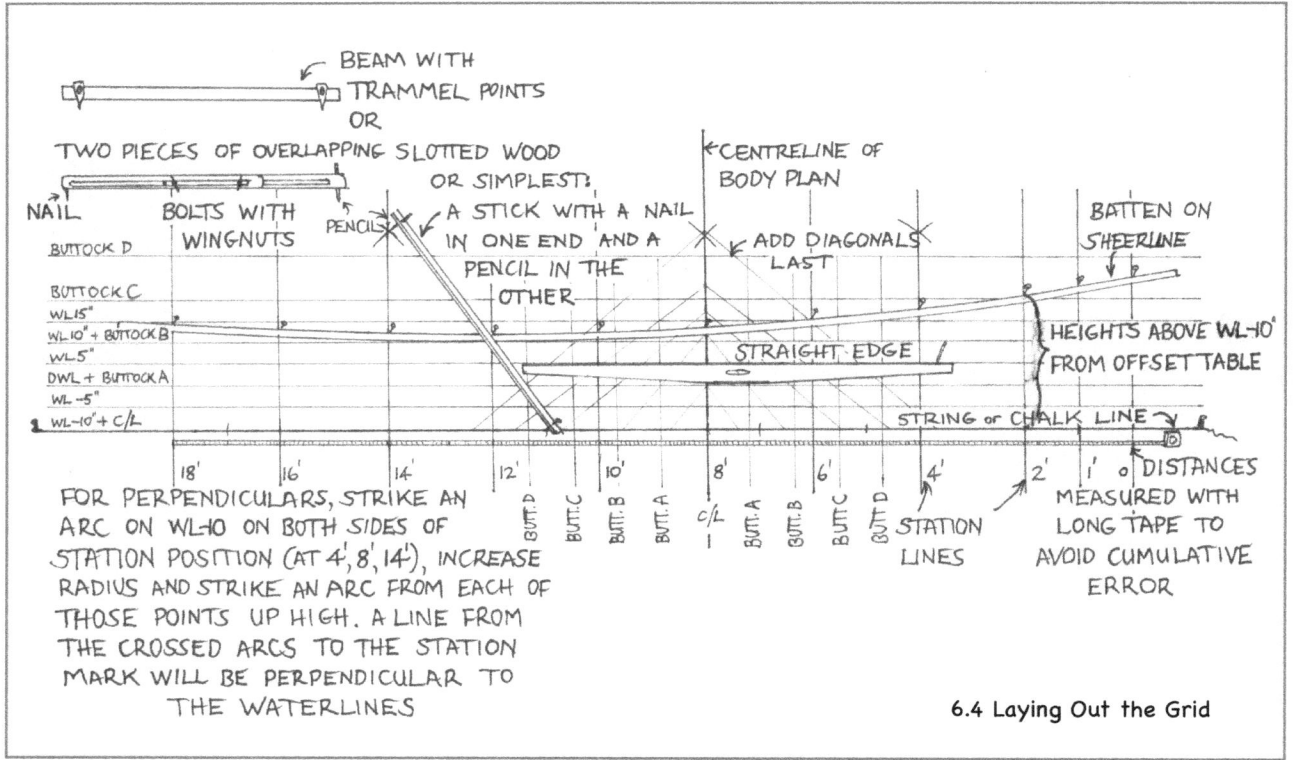

6.4 Laying Out the Grid

Sometimes this involves considerable time and effort.

More accurate moulds can be derived from full lofting of all three views of the boat. It can be laborious, but sometimes it will actually save overall time on the boat, and will certainly end up being closer to what the designer intended. There are even some people like me who actually enjoy it!

You will need an area just bigger than the boat. The process is called lofting because it was often done in a loft above the workshop. Without a proper loft, you will need to lay down a level surface of sheets of plywood or chipboard or MDF painted flat white or light grey or melamine covered, at least ½" (12 mm) thick. You will need a whole bunch of battens, clear oregon is best.

For an 18-footer you will need:
- one of 20-21' x 1 ½" x ¾"
- one of 20-21' x ¾" x ½"
- one of 10' x ½" x ¼"
- and several (you will break some) of 8-10" x ¼" x 1/8"

The longer ones will need to be scarfed. Fibreglass battens are great if you can get them. Buy a bag of 1 ¼" x 14g (30 x 2 mm) flat head bright steel nails and some carpenters pencils, some HB drawing pencils and some coloured biros and marker pens, and a steel tape measure longer than the boat. You will need a straight edge at least 8' long (one machined side of a sheet of plywood is ideal) and a string line.

The designer draws the three views separately, but to save space it is normal to loft the three views superimposed on each other. Your first line is the designed waterline (DWL). Stretch the string line in the required position between two nails, mark very carefully underneath it every couple of feet,

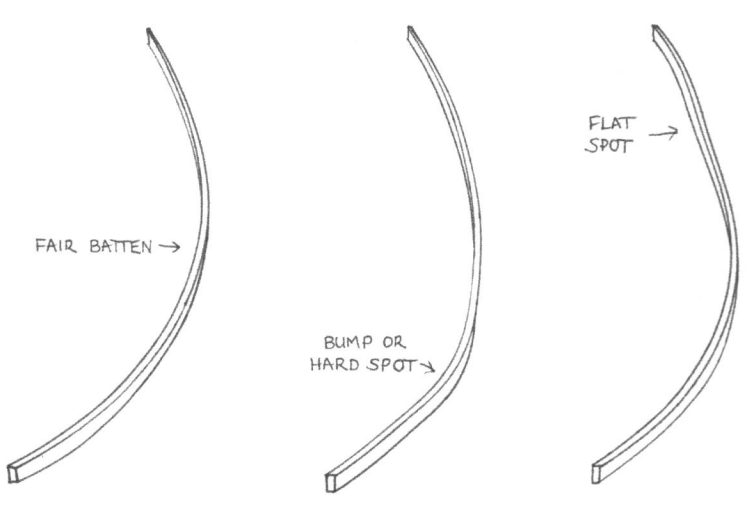

6.5 Sighting Along Battens

remove the string line and join up the dots! It is very important to take particular care to be accurate at this point- an inaccurate grid will make lofting difficult.

With either a set of trammel points or a homemade beam compass, establish a perpendicular which will become the 10' station somewhere in the middle of the lofting. Lay your tape along the base line and mark the position of each station, every 2'. Draw perpendiculars at the 2' and 16' stations, check your accuracy by ensuring that the distances between the stations are the same at the top as well as the base of the board, mark in the intermediate stations on the top as well and draw in the perpendiculars with the straight edge. Draw in the forward-most station which will be the line of the stem unless a fraction of an inch of rake of the stem is indicated (some builders did this to make sure they would be on or under the limit when the boat was officially measured). At the tuck draw the tuck station vertically or with a teensy-weensy bit of rake, with no part of it being more than 17'11 ¾" from the stem. This was also done to ensure the boat would officially measure at 18' or under. Wooden boats have a tendency to change shape ever so slightly when the boat is off the strongback and the moulds are removed and it was quite common for a boat to lengthen a fraction of an inch. Builders would run the planking just past the tuck and trim it back to measurement when the boat was finished, just prior to varnishing. If it still didn't come under 18' a bit could be planed off the stem.

All these lines can be inked permanently, black ink is best. Each line should be labeled with a marker pen in several different places, it is all too easy to lose track of what is what. With the tape and straight edge, mark in all the grid waterlines, I would suggest in blue ink. The vertical buttocks (in green) and the diagonals (purple ink?) come next. Give it a final check by measuring across the grid diagonally each way, the result should be within a small fraction of an inch (a millimetre or two).

The Sheerline and Profile

The first line we draw that actually belongs to the boat is always the sheerline. From the table of offsets, read off the measurement of the heights of the sheer at each station. You simply mark each of these off, tack nails in at the marks, and bend your longest and stiffest batten around the line of nails, holding it in place with other nails behind (not through) the batten.

Sight along from both ends, and see if the curve is fair, that is without bumps, hollows or flat spots. See drawing 6.5. Move any nails which appear to be holding the batten in a bad position. Make the batten continue to bend past the last nail at either end of the batten in the direction it was tending just before the last nail, to avoid flat spots in the ends. If no nails need moving, well that's friggin' unusual, but expect to adjust several nails by up to a quarter inch or so. The general principal where several nails are out of line is to adjust all to an average line of best fit. When you're happy your line looks good from all angles, ink it in permanently, this line will no longer change- so you'd better be happy with it- it's the most noticeable line of all on the finished boat, and in the past the beauty of a boat was often judged on the sweetness of her sheer.

The next line to draw is the same line, only in plan view, generally referred to as the Deck Line to avoid confusion. The same principles apply- once you're happy with the fairness of this line, ink it in, it will not change.

The profile of the hull is the next line to ink in, followed by the line indicating the half-breadth of the stem and the half-siding of the keel.

The Body Plan

You now need several flat straight strips of wood, about 5-6' x ¾" or so x 1/16" or a little thicker, known as tick strips or pick up sticks. As in the drawing you "pick up" the marks for the width of the deckline at each station and the height of the sheer at each station and realising that these are the coordinates of the one point on the sheer, plot them onto the body plan. When each has been done, use the same technique to locate the intersection of the profile and the half-siding of stem and keel and plot these points on the body plan.

Now turn to the table of offsets. At each station there is an offset given for the half-breadth of each waterline, for the height of each buttock, and for the distance along each diagonal. Plot each of these points onto the body plan grid, then throw away the offset table, you won't need it again. With your most flexible battens, pencil in **a line of best fit** through the shotgun scatter of the designers intended points. In some cases, most points will fit.

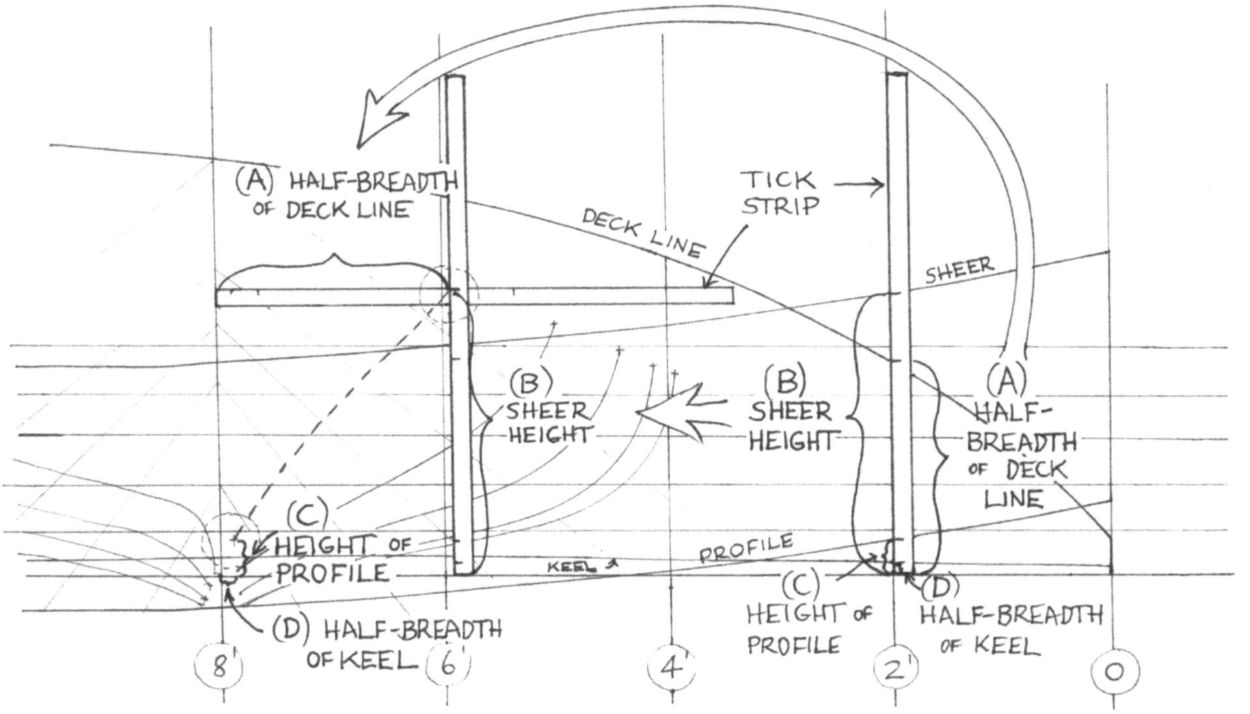

6.6a The Body Plan: Establishing Keel and Sheer Heights from the Profile View

6.6b The Body Plan: Table of Offsets

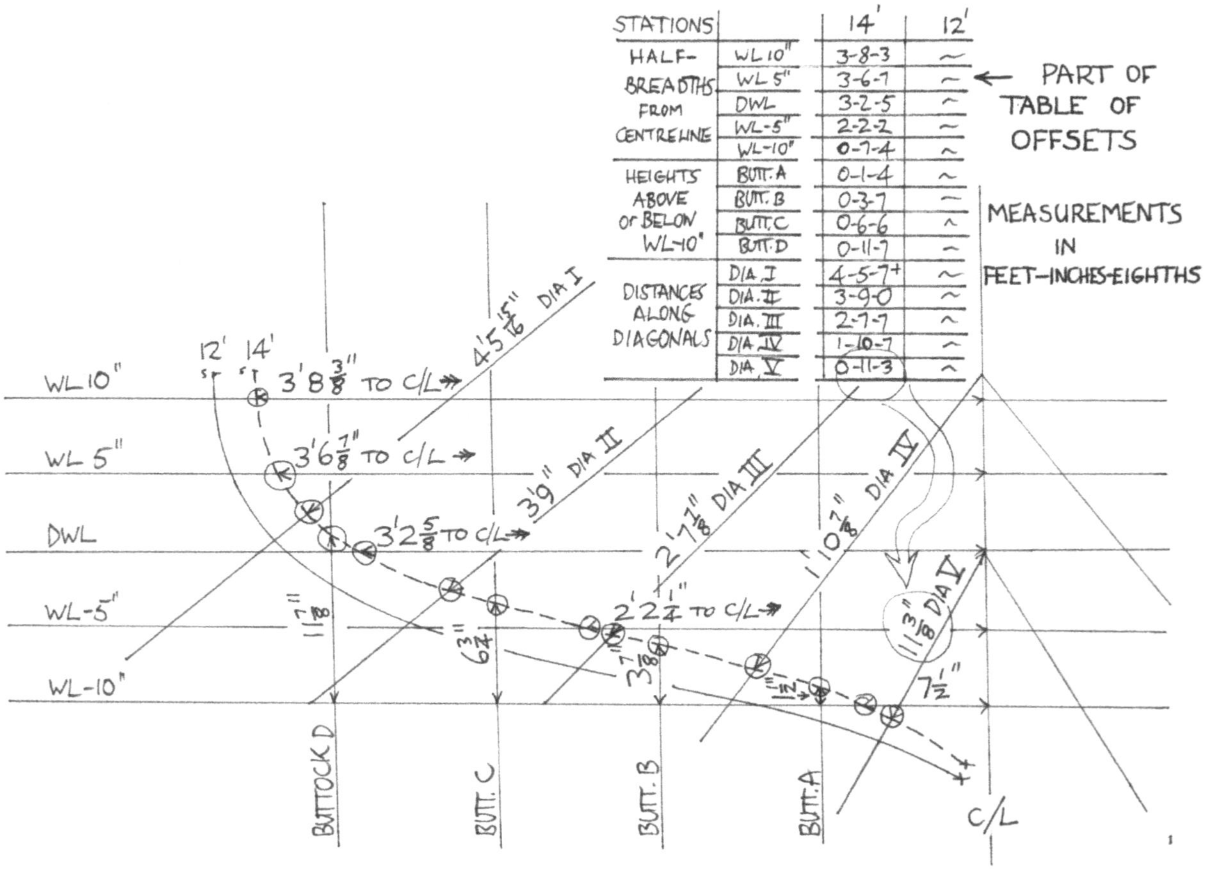

STATIONS		14'	12'	
HALF-BREADTHS FROM CENTRELINE	WL 10"	3-8-3	~	← PART OF TABLE OF OFFSETS
	WL 5"	3-6-7	~	
	DWL	3-2-5	~	
	WL -5"	2-2-2	~	
	WL -10"	0-7-4	~	
HEIGHTS ABOVE or BELOW WL -10"	BUTT. A	0-1-4	~	
	BUTT. B	0-3-7	~	MEASUREMENTS IN FEET-INCHES-EIGHTHS
	BUTT. C	0-6-6	~	
	BUTT. D	0-11-7	~	
DISTANCES ALONG DIAGONALS	DIA. I	4-5-7+	~	
	DIA. II	3-9-0	~	
	DIA. III	2-7-7	~	
	DIA. IV	1-10-7	~	
	DIA. V	0-11-3	~	

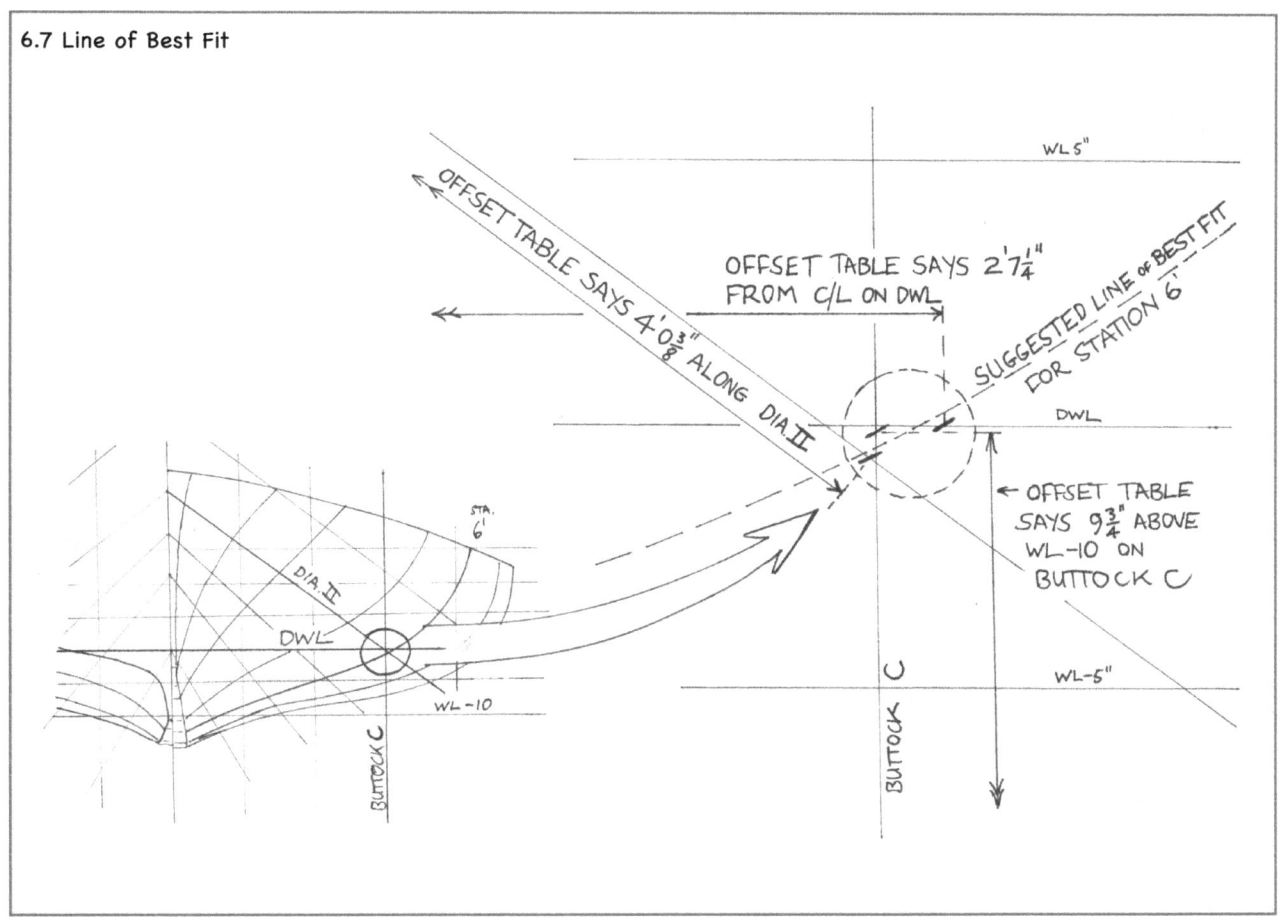

6.7 Line of Best Fit

In most cases most will not. Do not ink in these lines, they are bound to change.

Fairing the Diagonals, Waterlines and Buttocks

With old friends the tick strips, pick up all the distances along Diagonal A at each penciled station line, and transfer these out from the base line (use the line that is the DWL in the profile view) towards the bottom of the loft boards. A smattering of nails, a long batten, and we see how fair our diagonal is- the diagonals more than any other line follow the line of the planking- by plotting out this diagonal in the manner described we are finding out if the planking would lie fairly if we cut our moulds to the shapes we penciled in on the body plan.

Most likely, this first plotting will show one or two small corrections necessary to gain a fair curve. Note these, and mark them back on the body plan in red as a correction. Don't redraw the station lines in the body plan yet.

First do the same for the other diagonals, then do the same for all the waterlines, then each of the buttocks. When all corrections have been carefully marked on the body plan (mark them as soon as they are discovered), redraw the station lines in the body plan to the line of best fit.

Oh lucky you, if all the corrections agree and fit the new line! It's much more likely that several points will not. So with your tick strips, pick up the points of any corrected station lines and again plot out the diagonals, waterlines and buttocks.

If these longitudinal lines are still fair with these changes, well and good, but if not, new corrections need to be marked on the body plan and the whole process double-backed over again. Each time will bring you closer. You can ink the line in when you feel no further corrections need to be made.

Lofting Agreement

Every line on the lofting is repeated in each different view. For example, each waterline is a straight horizontal line in both body plan and profile, and a curved line in plan view. Each buttock line is a vertical line in the body plan, a horizontal line in plan view, and a curved line in profile. Wherever two lines cross in one view, this position in space (relative to the grid) should agree with the position these two lines cross in

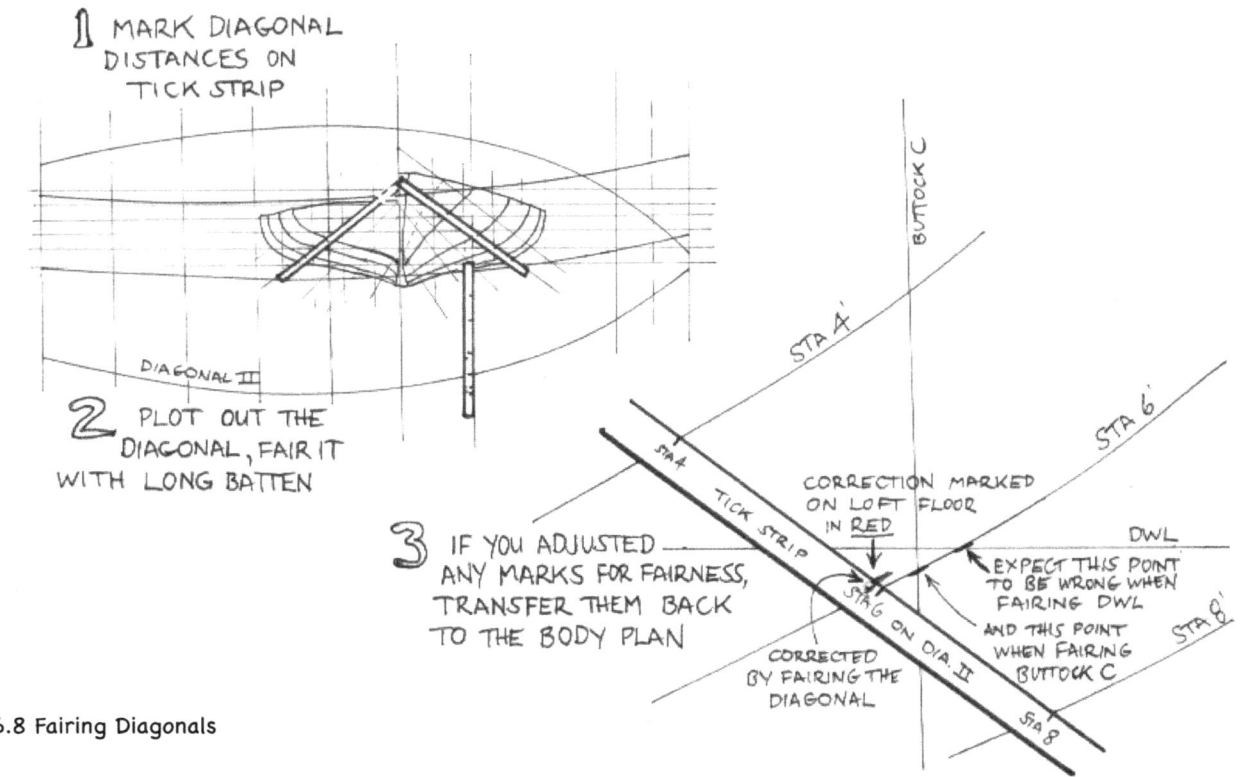

6.8 Fairing Diagonals

both other views. This is the essence of lofting, but some points are easy to miss. Being methodical is the only way!

Construction Plan

Once lofted to agreement, we can commence drawing in the construction plan, but only if your lofted stations are in the positions where you want to have moulds. In the case of *Britannia* the stations were at two foot intervals, closer than needed for mould spacing. So I worked out where I needed moulds to go, at 2'6" intervals from the stern, with an extra Station 1(18" from the bow, halfway to Station 2 at 3' from the bow). Station 4 at 8' from the bow is the only original one. I drew in vertical lines on the grid at these positions and plotted out each point where these lines crossed each waterline, buttock and diagonal and joined up the dots with a batten bent around nails to get the shape of the station where I would build a mould. This is the same technique you would use when lofting a yacht where you wanted to know the shape of an athwartships bulkhead not located on a station line. The construction plan is best drawn in red ink. Of course the lines on the original lofting are to the outside of the planking, so we must reduce these by the thickness of the planking plus the battens to get the mould shapes. But remembering each station is a section through the boat and well forward especially the planking crosses these stations at some angle, the actual planking and batten thickness deducted should be greater.

6.9 Agreement of Waterlines and Buttocks in Different Views

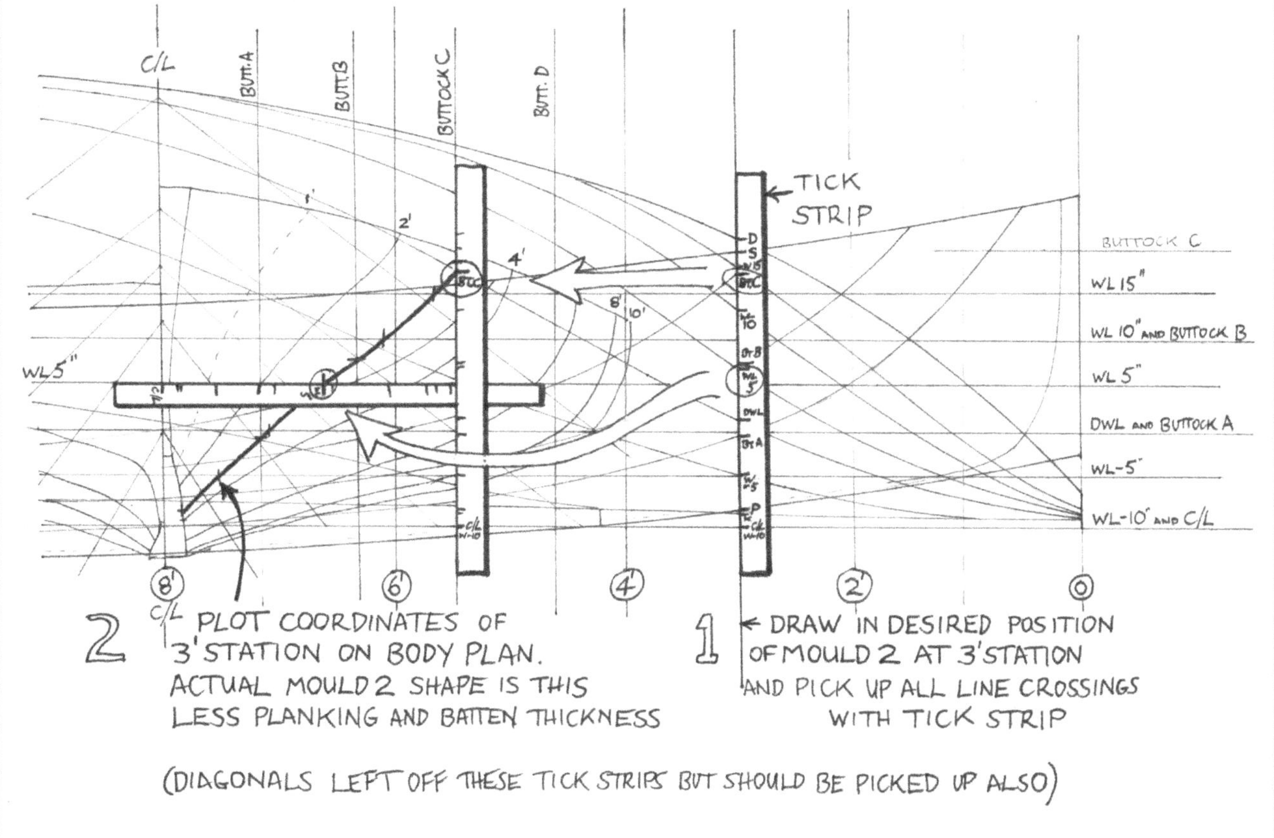
C/L
BUTT. A
BUTT. B
BUTTOCK C
BUTT. D
TICK STRIP
BUTTOCK C
WL 15"
WL 10" AND BUTTOCK B
WL 5"
DWL AND BUTTOCK A
WL -5"
WL -10" AND C/L
WL 5"
8'
6'
4'
2'
0
2 PLOT COORDINATES OF 3' STATION ON BODY PLAN. ACTUAL MOULD 2 SHAPE IS THIS LESS PLANKING AND BATTEN THICKNESS
1 ← DRAW IN DESIRED POSITION OF MOULD 2 AT 3' STATION AND PICK UP ALL LINE CROSSINGS WITH TICK STRIP
(DIAGONALS LEFT OFF THESE TICK STRIPS BUT SHOULD BE PICKED UP ALSO)

6.10 Drawing in Different Moulds

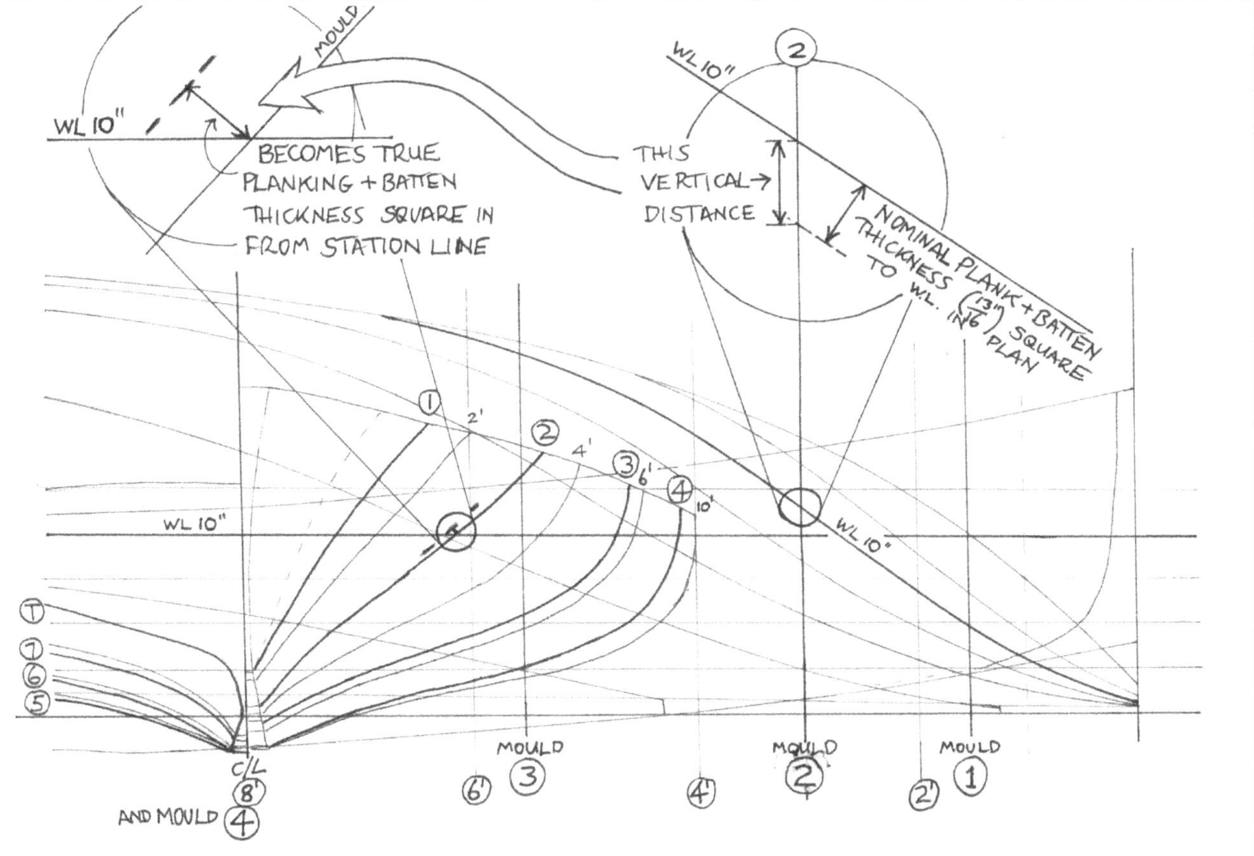
MOULD
WL 10"
BECOMES TRUE PLANKING + BATTEN THICKNESS SQUARE IN FROM STATION LINE
WL 10"
THIS VERTICAL DISTANCE
NOMINAL PLANK + BATTEN THICKNESS (13/16") SQUARE TO W.L. IN PLAN
WL 10"
WL 10"
MOULD
MOULD
MOULD
C/L
AND MOULD 4

6.11 Planking Plus Batten Thickness Deduction

Drawing 6.11 shows the method for picking this up. To get the bottom of each mould where it sits on the keel we need to draw in the keel, as in the drawing, simply a red line 1 ¾" above the outside line of the keel, being careful to transfer the correct heights to the body plan. From where the top of the keel in the body plan hits the inside of the planking you can get the width of the tapering keel to take back to the plan view for forward moulds, but you will find that for the midships and most aft moulds the actual wood keel will not need to be as wide as that. Draw in the rabbet line in profile and plan view, then transfer this information to the body plan as in drawing 6.12. You can then determine the shape of the planking rabbet at each station, and you will see that amidships the top of the timber keel does not need to go all the way to intersect with the planking as a decent-sized back rabbet can be had with the keel not quite as wide. By a decent-sized back rabbet I mean one that will be a big enough plank landing to easily hold a row of fastenings. The stem should be drawn in profile and body plan and several sections through the stem drawn in to determine the bearding line where the planking will land on the stem rabbet as in drawing 6.13. With the actual shapes to the inside of planking and battens marked on the body plan, you are now ready to cut the moulds, over which you will plank the boat.

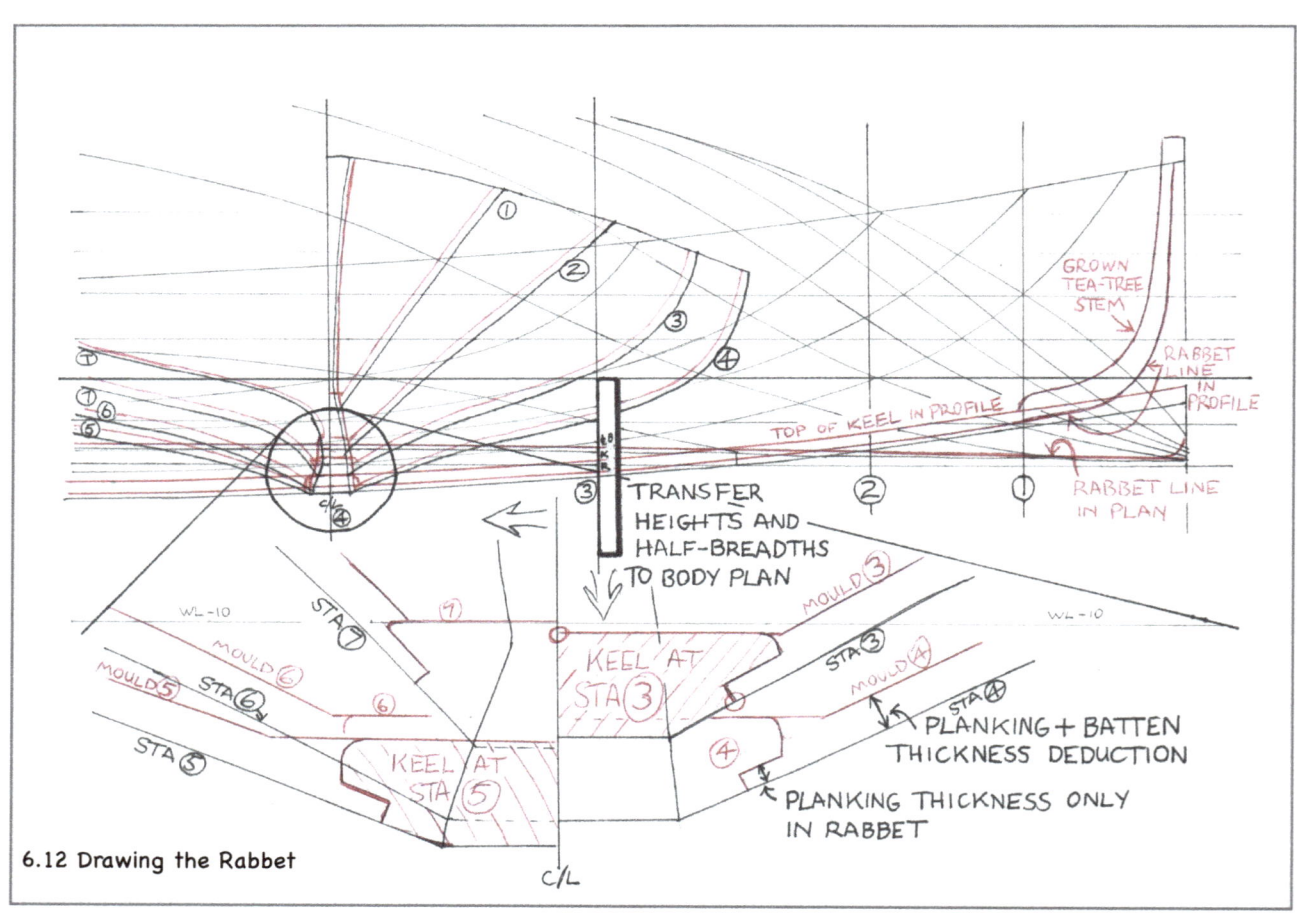

6.12 Drawing the Rabbet

6.13 The Stem

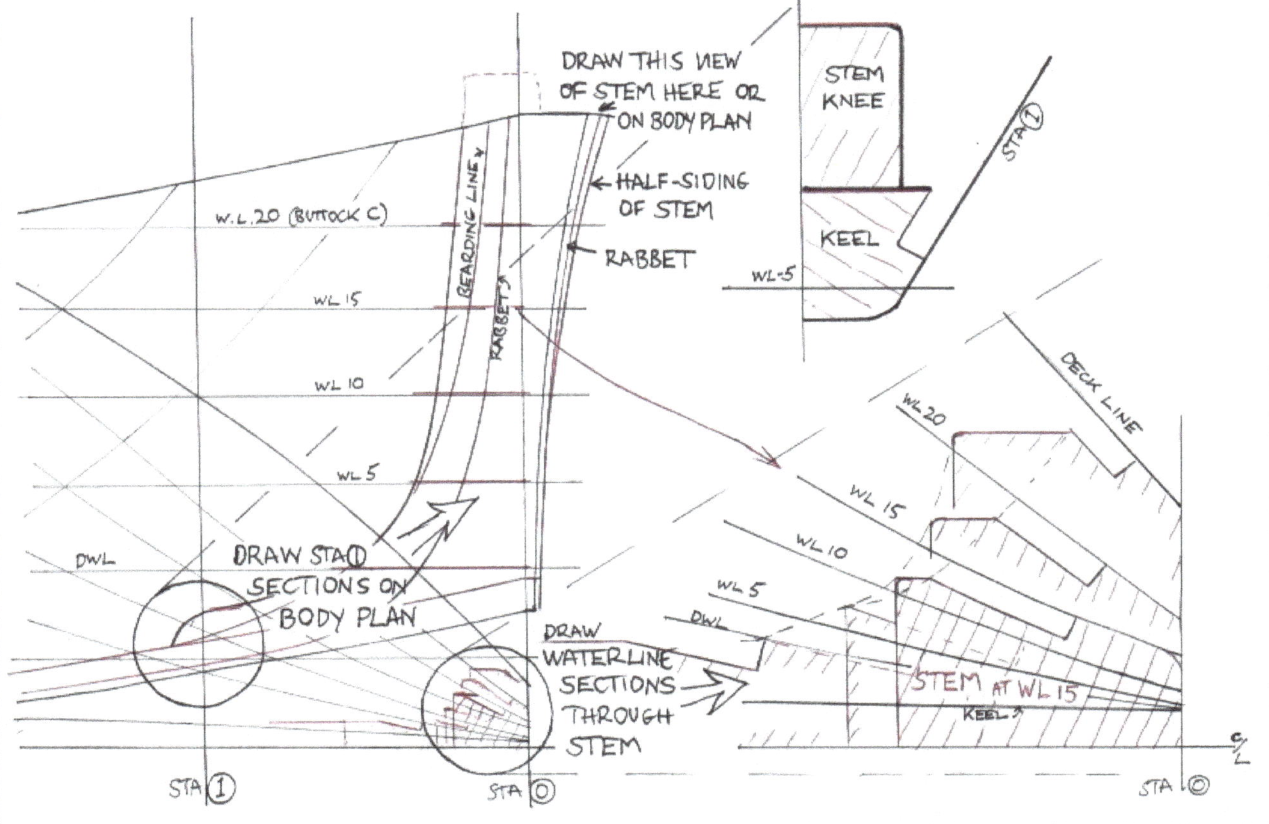

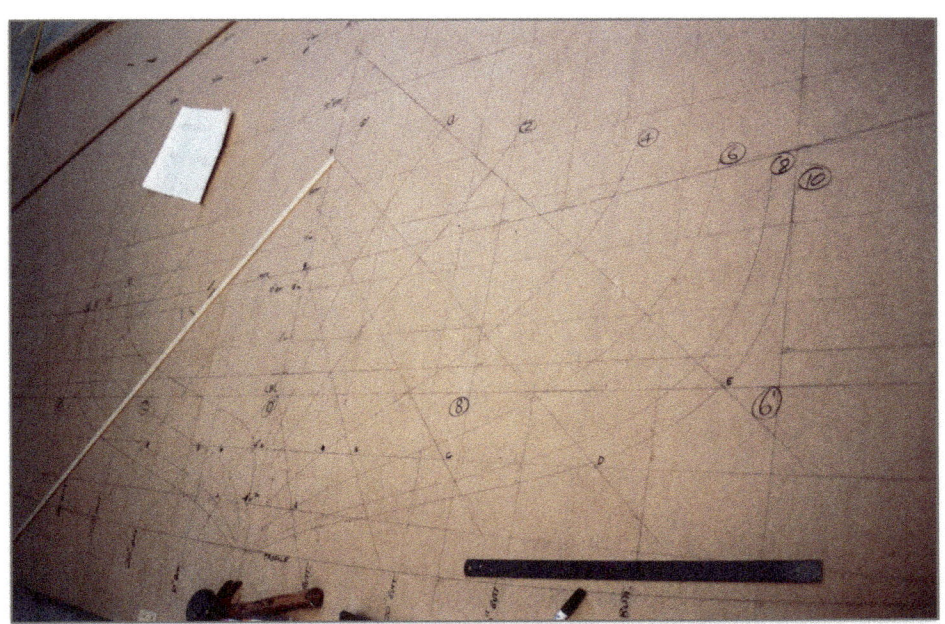

Photo 6B Britannia's body plan on the loft floor.

CHAPTER 7

The Moulds and Setting Up

These were traditionally cut out of wide cheap pine boards of around 3/4" finished thickness. Today you could cut them from sheets of plywood or chipboard or MDF but for the closest authentic experience I would recommend getting some lengths of radiata pine boards of 10-12" x ¾" for the shaped parts of the moulds and some 6" x ¾" for the cross spalls. Originally Baltic pine or Oregon would have been used.

Lay a section of wide board on the loft floor as in drawing 7.1 cut so that it reaches from just past the centreline to just past the turn of the bilge near the waterline, and with a minimum of timber to be cut off beyond the station line (so there is a maximum of timber in the mould). Lightly pencil around the board so you can relocate it, and remove it. If the board doesn't cover the whole line from centreline to sheer, draw a straight line roughly square to the station line where you want the two boards to join. Place flat-headed nails on the lines within the penciled area of the board as in the drawing and tap them to embed them. Remember you are after the line drawn to the inside of the planking (with closely spaced nails, say every 3 to 4 inches) as well as every straight grid line that crosses the board, the new joining line, and all waterlines, buttocks, diagonals and centreline (with nails spaced every 6 to 8 inches). Oh, and it's vital set a nail on the sheer mark on the station line. Check that you haven't missed any, then place the board down over the marked area and stand on it, squatting and tapping all around with a hammer or dead blow mallet to get the nail heads to imprint on the underside of the board. Lift up the board and have a look at the imprints. Many nails will be stuck in the pine. Before going too far from the lofting, carefully write near each straight line of imprinted nail heads to identify it, then ink these in with the same colour scheme you used on the lofting. Lay the board on the bench and tack nails into the nail imprints from the curved station line representing the inside of the planking and battens, tack a thin batten around these nails just as you did when doing the lofting and pencil or ink in the line. Lightly hatch the area outside this line so it is easily distinguished as the waste side of the line. Temporarily screw the board to another of identical dimensions and cut on the waste side of the line on the bandsaw. You could use a good jigsaw, but cut just clear of the line and plane back to it ensuring the edge is square. A good bandsaw used

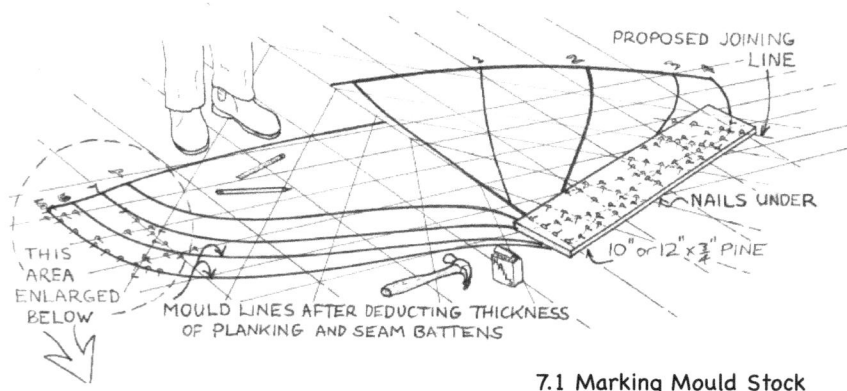

7.1 Marking Mould Stock

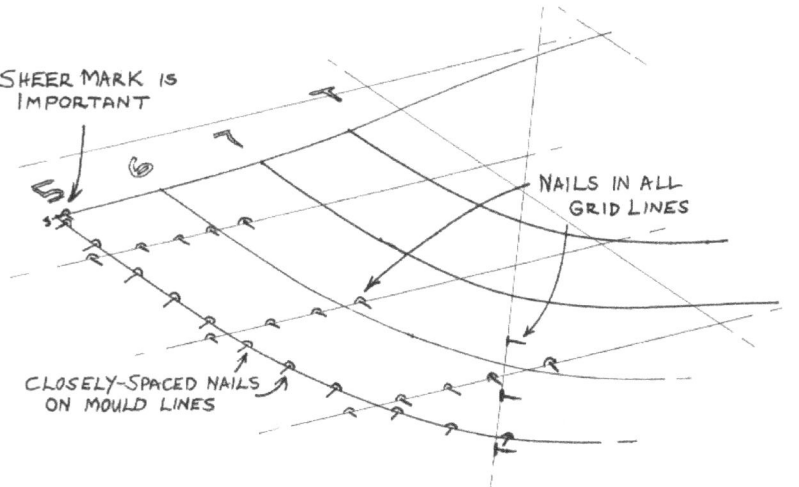

with good cutting technique will usually cut well enough to not need much edge planing. When cutting the centreline near one end of the board and the intended joining line at the other end, run the blade down the centre of the line. Before separating the pieces, square all grid lines around the edges.

That went well, didn't it? If not, perhaps your pine board was not flat enough, or the lofting floor was not flat enough for all nails to imprint. Or perhaps you didn't listen to me and were not careful enough identifying the grid lines and you got lost in the confusion of nail imprints. Flip the board over and try again.

On forward moulds your pine boards will probably be wide enough to cover the whole station line in one piece. On all other moulds you will need to repeat the process with short boards on the topsides.

Once you have all the pieces for a complete mould, take the first piece you imprinted and lay it on the opposite side of the centreline from where you imprinted it, so that its marked lines are facing up. See drawing 7.2. Locate it accurately by lining up all the grid lines you squared on the board edges with the grid lines on the lofting. Once you're sure it's in the right place (there may be slight disagreement between some marks, depending on how careful you've been marking out, but don't beat yourself up about it, some minor discrepancies are inevitable. The important thing is that the sheer mark should be exactly the same distance from the centreline and the same height above the waterline on both sides) temporarily screw it to the lofting.

Do the same for the upper piece (if there is one), then place the piece(s) from the other side exactly on the curved station line, checking that the grid lines marked on the edge of the timber line up exactly with the lines on the grid on the lofting. Screw these also in place. Then cut a cleat of pine or even better, plywood and screw it and preferably glue it (PVA is ideal) across the centreline at the bottom to fix the two sides together. Do the same at each side joint. Then cut and fit a cross spall out of the 6" pine with its top edge exactly at the level of

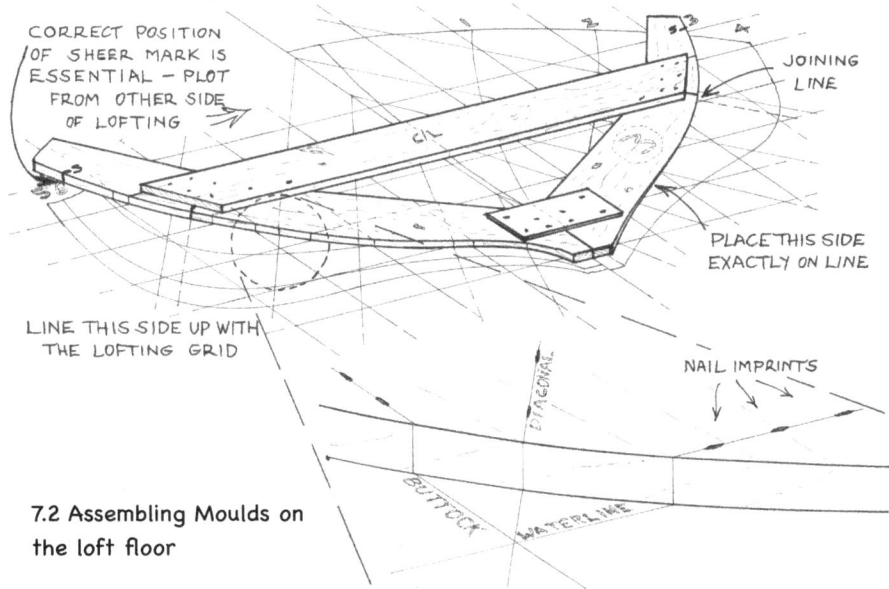

7.2 Assembling Moulds on the loft floor

the waterline one foot above the DWL, also screwed and glued. Before lifting the completed mould off, mark the centreline accurately on the cross spall and the centreline cleat. Undo the original screws holding the pieces down and lift off the mould so you can start on the next one. Uh-oh, you didn't fasten the cleats over those screws, did you?

If you choose to use plywood or chipboard as moulds, it is easier to transfer the shapes by tracing on mylar drawing paper (available at architectural supplies stores) and pricking through the lines with nails into the plywood mould stock, being careful to mark all of the required lines before removing the tracing including the centreline and the waterlines which you will then use to locate the other side of the mould when you flip the tracing over. After the moulds are done, lifting the shapes of the tuck and stem can be done easily with tracing paper as well.

Just repeat the process until you have a complete set of moulds, then you'll be ready to start marking and cutting the first wood that will become part of the boat.

The Tuck or Transom

Many types of boats and yachts have a transom (always known as the tuck to skiffies) that is sloping one way or the other, or curved, or both. This means some additional lofting must be done to develop the true shape of the transom before cutting wood, and it can be quite detailed work. You'll be pleased to learn that on Australian Open Boats the tuck is straight and vertical or close to it, so it can generally be treated just like another mould in the lofting. If your tuck is dead vertical, the shape of the tuck on your lofting is the true shape of the outside of the tuck, provided the planking thickness has been deducted (and only the planking thickness, do not include the thickness of the battens here as they will be fitted inside the tuck). But don't cut your lovely Cedar just yet. Because the planking approaching the tuck does so from the larger mould 7, the forward face of the tuck is actually bigger than the lofted shape of the outside. You could draw a line representing the forward face on the profile and plan views, 1 ¼" forward of the tuck station, and transfer every point at which this line crosses waterlines, buttocks and diagonals back to the body plan and connect up the dots for the true shape of the inside of the tuck. Or you can simply leave a guessed amount of extra wood outside your lofted line and shape the required bevel as each plank is ready to fit.

The top of the tuck should be marked in with a slight curve. Open boat tucks traditionally had a hardwood beam fitted across the top on the inside just below the top edge and were curved only slightly.

Tucks on Australian Open Boats were almost always in Australian Cedar, but occasionally a builder would use a nice piece of Queensland Maple if he had it. Generally both timbers were available in very wide boards, in *Britannia*'s case it needed to be two feet wide. In 2000 I couldn't find such a piece, so I joined three 8" x 1 1/8" boards together. I expect you will have to do the same, unless you are prepared to compete with the coffee-table market for wide Cedar slabs. Plane the mating edges of the three boards straight and square with your longest plane, preferably a Number 6 or 7, and check them when held together. There should be no light coming through the joint, possibly the slightest hint of light somewhere would be acceptable. Each mating edge now needs a groove 1'4" wide by just over 5/8" deep cut in it as in drawing 7.3 to fit a spline. You can do it on a saw bench, with an electric router, or if you want to be fully traditional, with a grooving plane (either a purpose-built wooden plane or a combination plane with a grooving blade fitted). Machine two spline lengths 1 ¼" wide by ¼" thick. Originally these would have been cut out of another piece of Cedar (usually on an angle as illustrated) or a soft pine that would swell to make the joint watertight if the

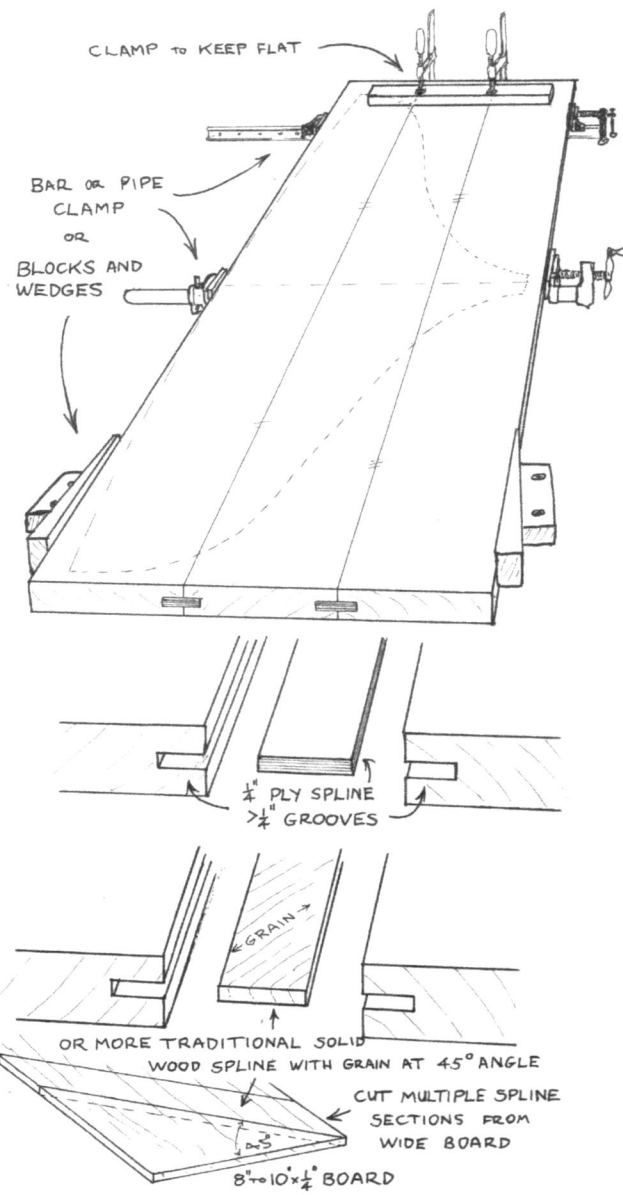

7.3 Gluing Up the Tuck

glue used allowed water in, which was often the case as the glue used was chiefly animal hide glue. With our access to modern epoxies it would be pointless not to use them, so we can cut our splines from ¼" plywood and they will be stronger across the grain and more waterproof.

Right here and now I'll nail my colours to the mast: epoxies or other modern glues can be used on traditional boats when it is necessary to make up a part that would have been a single piece of timber on the original boat, especially when such wood may be difficult or impossible to source.

<u>DO NOT</u> use epoxy to join together pieces of timber that were always designed to be separate

pieces of timber, such as planks and frames, or planks to each other. One of our replica builders made this mistake with a ten footer around 1990. Each plank was glued to the battens. On an early outing with a child aboard, a plank split with a loud bang and water started to bubble in. The child panicked, cried "We're all going to die!" And probably hasn't been near a boat since. Over the next few months, most of the planks cracked and the boat was retired.

There are some builders of some boats using particularly stable timbers in some places in the world with stable climatic conditions that have gotten away with it, but as a general rule trying to glue separate pieces of a traditional boat together will almost invariably end in heartbreak.

> **TIP ....Working with epoxies**
>
> Some people develop allergies to epoxy, but even if you don't they are not good for your health. Follow the manufacturer's instructions regarding safety precautions. At the very least this will involve gloves, masks and probably protective clothing. But even though you are wearing gloves, make a big effort to work as clean as possible. Change gloves as soon as they become slippery to save spreading epoxy on tools and everything else in the neighbourhood.
>
> Follow the manufacturers's instructions also on use. I spent part of my career trouble-shooting with home-builders for one of the bigger boatbuilding epoxy firms, and the chief problem was <u>not reading the instructions on the tin!</u> And particularly note the mixing ratio. Unlike polyester resins, epoxy will <u>not go off quicker by using extra hardener.</u> Stick to the ratio.
>
> It is often best to cleanup squeezed-out epoxy while still liquid. A putty knife for the bulk of it followed by wiping with a rag with methylated spirits, or even vinegar. But on open-grained timbers like Australian Cedar, wiping it up will actually spread epoxy into the nearby grain, and this will not often show up until the first coat of varnish. You may mask such areas, or if there is only a bead of residue you can leave it to cure and remove it with judicious use of a heat gun and triangular scraper. Heat softens epoxy, but you need to be careful because too much will soften the epoxy in the joint as well. On laminations such as that illustrated for a stem or other knee, the edges will be cut or planed off so no epoxy cleanup is necessary except to thin it out to save planer blades.

This rule is not to be confused with building laminated timber boats when that is what the boat was designed for such as cold moulding or epoxy encapsulation or glued clinker using plywood. These types of boats are meant to be monocoque construction which does not allow any water penetration and I have built plenty of them myself and agree the concept is sound and they can be excellent and enduring boats. Both methods are equally valid for building a wooden boat (unless you are trying to replicate a traditional type), the problems arise when a mixture of the two concepts is employed. A traditional planked boat is a collection of individual pieces of wood held together by metal fastenings. A laminated boat is a monocoque that depends on having no water penetration. **If the two are mixed, either by rigidly gluing together a traditional boat, or by penetrating a laminated boat by metal fastenings that leave pathways for water penetration, your boat will likely have a considerably shortened life.**

So... parts of a traditional planked boat that can utilise epoxy include: laminated stems or any other knees, frames or ribs, laminated keels, laminated deadwood, laminated thwarts and centreboard cases (to get the width needed), or getting back to the point of this chapter, tucks. Phew, glad I got that off my chest!

As always with an assembly requiring glue, do a dry run first, so that possible problems can be discovered. With the tuck, possible problems include having the splines too tight a fit (they need to be an easy slide-in fit to allow room for glue), and set-up problems such as not being dead flat when clamping pressure comes on. Clamp with sash or pipe clamps or simply with blocks of wood and wedges as in drawing 7.3. If it all checks out, mix the epoxy and apply, and clamp up for real. If you are using blocks and wedges on a flat surface make sure it is lined with plastic so that your tuck doesn't permanently become part of the surface. Once cured, usually the next day, remove the clamps and clean up both sides of the tuck to remove any glue residue and plane off any slight misalignment of the joined boards and sand it to about 150 grit.

Mark out the shape of the tuck from the lofting either by tracing with mylar film or more traditionally by making a pattern from light boards cleated together or cheap wardrobe-grade plywood pressing down on closely spaced nail heads the same as described for the moulds. Just trace or make a half-shape of course, and flip it over a lightly penciled centreline on the tuck stock to mark the other side. Making sure you've left enough stock outside the line for bevelling wood, cut around the perimeter with bandsaw or jigsaw. Don't cut the shape of the top of the tuck at this point, leave it oversize and straight as it will help with setting up.

The Stem

Stems were traditionally cut from Tea Tree (Melaleuca quinquenervia) or broad-leafed paperbark which happened to grow extensively close to the waterfront on the East coast of Australia. Knees were cut from the buttress roots to get the required curved grain and size. See drawing 7.4. They are not cut commercially any longer but many suburban streets are lined with avenues of these trees. Occasionally some are removed, and I am trying to establish links with a number of tree loppers. Curved branches cut where the branch leaves the trunk are great for smaller knees, but the buttress roots are the only part big enough for stems. The difficulty is that they need to be dug out and chainsawn below ground level. If the tree has been torn out by bulldozer, the buttress roots will have undergone incredible strain and it is almost definite that they will have invisible shakes which will render them useless for knees. There is a need for a niche business in urban forestry. Anyone interested? Outdoor job in all weathers, hard physical work, small financial rewards? Many trees are lopped or felled and turned into woodchips for mulch. I am trying to educate tree-loppers that there are certain timbers for which boatbuilders and other craftspeople will pay a premium. Cut knees are of course unseasoned. Boatbuilders would generally have quite a few in stock, seasoning. The process could be sped up by soaking them with the bark still on in salt water, usually under the wharf if a tidal pool was not available, and pulled out regularly to be cleaned off. A few months of this and a few weeks of drying out of the sun was considered about right for use. Native Honeysuckle (Banksia species) was the most common knee and crook timber in the

Photo 7A Tea-Tree is often an avenue tree in Sydney. This buttress root would make a big knee, but the local council might object!

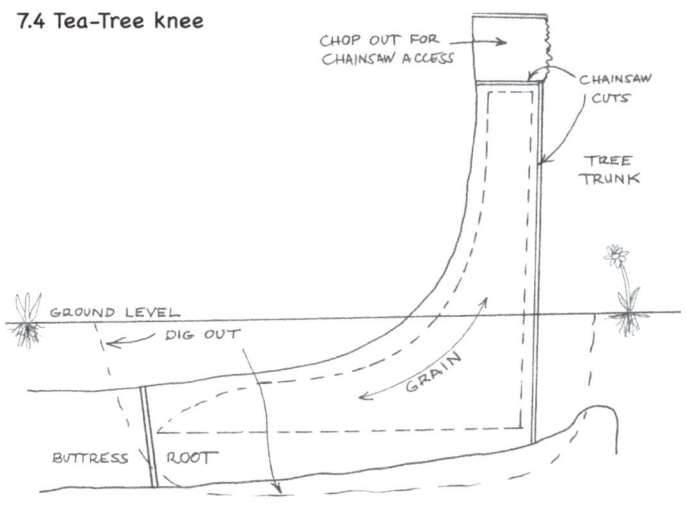

7.4 Tea-Tree knee

Photo 7B A cut tea tree knee. The Labrador is there for scale.

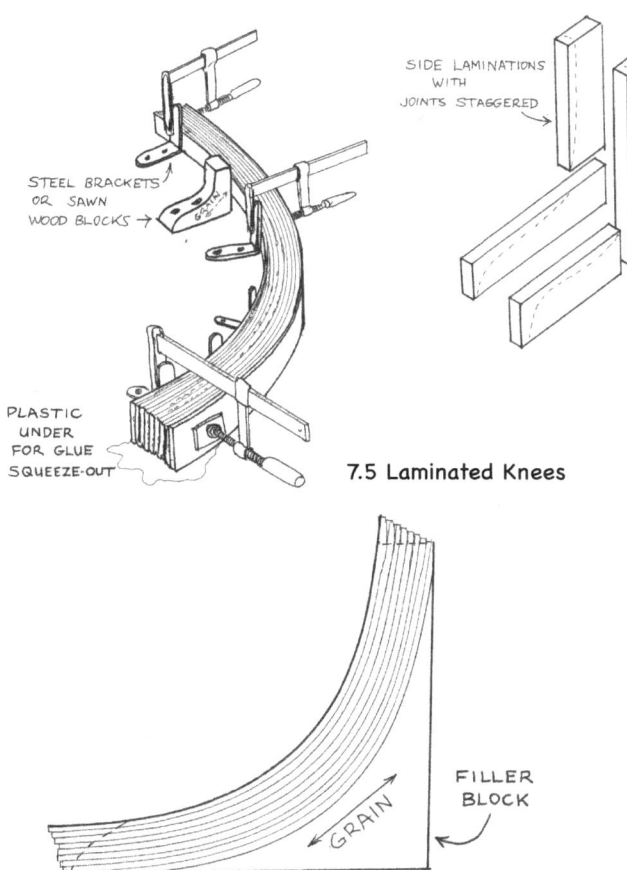

7.5 Laminated Knees

nineteenth century. Grey Mangrove was also occasionally used.

If you cannot obtain tea tree knees that is a great shame, but all is not lost, these can also be laminated. I would suggest Silver Ash or Flooded Gum (Rose Gum) which both glue well and are strong but not too heavy. If you can get straight-grained Tea Tree that would work even better as the colour would be dead right (make sure it is seasoned for gluing). Drawing 7.5 shows how to laminate around a series of angle brackets. Saw up laminates to a thickness that will comfortably take the bend individually. Straight off the saw is a good finish for gluing, there is no need for planing. Make sure the laminates are slightly wider than the finished piece to leave room for cleanup of glue and misalignments. On a 2" knee, allow at least 3/8" extra. Use enough laminates to more than cover the area your item will take up. You need not use the thin laminates for the total knee, as in the drawing you could use a filler block in the angled corner, with careful fitting to the curved laminate for close joints if varnishing. You could also laminate sideways from solid stock with the joints staggered.

Regardless of the material of the knee stock, when the knee is brought to finished thickness you need to mark out the shape from a pattern or tracing, including marking the rabbet line and bearding line, and back rabbet line if you have marked it. Also mark the waterlines which will help in establishing its correct height when setting up. The inside and outside faces of the stem should be planed to remove bandsaw marks to finish on the marked lines. It is critical to get the angle between the top of the keel and the vertical face of the stem exactly right, remembering that the face sitting on the keel will likely have an ever-so-slight curve as the keel is sprung to shape. A belt sander is good for finishing off the inside curve if you don't have a bobbin sander (I don't), and your closeness to the line is not as critical on this side. Traditionally compass plane and spokeshave would be used here. If you are confidant of your rabbet lines you can chisel them out a bit, but be conservative, it is safer to finalise these when fitting each plank especially towards the lower end of the stem where the rabbet must fair in to the rabbet on the keel.

Most Open Boat stem knees will be flared towards the top which adds an element of difficulty when cutting and marking. Your tracing or pattern cannot simply be laid on the knee and transferred unless you start out with a full thickness knee and then taper it down. Getting a tapered knee right is akin to sculpture. On *Britannia* the width of the stem knee is 2 ½" inside the boat but it flares to 8" at the stemhead. I simply could not find knee stock of that thickness, so I cut the side-on shape from a 2 ½" knee and glued on solid lumps of Tea Tree above the section where it begins to flare and tapered the upper section out of that.

Stern Knee

The tuck will be joined to the keel by the stern knee, also of Tea Tree or previously discussed substitute. This needs to be the full height of the transom and a slightly shorter distance along the keel. On *Britannia* and most other built-heel boats the garboard will land partly on this knee so there will be a rabbet to mark and cut here too. On heel-less skiff-type hulls the knee will be entirely within

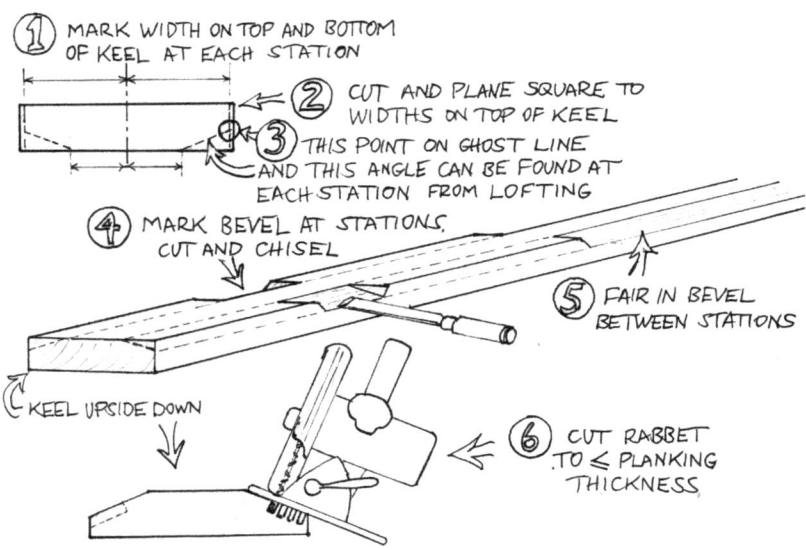

7.6 The Keel

the boat and no rabbet is necessary. Use the same techniques as in the previous section for marking and cutting, and laminating if necessary.

The Keel

On *Britannia* the keel is cut from a 8" x 1 ¾" piece of Spotted Gum just over 18 feet long. If you lofted the construction plan, you will have the amount of taper in plan view, and sectional views at each station to work out the exact shape of the keel. Mark out the stations along the keel, remembering that the keel will be sprung to a slight curve and so the station lines will be slightly further apart. Get the exact measurement by laying your tape along the curved line on the top of the keel as drawn on the loft floor or mark them onto a long batten bent to the curve. Mark the forward-most station where the stem knee will fit, and mark the tuck station at 17'11¾". Plot out the widths at each station on top of the keel on lines squared out from a straight marked centreline, tack nails into those marks and join them up by penciling against a batten just as you did in lofting. Do the same on the underside of the keel using the correct widths off the lofting for both the widths of the bottom of the keel and the width of the rabbet line, checking to ensure your centreline agrees with the centreline on top of the keel. Turn the keel back over and cut just clear of the line on top of the keel (cut square and right through) and plane back to the line making sure it is fair and square. The angle of the bevel each side of the keel can be lifted from the lofting as well as the the point of the ghost line of the bevel before the rabbet is cut as a double check (see 7.6), and the bevel can be chiselled out at each station. Then join all those spots by fairing in the bevel between with power plane and hand plane, remembering that it is constantly changing all the way along and the transition should be as fair as possible.

Then mark the rabbet line on the bevelled area (as always at each station then draw in the line with a batten). Set your circular saw blade to just a tiny bit less than the (7/16") plank thickness and make a series of cuts all the way along keeping the base plate of the saw as flat on the bevelled area as you can. Chisel out the waste and plane it fair. Be conservative at the forward end and if your boat has a built heel at the aft end as well because the fairness of the transition into the stem (and stern) knees is best judged after the knees are attached and the keel is set up in the strong back. You can even round over the line along the bottom of the keel and the corner of the top of the keel amidships (where it is not part of the rabbet), as it is easier to do on the bench than on the assembled boat.

Setting Up

Open Boats were traditionally built right way up. Only with the advent of glues were hulls built upside down. In summary, the keel with stem and stern knees attached is set up on a strongback and sprung to the required amount of rocker by forcing it down onto carefully measured blocks at stations with shores (called toms) down from the roof or an upper beam attached to the strongback when the roof is too high. The stem knee is temporarily fastened to the forward upright and the tuck is fastened to the stern knee and temporarily fastened to the aft upright. The moulds are then fitted at each station, carefully checking their height is correct and that they are dead on the centreline, then cross bracing is fitted making sure the moulds are square to the centreline.

The Strongback

The main parts of the strongback are cut from 6" or wider x 2" (150mm x 50 mm) sawn Oregon, structural grade. The best piece needs to be at least 18'6" long and dead straight (straighten any bumps and hollows with your longest jointer plane) on its top edge. Mark the station lines on both sides and the top before erecting it. The forward end will be notched or cleated to the forward upright, and it is best to allow an extra half-inch between the bow station and the aft face of the forward upright. Then, in *Britannia's* case I marked the stations as on the lofting at 18" and 3' from the bow, then 2'6" intervals to the stern. The last station is the outside of the tuck, but the keel in this case protrudes a couple of inches past the station in order to hold the bottom rudder pintle, so the aft upright will be a couple of inches behind station 8. Choose a height off the floor to locate the main beam which allows you to work under the boat in reasonable comfort when fitting the planking. From memory *Britannia's* strongback was about 18" off the floor. Fit three trestle-type legs to the main beam to suit your chosen height and set it up dead level. Erect the forward and aft verticals in their correct position, dead vertical and fasten them securely to the roof and floor, or to a braced frame as in the drawing. Join the main beam to them and fasten everything securely, ensuring the top of the beam is straight both up and down and side to side, and horizontal.

Now you need to cut 2" x 2" posts for each station to support the curved keel. These will be fitted forward of the station lines amidships and on the forward stations, and aft of the station lines aft of amidships, for reasons that will be soon apparent. Turn again to the lofting and measure the heights of the keel off the main beam at each station. You can either draw in the main beam on the lofting or measure down from a waterline, with the lowest point of the bent keel as zero. Pick up the bevel angle you need on top of each piece with a bevel gauge (on the correct side of the station of course) and cut the pieces to length. Fasten them to the main beam.

You might want to check that your keel will fit between the verticals without trimming, and then it is time to fasten the tuck to the stern knee, and the stem and stern knees to the keel, which is easier before fitting to the strongback. Clamp the stem knee to the keel exactly in position and drill the required holes for the fastenings you intend to use. In *Britannia's* case there were four fastenings, 3 of 5/16" copper rod peened over large roves, and one 3/8" copper bolt, head peened on one end and threaded for a bronze nut on the other. Copper rod

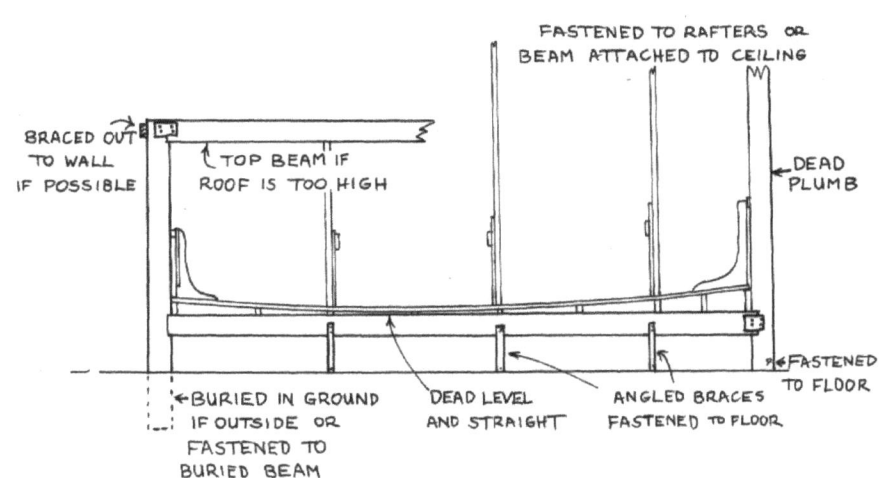

7.7 Setting up the Keel on the Strongback

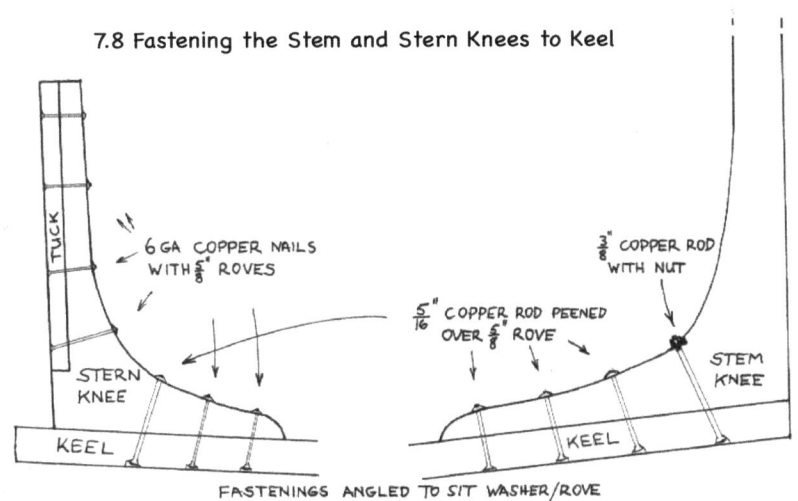

7.8 Fastening the Stem and Stern Knees to Keel

Photo 7C   Peening Tools

Photo 7D   Head Forming

can easily be peened to make a head with the round side of a ball peen hammer in a pipe-flaring tool held in a vice as in the photo, or a made-up flaring tool by drilling a countersink hole in a thick steel plate. <u>The golden rule in peening is to use the lightest hammer that will work to spread the copper into a mushroom shape.</u> Once you get to the small gauge nails in the planking, you will use a 2 oz hammer, the lightest there is. For 5/16" rod you will need about a 10 oz hammer which is about half the weight of the average claw hammer you will use to drive nails home. Make a good-sized head, at least ½" diameter on 5/16" rod. Tap a slight point on the other end. The holes you drill should be the same diameter. If you have a drill bit one sixty-fourth smaller, you could use that, but experiment in an offcut first. If a copper rod becomes difficult to drive it will rapidly seize up and if you continue you may never get it in, or out. You need a firm tapping fit. If any of your fastenings will be bolts, cut a thread to suit your nuts, usually UNC is most available.

With all holes drilled, unclamp the knee and lift it off. Countersink under the keel for the heads of the fastenings. They can either remain flush or be counterbored for plugging or puttying over. Tap the nails/bolts through the keel so that they just protrude and apply your chosen bedding compound to the mating surfaces. Originally this could have been white lead which is virtually impossible to get these days (and unhealthy to use), but usually in a boat that was designed to be varnished builders would use the thick gummy varnish in the bottom of an old tin, applied thickly to both mating surfaces. These days I would recommend a mastic or a low-modulus polyurethane sealant. Colours are available to nearly match the wood colour. Definitely do not use the harder polyurethanes generally promoted in the marine stores, and even more definitely do not use glue! Drive all nails/bolts in a bit with your claw hammer, using your heaviest dolly in line with each fastening as it is hit. This will locate the knee exactly where it was when you drilled it. It will help to then clamp the two parts firmly using G clamps (sliding clamps will loosen under hammer blows) as long as you can position the clamps to still get access to both ends of the fastenings. If a fastening needs a nut, drive this one home and fit the nut. Be careful not to over-tighten, copper threads can be stripped relatively easily.

Drive each of the other fastenings home and peen them over a rove in turn. The sequence to follow is illustrated in drawing 7.9. Roves are designed to fit tightly over copper nails, so if you are using copper rod you will have to drill out the roves one drill size under that of the rod. Use 5/8" or ¾" roves. Use a large rove punch to drive the rove over the protruding nail/bolt until it is flat on the knee surface. Cut the protruding nail/bolt with large end cutters, or bolt cutters if you have to. Do not leave much of the fastening sticking out otherwise it will take too long to peen it over and it

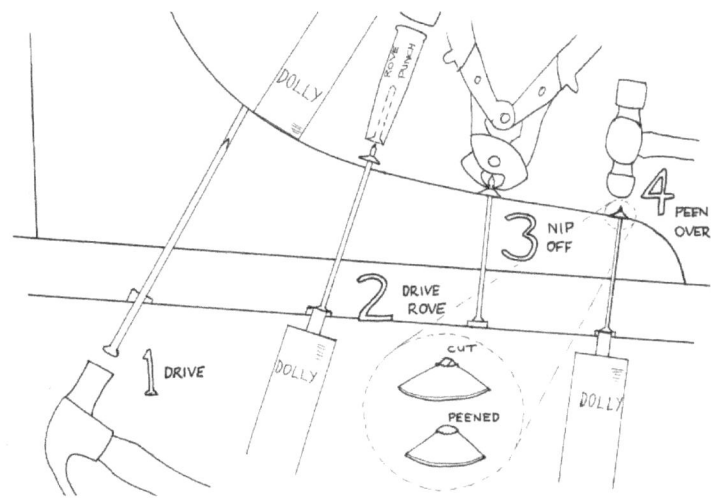

7.9 Sequence for Driving Nails and Roving Off

Fasten the tuck to the stern knee before fastening the knee to the keel. Use large gauge square copper nails here, say 8 or 9 gauge with 5/8" roves. The heads should end up dead flush on the outside of the tuck. Countersink a little less than the diameter of the head, as they will easily be driven in flush into the soft Cedar. Drill for these in two stages. Drill right through with a drill bit the exact size of the square section of the nail across the flats. Then drill through the hole in the knee with the next size drill bit 1/32" up. The Tea-Tree is tougher than the Cedar and there otherwise would be a chance the nail would bind and/or bend and that the knee might split. Bed the surfaces, drive home the nails, drive on the roves, nip and peen as before. Fit the knee and tuck assembly to the keel using copper rods/bolts as for the stem knee.

will end up an ugly haemorrhoid-like protrusion. Resting the jaws of the cutters on the rove is generally sufficient because of the way they cut. They will leave a hipped-roof type protrusion which will be enough to rivet over the rove and hold it for good. Use the same hammer you used to form the heads, back each nail up with a heavy dolly and peen it over. Aim most of your blows relatively centrally until the copper starts to spread, then hammer around the edges to flatten it down (just the nail, do not flatten the rove!). As mentioned before it is important not to use too heavy a hammer for peening. If you use too heavy a hammer it will just drive the nail or rod back into the wood if you are backing it up lightly, but if you are backing it up firmly (you should) it will just bend the nail or rod inside the wood.

You'll probably need a helper to lift the assembly onto the strongback. Clamp the keel down to its support blocks, making sure the marked station positions line up. The stem and the tuck will have a little clearance to the vertical posts, and these should be taken up with correct-sized packers, and the stem and tuck clamped in position. Check that the penciled waterlines on the tuck are level and that the marked waterlines on the tuck and the stem are at the same height, using a laser sight, or more traditionally with a water hose. See drawing 7.10. When you are happy, fasten off with temporary screws. Hopefully you left some extra wood on top for these temporary fastenings, otherwise you can drill through where you expect permanent fastenings to go later on, such as in the stem where there will eventually be a bolt through at the top of the stem holding the breasthook.

The clamps holding the keel down being only temporary, it is now time to fit 2" x 2" uprights at each station fastened to the roof or top beam. These are fitted, as mentioned before, forward of the station line in the forward part of the boat and aft of the station line in the aft part of the boat. Because....see drawing 7.11. Because the planking crosses each station at

7.10 Using a Water Level

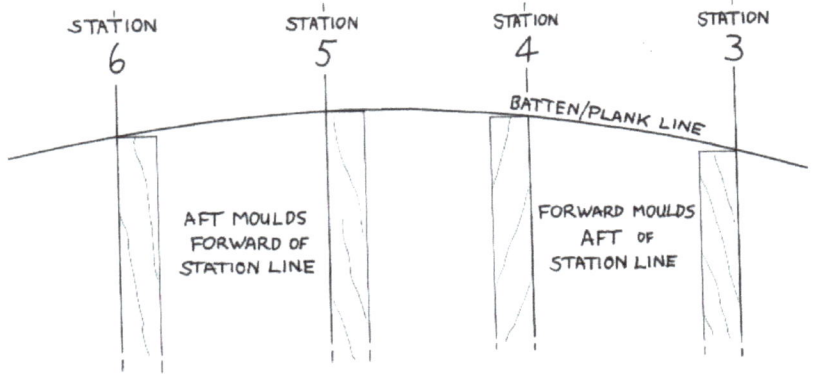

7.11 Positioning Moulds

an angle, the station lines must be located on the forward face of the mould in the forward sections and on aft sections of the moulds in the aft sections in order to land the planking right on the station lines. If they were located the other way around, you would have to bevel the edges of the moulds in order for the planking to lie on the station lines. This is unnecessary and a lot of work. It helps to brace the setup with a couple of beams from a couple of the verticals out to a wall, roughly halfway up the verticals but in any case above head height.

You are now ready to fit the first mould. (You may notice in photo 7E that I was impatient and erected the first mould before I had all uprights fitted).

Traditionally the midships or widest mould was always the first, in our case Mould 5 just aft of centre. The planking crosses this mould at close to a right angle towards the sheer, but from the buttock lines we can tell that the planking will be starting to rise up towards the stern at this point, so this mould will be treated as one of the aft moulds, and therefore it will be fitted forward of the line, up against the upright which is aft of the line. The cross spall will need a packer of an offcut of the mould material. Clamp it in place, making sure the marked centreline on the mould is on the marked centreline on the keel and that the straight top of the cross spall is level. Check that the waterline 1' above the DWL is exactly in line with those marked on the tuck and the stem, again using the water hose level or a laser sight level. You may need to shim the mould up off the keel with thin wedges, or you may have to deepen the notch in the mould to lower it (I always cut the keel notch on the bottom of the mould on the uppermost side of the drawn line as it is easier to shim than to remove the mould to extend the notch). When happy, screw the mould to the upright.

Photo 7E   Stem/Keel/Tuck

Photo 7F   First Mould

Now all you have to do is repeat the exercise for each of the other moulds, working forward and aft. Line of sight is perfectly adequate to line these up, you can pack the water level away, but if you have a laser level it could still come in handy. As you check the centrelines and waterlines, you may find that not every line agrees to the millimetre. If this is the case, the likeliest correct result is to average out the errors.

Bracing

The setup will be subject to some stresses and strains including shock loadings, so it is important to brace the moulds. Some builders would brace them up to the roof, but it is generally sufficient to fasten angled battens across the cross spalls, two forward and two aft, including the tuck. Clamp before fastening and check that the moulds are exactly square to the centreline, and the exact distance apart on the sheer as they are on the keel.

Stopwaters

Wherever the joint between two backbone members crosses the rabbet line a **stopwater** needs to be fitted, as in drawing 7.12, in our case the joint between the keel and the stem and stern knees. The hole for the stopwater is drilled right through from one side to the other in the joint between the keel and the knee in the back rabbet, that is, where it will be covered over by the garboard plank. The stopwater is whittled slightly oversize from a piece of softwood like pine or Western Red Cedar or a soft hardwood like Australian Cedar, slightly longer than it will finish up, and driven through a hole in a piece of steel 1/64" smaller than the hole in the

Photo 7G Ron Balkwell with his first 12-footer set up in the late 1940's. Note that the breasthook is already fitted (see Chapter 9). This boat, also named Ron, still exists. BALKWELL FAMILY ARCHIVES

boat, which will shave off the excess and compress the stopwater. It is then driven into the drilled hole in the keel-knee joint. The excess is then chopped flush with the back rabbet on each side with a very sharp chisel. Any water seeping along the joint will swell the soft stopwater and block off the joint.

Now you should take a little time to stand back and admire your work, and tip your hat to the original designer and builder for coming up with such a beautiful shape.

7.12 Stopwaters

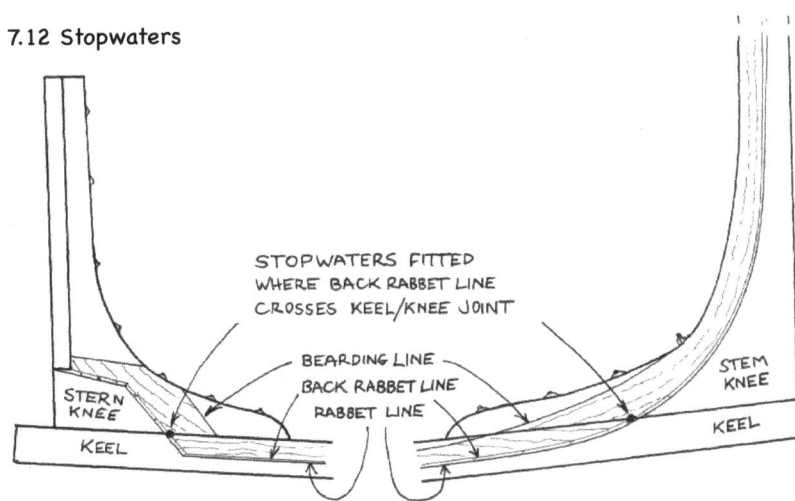

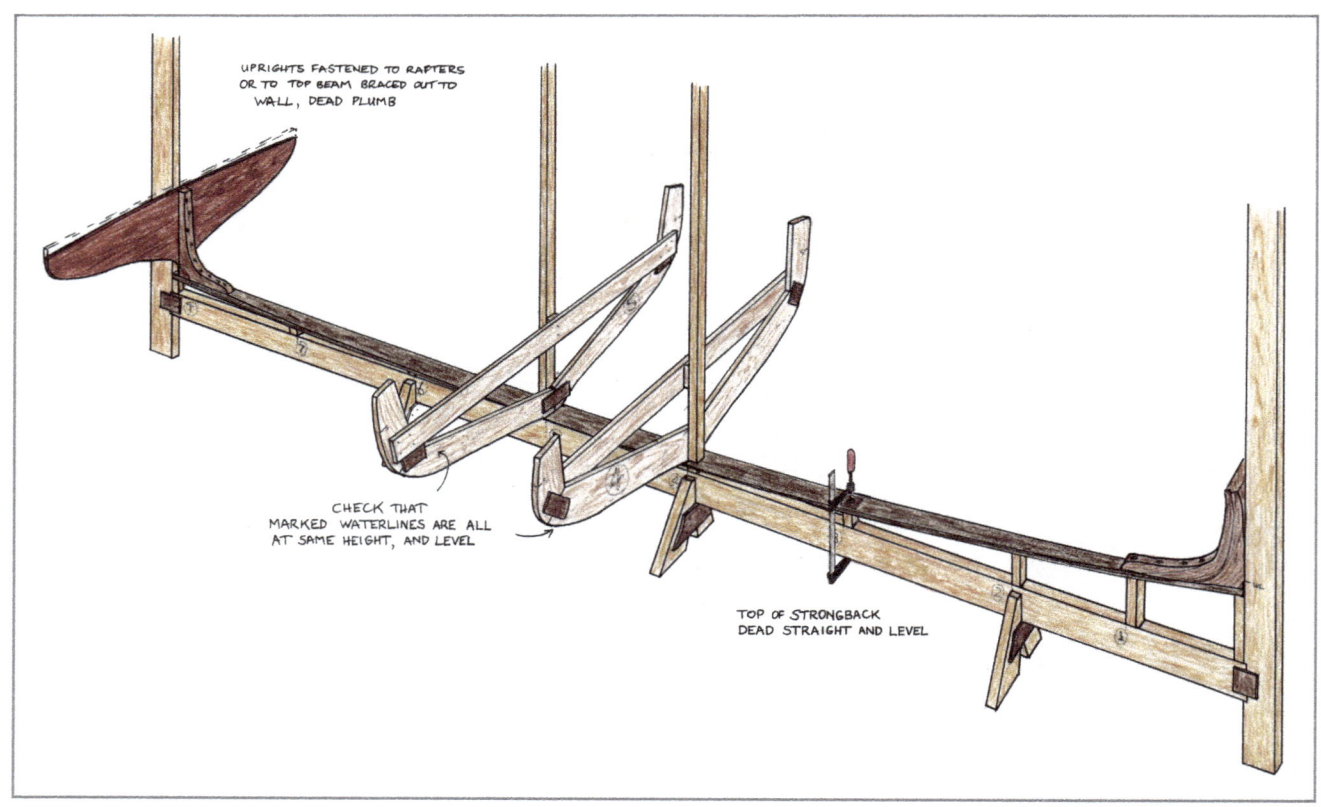

7.13 The first moulds set up on the keel sprung into the strongback

CHAPTER 8

Lining Out

Of all the procedures involved in building a boat, planking is the most satisfying. Every plank you add shows a bit more of the shape of the hull. It's like reading a good book, you just want to keep going to see how it turns out. But you have to know where each plank will be before you start. And you need to know the widths of timber stock you have available.

Timber Selection

You can't go down to your local timber yard and get long wide boards of Australian Cedar (or any Australian Cedar at all actually) but there are several yards supplying to craft workers in Sydney and Brisbane, and several sawmillers on the North Coast of NSW and the Queensland coast who can supply it. It is difficult to get full-length planks for an 18 footer (I had only a few for *Britannia*) but widths of 8-10" are not uncommon, and 12" widths can occasionally be found. You would not want planks any wider than this for reasons outlined below. An occasional plank of 7" or a healthy 6" might find a spot, but 8" is a comfortable minimum. Make up the lengths from 8', 10', 12' and 14' boards.

You may find Malaysian, Philippine or New Guinea Cedar more readily available, and I have no philosophical objection to using these as they come from basically the same species (confession: the tuck on my *Britannia* is made from Malaysian Cedar boards, but they were particularly good ones). However you do have to be more careful in selecting the boards, as they vary widely in quality. The colour can be considerably lighter than Australian Cedar, though it often is just as dark (freshly sawn and planed Australian Cedar is not as dark as some old folks remember it, it darkens with age and it was generally finished with dark finishes). But it often seasons (or has been kiln-dried) unevenly and has locked-in stresses which lead to it curling away from the saw blade in quite impressive curls. Reject any boards with uneven twists and turns or wavy surfaces. Also a lot of it has hairy surfaces which are difficult to plane and finish. Take a small block plane to the timber yard and plane any bits that seem a bit hairy. If the plane removes the hairiness and leaves a smooth surface, that is fine, but if tufts still stand up or the grain tears out reject the board.

The finished planking thickness for *Britannia* was 7/16", and later 7' beamers reduced this to 3/8". About half of your planking can be thickness planed to the finished thickness. Most of your narrower boards will be used near the turn of the bilge (and the hollow of the built heel) so they need to be thicker in order finish at 7/16" after rounding and hollowing, illustrated in drawing 8.1. You will not know exactly how thick until you know exactly where the plank will be hung, so have these planks sawn to about ¾" and have them thicknessed only when you are sure what their maximum thickness will be.

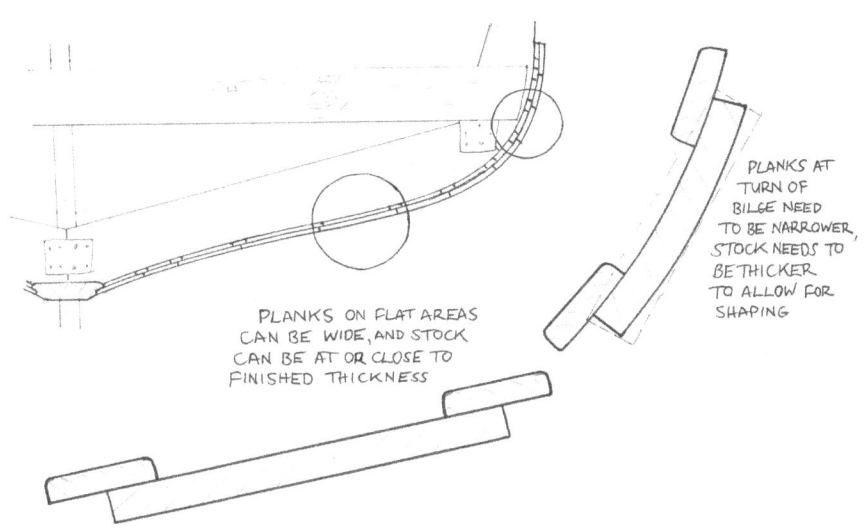

8.1 Thickness and Width of Plank Stock

If you have easy access to a thicknesser, have all boards other than the thicker ones sawn to 5/8" (or 9/16" for a 7' beamer) and you can prepare each board just before you intend you work on it.

The seam battens were generally of New Zealand Kauri Pine, and this can be difficult to source in Australia. I bought a load of used Kauri flooring which is still reasonably available. I had to scarf them together to get the lengths required, and I had to saw judiciously to avoid most of the stained flooring nail holes. I also suspect a couple of pieces were Rimu, another NZ timber but still useable. Fijian and Malaysian Kauri (Damar Minyak) are currently readily available, and in reasonable lengths, but be aware that these timbers are not as durable in the marine environment as New Zealand Kauri. The seam battens need to be prepared before starting planking as they are fitted concurrently. Cut and plane to size (in our case 1¼" x 3/8") and cut or scarf join to length. Ease the corners that will be on the inside of the boat.

Lining Out

This is the process of working out where each plank will be. With *Britannia* I had the original boat to copy, but if you don't have that, here is how to go about it.

Depending on the width of Cedar stock available, 18-footers were generally planked with about eleven or twelve planks a side in the big beam era, down to nine or ten when the boats got narrower.

You might assume that with twelve planks a side, all you would need to do is measure the girth from keel rabbet to sheerline at each station and divide by twelve. This would give you a series of tapered planks as the girths amidships are larger than those towards the ends. But although the taper of each plank is the same, the planks will definitely not be the same shape. This only works on a barrel which is perfectly round. Any boat has variations in shape along its hull that make it far more complicated. But even if you did decide to shape each plank individually to this lineout, you would have problems, mainly because when you lay out planks cut to fit this lineout flat on the floor, most of them would have considerable curve, some would have S bends, and most would be so curved that you would not be able to find stock wide enough to cut them out of.

Thickness and Width of Plank Stock

You need a straight batten longer than the boat about 3-4 inches wide by about ¼" thick. Plywood scarfed or cleated together for length would be fine, but solid lightweight timber is better. Wherever you wrap this around the moulds it will tell you where a straight plank would lie. You are aiming at getting the straightest planks you can for several reasons.

1. You will get them out of narrower stock, which is more available and desirable because….

2. Planks that are too curved will mean that the grain towards the ends will run out and be too short which is weaker and more likely to split. And this is even more the case with…..

3. The seam battens which are narrow and parallel sided and are penetrated by two lines of closely spaced nails and it is imperative that they be as straight as possible.

Stand back and look at the boat from just to one side of the tuck. You will see that from the tuck forward, the turn of the bilge where the bottom of the hull grades into the topsides forms a sort of

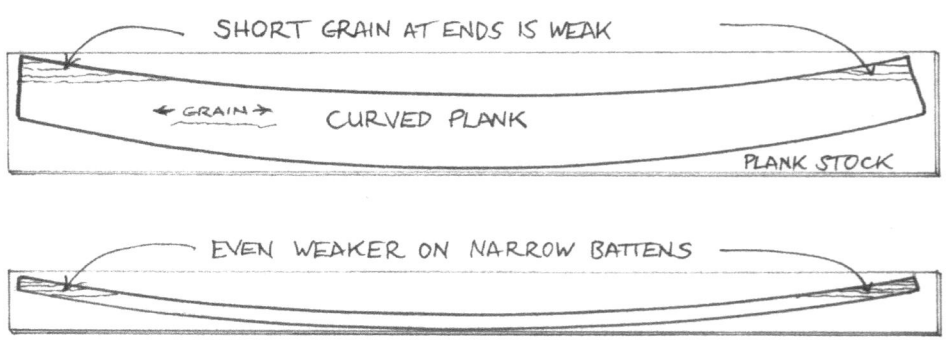

8.2 Why You Need Straight Planks and Battens

8.3 The "Ridge Line" of the Turn of the Bilge

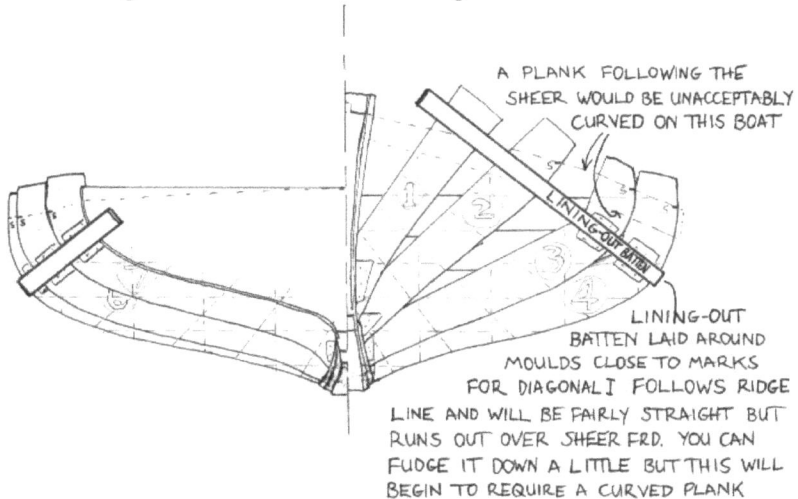

ridge. On *Britannia* it closely follows the line of the uppermost diagonal on the body plan. It would be difficult to lay a plank that starts on the topsides and ends up on the bottom and crosses this ridge. Any plank will lie far more comfortably when it lies as close as possible to the top of the ridge. Pick the side of the boat with the best access and light, and lay your batten as close as you can to the line of the top of the ridge. The ridge line fades away on the forward few moulds, and on a boat with a lot of bow flare like *Britannia* you will find that the forward end wants to climb high on the stem, even to the point of running out above the sheerline before reaching the stem. This is not a problem on a seam-batten boat (it might be on a clinker boat). Mark the moulds in pencil on either side of the batten, remove the batten and mark the centreline between those marks. We'll refer to this again as the <u>ridge line</u>. If you find that the batten can't exactly follow the ridge, that is the peak of the ridge line may be a slight curve, remove the batten and replace it with a narrower batten (say 1" x ¼") that you can bend around the moulds and make a fair curve of the ridge line. Mark one side of this line on the moulds. **Hint:** work out a notation system for your marks, because eventually there will be quite a few of them and it easily gets confusing. Rub or sand off any marks that have been corrected or are no longer needed.

Whichever batten you used to mark the moulds, work out how many planks would be required to cover the territory above your marks on the mould, probably three or four. Do not expect every plank on the boat to be the same width. Planks on parts of the hull that are tightly curved in section will have to be narrower to be able to be cut from stock which is not too thick, and on *Britannia* this involved four planks at the turn of the bilge which were no wider than 4" at any point. Planks on flat sections of the hull can be quite wide, up to about 8" at any one point. Planks with a little sectional curve can be somewhere in between. Refer again to drawing 8.1.

Divide the distance from your ridge line to the sheer on the midships mould (5 in our case) and several other moulds, say 1, 3 and 7 by the number of planks and mark those plank widths on the moulds. Wrap your wider planking batten around the moulds starting above the mark on the amidships mould and below the first plank width mark above that, running it so that it is an even distance from the marks on the forwardmost and aftermost moulds (it will probably just cover the lower ones). Check that the batten lays comfortably by imagining it is a plank, would it be happy there? And would the width needed to cover your plank width marks on the moulds be within the plank stock you have? (You do have something up your sleeve if you will be scarfing planks to get the length. As described and illustrated in the next chapter on Planking you can scarf the stock together at an angle to allow curved planks from narrower stock.) If so, move the batten upwards to between the next marks on the midships mould and wrap it around in a similar manner, and the same for each remaining plank. It's unlikely there will be a problem here, but if there is, try slightly different angles to the planking, i.e bow up or bow down to see if there is an improvement, which would mean the planks would taper more at one end than the other relative to your original marks. You may need to consider using an extra plank, say if you started by lining out for three planks and they seem too wide or too curved, line it out again for four planks.

If your planking batten on the ridge line did not run out over the sheer, you may decide to see if you can work it so that the uppermost plank runs all the way from bow to stern. Almost all 7 foot beamers and all of the 6 foot beamers were done this way. This was possible because they were narrower and less flared forward than most of the big beamers. In

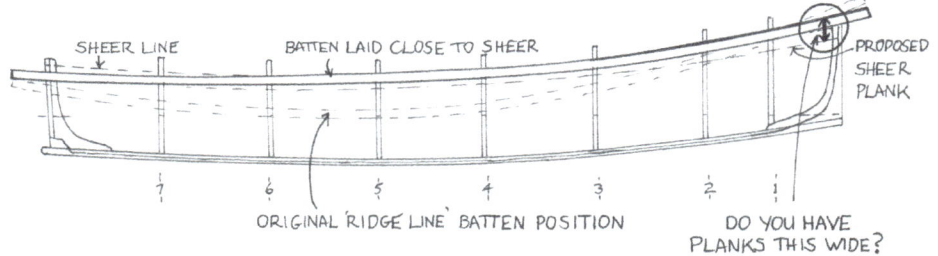

8.4 Measuring Proposed Plank Widths Off Planking Batten

fact Bill Barnett made it a point of honour that the sheer plank finish on the stem. To see if you can do this, wrap your planking batten around the moulds just below the sheerline and see where it wants to lie. You will probably find that it lies reasonably well at the stern, but wants to rise up a fair bit at the bow. This means that the actual sheer plank will curve down considerably at the forward end when laid flat. Careful measurements off your planking batten will determine how much curve is involved and whether you have the planking stock available to cover the territory. If the batten suggests it can be done, lining out the topsides planking area will involve measuring the distance from your original ridge line marks to the sheer on the stem and tuck as well as moulds 1, 3, 5 and 7 and dividing those distances by the number of planks. If the resulting planks are less than 1 ¾" wide on the stem, you will have to start all over again with your ridge line with your flexible batten and try to bend it down forward until the planks above it are all at least that wide. This is because if they were any narrower there would not be room for two fastenings on the stem which is the minimum.

Do the same to the area below your original marks. But first you need to work out where the first plank, the garboard will go. This plank can be reasonably wide (about 5 or 6 inches) as long as any hollow towards the stern doesn't start too low. It should keep its width well towards the ends, particularly at the bow where the upper planks will try to rise and there is a lot of territory for the lower planks to cover. You will almost certainly need your more flexible batten to mark the upper line. Make sure you're happy with what you've proposed, that is that the stock you have will cover the territory and that the plank will lie comfortably, remembering there is a lot of twist in the garboard. Mark the top of the garboard on all moulds, stem and stern.

Now check, if your boat has a built heel like *Britannia* there will be a hollow developing towards the aft end where a narrow plank will be required to lie in the bottom of the valley of the hollow just as one had to along the ridge of the turn of the bilge. Lay your batten just above your proposed marks for the garboard forward and amidships and see where it wants to lie aft. On *Britannia* it separated from the garboard aft and ran along the upper edge of the tight valley at the stern. On a boat with a deeper heel such as Western Australia's *Mele Bilo II* it may stay close to the garboard and not reach the tight hollow aft. The solution on *Britannia* and *Yendys* was to fit a stealer plank. This is highlighted in photo 8A. The stealer runs along the valley bottom which is very much hollowed at the stern knee and fades rapidly forward. This plank had to be sculpted out of a much thicker piece to allow for the hollow and twist. It also was notched into the garboard, which means your have to redo the marks you made for the top of the garboard to incorporate this. The line you should lay out with your flexible batten will actually be the bottom of the main second

Photo 8A Stealer plank, second from bottom.

Photo 8B Tapered stealer, fifth from bottom.

plank. Tack the batten on moulds 1 to 5, then allow it to rise up to the tuck along the top of the hollow, so that the plank above this will have way less hollow than the stealer. Mark this on the moulds. More details on fitting the stealer later.

If your boat doesn't have this feature, and most heel-less 7' beamers will not, simply divide the distance from the bilge mark to the marks you made for the top of the garboard on moulds 1, 3, 5 and 7 by the number of planks you expect to use (say 7 or 8) and mark these spacings on those moulds. Wrap your batten around each of these hypothetical plank areas in turn and check how the plank will lie, and how wide your plank stock will need to be to cover the territory you have marked. Adjust your marks if any proposed plank would need to be too wide and try again. You may need to adjust everything a number of times. You may even need to redo it for a larger number of planks, each of which can then be narrower.

If your boat is beamy and well-flared towards the sheer at the bow like *Britannia* you will find that the upper planks rise up towards the bow and the upper planks run out over the sheer. But the lowermost planks do not want to rise up without being unnecessarily wide. A stealer is also employed here, in *Britannia's* case as the fifth plank up from the keel. This is highlighted in photo 8B.

It is important to lay the planking batten in the position of every proposed plank to check that the measurements you make from the batten to the proposed plank marks will be within the plank stock you have available. And it is important that the batten lies comfortably. The garboard and the next few planks will have considerable twist in them up forward. Your ¼" batten should take this twist with a bit of persuasion from clamps, but it is important to wrap the batten around the moulds, being careful not to edge-set it as the twist develops. You also need to check that at any point the planking stock thickness will be enough to allow for any hollow and rounding on curved sections of the hull. Check your lineout marks on the moulds by placing a rule across the span of the marks. Your planking stock thickness at this point needs to be the finished planking thickness plus the distance from the ruler to the curve as in drawing 8.5. But once you've checked that you've done this (and of course you only need to do it on one side of the boat) you are ready to start planking.

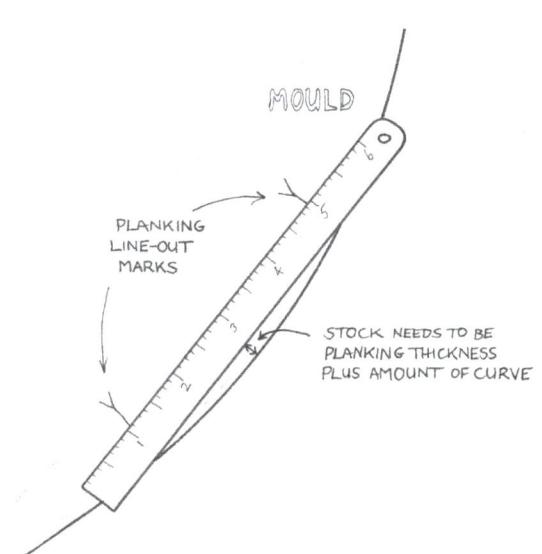

8.5 Checking Plank Stock Thickness Required

Summary:

1. Keep in mind that you will use narrower planks on hull areas with sectional curve (turn of bilge, any hollow heel), wider planks on flatter areas. Consider the width of stock you have available.

2. Lay your planking batten along the crest of the ridge that follows the turn of the bilge. When happy with how it lies, mark both sides on each mould then more noticeably mark the centreline which we will call the ridge line.

3. Divide the distance between the ridge line and the sheerline on stem, tuck and alternate moulds by the number of planks you intend to fit and mark these proposed plank widths. If the marks on the stem are closer than 1 ¾", start again with a flexible batten on the ridge line, curving the forward end down until the planks landing on the stem above it will be at least this wide. Check that the proposed new plank on the ridge line can still be got out of the stock you have. If your original plank batten landed on or above the sheer at the stem, you are going to need to run all planks above it past the sheerline forward.

4. Lay your planking batten just above the keel to work out how your garboard will lie. You may need to use a flexible batten to mark out the top of the garboard as it should rise up the stem as much as you can comfortably make it, and because if there is a heel and therefore a hollow aft you will probably need to fit a stealer plank, and this line you are marking will actually be the underside of the main second plank.

5. Divide the distance from the top of the garboard (or bottom of the second plank) to the ridge line by the number of planks you intend to use and mark these proposed widths on the moulds. Lay your planking batten on each of these areas in turn to check that the stock you have is wide enough and that each plank will lie comfortably. If your boat has a flared bow you may need to fit a stealer here also.

6. Check that you have enough thickness in your plank stock to allow for rounding and hollowing in the most curved sections.

CHAPTER 9

Planking

The Mystery of the Queensland Bow

In the 1930's when the Queensland-built *Aberdare* revolutionised 18-footer racing (see previous Chapter 5 and Robin Elliott's *Galloping Ghosts*), many owners and skippers went to the Queensland builders for their new boats, but some went to Sydney builders. The Queensland boats featured bows that were very sharp on the waterline at the bottom of the stem, and very rounded on deck which made a very flared bow which was difficult to plank. The advantage of the great flare was to keep water from coming aboard and to help lift the bow if the boat nose-dived. According to Ken Minter the first Sydney builders trying to copy the Queensland designs could not get the same amount of deck rounding and hull flare. At some stage (I suspect sooner rather than later) they either were told or figured out the Queenslanders' secret: the breasthook which joins the planking at the sheer to the stem and each side of the boat to the other (see Drawing 9.1) is fitted <u>before</u> planking reaches that level! Several closely spaced ribs (3 or 4 per side) are then steamed in place, notched into the breasthook and either fitted into notches cut before planking in the stem knee or simply jammed into the tapering gap between knee and the garboard.

When to fit the ribs needs to be finely judged. Too early, with only a few planks on will make it difficult to get the right shape on the upper part of the ribs. Too many planks fitted and the top one or two of those will not be starting to flare enough. Roughly halfway up the stem is the best time, as the lower planks will still have a bit of the sharpness of the waterline, and the upper part of the steamed ribs will tend to take exactly the bend they need to land on the breasthook. The technique is to put a slight bend in the top half of the rib over your knee or the bench as it comes out of the steam box, jam its lower end down behind the planking and bend the top end outwards holding it close to the top so the curve tends to fair itself out, overbend it slightly then allow it to rest back into the notch in the breasthook. Be careful not to have it kink over the uppermost batten, as it is vital that the rib be a fair curve. I mention this because it is quite likely, and you may even have several attempts before you get it right. No clamps are necessary or indeed possible, so drill and fasten these ribs before they cool, at least drive enough nails to hold the rib against the battens as it cools. Details on steaming, ribs and fastening will soon be dealt with. But my point in describing this process here is to point out that the breasthook was usually fitted during the setting up stage, before planking commenced. Its shape is cut as per lofting or scaled up from a model, but the changing bevel can only be estimated and it is best left a little oversize until the ribs are fitted. A little extra wood should still be left on until the saxboard is fitted, see below. The saxboard was sometimes butted up to the back of the breasthook, so the breasthook needs to be proud of the ribs by the saxboard thickness. Boats designed and built before the early 1930's had their breasthooks fitted after planking was finished.

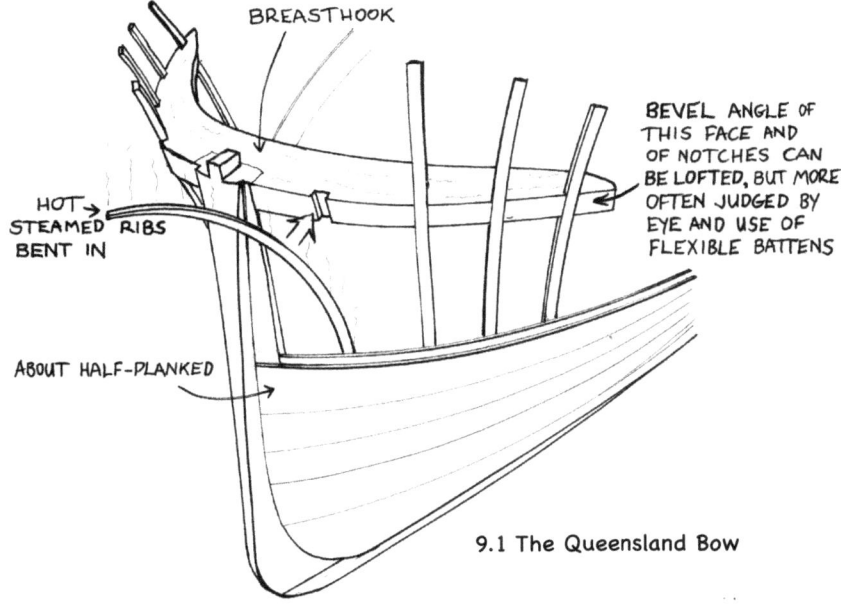

9.1 The Queensland Bow

The Garboard

You know where the first plank, the garboard, is supposed to land, on the stem, in the keel rabbet and on the stern knee if your boat has a heel or on the tuck if heel-less. But you need to work a bit more on the rabbet before you start fitting the plank. Using short offcuts of the planking, at 7/16" thickness, chisel and rabbet plane, trim the keel rabbet at each mould until your test piece fits well up against the back rabbet and an offcut of a seam batten centred on the proposed line of the top of the garboard on the mould as in drawing 9.2. Then fair it in between moulds. Chisel the rabbet where it crosses the joint between the keel and the stem knee, making sure the rabbet line is a fair curve because this is where you will fit the plank edge to. See photo 9A. Chisel right to the rabbet line, but leave a sixteenth of an inch of wood on the back rabbet forward of the first mould to be faired in when you have the plank steamed and ready for final fit. The steamed plank may want to lie slightly differently on the back rabbet compared to any test piece you may offer up.

At the stern, if the boat has a heel, be conservative with chiseling the back rabbet on the stern knee the same as you were for the stem. If the garboard will land on the tuck, bevel the edge of the tuck to suit the angle at which the garboard will land, testing with a batten held across the tuck and the aft <u>two</u> moulds (a line between the tuck and the last mould will not give the correct angle). Be careful to hold the batten as lightly as possible on the tuck landing as any finger pressure may distort the fairness of the batten and give a wrong reading. Remove timber until the batten lies fairly right to the lofted line drawn on the outside of the tuck.

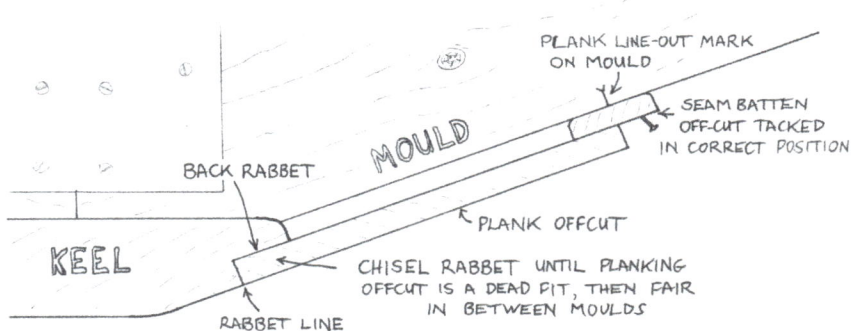

9.2 Fashioning a Landing for the Garboard at Each Mould Using a Plank Offcut

Spiling

This is the method we use for working out the shape of the garboard. Make up a spiling batten from a piece of softwood about 3" to 4" wide by ¼" thick. If the boat has a heel, the spiling batten needs to fit within the area of the garboard that lands on the keel. If heel-less, it must be longer as it must run out just beyond the tuck. It need not be a continuous length but can be two lengths cleated together. You may choose to recycle your original plank-mark-out batten. Tack the batten at each mould within the area of the proposed garboard starting in the middle and working out, ensuring that the batten lies flat on each mould and that you are not edge-setting it in the slightest. If the twist is such that lightly tacked nails will not hold it, use temporary screws.

Spiling, illustrated in drawing 9.3 involves using a set of compasses with pencil attached to describe a series of arcs on the spiling batten with the point of the compasses held hard against the back rabbet. Make an arc every 8" or so. When you take the batten

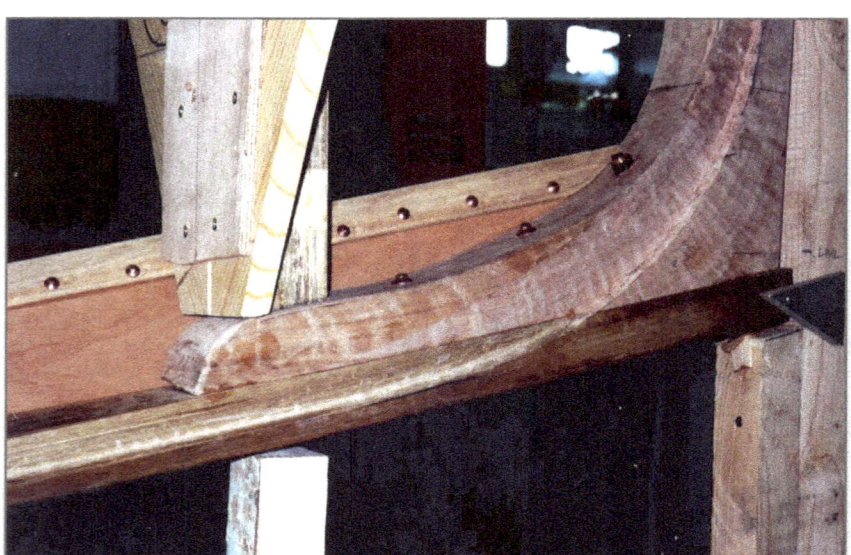

Photo 9A   Rabbet on keel and stem.

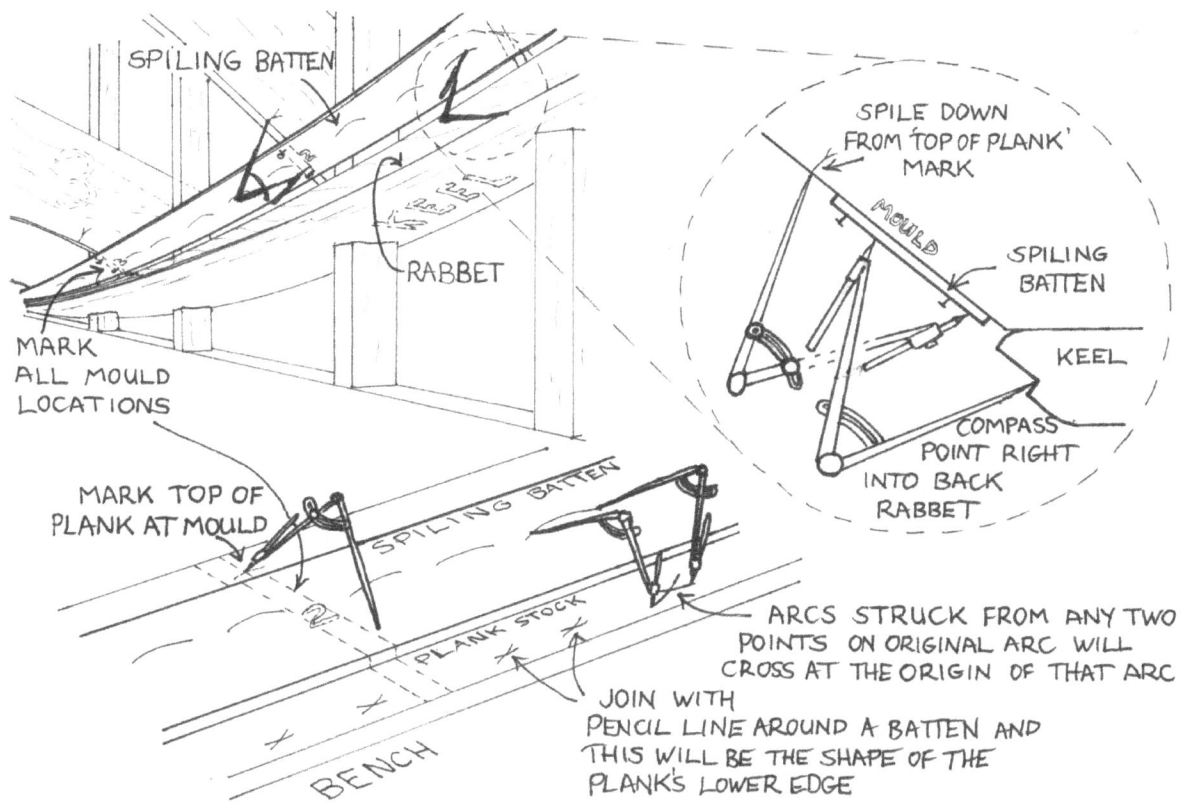

9.3 Spiling the Garboard

to your plank stock (do not remove it yet), you will describe two arcs from any two points on the original arc which cross, re-establishing the origin of each arc, and these crossing points therefore represent the relationship of the back rabbet to the batten. A fair line around a batten held by tacked nails to these points will therefore give you the line to which you will cut. But first you need to get a template of the forward end where the garboard lands on the stem, and the aft end on the stern knee if necessary. You need a piece of timber or very thin plywood or MDF about 2'6" to 3' long, at least as wide as the garboard and flexible enough to take the twist from the mould to the knee comfortably. You need to make this fit into the rabbet as an exact template of the garboard. You could practice your spiling by roughly fitting a smaller piece of the same material to the area as a spiling batten, then transfer the arcs to your bigger template, which should be accurate enough to need only a few trial fits with a little planing in between to get a perfect fit. Or you could roughly fit the bigger piece and scribe it, cut and plane to fit. See drawing 9.4. You will need to withdraw the tacks on your main spiling batten while fitting your template, or you could do the end template(s) first. Make sure the template is packed out from the mould by the thickness of the seam battens, but it should lie hard up against the back rabbet on both the keel and the stem. The long spiling batten is then fastened and/or glued to the end template(s) (hot-melt glue is good). Check that you have drawn arcs all the way up to the template(s). Mark the batten where it crosses each mould, and describe an arc from the mould marks representing the top of the garboard. Double check everything. The whole thing can now be taken to the bench where you have your plank stock, laid flat on it, clamped so that it cannot move, and marked out as in drawing 9.5. It is important to transfer the mould positions to help locate the plank. A penciled line around a fair batten around tacked nails will give you the shape of the garboard. You can confidently cut and plane close to the line which will fit along the keel, but leave a little extra wood (about ½" if you can) on top and about ¼" on the knee end(s). You will be steaming the plank into position and steamed wood has a habit of changing shape in unexpected ways, and this extra wood gives you the option of trimming the other plank edges for a perfect fit. If you are scarfing the plank (see below) you could make a separate pattern for each end, but it is better to make one complete pattern and mark each half-plank off each end separately, to ensure that the plank edges will be fair near the scarf.

You could cut out the sister plank for the other side of the same template but leaving a little extra wood all around, but I suggest you make a separate spiling and template arrangement for the other side. Have both planks ready before steaming.

Each plank must be fitted for the final time along with its upper batten, but for the trial fits and for steam bending and twisting it is easier to tack some offcuts onto the moulds.

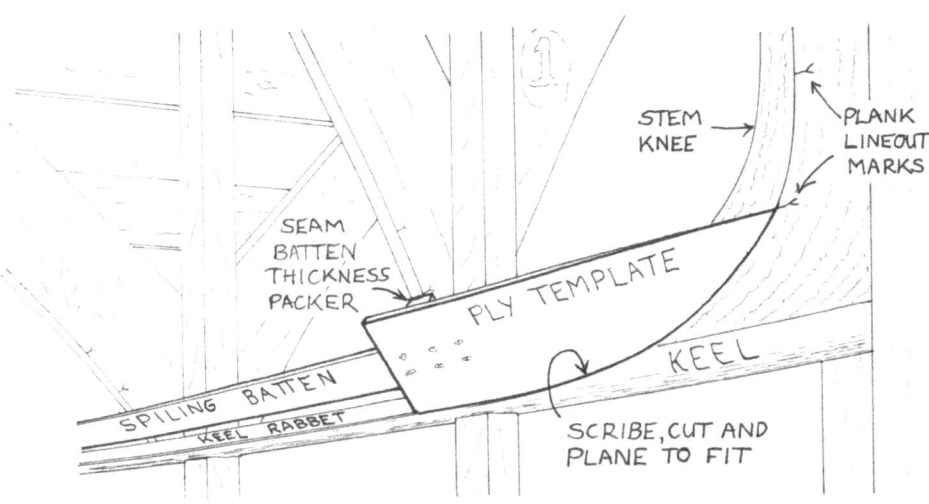

9.4 Pattern of Template for Garboard End

Experience helps

Bill Barnett built several boats a year for himself and others, often off the same or similar moulds. He clamped his garboard plank stock in place and simply scribed the edge off the rabbet. He used his experience to draw in the curve at the stem end, then steamed the plank and usually had very little trimming to get it to fit after cooling. He was considered the best and quickest planker there was. Len Heffernan, who worked alongside him on a number of boats said that Bill would often fit the plank after scribing with no further adjustment, and very rarely had to do more than one trial fit.

Steaming

The garboard will need steaming to take the twist towards the bow (and the stern if the boat has a heel). Some builders simply wrapped the plank in towels soaked in boiling water and kept pouring boiling water as they forced the plank around, but if you have a steambox (you will definitely need one for bending the ribs) it will be easier. A steambox can be as simple as a large metal tube sealed at one end propped up at an angle with the lower part full of water and a gas burner or fire lit under it. It is better to have a remote boiler which can be as simple as a large metal container like a lidded pot or a converted old gas cylinder. The box can be metal or wooden. For an eighteen-footer, the box needs to be wide enough to fit in one end of a 6"plank with a bit of a curve, so no narrower than say 8" x 6", and long enough to fit in ribs which will go from gunwale to gunwale, so at least 12' long. Photo 9B shows such a simple but adequate setup. Some steam generators might be available sold as wallpaper removers or carpet cleaners. You need to be able to generate enough steam so that it

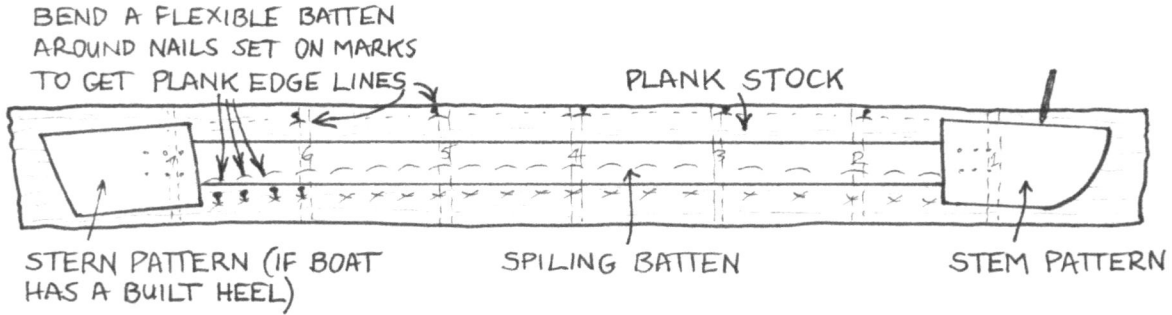

9.5 Schematic (Not to Scale) Drawing of Marking from the Garboard Pattern

Photo 9B   A simple steam box.

are good but it can be done alone if necessary. Support the aft end about the same height as the keel with a box, crate or helper. Clamp the plank to mould 3 (with a wide pad protecting the plank surface and spreading the load) with the mould marks you transferred from the spiling batten about 1'4" behind the mould (or a fraction over the amount of extra timber you left beyond the template line at the forward end). Start to twist it at the bow and clamp or hold it close to where it will live, which will probably bow it out at moulds 1 and 2, so go back and clamp it to the moulds here. If you have enough helpers you could have someone at each mould. It doesn't have to fit perfectly into the keel rabbet but it must be close. A little judicious tapping with a rubber mallet or a metal one hitting a wooden pad may help. Try not to put local pressure on too narrow an area, it is possible to split the plank. If you found the first part of the clamping took too long, or for some other reason the plank doesn't want to take the twist, no harm done, you can return it to the box and start again, with perhaps a little less time in the

escapes from the box under slight pressure. If steam only rises up in wispy tufts it will not be hot enough. Some barbecue burners do not produce a hot enough flame. Professional shops will have more sophisticated arrangements, often with boilers containing copper coils, and larger boxes. Round up some cloth or leather gloves (gardening gloves are ideal) and several quick action clamps and wooden pads to spread the load. You should experiment by clamping your template in place so you know where you can fit the clamps. You may find you need to have wooden cleats ready to screw to the stem to hold the plank into the rabbet.

Unless you have a large enough box to fit the whole garboard in and several helpers, you will have to steam and fit each end of the garboard separately. Fit the forward end into the box (which may or may not already have steam up) and support the other end. The old rule is to steam planks for an hour for every inch of thickness. Some Australian hardwoods require longer than this, but for Cedar it is about right, so for 7/16" planks you need to leave them in the box for about half an hour after steam is fully raised. Test it: if it is hot enough to touch with bare hands it is <u>not</u> hot enough to bend properly.

When ready, pull the plank out of the box and take it to the boat as quickly as possible. Helpers

A Note on Symmetry of Planking

Many boats up to 12-footers were built with only one mould plus the tuck, and plank shapes were got out by experience. Planks were got out in pairs, generally sawn out while held together and planed together to be identical. This way the shape of the boat would be symmetrical as long as great care was taken. The bigger the boat, the more moulds are needed and the more likelihood that small cumulative errors will creep in and identical planks will not fit exactly the same on both sides. With super-careful setting up, just a little adjustment to the matching plank might be sufficient to fit it. But not all of the original builders could get it right every time. Ken Minter told the story of how in 1947 boatbuilder Lester Woodforth measured up one side of the 1933 boat The Mistake built by Jack Whereat, and built No Mistake off those lines. No Mistake was a bit of a disappointment, it couldn't perform as well as the original. When they checked the measurements, it was discovered that one side of The Mistake was different from the other. The joke was told that they had measured the slow side!

box. When you're happy with it you put the matching plank for the other side into the box and repeat the procedure there.

It will take less than an hour to cool right off, but leave it for at least several hours to dry more, preferably overnight before removing the clamps. Too soon and it will straighten out more. If you fitted it early enough in the day you could fit the aft end (if it is a one-piece garboard) late in the day. If your boat is heel-less you only have to fit the forward end. Any small adjustments you make there by removing timber can be made up by tapping the plank forward a touch. If there are gaps between the plank and the rabbet, set your compasses or dividers to the widest gap and scribe a continuous line all the way along the plank, then plane to that on the bench and offer it up again. With any luck you will need only very minor planing adjustments to get a tight fit. A block plane is best for the edges of these thin planks, with the plank held flat overhanging the edge of the bench and the plane held dead square to the plank while planing. **It is better to work to a line than it is to guesstimate how much wood to remove**. Scribing with just a pencil for that last thirty-second of an inch is better than guessing. **But the secret of getting accuracy through guessing is always to guess, then remove half of what you think should come off, then try another trial fit.** If your garboard has to fit between the rabbets in the knees at both ends you have to be especially careful. Fit one end perfectly, then the other. You will be glad you left extra wood on each end.

Once you are happy with the fit, draw a penciled line on the inside of the plank at each mould, and mark where the inside of the plank disappears into the stem knee and stern knee or tuck (this mark is to give you the positions of the ends of the seam batten), remove the plank and measure (with either ruler or dividers) the distance from the back rabbet up to your plank width marks on each mould and transfer them to the inside of the plank along the lines you penciled where the plank lay close to each mould. Tack nails in, bend a batten, check for fairness, and adjust where necessary. Cut to this line and plane exactly to the line, sighting along it to ensure it is fair. If you have fitted the other side home as well, you may choose to lay the planks together and simply draw the top of the first plank onto the other one. This will only work if the rabbet sides of both planks are very similar in shape. If they are identical, give yourself a huge pat on the back, it's something I have never done though I've come close. If the planks are considerably different you'd better check everything and if you can't see a problem that needs correcting, mark the second plank individually off the lineout marks on its moulds

Scarfed Garboards

If your garboard is a full length plank, great, that is more traditional, but you may find (like I did on *Britannia*) that if your garboard has to fit into a rabbet at both ends, it is easier to fit the garboard in two pieces scarfed in the middle. Whaleboats were generally built this way because easier and quicker means cheaper. You certainly could scarf the stock together on the bench and treat it like a continuous piece of timber. Just don't let the glued scarf anywhere near the steam box because if you used epoxy it will come apart, epoxy does not like high heat. But it is easier to fit each end in turn with a good overlap on your plank in the middle where there will be hardly any twist. Spile each end individually and cut them out leaving a little extra timber on the top edge. Ensure that the planks overlap by at least the length of the scarf and preferably more, because for the cleanest look, you will land the inner joint of the scarf under a rib so that it is not seen and you may need to adjust the scarf area to suit this. Therefore you need to know at this stage where the ribs will be.

Rib Spacing

Britannia's ribs are 1" x ½" spaced on 8" centres. *Yendys* had 3/4" x 7/16" ribs on 5"-5 1/2" centres. *Top Weight* had 1" x 7/16" ribs on 7" centres. A good place to start is right against where the back of the fin case (centreboard case) will be. Start measuring along the keel each way out from there. You need all of them, including any extras. Most eighteens had extra ribs in the spaces between the others under the mast step and often just behind the fin case. The reason you need them all is because it determines your fastening pattern. Three nails will fit evenly spaced between the ribs, so where the rib will land is left undrilled at this stage. Mark the rib positions squarely up from the keel onto the garboard, and mark your fastening positions ensuring they are evenly spaced. Leave out the middle one wherever you will be adding extra ribs. They need to be parallel to the seam, and with battens 1¼" wide, the fastenings should be drilled 5/16" from the seam. Mark a continuous line this far in from the edge before final fitting with a pencil held against a combination square sliding along the plank as a marking gauge. The nails for the keel and stem/stern knees are different: the back rabbet of the keel is generally wider than the plank landing on the battens, so its fastenings are drilled at a distance from the edge that will penetrate the back rabbet in the middle. Towards the forward end (and aft on a heeled boat) some nails will eventually land at such an angle that they will not go through the keel so as to be roved over. These nails are therefore drilled and fitted blind, that is the points remain buried. On stem and stern knees, the back rabbet is even wider than on the keel, especially low on the stem, so there is usually room for two lines of blind fastenings, staggered.

Plank Scarfing

Before reliable waterproof glues any plank scarf was generally bedded on some sort of compound and fastened through a backing block. You could certainly still do this, perhaps with a polyurethane bedding compound, but I epoxied all mine to pretend they were one continuous plank.

A plank scarf should be a stepped or notched scarf, the steps being about 1/16" deep and the length of the scarf 6 to 8 times the plank thickness, shown in drawing 9.6. Traditionally the scarf end on the outside of the plank was aft, probably so that any edge lifting would not be as susceptible to damage as the boat moved through the water. Mark the scarfs on your garboard with the planks on the boat by having the forward end (which you will have trimmed to a square edge at a distance which ensures that the inner joint of the scarf will be under a rib) overlap the aft end and pencil in where it lands. Take the planks to the bench and mark the areas to be scarfed carefully, the cut them with chisel and rebate and block plane. You may even want to knock a bit off with a power plane but the soft cedar is easy to work and a bit of chiseling and planing will have it halfway there before you can find and plug in your power plane and find your hearing and eye protection. Test fit on the bench. Fit the planks onto the boat exactly where they will live (still with the batten-thickness packers on the moulds along the upper plank edge), clamp them in place and apply glue and clamp up the scarf with wooden pads to spread the load, and plastic sheeting under the scarf so no glue attaches the plank to the boat. Repeat the procedure for the matching plank on the other side.

The next day, check that you have a penciled line across the inside of the planks at each mould, remove the planks and cleanup the glue residue. Measure the plank widths at each mould from back rabbet to lineout mark, and transfer these to the plank along the marked mould lines. Tack in nails, bend a batten, check for fairness and adjust if necessary. Mark, cut and plane to this line sighting along the line to ensure fairness. Clamp the planks together, and as discussed before, you may decide to cut the top edges of both planks identically.

Fitting the Batten with the Plank

The batten on top of each plank must be fitted together with the plank. As mentioned before, you will have marked on the inside of the plank the position where the batten will fit up against the stem and either stern knee or tuck. On the bench, clamp your batten to the plank edge with exactly half its width on the plank, mark each end where you expect it to finish and cut just outside the line so you have a little extra timber to play with when fitting. It is important that the batten fit tight to the knees/tuck for watertightness. Remove any clamps you've fitted within about three feet from each end. Fit the plank plus batten to the boat (making sure you've removed the temporary batten-thickness packers on

9.6 Plank Scarfing

Photo 9C The batten is fitted with each plank. The upper batten here is a continuation of the one on top of the garboard forward. The lower one is added here aft for the stealer.

the moulds) being careful to bend the unclamped batten ends well into the boat when fitting the plank ends. Trim the ends to fit against the stem and stern knee or tuck. There will be a bevel. It will be awkward to get your tools to the end, and you can try small sharp saws, block planes or even careful use of a small sanding disc on a grinder. It may be necessary to mark the amount you expect to remove, and take the whole thing off the boat. I will also repeat, it is better to work to lines than it is to guess. When the batten fits tight, replace a few small clamps and check all around that you are happy with where the plank and batten are going to live. If you will be fitting a stealer aft, remember the garboard has to be notched to house the thin end of the stealer. The batten in this case continues to sweep up towards the stern because it will back the seam on the upper edge of the stealer. Fit the batten that will support the lower edge of the stealer as in drawing 9.7 and fasten it off when you do the rest of the fastening.

Mark out the rib spacings onto the plank, then plot out the nail positions as described before. The nails will be 14 gauge, so drill each hole where a roved nail will fit with a 5/64" bit. On the stem knee and tuck and possibly some parts of the keel near the ends there is no chance of a through fastening, so some builders used a slightly larger diameter nail, usually with a twist in it (twist them in a vice with pliers), some used bronze screws. Whatever the fastening, drill for them, drill the plank only out to screw shank size and countersink slightly for the heads. Cedar is quite soft and it is best to make the countersink just slightly less deep than you think, as the force of screw-driving or nail fastening will pull the heads in a little and your aim is to have the heads flush with the surface.

Some builders would fasten off at this stage, without putting any bedding compound between the mating surfaces, and not removing any drilling swarf. It was explained to me by Jack Boyd, not a boatbuilder but a top skipper, in terms of: why would you bother trying to keep a little water coming through the seams when you're always getting plenty of water over the sides and the bow? However some builders like Ken Minter would remove the plank and coat mating surfaces with old gummy varnish. Some would add a thin line of caulking cotton on the keel and stem and tuck near the fastening line (not hammered into the seam itself). In the twenty-first century I can see no reason why you would not lay a bead of a low-modulus polyurethane sealant or a mastic. As mentioned earlier, do not use glue or any hard sealant such as those usually sold in the marine stores. *Britannia* had the soft sealant treatment and did not begin to leak until after six or seven hard seasons.

When you replace the plank for final fitting and fastening, you should fasten off three or four nails amidships through the top of the plank and through the batten while on the bench. This will locate it exactly where you drilled it. Clamp the plank and batten back in place, and **use narrow gauge steel nails as feelers to make sure that when you start driving nails you go through the drilled holes.** If you miss, I can almost guarantee that the batten will split. If you miss on the hardwood keel the copper nail will just bend. Follow the nailing and roving sequence as described in Chapter 3, remembering that with the 5/16" or 3/8" roves you will use and the 14 gauge nails, you can only use the lightest possible ball peen hammer. You will have to leave out an occasional nail when it is meant to go where you currently have a mould.

Once you've roved all nails and driven any screws, you are ready to start work on the second

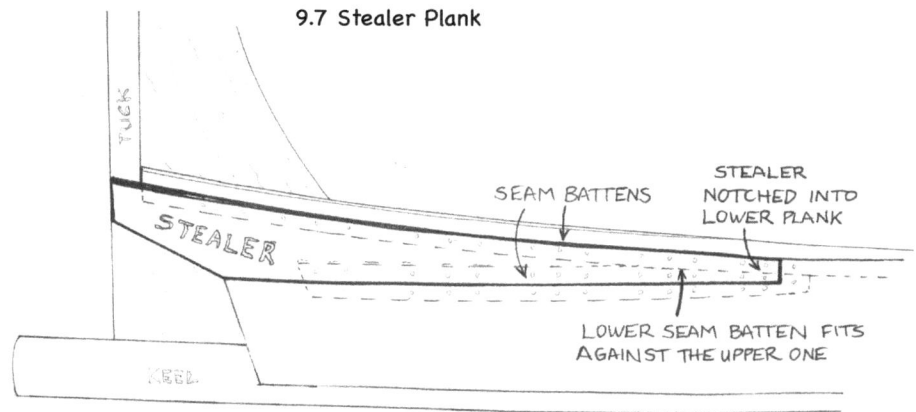

9.7 Stealer Plank

On *Britannia* and most other heeled boats the stealer must fit in a very tight hollow which means the back of it will have to be well rounded and the outside hollowed. But also there is a twist from one end to the other, roughly 20 degrees over only about 3'6". It would be impossible to twist a hollowed and rounded plank to fit here even with steam, so the answer is to carve it out of a thicker piece of Cedar. To determine the thickness you need to start from, fit two short straight edges at either end of the landing area and make a close guesstimate of the angle by sighting with a protractor.

Plot this out on paper with the sectional area at each end drawn in superimposed. Your stock will need to cover the combined sectional areas as in drawing 9.8. You should also check on the amount of curve fore and aft. It will likely only be slight, but you should add this amount onto the stock thickness as well. Add another fraction for safety and you have your thickness. On *Britannia* it worked out at a bit over 1 ½". Cut the taper first, but leave a large margin of error. Don't attempt any hollowing until the rounding on the back is complete and the plank fits. Round the back with hand planes slightly including the twist and fore and aft curve, plane the bottom edge to fit the garboard, and give it a trial fit.

plank, often referred to as the First Broad because on the majority of boats it is on a flattish area of the hull and can be cut from quite a wide (broad) plank. This case applies to most 6 and 7 foot beam eighteens, and to sixteens and twelve-footers. Built-heel eighteens such as *Britannia* however need a narrower plank here as the heel hollow extends well forward. In fact *Britannia's* heel hollow is so tight aft it needs a stealer plank.

Fitting a Stealer Plank

The basic layout of a stealer plank is illustrated in drawing 9.7. The stealer is notched into the lower plank such that the adjoining upper edge of the host plank and the stealer are a continuous fair line against which the next plank will fit. The batten at the top of the host plank follows this line and is therefore the batten for the top of the stealer as well. An additional batten is added to the lower seam of the stealer, extending just past the notch so that there is room for fastenings.

Sight it up, mark where wood should be removed and remove less than you think you should before another trial fit. Keep whittling until it fits. Trim the top edge to fit the middle of the upper batten, making sure the transition between the stealer and the host plank is a fair line to which you will be able to fit the next plank, that is, parallel with the batten, then start hollowing it, ensuring you don't go below the 7/16" thickness on any edge (or anywhere on the

9.8 Carving a Stealer

plank in fact). Hollow it with round-bottomed planes, or less traditionally with a 4" grinder, but be very careful. It helps to have templates of the shape at the mould and the tuck as illustrated. Drill and fasten it off then repeat for the other side.

The First Broad Strake

As I mentioned, the second plank is referred to as the first broad because on most carvel boats it lands on a flattish area to which wider planks can be fitted. This is the case with most seven and six foot beam eighteens as well as many other classes. But on heeled boats it will generally be narrower, and require a little rounding and hollowing. You should have determined the extent of this before starting planking by holding a straight rule on each mould across your marked plank widths and selecting your stock accordingly. Most likely the forward end of the plank will require steaming to take the twist. You have two alternative ways of marking out the plank. You can spile the plank shape as for the garboard, then mark and cut your plank (leaving the top edge a little oversize) and steam it before fitting and twisting it into place. Or see if this works: steam your plank stock and clamp it to the moulds to get the twist, just above where it wants to live such that it touches the previous plank in a couple

Photo 9E   Garboard, stealer and first broad fastened off.

of places (at the stem, you will have picked up the rough angle of the top of the previous plank to the rabbet with a bevel gauge and marked and cut the plank stock before steaming). Once it's cooled, readjust its position if necessary to ensure that the stock is lying naturally with no edge set, and make sure the upper part is packed out by the batten thickness just where the top batten will live. Tap it forward so the forward end is touching or very close to the rabbet line. Set your compasses to the width of the greatest gap and scribe a pencil line all the way along the stock with the compass point running along the previous plank edge as in drawing 9.9. Scribe the rabbet with the narrowest set of the compasses that will draw a line across the plank. If the plank is a true broad strake, that is one that lies on a flattish area of the hull, cutting and planing to this scribed line should give you a very close fit to the previous plank. If the stock cannot be held close to where it will live, the scribed line is less likely to be accurate. But it will enable the plank to be clamped closer to its eventual position for a second scribed line (which will be more accurate) as long as there is enough width on the plank stock to cover the territory. If there is much of a hollow where the plank will live, it is generally better to spile the plank, but if you can do it, scribing off the previous plank is quicker. Of course you should mark the mould positions

9.9 Scribing Off Previous Plank

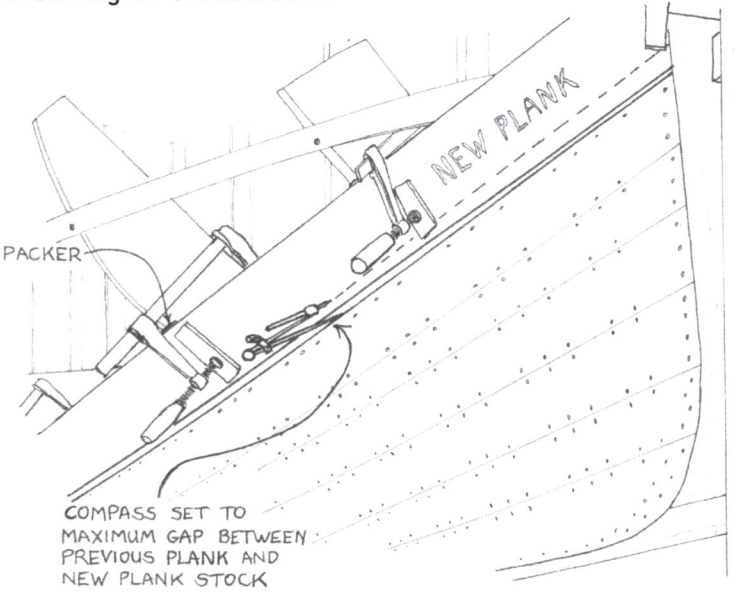

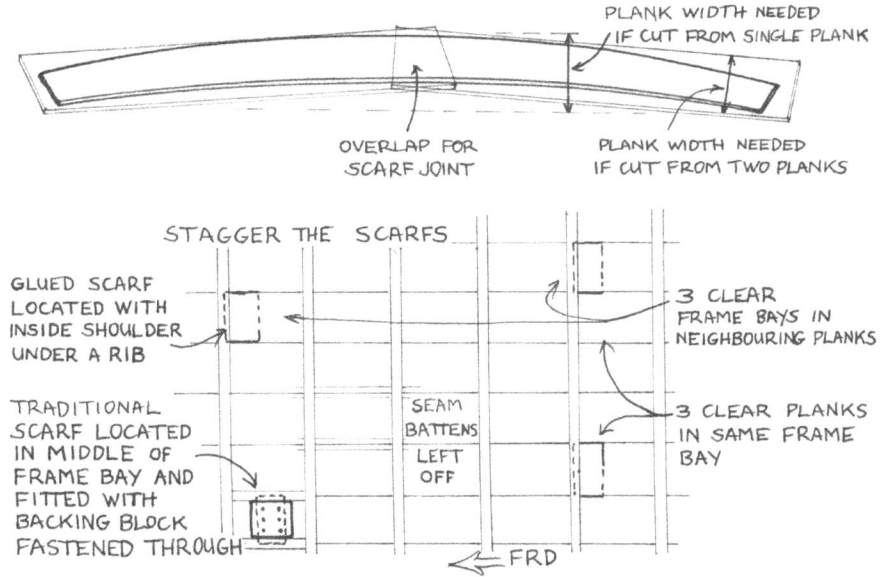

9.10 Scarfing Plank at an Angle to Allow Use of Narrower Stock

across the back of the plank so that when you measure the plank widths at each mould you can lay them off on the inside of your plank, cut and plane fairly to this line.

If you need to scarf the planks for length, spiling is easier as you can join the planks on a slight angle to enable use of narrower stock as in drawing 9.10. Lay your spiling batten on the bench and draw the arcs and draw in the whole plank. Lay your two plank stock pieces to check that you can cover the territory. Once you've established that the spiling will fit you can glue the planks together on the bench. If you are happy that your plank stock will cover the territory if joined in a straight line, you can cut the scarf and join them together on the bench and treat it as one long plank, either spiling or marking it off the previous plank. But it is more difficult to locate the scarf joint behind a rib. What I did was to spile the forward part and fit it, and clamp on the aft part and mark it off the previous plank. When both were fitted individually I marked and cut the scarf where I wanted it and glued the scarf together on the boat. It is better that scarf joints in adjacent planks are not in the same position along the hull. A bit of planning is necessary to make sure they are several ribs apart on adjacent planks, and several planks apart in the same frame bay (the space between a pair of ribs).

If there is hollow in the moulds, work out how much rounding is needed on the back of the plank at each station as described in the previous section on the stealer plank, plane conservatively at each station, then plane away the excess between stations to fair it in. Offer the plank up for a trial fit, remembering to clamp on its upper batten as you fit it. Mark any areas that need further stock removal, and keep whittling it down until you're happy with the fit. Then remove it to the bench and hollow it on the outside where necessary, again making sure you do not go below the intended plank thickness. Then fit it for marking and drilling, then fastening it off.

The same procedure can be followed for the next few planks on most boats. During the lineout, you may have decided to fit a stealer up forward as well, in *Britannia's* case it was required as the fifth plank to fit up forward. A forward stealer will not require much hollowing and rounding, but you should check how it fits against the top and bottom batten. It is possible that a little bevel will have to be taken off the back of the stealer to lay flat on each batten as in drawing 9.11. You may need to start with slightly thicker stock to allow for the amount beveled, or even thicker stock and round the whole back of the plank as for the aft stealer.

Even if you are going to spile a plank, it is useful to wrap the plank stock into the position it is going to live forward of amidships to determine when you can stop steaming the planks. If you can twist the plank into position with firm hand pressure you will not need to steam it, and usually none of the following planks either.

Rib Positions Continued

As you plank up you need to keep working out where the ribs will be, to work out where your fastenings go. For the first few planks, the ribs will be laid right across the boat so the intended rib line will have to reflect this, i.e square with the centreline. Towards amidships the higher planking is still fairly square with the centreline so the ribs will be roughly parallel to the moulds. However towards the ends of the vessel, particularly forward, the diminishing beam measurement and the rise in the keel mean that the flat ribs will want to cant aft a little as they approach the sheer up forward, and cant forward a little up aft. When each plank is clamped up ready to mark and drill for nails, make a thin flat batten to represent the rib that you can bend around by hand, visualising how it will lie flat on the upper planks (which aren't there yet) with as little edge set as possible. There will be increasing twist towards the ends. Mark each rib position on the plank. Mark all rib positions before marking and drilling for the plank/batten nails to check they are visually roughly parallel (although probably slightly diverging), and check that both sides of the boat are done the same.

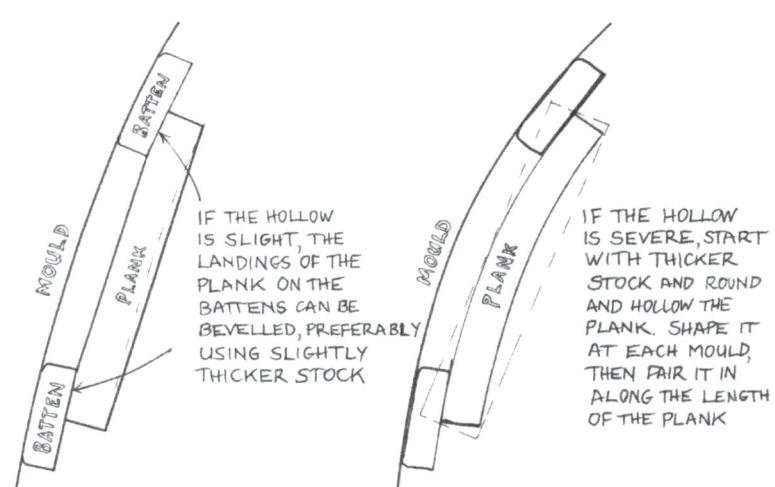

9.11 Fitting Planks to Seam Battens when Planks are Hollow

Running the Planks out over the Sheer

Before we get to the narrower planks at the turn of the bilge on a wide flared boat like *Britannia* the planks begin to run out over the sheer at the forward end. In fact on *Britannia* the seventh plank up the stem (including the stealer) is the first to run out. This plank and those above it need to have something to fasten to at the sheer, so a saxboard or sackboard is fitted around the sheer. This is generally fitted on all eighteen-footers sometimes just as an upper batten on the sheer strake, sometimes of the same material as the other seam battens, but more traditionally from the same timber as the planking, but planed down to the thickness of the battens. On *Britannia* the saxboard is 3/8" thick and 1¾" wide. Because of the rise in the sheer, this width of Cedar cannot be edge-set to fit the sheerline, so a wider board is clamped around the moulds as in photo 9F so that it covers the sheer marks and also covers at least 1¾" below each of the sheer marks. Mark these positions directly onto the Cedar, then follow the usual story of tacking nails in the marks, pencil the line along a fair batten held to the nails, cut, plane and fit, and it will finish up as in photo 9G. **(Hint: when making such marks always draw a T or an X to locate the point, a simple dash or dot may lead to inaccuracy).** You can see in the photos that I did it in two sections, only the forward section needed to be marked onto a wider piece. I simply scarfed a 3/8" x 1¾" length of Cedar onto the back of the forward piece, glued and clamped on the boat. If the breasthook was fitted first, the saxboard needs to fit around that and will probably require steaming, as will the planks in this area.

As noted at the beginning of the chapter some builders ended the saxboard at the aft end of the breast hook but left the breasthook proud of the ribs by the saxboard thickness. Continue planking with the broad strakes,

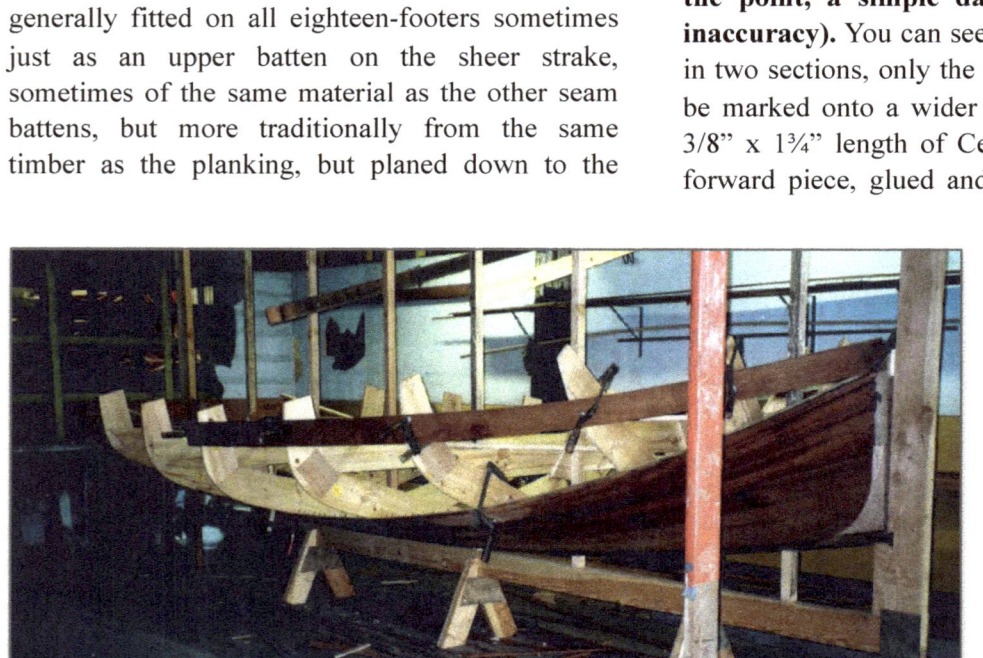

Photo 9F   Saxboard stock ready to be marked for sheer curve.

running them out over the sheer. Fasten the planks to the saxboard with only two roved nails, one forward and one aft. There will be plenty of other fastenings right through these two bits of timber later. The seam battens are cut to an angle that simply butts up to the underside of the saxboard. The part of the plank appearing above the saxboard can be cut off 1/8" to 1/4" above the saxboard.

At the tuck you can simply leave the planks long at this stage or you can cut them no closer than about 1/2" aft of the tuck. Carvel planked boats in Australia generally had their planks run past the tuck and were then cut and planed evenly to protrude slightly beyond the tuck. The reason for this on most boats is lost in the mists of time, but for racing skiffs it was because the overall length which was the main class measurement was measured from the stem to the back of the planking. Boats were set up with their tuck a fraction of an inch under the maximum length as we described earlier. The planks protruded a bit and could be planed back to get the correct length. It is possible that its prevalence on other types of boats was simply that most boatbuilders built some racing skiffs and carried the tradition over to other types of boats.

Photo 9G Saxboard trimmed to shape.

Fitting Narrower Planks at the Turn of the Bilge

The planks at the turn of the bilge are narrower as discussed in Chapter 8. The original builders varied in their techniques for these planks with regard to hollowing the backs: some did and some didn't. Ken Minter and Jim O'Rourke generally did not hollow the planks, and simply planed a little off the seam battens so they were in the one plane as in drawing 9.12, or planed a little off the exposed half of the lower batten and simply fastened the next batten unmodified to the top of the plank when fitting it. Bill Barnett generally hollowed the back of the plank to remove a little extra weight and so that the plank would lie fairly on unmodified seam battens, but he also said that occasionally he took a little off the battens. On *Britannia* I didn't hollow the planks and took it all off the top half of the lower batten. The extra thickness of Cedar in the middle of each plank adds negligible weight.

The rounding over of the outside of the plank is generally judged by eye, or it can be templated at each mould, the plank shaped to fit the template at each station, then the intermediate areas faired in. On *Britannia* I was careful to get the edges exactly to 7/16" thick, and judged the round in the middle of the plank conservatively by eye. After all planks were on a little fairing with hand planes and torture boards removed any bulges. Which is where we're at once you've continued the process all the way to the sheer strake.

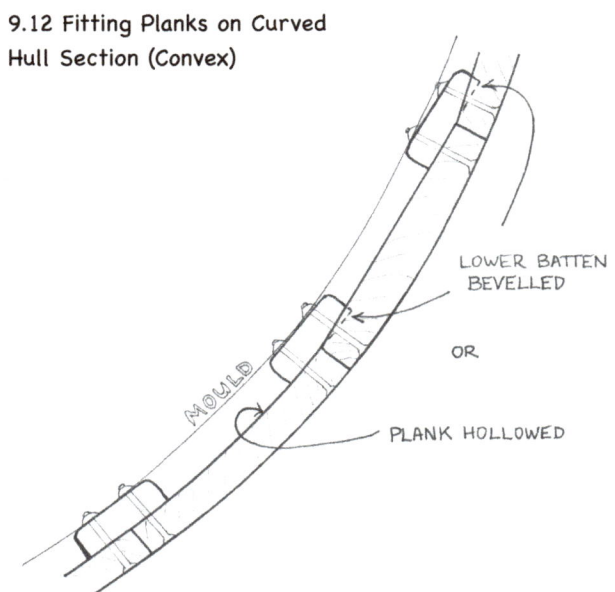

9.12 Fitting Planks on Curved Hull Section (Convex)

Fairing the Planking

There shouldn't need to be a whole lot of work here. A thorough sanding with a random orbital sander should take care of the minor raised edges at seams, but a little planing will be necessary on those curved areas of the hull just mentioned. Alternate diagonal planing with a fine-set No 3 or No 4 plane is best. If you find the plane blade is catching on any nail heads you will have to go straight to sanding with torture boards or more traditionally the biggest dreadnought file you can find which will remove Cedar and copper at about the same rate. You should pause often to rub your fingers and palm of the hand over the area to feel bumps you cannot see. You can also bend a thin batten vertically around the hull with a light source beyond to show up the bumps and hollows. Remove the plane marks with a torture board, sandpaper attached to a thin flexible board about 2' long with handles at each end, a tool quite familiar to modern boatbuilders. Finish with orbital or random orbital sanding. Give yourself some time to admire your work. Planking has been enjoyable, but we're ready for a change and we can start to get excited about fitting the ribs. But on a sobering note, you've still got more than half the project ahead of you.

Mast Step Floors

Before we can start bending in the ribs there's several things we need to do. The horizontal bracing connecting the moulds needs to be removed for access. The moulds will stay in until all ribs are

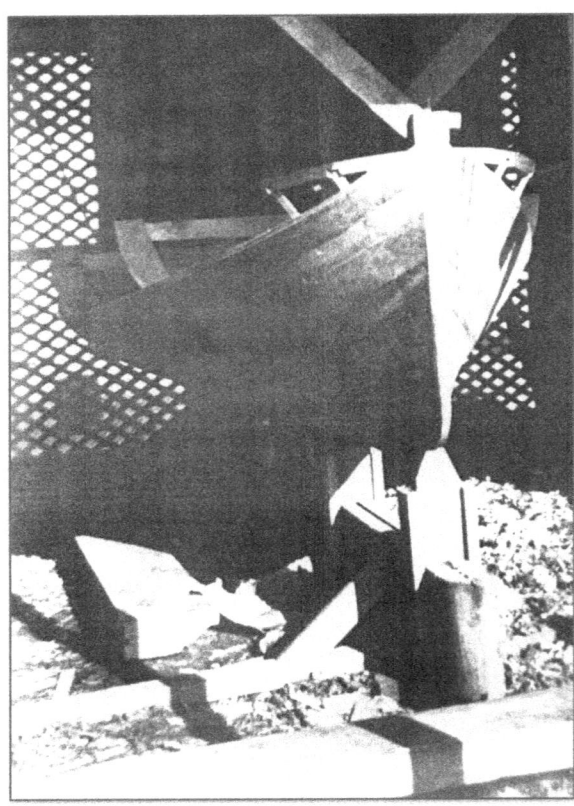

Photo 9H Ron Balkwell's 12-footer Ron almost planked up, 1940's. Notice the breasthook and forward ribs are already fitted. BALKWELL FAMILY ARCHIVES

in the accessible places between the moulds, then the moulds are removed and the rest of the ribs fitted. The moulds are a check on possible distortion of the hull from the force applied when bending in the ribs and the combined effect of the ribs trying to straighten out. If your boat has any hollow, you should reinforce it from outside by shoring up a stiffish batten running through the bottom of the "valley" of the hollow, especially aft, as in drawing 9.13.

Up forward, all eighteen footers and most other Open Boats will have several athwartships floors to spread the load of the mast step. These are fitted before the ribs and will hold the shape of the hull in that area exactly. See photos 9I, 9J and 9K. You can either loft the shape out and cut

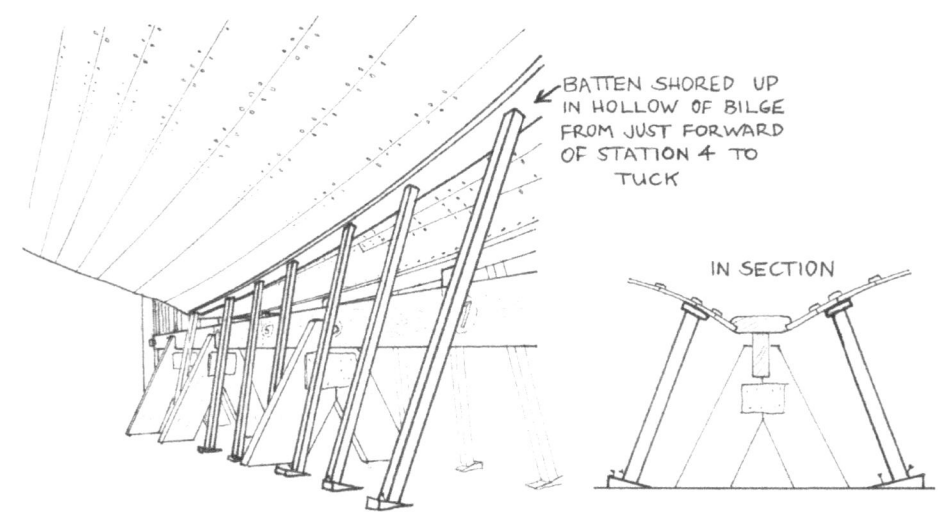

9.13 Bracing Hollow Bilges Against Strain of Bending in Ribs

106

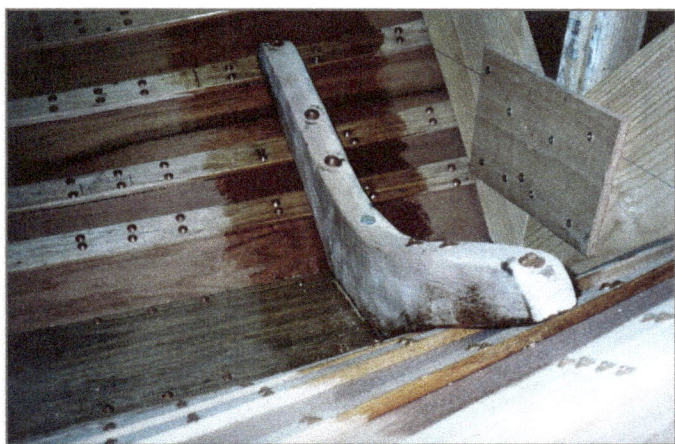

Photo 9I   Mast step floors are fitted before timbering out (fitting ribs).

Photo 9J   Note the stealer seam battens.

Photo 9K   Note the varnish under the floors.

and fit these floors, remembering that there will be a changing bevel on the underside, or you can make a template from the hull. The floors will land on the keel and the battens, it is not necessary that they touch the planks. They are cut from Tea-Tree crooks or laminated and fastened through each batten with large gauge copper nails, drilling from inside aiming the drill to come out either side of the plank seam in the middle of the batten. If you planned ahead and left the planking nails and roves out of these positions you can drive a small gauge blind nail into the plank, batten and floor on the other side of each seam to the larger nail. If, as I did, you had fastened off the planking nails in the way of the floors, you will need to notch the underside of the floor to allow room for the roves, and drill for your large nails so that you just miss the small nails. Each floor will be eventually fastened with a central bolt right through the keel and the mast step, but at this point you have no access and no mast step, so each floor is temporarily fastened to the keel with a coach screw of the same diameter as your eventual through bolt, in our case 3/8".

Fin Slot

Most original builders fitted the ribs in the way of the fin case in one continuous length across the keel and cut them later to a length that would notch into small mortices in the keel logs (or keel grounds). Others would fit the fin case first and fit the ribs on either side. Bill Barnett did a bit of both but mostly fitted the case later. But it is easier to cut the slot in the keel before the ribs go in. The slot is a bit wider than the fin, in *Britannia* the fin is ½" thick so I made the slot ¾" wide. A hole is drilled at each end to the size required, and a good jigsaw will cut out the waste in between. Be conservative as most jigsaws will never cut dead vertically, and you will have to finish off with chisel work. It is of course possible to cut the slot on the bench before setting up, but apparently this was not often done. Some early builders may have followed whaleboat practice and cut the slot before setting up leaving an uncut section in the middle to eliminate widening of the slot while building, but no builders still alive in the early 21st century could remember anyone doing this. There will usually be a mould in the way, and this can be temporarily removed and replaced. All of the mould-to-mould bracing has to be removed anyway before fitting the ribs. It is possible to make up the fin case (see below) at this stage and scribe, cut and plane its mating surface with the keel, but this can also be done with only a slight degree of difficulty more after the ribs are fitted.

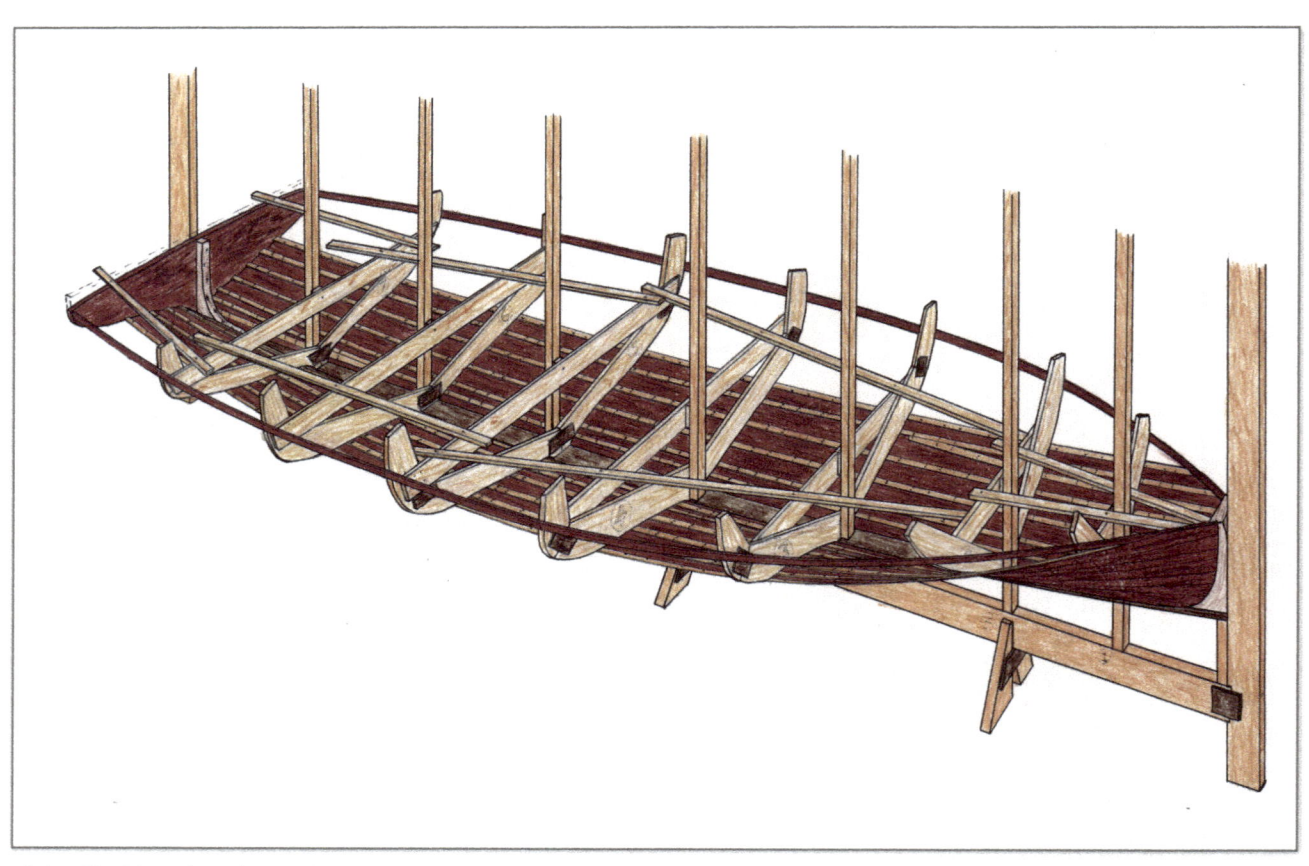

9.14 Planking almost complete

Summary of Planking Procedure

1. Spile the garboard plank shape onto your planking batten, with templates shaped and fitted at the stem (and stern if a built-heel boat).

2. Mark the spiling onto your garboard stock in one or two pieces, and cut and plane to your lines on the lower edge, leave a little extra on the ends, and along the top edge.

3. Steam the plank and immediately clamp it in place.

4. Final trimming after it cools. Mark where the top edge will be if any correction is needed. Mark where the ribs will be, and mark and drill for fastenings into the keel and stem and stern. Remove from the boat and cut and plane fair the top edge if necessary.

5. Fit the seam batten to the inside top of the plank, nailed and roved in the middle, clamped most of the way along.

6. Clamp the garboard in place, feel for your drilled holes with a thin steel nail, drive the copper nails home starting from the bow and working aft.

7. Mark the rest of the planks by wrapping the stock around the moulds and scribing off the previous plank. Repeat the balance of the procedure above on each plank.

CHAPTER 10

The Ribs

Eastern Australia has two perfect timbers for ribs. Spotted Gum (Corymbia maculata) and Silver Ash (Flindersia schottiana). In Sydney boats Spotted Gum was dominant until the late 1930's. Brisbane boatbuilders had been using Silver Ash at times before this, but by the time of *Aberdare* and the narrower boats that followed in the early 1930's Queenslanders used Silver Ash exclusively and eventually NSW boatbuilders followed suit. Silver Ash is slightly lighter but with an equal strength to weight ratio, and the boats were getting lighter and this became the main factor in the choice. Even keels were occasionally cut from Silver Ash, but this was more common in the sixteen-footers and twelve-footers than in the eighteens.

Nineteenth Century sources nominate native Honeysuckle for worked or sawn frames (utilising the natural curves), and native Hickory for steam-bending material in open boats. Native Honeysuckle is several varieties of Banksia, which grows prolifically in coastal areas and with its natural curved shape and large size is ideal for worked frames. Native Hickory is one or more species of Acacia, particularly Blackwood (Acacia Melanoxylon), and that timber is certainly a good bending timber. It was popular because it bent easily and was quite strong, but unfortunately it does not last well in the marine environment, and it dropped out of use by the end of the nineteenth century. Imported elm was popular until Spotted Gum took over in the 20th century.

Timber Selection and Machining

The timber stock of whatever species for ribs has to be the best quality. There can be no knots, cranky grain, shakes, gum veins, checks or grain sloping steeper than 12 to 1. It should be sawn out flat sawn, that is with the growth rings closest to parallel with the wider surfaces as in drawing 10.1 and dressed all round to the finished size, long enough to go from gun'l to gun'l across the keel plus a bit to hang onto. Twelve feet was ideal in our case. It is definitely preferable that it be green timber, i.e unseasoned, but good seasoned timber will bend quite well as long as you give it a bit of extra time in the steam, or even better, soak it in water for a few days before use. I can't stress enough the need for good straight-grained timber. A good bit of a bad bending species like Mahogany will bend more successfully than a bad bit of a good bending species like Spotted Gum. Read that again slowly. Prepare at least one third again as much timber as you will fit in the boat, there will almost definitely be breakages. In one recent class on traditional clinker dinghy construction we broke half the rib stock and had to machine more to finish. It wasn't the best timber but it was all we could get for the scheduled class.

I've got to tell you the story about the best bending timber I ever had. In the late eighties I purchased a load of Silver Ash, 1" thick boards which had originally been intended for paneling in the new Parliament House in Canberra then under construction. Somebody realised it was a rain forest littoral species which was under threat (which was slightly true at the time) and decided they couldn't

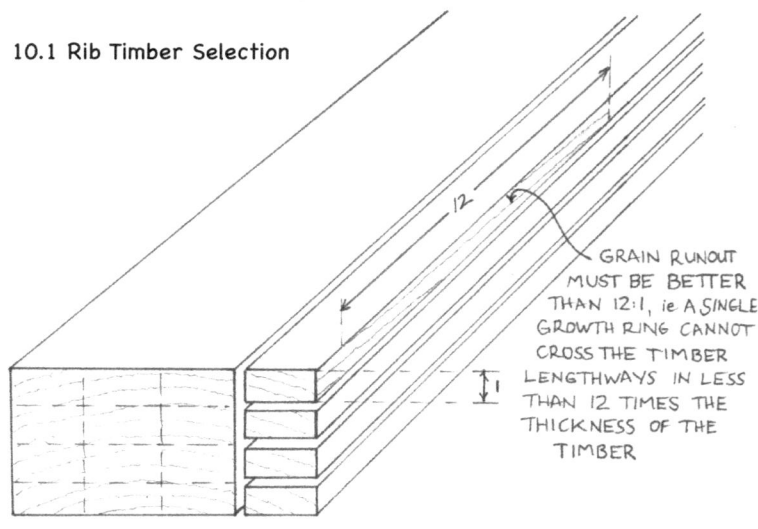

10.1 Rib Timber Selection

GRAIN RUNOUT MUST BE BETTER THAN 12:1, ie A SINGLE GROWTH RING CANNOT CROSS THE TIMBER LENGTHWAYS IN LESS THAN 12 TIMES THE THICKNESS OF THE TIMBER

Photo 10A Ready to fit ribs.

use it (even though it had been cut). Eventually I purchased it and it was some of the best timber I have ever used, even though it was well dry. As ¾" x 5/16" dinghy ribs we didn't break one! At the first Sydney Wooden Boat Show at River Quays Marina in 1990 I held a demonstration of steam bending and used some of this timber for a circus trick. I claimed that I could tie the dinghy rib into a knot but suggested to the crowd that it might break. I pulled out of the steam box one rib I had prepared earlier that I knew would break. When it did, there was a loud sigh of disappointment from the crowd. A second planned breakage got a larger sigh. On the third try with one of the Parliament House ribs I pulled the ends into a loop and passed one end through the loop and pulled the ends tight enough to form a circle of about ten inches diameter. The crowd went wild! I think I still have that loop somewhere in the shed, but I haven't seen it for a while. But not all timber is that good, so prepare extra.

The boat needs to be ready to receive the ribs. You will have already marked the rib position on the outside while planking up. Run a thin flat batten around these marks from rabbet to gun'l to check that they are all in line, or at least close enough to land in the middle third of the rib width. Drill these holes (same nail gauge as for plank to batten) square with the planking surface. Climb inside the boat and pencil a couple of marks either side of a short piece of rib stock, as a guide to where the rib should land, on about every third batten, including the keel and the saxboard.

Many original builders, probably a majority, would drive the nails straight through the hot ribs, and this is definitely the quickest and easiest way to do it. So at this point they would tap all the nails into the drilled holes in the planking ready to drive them all through each rib as it lands, backing up with a dolly close to where the nail will come through. The fibres of the hot rib mostly separate enough to allow the nail through without damage, but in quite a few cases the rib will start to split. In my experience this happens enough to require a lot of ribs to be rejected and replaced. But more importantly, in many years of repairing and restoring boats I became convinced that even if the rib didn't split while driving the nails, and didn't split when the rib cooled and shrunk, it was far more likely to split as it aged because of the distortion of the fibres than those ribs that were drilled. A case in point is that the Swanson boats (yachts, launches) have far less rib splitting for their age than most other boats, and the late Ken Swanson insisted that they drilled for all rib fastenings. Bill Barnett also drilled his ribs.

Round up all the quick action clamps you have plus small timber or plywood pads so as not to mark the timber, lay them near where they will be used. Have a drill, 5/64" bit, countersink and claw hammer and 14g x 1½" copper nails handy.

The setup for steaming has been described in the section on planking. With eighteen footer ribs being 1" x ½" or a little smaller (except sometimes for wider ones under the mast) they need to be in the steam for at least 40 minutes. It is _essential_ that they are hot enough, they must be too hot to touch with bare hands. Except for the shortest ones forward and aft you will not be able to bend them in alone, at least one helper is necessary. One person should be in the boat, one outside to draw the ribs out of the steam box (and close it again). Both should be wearing gloves.

Start in the middle of the boat. Ignore the fin slot, run all amidships ribs from gun'l to gun'l. The outside person passes one end into the person in the boat who centres it and pushes the centre down towards the keel while both workers start to bend the sides out to the turn of the bilge. Make sure it follows the line of marks you put either side of the

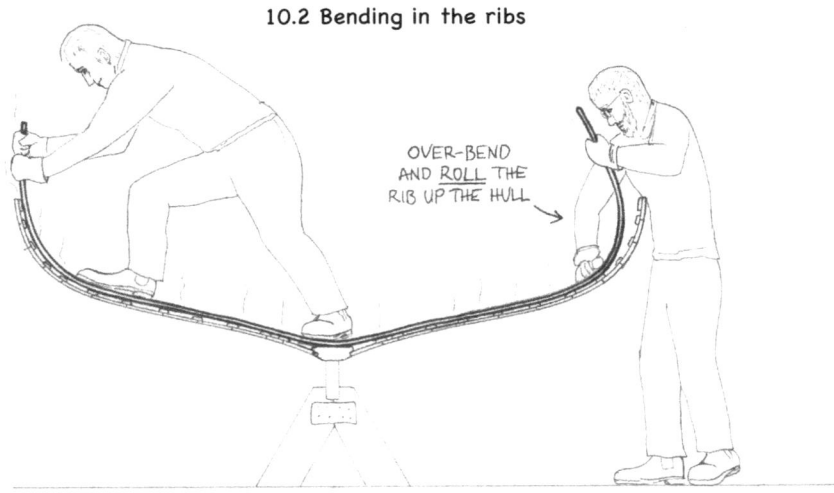

10.2 Bending in the ribs

OVER-BEND AND ROLL THE RIB UP THE HULL

If the keel is higher than the first batten (only amidships on some flat-floored boats) you need to force the rib down on both sides of the keel. On most Open Boats this will not be the case seeing there is considerable 'V' in most hulls. In fact you will have to try to flatten the rib onto the keel with your broad Blundstone boot to avoid kinking the rib here. On heeled boats towards the stern the opposite will happen: the hollow in the garboards will mean that the rib has to be forced down into the keel with a reverse curve over the garboards. Variations and eventual fastenings are illustrated in drawing 10.3.

drilled holes, but don't waste time on getting it dead right over the holes, it is far more important to get the bend into the timber. The insider stands on the rib over the keel with his foot and both concentrate on forcing the rib out to the turn of the bilge. The upper section should be overbent and sort of *rolled* out up the hull. Each person clamps the rib to the gun'l, preferably with wooden pads protecting the rib and the outside of the planking, and each end is tunked with a large mallet which also helps force the rib out to the hull. Tap the rib where necessary to centre it over the holes, using the pencil marks you did earlier. Select a nail hole on each side at the turn of the bilge and drill and drive a nail each side through plank, batten and rib. Don't clench or rove it at this point. These nails and the clamps at the gun'l are enough to hold the rib as it cools. You could also drill for and fit a narrow screw, say 8 gauge through the centre of the rib into the centre of the keel.

Get out the very next rib, either forward or aft of the first and fit it in the same manner. Keep working forward and/or aft until you've done all you can do in the bay between the two moulds. Then move into the next bay. Work each bay alternately aft and forward. When you've done the three central bays, make a couple of temporary beams across the boat, notched over the gun'ls just adjacent to two central moulds, the remove those moulds. Then fit the ribs that you couldn't get access for while the moulds were in. When you run out of clamps, drill for and drive copper nails through the earliest ribs through one of the uppermost planks or at the turn of the bilge to free

Hints and variations: Bend the rib quickly, you will need to have the major bends in no longer than 30 seconds after leaving the steam box. Minor adjustments can happen for a few minutes longer. By quickly I do not mean suddenly, use steady firm pressure and do not work it so that it bends and straightens multiple times. Be careful not to make the bending pressure too local, it is easy to kink a hot rib.

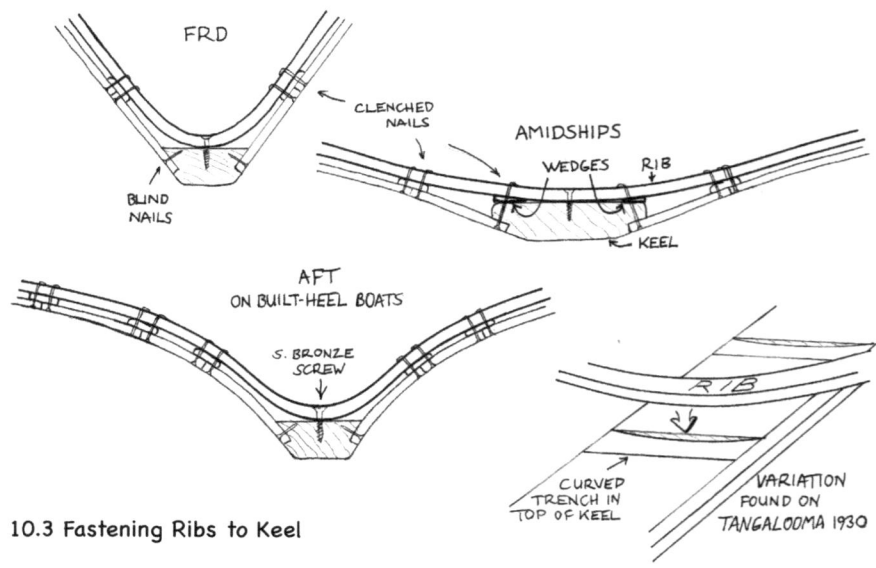

10.3 Fastening Ribs to Keel

up those clamps. Remove the other moulds but only after ribbing out the bay beyond the mould, and replacing it nearby with a temporary beam notched across the gun'ls.

The Breasthook

If the breasthook was not fitted before planking, now is the best time to do it before the forward ribs are fitted. But only dry fit it until the ribs are in because it must be notched over any ribs in the way. It is a lot easier to scribe and fit it without the ribs there, although it can be done. In fact it can be fitted anytime between now and when the inwales go in. As discussed earlier, it is cut from a Tea Tree crook with the grain following the curve, or laminated. In fact if your boat will be decked and you are light on for Tea-Tree crooks this is a good one to laminate as it will never be seen. Making a thin plywood pattern is the easiest and safest way to start. Scribe it as in drawing 10.4 and note the bevels. Transfer these to your stock, cut it out and bevel it to the angles, and offer it up for a trial fit. It must bear well on the saxboard and the back of the stem for strength. It is worth spending a bit of time on this. Chalk rubbing is a useful technique to employ. Apply chalk to the landing area on the boat and rub the breasthook against it. If the chalk has marked only a few areas, plane those off (just a couple of strokes). Repeat. You are ready to fit it when the chalk marks all mating faces of the breasthook evenly. After the local ribs are fitted, notch out the breasthook to clear them. A tight fit is not necessary. Fasten through the stem with a 3/8" copper bolt, and right through the planking, saxboard and breasthook with large gauge copper nails. Use at least two per side. You will probably fit a third one right through from the inner sponson when fitted.

Shock! Horror!
Modern variation creeps in!

Bending ribs still puts a great strain on the timber. The fibres on the inside of the curve are compressed, and the fibres on the outside of the curve are stretched. You may find some of your ribs cannot take the bend even amidships, if so just replace them when they break, or if you notice cracks after you have fitted them. On the original *Britannia,* when the hull was restored in the late 1980's, all of the ribs well forward where there was a sharp V, and aft where there was a tight reverse curve into the keel over the hollow garboards the ribs had long given up. In fact most ribs aft and forward of the fin case were found to be in three sections, with the central section lapped over the tapered upper sections, just inboard of the bilge stringer. This suggests to me that these central sections were replaced during the active life of the boat. These newer sections had also disappeared, therefore these tight bends had caused two sets of ribs to give up.

For ease in fitting and for greater strength and longevity, I invoked my reasoning mentioned earlier that I have no objection to laminating any piece of timber that would have been a single piece in an original boat. When the ribs in the aft third of the boat and the forward third began to get hard to bend over the keel, I began to laminate them from two layers. For the aftermost and forwardmost several ribs, I went to three layers. The process was thus: I machined the timber so that the eventual combined

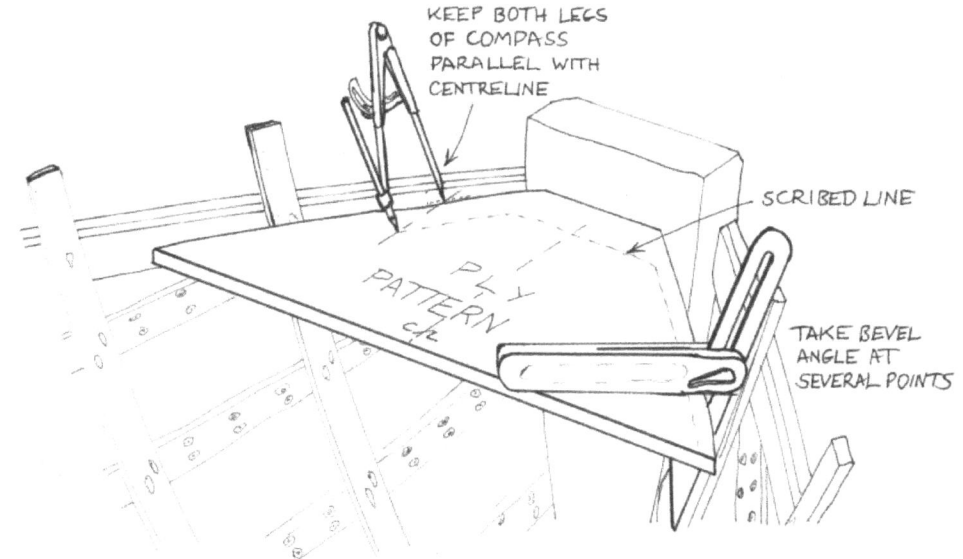

10.4 Scribing the Breasthook Pattern

thickness was ½", the same as the one-piece ribs, but just over 1¼" wide to allow for cleaning up misalignments of the laminations back to the finished 1". I steamed the laminations and bent them into the boat and drilled and drove narrow gauge chipboard screws from the outside through the rib at every second or third batten (through a hole that would become a nail hole, with a plywood pad under the head to protect the planking) until they lay well on the battens. I left them there until next day, when I removed them from the boat, separated the laminations slightly and laid them out on the floor, with a couple of blocks screwed in position so that most of the bend is held in them while they completely dry out which will take at least another whole day. A bit of gentle application with a heat gun can speed this up. I then coarsely sanded the mating surfaces, applied epoxy glue and fitted them back into the boat with a layer of builders' plastic between the rib and the hull, screwed through the same holes that held the steamed laminations in, being careful to find the holes with a thin steel nail before driving the screws. I then drilled extra holes and added more chipboard screws, one through every batten so that the laminations pull down (check that the last lamination doesn't get held up on the thread). Next day, the cured laminations are removed, the edges are trimmed back to remove glue dags and finish the ribs to 1", and edges eased. They are then fitted back into the boat and copper nails driven through the same holes that held the temporary screws plus additional nails so there are two nails in every batten, either side of each plank seam. In *Britannia*, none of the ribs thus treated have shown the slightest sign of cracking after 14 hard seasons of racing.

In between the stages of fitting these laminated ribs you will have found plenty of time to fasten off the earlier-fitted one piece ribs.

Fastening the Ribs

Start from the centre, on the keel and work outwards evenly. Rib fastening requires a helper for all nails except on the upper few planks where you can reach over the gun'l. If you didn't fit a narrow gauge screw in the centre into the keel, do so now.

Then you will have to make up wedge-shaped packers under the rib where it separates from the keel on each side, as illustrated in drawing 10.3. A nail goes through each of these starting along the line of the other nails close to the lower edge of the garboard.

Some original builders (such as Ken Minter) roved the rib nails as well as the batten nails. But the majority, including Bill Barnett simply clenched the rib nails. This was not especially because it is a bit quicker, but because most sailors sailed barefoot, and the ribs which took most of the foot pressure were smoother when clenched. Unlike European and American clenching where the nail point is tuned by a dolly when it first appears, Australian clenched nails were always done thus: the nail was selected to protrude past the rib surface about ½" (for 14 g, longer for bigger nails) and was driven with the flat sides of the square section parallel and at right angles to the direction of the rib. The point was cut off about 1/4" to 5/16" above the surface. The head was backed up by a dolly outside and the protruding nail was bent straight

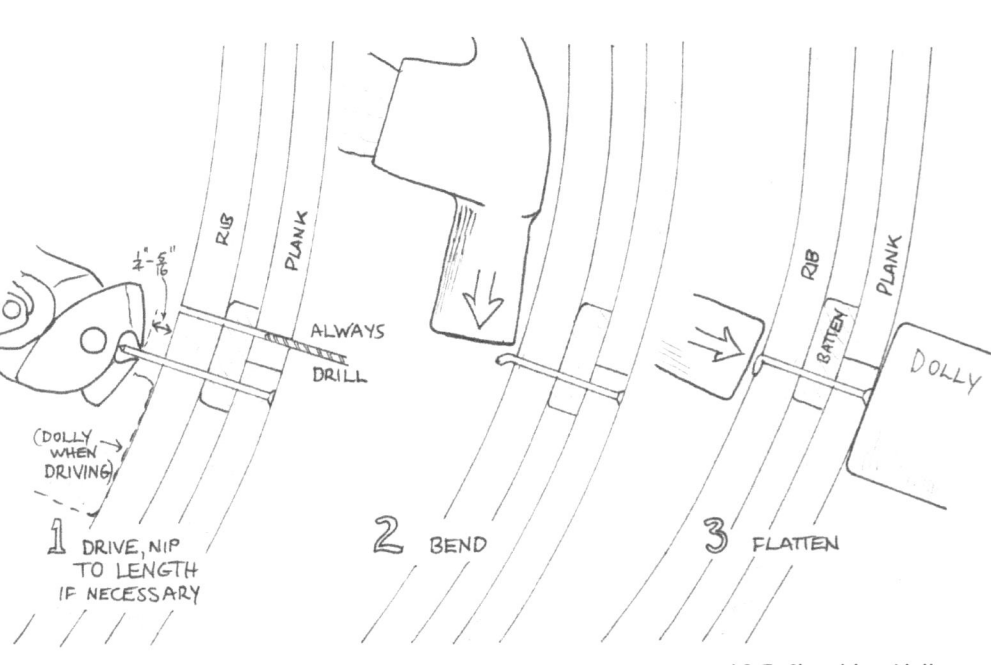

10.5 Clenching Nails

down the rib and then hammered flat with multiple blows from a claw hammer. Some builders took care to use the flat striking surface of a similar-sized ball peen hammer here as the striking face of such hammers is generally slightly more rounded than those on claw hammers, and this means there was less chance of leaving crescent-shaped indentations in the rib if the hammer hit the surface off-square. Some builders also took care to bend the nail slightly to one side or the other of a line parallel to the grain direction of the rib in a quest for less splitting pressure on the rib's grain. When done this way the bent nail can be barely felt above the surface. Do not leave more than the called-for 5/16" protruding for 14g nails or the extra length will not easily flatten into the rib. The process is illustrated in drawing 10.5. You can leave out the uppermost nails through the ribs at the sheer as these will be pinned by larger nails that go right through from the inner sponsons to the inwales (see below).

Leave the ribs protruding above the sheer line at least a couple of inches until after the inwales and inner sponsons are fitted.

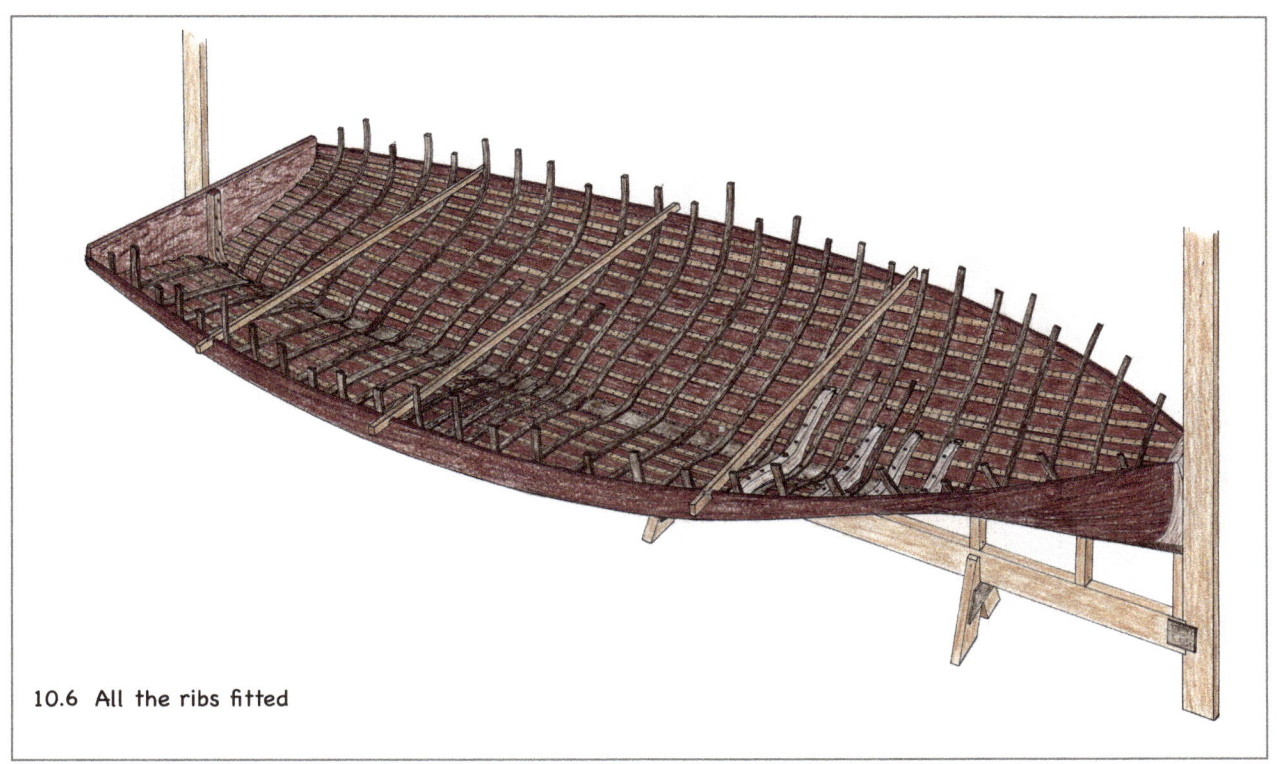

10.6 All the ribs fitted

Ken Minter (right) and Ron Balkwell (left) fasten seat riser into a 16-footer in the 1940's.
BALKWELL FAMILY ARCHIVE

CHAPTER 11

Stringers and Other Internal Structures

There's a fairly set sequence in which the internal structural pieces are fitted as any one item depends on the previous fitting of another, with only a bit of minor juggling in starting the fin case and the foredeck framing.

Stringers and Risers

Stringers are longitudinal strength members. Their function is to support the flatter areas of the hull and to resist racking (longitudinal twist). Most Open Boats had a single stringer each side pretty much in the middle of the flat area of the bilges. On most Open Boats they tended to follow the line of the plank underneath it, generally up the middle of the plank. On most boats there is a bit of a bend to get it to lie down on the ribs given sizes of between 1½" and 2" wide and ¾" to 1¼" thick. Steaming is advisable, particularly at the forward end and middle, but not necessary in the smaller sizes. It might be a wriggle to get them into the boat with the temporary beams in place, but if you have to remove any of these for access, replace them as soon as you can. They are meant to stay in place until the thwarts are fastened off which will lock in the hull width. Otherwise it is quite possible that the hull will change shape.

Stringers were usually of Silver Ash, Oregon or Kauri. On *Britannia* the originals were Kauri, so I scarfed up some old Kauri floorboards, and being only ¾" thick, bent the first one into the boat. The timber under my boot touched the hull, and then exploded into multiple pieces. Perhaps it would have been okay had I steamed it. However Kauri is a relatively brittle timber compared with Silver Ash, so I remade the stringers in Silver Ash and fitted those without a problem. This is the only time I varied the timber species in the replica from the original, but I have no regrets. Wee Georgie must have had better Kauri.

The stringers don't need to be cut precisely to length as long as they extend past the aftermost rib and past whichever forward rib they land on. They generally did not go as far as the forward most few ribs as the bend there would be excessive and as they converge on the seat riser, that area of the hull is already supported. Ease the edges that crew feet will land on (well-rounded on each edge). One person inside can hold the stringer in position centrally (on the rib that crosses the boat immediately aft of the fin case) and drill for the nail, locating it one-third of the stringer width in from the edge. Another person is needed outside to hammer the nail through. There must of course be a packer between the rib and the plank. In *Britannia's* case these were rib offcuts planed down to the 3/8" batten thickness and extending across the plank from batten to batten, occasionally hollowed a little to fit a particularly curved rib. Blocks of wood clamped to ribs (or other helpers) can hold both ends in position while you start to fasten your 10g nails through every rib with ½" roves, working from the centre out to the ends. The nail positions are staggered or **reeled,** that is every alternate nail hole is drilled one-third from the top edge of the

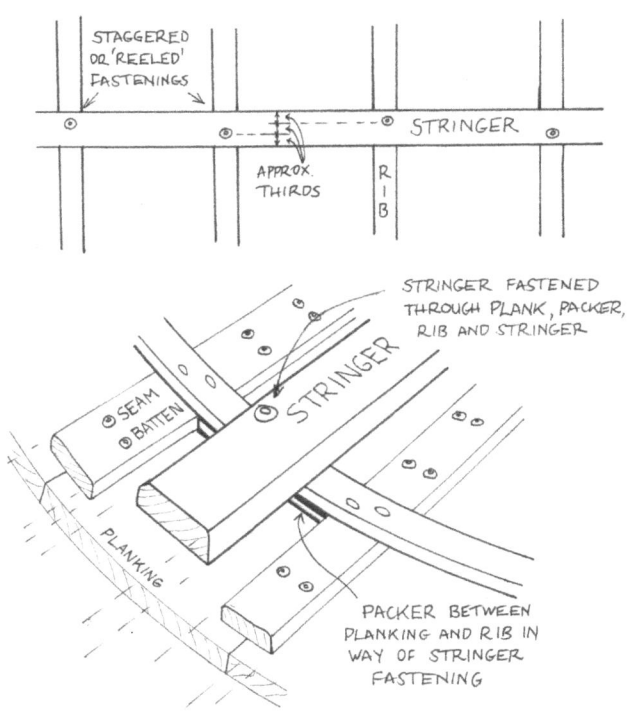

11.1 Stringer Fastening and Use of Packers

stringer and the next is drilled one-third from the bottom as in drawing 11.1.

Risers

These are the near-horizontal stringers along each side of the boat that support the thwarts. They sweep up towards the tuck keeping roughly the same distance below the sheer, or diminishing a little. They keep roughly the same distance below the sheer forward as well so they do not follow one plank but cross some seams. Packers are needed wherever they are not backed up by a batten. There is usually less bend in the risers than the stringers and the size of the risers is either the same or narrower, so steaming is generally unnecessary. Fitting and fastening procedures are exactly the same as for the bilge stringers. In fact the order of fitting stringers and risers can be reversed.

Photo 11A Riser being fitted, alone with clamps.

The Fin Case

This could have been constructed earlier and even dry fitted before the stringers go in, but should not be finally fitted and bedded down until the risers are in and the two forward thwarts are ready to fit. The case is built up as in drawing 11.2, from Cedar boards with Spotted Gum vertical members and logs (or grounds) and top edging and fin handle rack. The space between the sides is wider than the slot in the keel and in the top edging, and thin vertical strips are usually added to narrow the gap and to take the wear from the metal fin. The inner surfaces are varnished with a few coats before being fitted together (you could use a clear coating epoxy as I did for greater waterproofing. The case is not glued together. Because it is built up from wide boards of solid timber it is through-fastened with a bedding compound on all mating surfaces. The sides themselves can be one wide piece if you have the stock, but otherwise should be edge-joined as mentioned for the tuck.

Length of the Fin Case

The length of the case and slot is well in excess of the size of the fin. This is because it is impossible to locate the exact position of the fin before rigging and sailing the boat. The sail areas are so large and so far beyond the waterline of the boat that unless the sheet hands are working together to balance the forces, the sail pressure will completely overwhelm the steering. A long slot means that the centre of lateral resistance can be moved fore and aft to help balance the sail plan on the wind. Len Heffernan told me that the old rule of thumb was that the mast should be about 1/3rd of the hull length from the bow, the fin

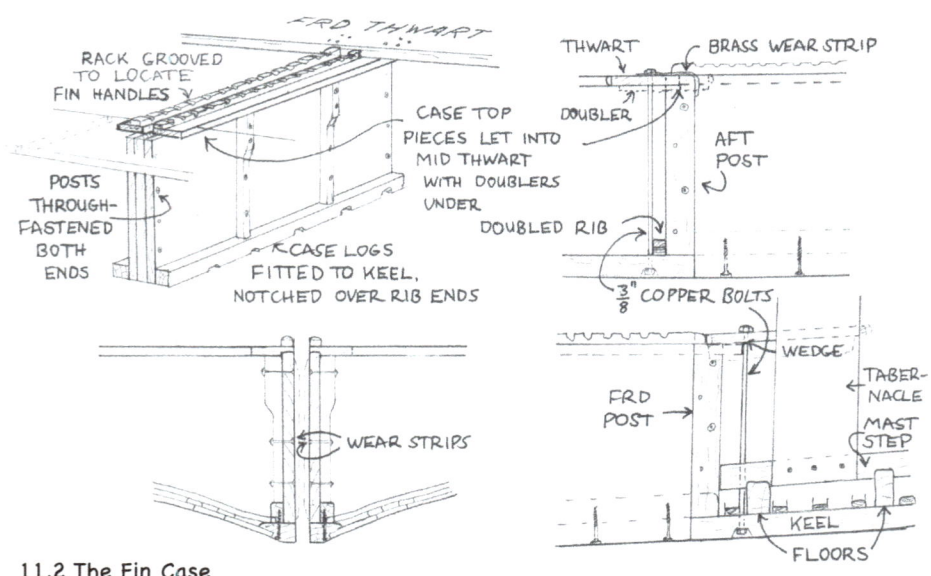

11.2 The Fin Case

should be in the middle of the boat, and the boom should be about the same distance behind the tuck as the jib is beyond the stem. This does seem to work very closely. *Britannia's* mast is centred just 2 ½" forward of 1/3rd back, and the centre of the fin when the rig is balanced is exactly at 9' from bow and stern. At this point the fin is as far back in the case as it can go, suggesting the slot could even have been made longer aft, or the mast could go forward. The current positions work perfectly, the tiller can be let go for brief periods in flat water and light steady breeze.

Shaping the Case to Fit the Keel

The boards and case logs have to be shaped to fit the curve of the keel. If you had enough foresight to do this about the same time as you cut the slot before fitting the ribs it would have been a little easier. If you didn't, you can still sit it on top of the ribs and scribe the keel between the ribs and cut and plane to this almost continuous line. Make sure the case is dead vertical when you do this. A spirit level helps but a plumb bob from a central string line between the top of the stem and the centre of the tuck will be the most accurate guide. Cut the ribs in the way of the keel slot back so that they will just notch into the case logs. Drop the case over these and mark and cut the notches in the logs. Offer it up again and check all around that there is no gap between the logs and the keel. If there is, scribe it closely and plane it again. There will be copious amounts of bedding compound on the mating surfaces but you need good wood to wood contact all around. Drill for the fastenings which will generally be large gauge bronze screws drilled from underneath the keel, but do not bed and fasten the case at this stage.

Thwarts

The three thwarts in the older boats were generally quite wide and were continuing the tradition of wide and reasonably comfortable seats from other types of working and pleasure boats. The forward thwart on these boats was generally cut from a board about 12-15" wide which was cut away forward to house the mast tabernacle and was tapered out to about 8" wide at the risers. After the mid 1930's the thwarts began to get narrower until they were only about 4" wide and the aft thwart was often dispensed with entirely. The boats were narrower by this time and the skipper could always steer from the rail. The thwarts land on top of the riser or are notched into them in a very shallow notch. The ends do not need to touch the hull planking or the battens but land against any ribs in the neighbourhood. The ends are scribed to fit against the ribs as illustrated in drawing 11.3, one side at a time, with the accurate distance across the boat being measured with two sticks clamped together. Cut conservatively at first, and work it down after a trial fit. A couple of screws at each end vertically down into the riser are enough to hold it until the knees are fitted.

Most Sydney-built boats of the 1930's and 40's had a feature called a fishplate (see drawing 11.4) fitted under the mid and often the forward thwart on each side, beveled to fit along the riser and bolted through the riser and the thwart.

The main (mid) thwart supports the aft end of the fin case, and the upper Spotted Gum case trim can be housed into the front of the thwart, or land on it and be fastened through. The forward thwart is either treated the same way, or as often happens, is higher than the front of the case and therefore needs packers to connect the two. There is always a long bolt, usually copper, at each end of the case going from the thwart and/or supporting structure vertically down

11.3 Fitting Thwarts

outside the case through the keel. This can be riveted or threaded and nuts fitted, mostly threaded so it can be adjusted later if the case shrinks or moves. The top end of the aft bolt often goes through a brass strip that acts as a washer for the nut and also bends into the back of the case to form a wear strip for sliding the metal fin in and out. The forward nut on the *Britannia* replica is an eye nut which doubles as the anchor point for the boom downhaul tackle. Both these thwarts and the case should be fitted now for good with bedding compound especially between case and keel. The aft thwart can also be fitted, and all temporary beams removed.

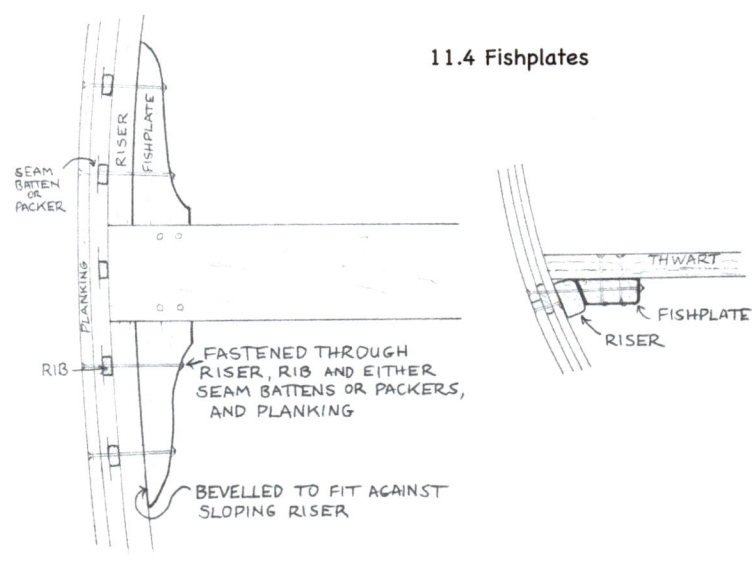

Photo 11B Case

Photo 11C Thwarts

Inwales and Sponsons

Open Boat classes with no side decks (16's and 12's) generally had no inwales which are longitudinal pieces at the sheer inboard against the frame heads. All boats had sponsons, which are the longitudinals outside the planking at the sheer. Various combinations are illustrated in drawing 11.5. On earlier boats like *Britannia* the sponsons were usually built up from several pieces, and the inwale and inner sponson were sometimes fitted together, sandwiching the planking and rib heads and fastened through all four components. An easier technique is to fit the inwales first and fasten them off through every second rib head. Then the sponsons can be fitted and fastened to the other rib heads. Norman Wright and Sons' boats had a two part inwale fastened through the planking and rib heads. If you see that any later knee fastenings are going to go through the same spot, leave that nail out at this stage. If your chainplates are going to run up the planking without cranking around the sponson, it is best to notch out the back of the sponson before fitting. Both inwales and sponsons are generally tapered in one or two dimensions towards the bow, and sometimes towards the stern. All were generally cut from Oregon.

The inwales generally touch the tuck or the tuck beam aft and butt up to, or are notched into the breasthook forward. It is best to fit one end correctly, then clamp the inwale all the way along the sheer with the other end left longer than it needs to be. Allow this end to rise so that it just lands on top of the breasthook or the tuck/beam, mark where you think it should be cut to drop into its final position, then cut at least 1/8" outside that mark and give it a trial fit, making sure it is pulled out to all of the rib heads. If there is still more to cut, repeat. Always worry it down by cutting a little less than you think you should. The sponson on the outside is easier, it simply wraps around and runs out past each end. If you are going to fit both together, clamp right across the group at each rib head, tap it where necessary to adjust for height, then

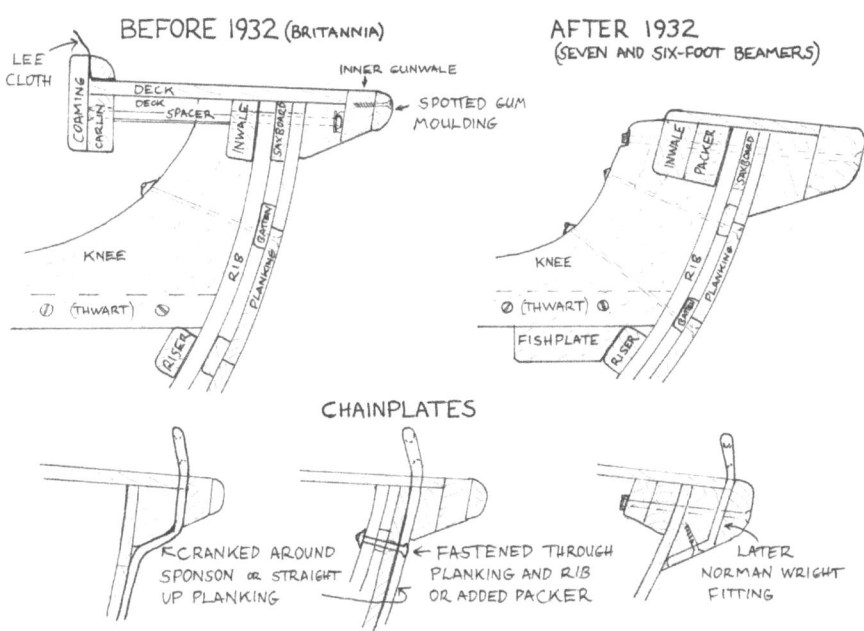

11.5 Gunwales

remove each clamp one at a time, usually starting in the middle and working out, drilling for and roving 12g copper nails with 7/16" roves. On *Britannia* the inwale stops at the forward deck beam which was fitted first as it butts up against the saxboard on each side, an unusual feature but sometimes found on small launches. As mentioned before, I fitted the inwales first, fastening them off through alternate ribs, then fastened off the sponson through every other rib. In fact I left off the sponsons until after the fin case, thwarts and thwart knees were fitted, just leaving the uppermost thwart knee fastenings out until the sponsons were fitted and then fastened through all. So there are variations in the sequence that you can try, but think it well through in advance. The sponsons are also generally fastened right through the breasthook and the quarter knees.

The Tuck Beam

On *Britannia* this was fitted before the inwale. It is a strength member as it braces the tuck for the immense strains of the rudder, holds the mainsheet horse which takes much of the force of the mainsheet and supports brass pins to which the peak spinnaker halyards are cleated off. One or two of the replica boats have had this beam torn out of the boat. In *Britannia's* case it is a piece of Spotted Gum 2" x 1¾". The top of the tuck has a slight curve, and although the Cedar of the tuck protrudes slightly above the tuck beam, the beam needs to be curved as well. Cut it overlength at this point. Steaming is necessary, and it is bent around a simple jig on the bench or floor set out for a bit more bend than the tuck as the timber will relax back a bit straighter. When it is cool and dry, cut a notch for it to fit around the top of the stern knee. It is important that these parts all lock together. Cut the ends to fit against the planking (or inwale if fitted first). It is then clamped and fastened through the tuck with 10g nails and ½" roves. Do not put any fastenings in the outer 1' each side as there will be quarter knees fitted here which will be fastened right through.

Foredeck Beams

As I mentioned, on *Britannia* the forward deck beams were fitted earlier, after ribbing out was completed. On other boats the inwale is fitted first and the deck beams are fitted inside that. There is not enough meat on the inwale to check the deck beams in, so a simple butt fit is made by picking up the required bevels both horizontally and vertically and cutting conservatively. It is a rapidly diminishing fit so the beam won't move forward much with a small amount of trimming. The main beam is fitted with knees, a hanging (vertical) knee underneath on each side (or attached to its aft face as on *Britannia*) and a lodging (horizontal) knee each side on later boats with narrower decks and no rounded coaming.

Knees

There are numerous knees bracing the internal structure, and they all need to be fitted now. As well as the knees bracing the foredeck main beam, there are horizontal quarter knees bracing the sheer to the tuck, vertical knees bracing the thwarts to the side of the boat, and on later boats with narrow thwarts, lodging knees at each end of the thwarts bracing them to the risers. As discussed earlier, they were always cut from Tea Tree crooks, but you may find you have to laminate them.

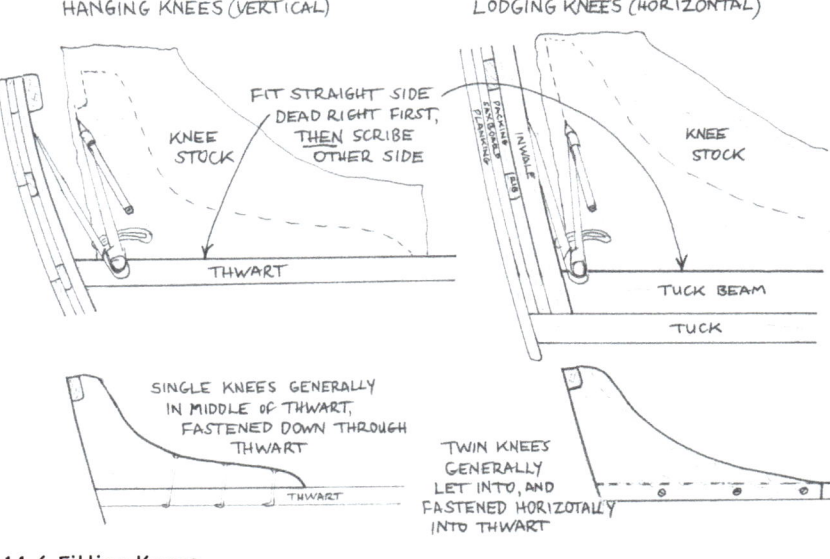

11.6 Fitting Knees

There is a trick to fitting knees, but it is simple. Every knee (except breasthooks and floors) has one side that is either straight or at least straighter than the other side (I was going to say other arm, but surely the extension of a knee would have to be called a leg, but for some reason we do not hear that). <u>Get this side fitted dead right first, with both its edge shape and its bevel correct.</u> Then work on the other side, as in drawing 11.6. The completed side can slide in a little without changing its fit.

Thwart knees are the easiest as one side is dead straight and square and can be slid any distance without changing. Often on Open Boats (as on *Britannia*) they were fitted beside the thwart and fastened horizontally. A number of scribes, cuts and trial fits might be needed to get the other side dead right. It is important for knees that they are a dead fit across their mating surfaces for strength. Thwart knees maybe fitted up against the planking but need to be notched for the inwale and any seam batten in the way, unless the seam batten in the neighbourhood is exactly in the best position for a through fastening in which case the part of the knee in between the fastenings (the upper one will be through the inwale, saxboard, planking and sponson) can be left off the planking. Or they may land on a rib, which is easy to fit against but may require a packer between the rib and planking. It is vital for all knees that anywhere a fastening will go through a gap, a packer is fitted. Through fastening is always better, but knees in some positions require occasional blind fastenings.

Quarter knees are fitted to the inwale first, then to the tuck or tuck beam. On *Britannia* they are let into the tuck beam so that side

Photo 11D   Quarter knee trial fit.

Photo 11E   Quarter knee fastened off.

must be trimmed to exact length before finalising its edge shape. All knees should be left oversize where possible until both sides fit, then the final shape is drawn and cut. See Photos 11D and 11E Quarter Knees.

Lodging knees on thwarts should be fitted to the thwart first and then fitted to the riser which will necessitate considerable bevel. All knees should have their exposed edges eased, at it is best to sand them before final fitting. Varnish or put some bedding compound between the mating surfaces.

Thwart Trim

On boats with wide Cedar thwarts a rounded moulding of Spotted Gum was fastened to the edge of the thwart to protect the soft Cedar. On *Britannia* these were tapered off across the thwart knees and shared several blind nails. Later boats often used Silver Ash for the same purpose.

Carlins

The earlier boats with wider decks had to have a carlin to support the inner deck edge. In section this is illustrated in drawing 11.5. It is fitted to a shallow notch in the quarter knee aft as in photo 11F and a shallow housing in the main deck beam forward. It is pulled out towards the gun'l with long clamps and will need some temporary props on the mid and forward thwart to hold it at the right height. Cedar props are then notched to support the carlin from the riser every few feet, seen in drawing 11.4 and in photo 11G. There's going to be a lot of large arses sitting on this deck! Short deck beams are then dovetailed into the carlin and the planking/saxboard combined. The dovetails and housing for the inwale are only half the depth of the beams. Several tie rods, 3/8" copper bolts are fitted right through from the sponson to the carlin to resist spreading of the side decks. The rounded outline of the foredeck is drawn out on two pieces of Oregon fitted to carlins and deck beam, as in photo 11 I.

Photo 11G Carlin supports. Note vertical prop to riser, dovetailed deck beams and copper tie rods. BOB CHAPMAN

Photo 11H Forward end of carlin.

Photo 11F   Knee/Carlin. BOB CHAPMAN

Photo 11I   Carlins and deck beam. BOB CHAPMAN

Mast Step and Tabernacle

Make up the mast step from Spotted Gum leaving out the trench in the top for the mast heel tenon at this point. Make up the parts for the tabernacle including the slots for the lugs on the mast band on which the mast will pivot, and cut the housing for the tabernacle in the front of the forward thwart. Some boats had the tabernacle sides dead vertical with just enough clearance for the mast. Some were let in or dovetailed into the sides of the mast step, some were simply fastened to it. *Britannia's* was splayed out, screwed to the mast step and also to solid packers

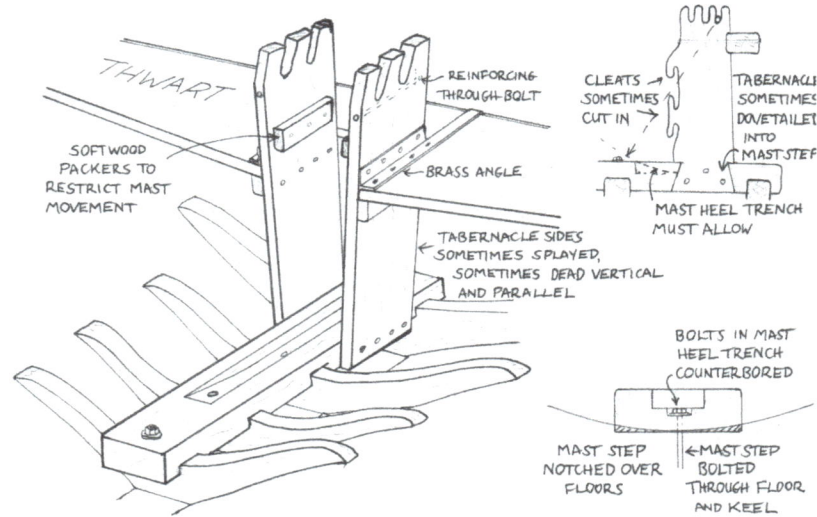

11.7 Mast Step and Tabernacle

underneath the thwart and brass angle on top of the thwart. Two softwood packers on the upper inside faces of the tabernacle left just enough room for the mast. Some tabernacles incorporated cleats for halyards. All had multiple slots for mast band lugs, mostly two but sometimes three alternate positions. Some were bolted longitudinally through the thwart, but if not a bolt was fitted longitudinally just above the thwart to resist the splitting pressure of the mast pivot lugs.

Remove the temporary coach screws in the centre of each floor timber and drill the holes out right through the keel for 3/8" bolts. Notch the mast step over the floors as in drawing 11.7. Assemble the mast step and tabernacle temporarily. Work out where the heel of the mast will land when the back of the mast is dead vertical (the centreline of the mast will be directly below the resting position of the lugs on the mast band) and mark it. Disassemble everything and mark and cut a trench 1" deep by 2" wide for the mast heel on top of the mast step, stopping it where you marked it at the aft end, and making sure the forward end will allow the mast tenon to clear it when it pivots on the tabernacle. It still needs to have a vertical ending at the forward end as the most common way to hold the heel of the mast in place was to drop in a block of wood that filled the trench and lash it or pin it in place. Occasionally on the smaller classes a bolt was slid right through the centre of the tabernacle and mast, or sometimes just a retaining bolt through the front of the tabernacle.

Hull Varnish

Now is a good time to sand the outside of the hull and apply several coats of varnish. I actually did it after the inwales, thwarts and knees were in, but before the sponsons were fitted. Add a few extra coats on a couple of areas along the keel and a couple of areas under the bilges where you plan to block up the boat when the strongback is dismantled. The plank ends at the tuck have not yet been trimmed, so varnish the planks just past the tuck at this stage. You could apply a few coats to the aft face of the tuck at this stage or leave it until it is out of the strongback.

Photo 11J Hull varnish starting.

Remove the Strongback

You need to get at the bottom of the keel for some of the next procedures, so this is the time to get rid of the strongback. Chainblocks and slings allow you to do it alone, but ordinary blocks and tackles can do it with a few helpers. Sling the boat first, then remove any temporary fastenings you had holding the boat to the strongback (top of stem, top of tuck) and any cleats or packers. Take the weight of the boat and dismantle the strongback. Lower the boat onto blocks at a height that will enable you to drill up through the keel through the mast step. Aim for level fore and aft but it is not critical any longer. Shore up the bilge with other blocking so that it will be sturdy with one or more workers inside the boat. Make it easily removable for access when sanding and varnishing.

The mast step should be fitted back in place and the 3/8" holes through the keel and floors should be drilled up through the mast step. The keel end of the holes should be counterbored for the head of the copper bolts, and those at the mast step end that are located in the mast heel tenon trench should be counterbored for the nuts so that they will leave clearance for the tenon. Bolt the step down with copper rod, headed below and threaded above.

The tabernacle parts can now be fitted for good. You could cut the slots for the mast pivot lugs on the bench or after it is fitted, on the bench is probably easier. There were always multiple slots in tabernacles. As for the fin case discussed earlier, the exact position of the mast could not be determined before sailing. Sometimes different rigs would require the mast to be in different slots. Different-sized packers were used at the heel (or different heel pin positions). Most surviving boats show more wear in one pair of slots. *Britannia,* as restored at the ANMM has only one slot extant. But Ron Robinson told me that there had been two slots until the front of the forward slot broke off and seeing that they only used the back one, they simply cleaned the damaged part off. On the replica *Britannia* we use only the aft slot with all rigs, other than in the first few seasons where the jib that worked with 3rd and 4th rig didn't balance the 3rd rig main, so we located the mast in the forward slot which eased the helm slightly. A new larger 3rd jib now balances the 3rd main from the aft slot.

Top of the Tuck

This can now be trimmed to a cambered curve just protruding above the tuck beam. Take care to sight it up from different angles to ensure it is a sweet curve. Where the deck will land on each side should be a continuation of the slight curve.

Plank Endings at the Tuck

The boats were measured by the builder at this stage as they were out of the strongback, sitting on their keel and unlikely to change shape. They could not be greater than 18 feet long between perpendiculars when propped level, in most cases this meant that the stem heel would be about 2" closer to the level floor than the bottom of the tuck. If the aft face of the tuck was less than 18' from the stem perpendicular, the ends of the planks could be trimmed, up to that distance off the tuck. In all cases I have seen, this was less than 5/8". It was not always performed slavishly to the exact measurement. Official measurements for the Sydney Flying Squadron for the season 1938-39 show that *Britannia* measured at exactly 18' (Wee Georgie was the official measurer) but most other boats in the fleet of 24 boats were either 17'11½" or 17'11¾", one was 17' 11¼", two were 17'11" and two were 17'10½"! If any boats had been a fraction over, the stems were solid enough to allow a bit of planing off, up to about ½" would not be missed, but the stemhead bolt through the breasthook could be a problem. Having said that, I can find no mention of boats having to be altered.

The edges of the planks should be eased but only slightly. Then the whole tuck and the plank ends should have several coats of varnish applied if this has not already happened. I considered this a good time to get the name written on the tuck. A few coats under it make a good base, a few coats over it mean you can lightly sand each season or so and re-varnish without damaging the lettering. It was generally professionally sign-written on the Port side or the lettering spaced out across the whole tuck with a gap for the rudder. Signwriters who paint by hand are scarcer than wooden boatbuilders (the last guy I used for the ten-footer *Republic* in 1995 won the lottery and retired!) so I compromised with computer-cut vinyl lettering. I asked Ron Robinson if he remembered the kind of lettering the original *Britannia* used because the only photograph with a close-up of the boat in the

1940's showed no name painted at all. Ron's answer was that he had never seen a name painted on the tuck. Apparently some time in the 1930's a spinnaker pole had come flying back and punctured a hole straight through the tuck. When it was repaired the name was left off. I chose gold lettering with black shadow lines which is seen on several surviving Open Boats.

Photo 11K   Name on tuck.

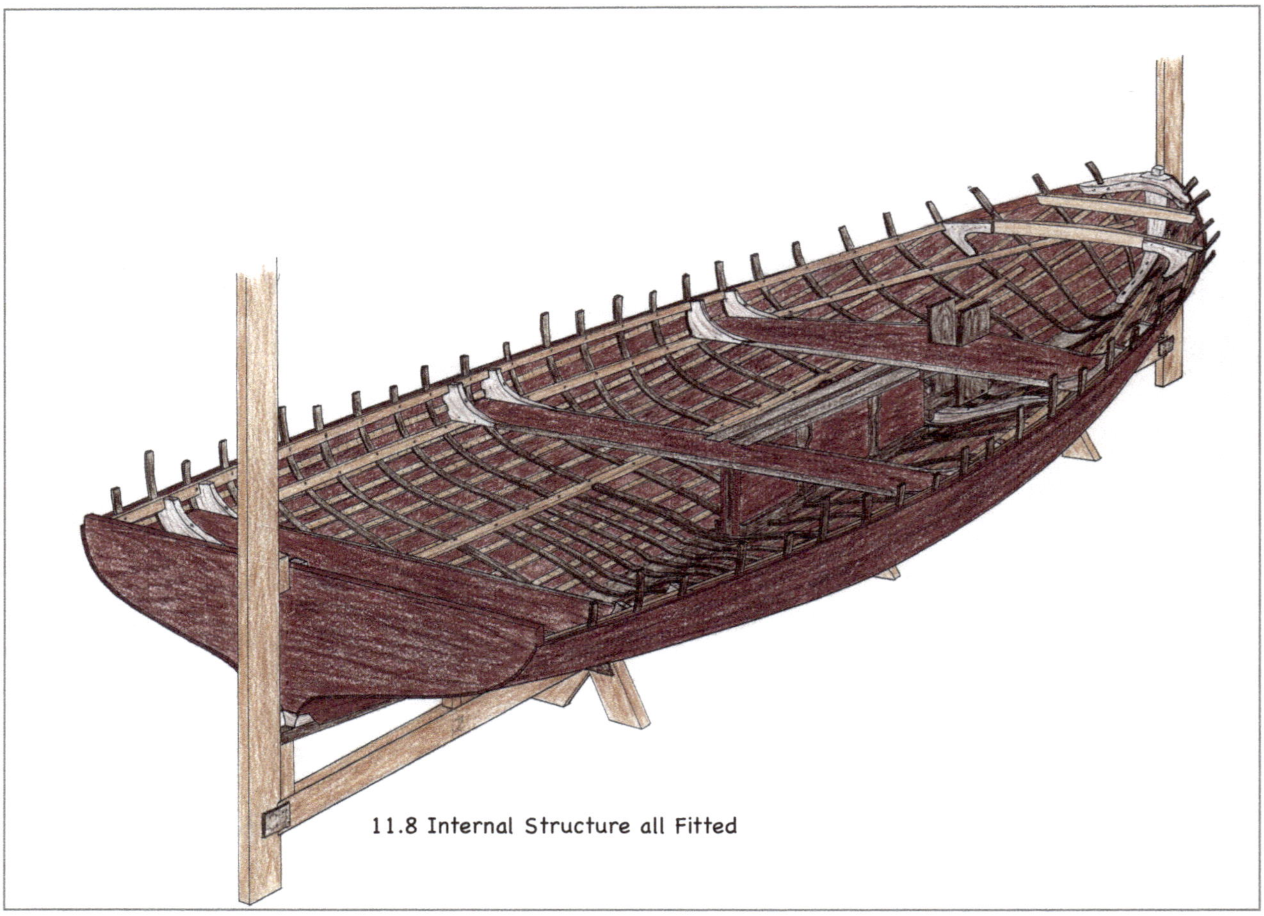

11.8 Internal Structure all Fitted

CHAPTER 12

The Deck, Sponsons and Coamings etc

The landing areas for the deck will need to be planed to be fair. Test with offcuts that the deck will land solidly on all supporting parts. Any rib head that protrude must be cut back to the surface, or preferable just below it to make planing easier. I found that a touch with a 36 grit disc on a 4" grinder was ideal, but extremely sharp chisels would be more authentic.

After the detailed woodwork so far, fitting the deck is a breeze. The side deck stock pieces (same thickness as the hull planking) are simply laid onto the side deck framing and the perimeter penciled underneath. Two lengths butt on one of the central dovetailed deck beams. The forward pieces will need to be cut from fairly wide boards. The foredeck is made up of several angled planks, with battens under the seams let in to the deck beams, as illustrated in photo 12A (which is actually of the ten-footer *Republic* but is of similar style, other than *Britannia* has no central king plank). The central tapered plank is tunked forward like a wedge which forces the foredeck planks hard up against each other. The planks are fastened down with copper nails (or bronze ring nails) driven blind into the carlin, inwale, sponson and deck beams, and copper nails driven from above and clenched under the foredeck battens. Coat the undersides with several coats of varnish before fastening down. Trim the edges back in line with the carlins and the inner sponsons remembering that the outer sponsons will be fitted up to the deck edge as will the coamings on the inside.

Photo 12A Foredeck structure.

Photo 12B Fitting the deck.   PHOTO BOB CHAPMAN

Sponsons

There were generally two more parts to the sponsons on each side outside the deck planking which landed on the inner sponsons. This has been illustrated in drawing 11.5, including the chainplates, which must be fitted before the outer sponson goes on. The fastenings for the chainplates were generally ¼" copper rod with a peened head fitting a countersink in the chainplate and polished flush, and threaded for a nut on the inside, where all fastenings went through a reinforcing block fitted against the hull planking hard up under the inwale. The first part, the outer sponson was generally Oregon Pine or sometimes Huon Pine, beveled underneath to continue the bevel of the inner sponson, tapered forward and screwed or blind nailed to the inner sponson. The outer part was a half-round Spotted Gum moulding always referred to as "the moulding" and available as such from the local timber yard. Later on Silver Ash was used by some to save weight. It is screwed or blind nailed to the rest of the sponson. All parts need to be steamed when the bows are full.

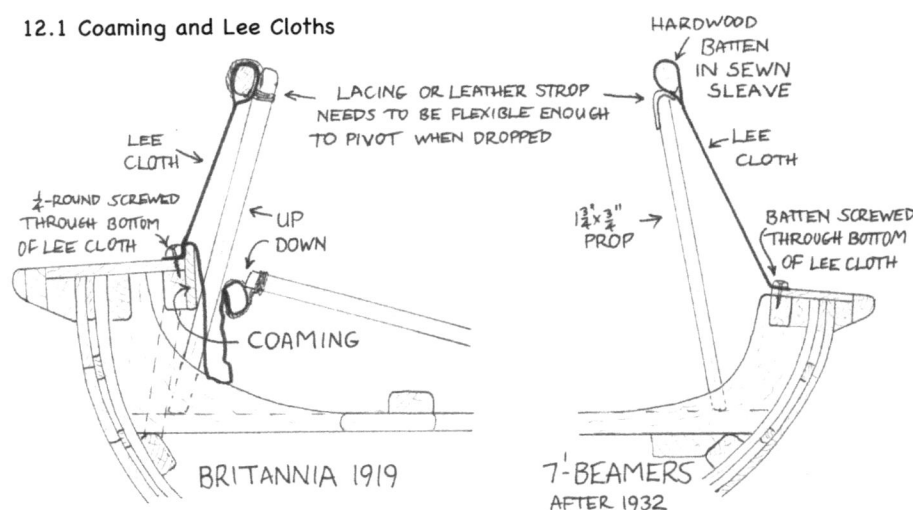

12.1 Coaming and Lee Cloths

The Coaming

Most later boats did not fit coamings on the inside of the deck, but early on they were invariably fitted protruding above the deck for ¾" to 1½". Before the general use of lee cloths they were even higher as they functioned to help keep the water out. They often continued in one piece around the curve of the back of the deck. *Britannia's* coamings were of Kauri protruding only ¾" above the deck, the same height as the quarter-round moulding that held the bottom of the lee cloths (see Drawing 12.1) and were not continuous up forward across the centre. They almost met in a curve, with a short filler piece in the gap. They finish at 3" wide but needed to be cut from wider boards. The shape was found by clamping the over-width stock to the carlins and penciling under the carlin where it finishes flush, and scribing a line ¾" above the deck. It is simply screw-fastened to the carlin. Later boats without a coaming would have a breakwater fitted across the back end of the foredeck to serve the same purpose up there, generally fastened against the back of the deck beam and sometimes notched over the side decks.

Swinging-out or Hanging-out Battens

The unballasted boats could only be held up against the pressure in the sails by the crew weight on the side decks, and it helped if they could swing their weight as far out as possible by hooking their feet (or rather one foot….the other foot was left free to enable a rapid leap inboard if the wind shut off suddenly) under a batten fastened above or below the three thwarts. *Britannia's* is 1 7/8" x 1 1/8" Spotted Gum, chamfered on the underside for the crew's bare insteps. Later boats generally used Oregon of about 2"square, as on *Top Weight*. Some 16 and 12-footers, and some later 18's had their swinging-out battens held just off the planking by a large block of wood each end. These were generally referred to as toe rails, and were in short sections in each bay between the aft and mid thwarts

Sole Boards

Before the 1930's most eighteens were fitted with sole boards made from planking offcuts, generally only between the forward and mid thwarts and inboard of the stringer. This was a largish flattish area that copped a lot of heavy foot traffic. The boards were simply screwed to the ribs. They were left bare or oiled (linseed) so were not fitted until after varnishing was completed. For the best look, divide the distance from the keel to the stringer on at least four points fore and aft, subtract the total of the intended gaps and the result is the width of each board at that point. Scribe the inner edge of the first plank along the keel or case log, mark off the widths you just worked out, and cut and plane to these slightly curved lines. The outer edge of the inner plank can be used to mark the inner edge of the next plank and so on. Or you can just use parallel-sided boards and accept the slightly agricultural look. Some boats also had a flat slatted platform forward of the mast, possibly an attempt to help the spinnakers stored there to stay dry. I can't think of another reason. We tried it for the first couple of seasons on *Britannia* and it was more trouble than it was worth, ropes would hook under edges, clips would jam in the gaps and so on, so we left it out. Smaller crews and narrower boats later meant less pressure on the planking from feet, so sole boards dropped out of use.

Finishing the Stem Head and Tuck

The bumpkin fitted to the foredeck had its aft end held down by a bolt through the deck and a reinforcing block firmly fastened to the forward side of the main deck beam. The stem knee protruded above the deck to form a squared tenon that located in a mortice under the bumpkin. The forward end cap of the bumpkin is held by two whisker stays back to the top of the sponsons just forward of the mast, and a bobstay back to a fitting on the base of the stem, and joined there by a preventer starting a bit more than halfway out on the bumpkin. This stem heel fitting was sometimes just a bronze strap under the keel fastened up through the stem knee, but the strap often was cast with sides so it formed a sort of shoe and was referred to as the shoe. This is best fitted, at least dry-fitted before final varnishing. Some boats had an eye bolt or some similar bolt fastened horizontally through the stem knee 3 or 4 inches up from the keel. The aft end of the keel must be trimmed to take the fitting for the lower rudder pintle which can also be fitted now. If you didn't trim the plank ends at the tuck earlier, or have the signwriting done, now is the time to do those things too. The top of the tuck should be planed back to just above the level of the tuck beam and if the top of the stern knee is still protruding above the tuck beam it should be cut back flush.

Varnishing

Finishing work is one part applying varnish, nine parts preparation, mostly sanding and

Photo 12C Britannia's stem shoe.

vacuuming up the dust. So get cracking inside (hopefully you were clever enough to sand the inside of the planking and most of the other components before fitting). There will inevitably be some bedding compound that needs to be cleaned up, and as you crawl through the boat you will probably find some fastenings that need to be smoothed down. If you applied a few coats of varnish to the hull earlier you will need to check that the borders will blend into the new varnish, which is why you will have located these borders on edges involving a change of direction. Ease those edges and feather the varnish edge. Dusting out is very important, there are plenty of nooks and crannies for dust to gather.

I applied the first internal coat by brush and made sure it got into every nook and cranny and behind and under every part I could reach. I then sanded lightly with 320 grit to remove the nap and raised grain that Cedar in particular is subject to, then had a friend spray multiple coats throughout the interior.

Photos 12D and 12E Freshly varnished boat. BOB CHAPMAN

Because the boats are sailed hard for 25-30 afternoons in the Summer, every Winter a touch-up is necessary. For eleven seasons I simply spot-sanded bare areas and minor scratches etc and built up five coats locally, then got the crew around for a day when we completely sanded the interior and deck. I then brushed one all-over coat. After the eleventh season the main foot traffic areas needed stripping back to the bare wood and starting again. The outside of the hull was touched up with one all over coat every second or third season, until after the twelfth season I stripped it back to the wood and started again.

Photo 12F Freshly varnished boat. BOB CHAPMAN

The Rudder

Rudders were generally made from wide Cedar boards and the cheeks cut from Tea-Tree knees. The earlier rudders were "barn door" affairs, as long or longer fore and aft than they were deep. By the 1930's they began to be swept back in a shape referred to as "tear drop", but the essential structure of Cedar blade and Tea-Tree cheeks was retained. *Britannia's* blade was 1¼' thick, with cheeks of 1½" Tea Tree. It was tapered to 3/8" on the trailing edge, and rounded on the leading edge, but a NACRA foil it is not.

Hawk-eyed observers will notice that the original rudder displayed on the original boat hanging up in the ANMM is not as long fore and aft as the drawings, or the replica. This was explained by Ron Robinson. After conversion to a motor launch the boat was returning to Balmain after a trip out, after dark. A dredger was not particularly noticed, until it hauled hard on one of its steel hawsers which rose up rapidly under the boat and tore of the back part of the rudder! As a motor boat *Britannia* didn't need such a big rudder so Wee Georgie simply cleaned up the trailing edge and used it as it was.

Photo 12G Builder with rudder and fin. BOB CHAPMAN

12.2 Rudders

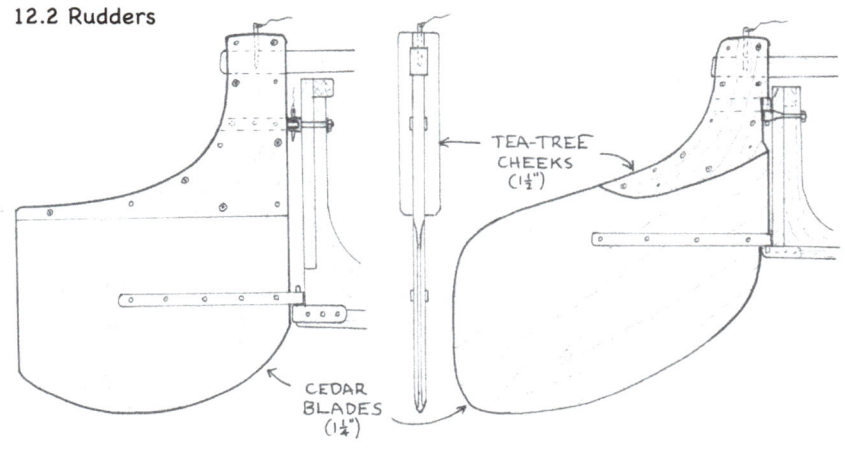

'BARN DOOR' PRE 1932   'TEAR-DROP' AFTER 1932

The Tiller

The tiller was almost invariably made from Spotted Gum and was substantial as the loads are immense, particularly off the breeze before or after an extra is flown. On my *Britannia* in fresh breezes a crew member sits the other side of the tiller off the wind and assists in pushing the tiller when called for. Lately I have been using a 3:1 tackle set up each side (Ron Robinson said that Wee Georgie used a tackle). The first Spotted Gum tiller was tapered to 1 ¼" to fit between the cheeks. On a hard broad reach I pulled the tiller hard to weather to allow for the increased load when the balloon jib came down before the turning mark and the tiller snapped off! I wouldn't have believed it. I made a new tiller before the next race and it lasted two seasons before the same thing happened. This time I chiseled out the mortice in the rudder head to 1¾" wide, and the tiller that fits that has lasted to date. A rope is spliced around the inboard end so the skipper can steer from the rail, usually with a foot on the tiller for pushing when necessary. The tiller is locked into the mortice by a brass or copper pin in a hole drilled vertically down into the tiller through the centre of the rudder head.

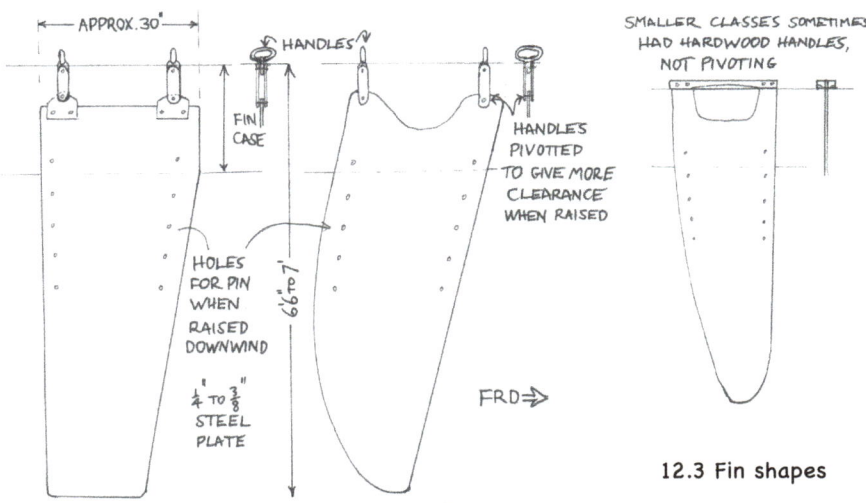

12.3 Fin shapes

The Fin

The metal dagger board was always referred to as the fin. It was cut from boiler plate steel, 3/8" or 5/16" thick, or even ¼" later according to Alf Beashel, and shaped with a tapered leading edge. Later the trailing edge was commonly rounded. The top had steel handles up to about 1' above the top

---

Dixon Kemp's "Gin"

In the late nineteenth century Dixon Kemp's "Manual of Yacht and Boat Sailing" was a popular and influential book in the English-speaking boating world, full of fabulous detail of yachts and boats of the time, and is still available through second-hand dealers (I have the 8th Edition, 1895). In a section which covers boats from different parts of the world he discusses the Sydney boats which he saw in what I suspect must have been a short visit (if he came at all, I can find no newspaper reference to his visit, which would be unusual given his fame, so I conclude it was probably written by a correspondent). He refers to "the centreboard-locally termed the 'gin'"...what?!? I puzzled over that one for a while till I realised that he must have made notes and not deciphered his own handwriting (or his correspondent's) when he got back to Blighty and wrote the book. An "f" in handwriting of the time could easily be mistaken for a "g", but usually not by the writer himself. Perhaps a secretary was involved. I originally thought that the sizes he gives for the centreboards were also suspect, for example 8' by 5'6" for a 24 footer, thinking he had assumed that the long slot for the fin is filled all the way fore and aft, but my research suggests that 19th century fins generally were long fore and aft. He also mentions outriggers for the boom sheeting (like the US sandbaggers), but I have never seen a single photograph of a Sydney boat with stern outriggers. There are reports that the 24' Willia had one, as did Bronzewing V, a very short-lived imported boat. Most of the article seems to be spot on, but it is a reminder that all written information should be checked. Or know the background of the commentator. Or don't trust strangers.

of the steel fin which pivoted to keep below the boom when hauled up downwind, and also to save a bit of weight. Alf Beashel wrote that even a ¼" fin weighed 142 pounds (65 kilograms). It took at least two men to lift the fin and at least three to haul it out. Often a derrick would be employed to lift it out at the home shed. In the replica fleet we use aluminium fins of ½" thickness and about 40 kg due to a shortage of derricks!

Belaying Pins

Halyards and the kicker are cleated to belaying pins set through holes in the forward thwart and on some boats in the mid thwart for the runner tails (full details of running rigging will be found below). They were usually turned from Spotted Gum with proportions as illustrated in drawing 12.4. Also illustrated are 3/8" brass pins that were fixed through the tuck beam to cleat the spinnaker halyard tail to as a backstay, and on some boats on the boom jaws to cleat spinnaker halyards or topsail gear.

Mainsheet Horse

A double block as part of the mainsheet tackle traveled on a bronze horse spanning about 2' bolted through the tuck beam, high enough to easily clear the tiller which fitted through it.

Lee Cloths

Lee cloths came into use around 1900 as an aid to keeping the Harbour out of the boat. The leeward one had to be propped up, and when tacking the first man across dropped the newly windward lee cloth so all could sit on the deck and the last man to leave propped up the new leeward one. They were made from heavy canvas, and both Post Office bags and NSW Railways tarpaulins were popular sources (NSW Railways supplied most of the canvas for the canvas dinghies also), quite unofficially obtained. A Spotted Gum batten of around 1 ½" x 1 ¼" ran in a sleeve in the top of the lee cloth and pivoted in a metal ball joint fitting with the forward end on the foredeck coaming and the rear end on the tuck beam or quarter knee. This was steam-bent to the shape of the side coaming, and in use was propped up by a stick lashed flexibly to the batten at the mid thwart to be 12-14" off the deck. When dropped it rested just inside the coaming just below deck level. The lower edge of the cloth was held to the deck all the way along the outside of the coaming by a pine (Kauri or Huon or Oregon) quad of about ¾" radius or a batten of about ¾" x ½" on later boats without coamings, screwed into the deck and carlin. See Drawing 12.1.

Some boats, particularly ten-footers but also some eighteens also rigged a canvas "booby hatch" across the aft end of the foredeck lashed up to the mast to keep out water coming across the foredeck.

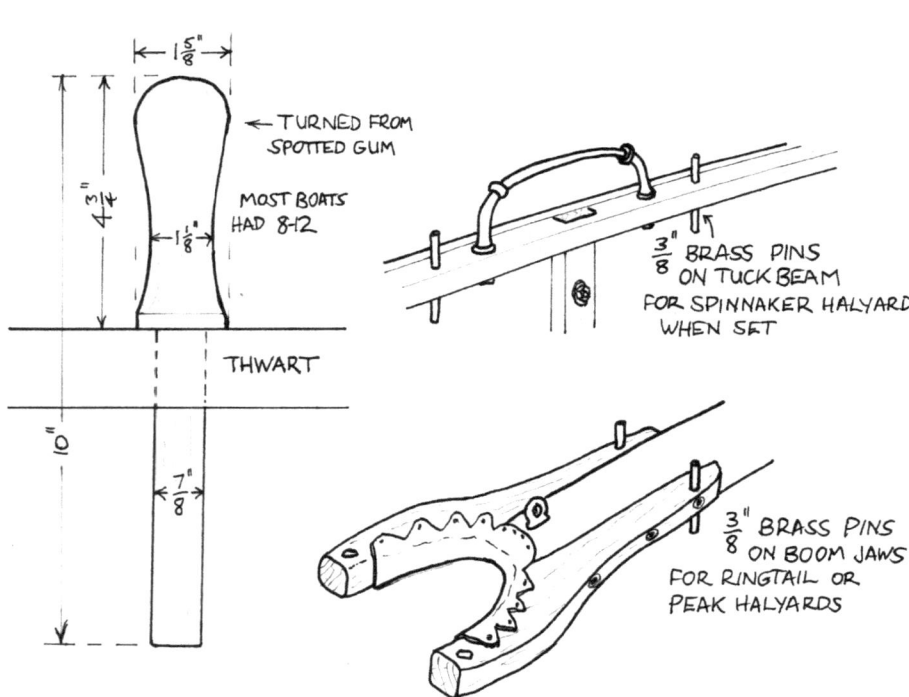

12.4 Belaying pins, Mainsheet Horse and Boom Jaws

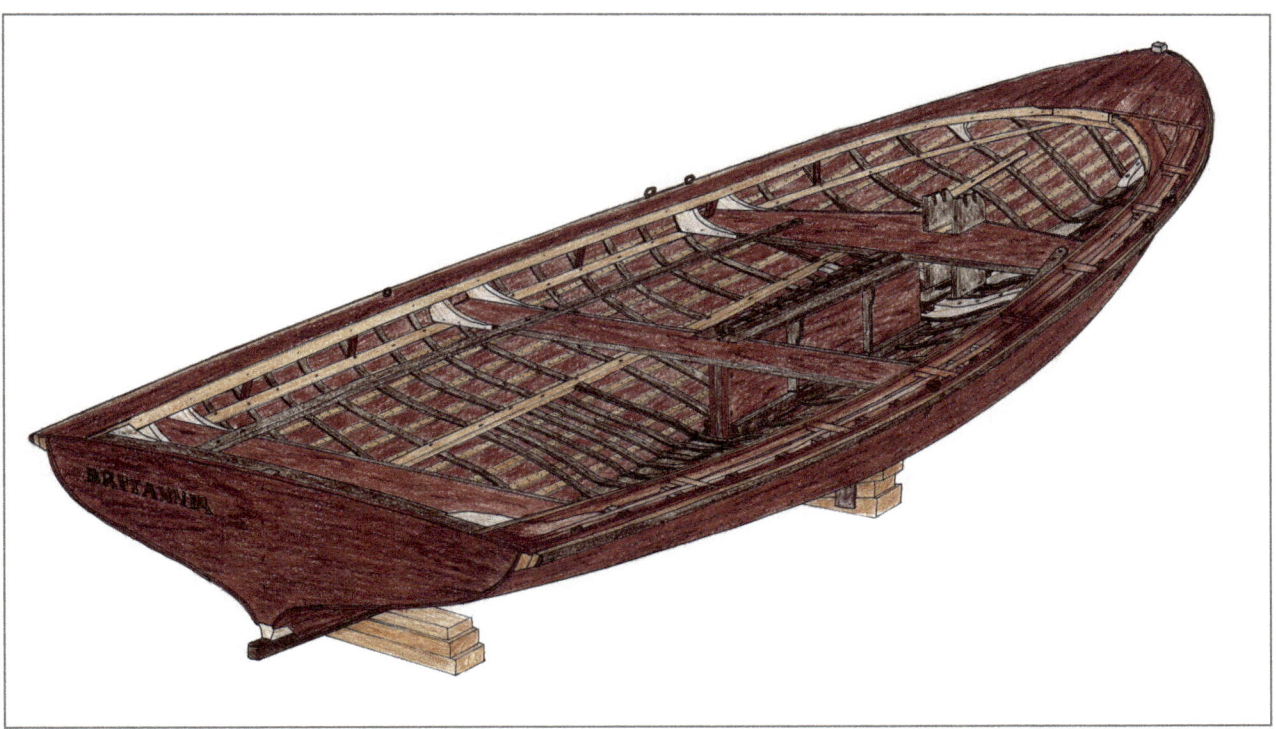

12.5 All Decking Complete

Photo 12G   H C Press was one of a few 18-footers that carried a canvas booby hatch across the foredeck.
HALL COLLECTION ANMM

CHAPTER 13

Masts and Spars

I really enjoy building masts and spars, and I am not alone: in boatbuilding yards the head shipwright normally reserved that task for himself. I hope you enjoy it too because an historical eighteen-footer has a *shipload* of masts and spars. Each boat usually had three rigs, a first or big rig for light weather (under 12 knots), a second or intermediate rig (12-20 knots), and a third rig (over 20 knots). Occasionally some boats had reef points in mainsails and additional jibs to give more combinations, either intermediate to the three main rigs or smaller for really fresh breezes. Boats usually had:
- two bumpkins
- two or three masts
- three gaffs
- three booms
- four sections of spinnaker pole
- two or four ringtail spars (for two different ringtails).

As discussed elsewhere, masts and spars were made from Oregon Pine, Bunya Pine or Riga Spruce.

Masts

Throughout most of the nineteenth century masts and spars were solid, most commonly of Riga Spruce (Pinus sylvestris), pronounced locally as Ricka Spruce which were imported specifically for mast and spar-making. The first reference to hollow masts I have found is from an article in an 1899 newspaper claiming that one of the crack 22 footers had a new hollow mast for the coming season. It was expressed in terms that this was something to be noted but not revolutionary, so until more evidence is found I would suggest that hollow spars had been in use, but not for all boats, since sometime in the 1890's. The only glues available were animal-derived hide and hoof glues which needed heat applied before use and were not particularly waterproof. I would suggest that plenty of varnish would have been applied to aid in waterproofing, and the metal cap and bands at spreaders and tabernacle would be relied upon to hold it together. The original *Britannia* had mostly hollow masts and spars, but according to Ron Robinson the smallest mast was a solid stick of Riga Spruce.

In the 21st Century there is no real reason to use anything other than epoxy glue, though resorcinol has its adherents (zig boom!) even though the glue lines are dark and prominent.

In the late 1930's when the boats became lighter masts were built between 4½" and 4 7/8" diameter. *Britannia's* masts are both 5" diameter.

The easiest way to build a hollow mast is to hollow out two sections big enough to form the outside diameter of the mast. This will require

13.1 Mast Cross-Sections

two sides from standard 6" x 3" stock. However this is not always available in suitable spar timber in Australia, so the sections may have to be built up from smaller stock. Drawing 13.1 shows some of the possibilities. Two-inch thick stock is more readily available. There are other possibilities as well, however some of the sections drawn in textbooks and on the internet do not allow for easy clamping up. Any section made up of four or more pieces needs

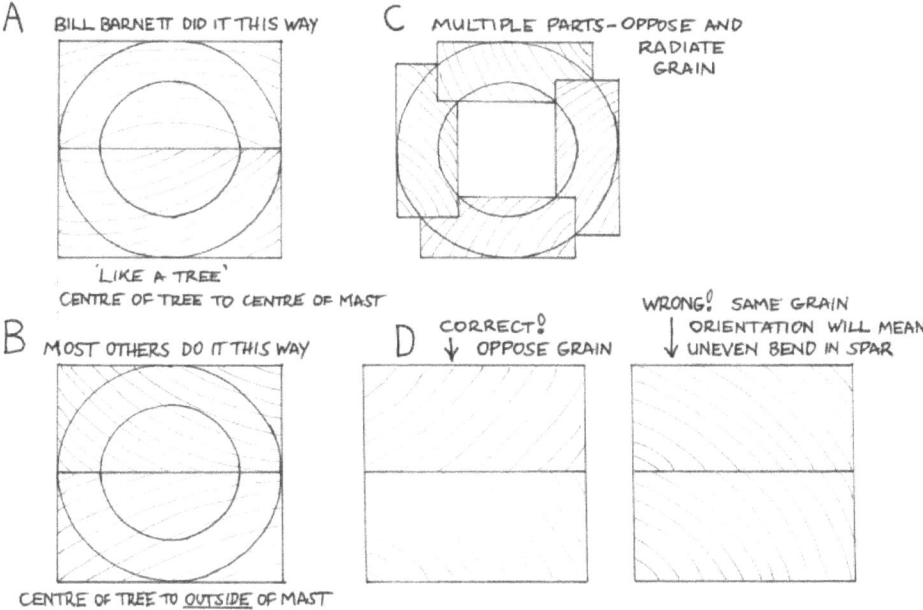

13.2 Grain Orientation

some form of rebate in at least two of the parts so the parts will not slide around while gluing up. Four-part sections usually use less timber so can save a bit of cost. You can draw up sections to suit the timber you have.

The internet is alive with "bird's mouth" spars, built up from machined sections as in the drawing. I did it once. It takes away most of the pleasurable bits in shaping a spar and increases the unpleasant bit, the glue-up. The extra machining time results in very little time saving overall. It may make sense for professional yards that have proper machining setups and lots of jigs for holding while gluing up, but for others I would only suggest it if you happen to find a whole heap of cheap long small-section timber and have a good machining setup.

Grain Orientation

Bill Barnett told me that he always aligned the grain in hollow spars so that the centre of the tree was in the centre of the spar, that is, mimicking the tree as in 13.2A. Most twentieth century written authorities suggest putting the inside of the tree towards the <u>outside</u> of the spar as in 13.2B and C. I have always done it this way. Bill Barnett didn't break many masts, and neither have I, so I'm not sure it matters a hell of a lot. But I will say that into the 1950's with Bermudan rigs and <u>very</u> thin-walled masts (a lot thinner than any I've done) Bill still didn't break a lot.

But the important thing is that the orientation of the grain should be as close to a mirror image as you can get. If the two sides have the grain in the same direction as in 13.2D, the spar will bend differently to different sides. This is a real problem in a boom. Mirror-imaging the grain will give the spar similar resistance to bending each side and will be stiffer. With four or more pieces try to radiate the grain from the centre.

Scarfing

Any mast and most spars today will need timber scarfed together to get the length. This was not a problem for the original builders. Up until the 1930's Oregon Pine logs of up to 100 feet were still being imported (until the 1920's often in sailing ships!) and cut down by the sawmills in Rozelle Bay. Now it is rare to find any lengths over 20 feet. Plot out the mast sides as in drawing 13.3 to work out where the scarfs will go as well as the grain orientation. Make sure scarfs are not close in adjacent sections. If you have a thickness planer with enough access to run your stock through, it is best to finish all pieces to the maximum diameter on the wider dimension, and to exactly half the maximum diameter on the smaller section. This will save a huge amount of work. You will just need to be careful to align the pieces perfectly when gluing up the scarfs. And of course you will need to have one side dead straight and square before putting it to the thicknesser. If you are building up from four pieces in section, thickness them all to your maximum dimensions on your diagram. If you can't thickness them, leave them very slightly oversize (to the maximum diameter dimensions) and plane them to size after they are scarf-joined to length.

Scarfs in masts and spars need to be cut to a ratio of 12 to 1, that is, the scarf will be 12 times longer than the thickness of the timber it is cut on. For 2" timber each scarf will therefore be 24" long. Mark out the scarfs, being extremely careful to mark them on the correct side. There are many ways to cut scarfs. I always cut just clear of the line with a circular saw (which gives you lots of wedges, always useful in boatbuilding), then power plane very close to the line, then finish off with a hand plane, for mast scarfs a No5 bench plane is about right. You can find various jig designs on the web, but by the time you're well into building the boat your skills will be more than adequate for scarf planing. When gluing up, as always, do a dry run first. Use a string line or laser sight or just your eye to make sure the two parts you are joining are in line and not kinked. Clamp sideways across the scarf to line the edges up. Clamp the piece with upward-facing scarf to the bench (on blocks to give room for clamps) and locate reference blocks so you can replace the other piece in exactly the dry-fitted position. Apply epoxy using the instructions from the manufacturer! Then clamp up the two pieces and leave for 24 hours.

13.3 Scarfing

Marking the Taper

All of the masts and spars you will build for an Australian Open Boat will be tapered (except for all but one of the spinnaker poles). The intermediate stages of a taper are working out as in drawing 13.4. Eighteen footer masts of 4 7/8" diameter held this diameter constant from the tabernacle band to the spreader band. They generally tapered only slightly from the tabernacle band to the heel to no less than 4", and above the spreader band they tapered to 3" to 3 ¼" at the lower end of the mast cap. At

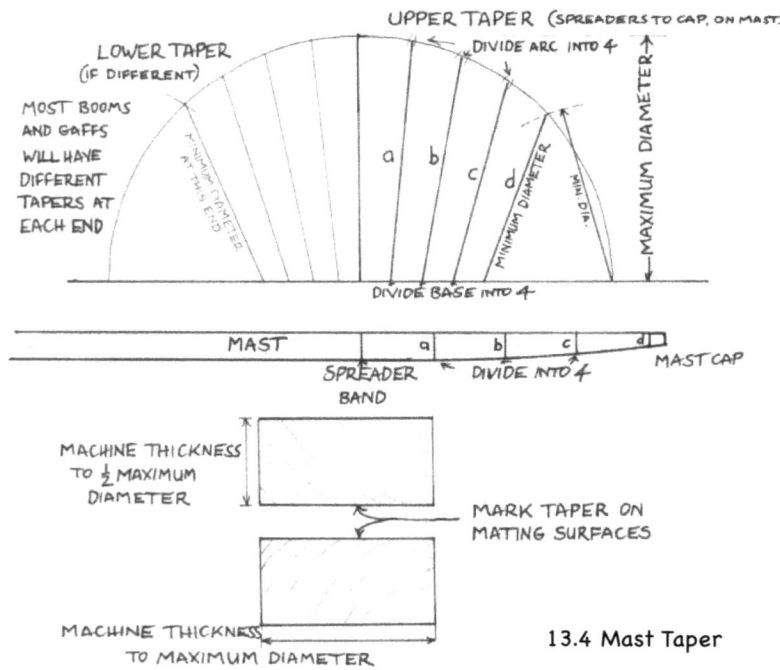

13.4 Mast Taper

the head the aft side of the mast is often made straight in a continuous line from lower down and the taper is all taken off the front of the mast, but this is not necessary in a gaff rigger so the taper can be even all round. Plot the taper out either side of a straight centreline on the mating surfaces, tack nails into these points and bend a batten around the nails and pencil the lines in, then cut close to the lines. It is best to then clamp symmetrical pieces together and plane the sides down to the lines constantly checking by eye that the surface is fair. Or plane one half very close to the line and very fair, then clamp it to the other piece and plane it down to the other. Colour in the smaller finished one by hatching with a pencil so you can see when you are cutting into the smaller piece. If you are using a four-part section, plane each pair of opposite pieces as an identical pair, separate from the other pair (too hard to plane all four together). Ensure that you are keeping the sides square to the mating surfaces. The surfaces of the mast opposite the mating surfaces do not need to be tapered yet, that will happen after gluing the two (or four) sides together.

Hollowing

Wall thickness in masts was standardised in the early twentieth century by Skenes and others at 20% of diameter. I used this figure, so *Britannia's* 5" masts have 1" thick walls through their main sections. As discussed later, gaffs and booms can have thinner walls. I have not found any references before 1945 to wall thickness in 18-footers, but by the late 1940's Bill Barnett was building his masts

Photo 13A Brit mast ready for gluing

about 4 ½" in diameter with ¾" walls, so just under 17%. Later when Bermudan rigs came in (1950's), builders experimented with thinner walls but by the time they got down to 12% the masts were exploding regularly. The replica *Top Weight* had its first mast built with 12% walls and it did not last the first season. So I'd suggest you don't go less than 17%, but 20% is even safer. Masts are solid from about one foot above the position where the boom jaws will be to the heel, and from about 6" to 1' below the bottom of the mast cap. Often they are also solid for a foot or two in the way of the spreaders. I did not do this on *Britannia*, but left it hollow. Any crushing load from the spreaders is taken by the aluminium spreader band and bending strains have not proved excessive in the sense that the smaller mast has been used hard for 14 seasons without breaking or straining. Every termination of the hollow should be tapered over at least 6". Masts made up from parts which do not meet in the intended solid sections should have fillers fitted before gluing up.

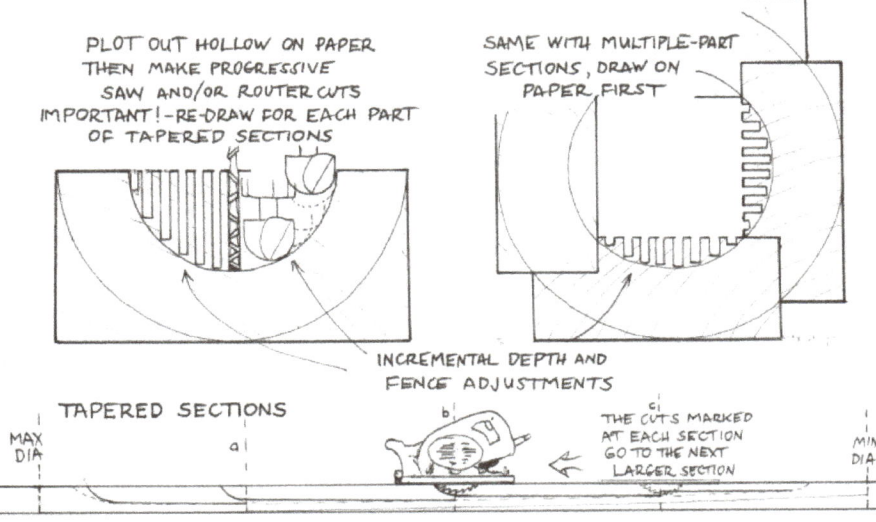

13.5 Hollowing

They sure can bend though

Masts can bend alarmingly in fresh conditions. Plenty of photos show lots of bend. There are stories of breakages under spinnaker. In a replica ten-footer on the Brisbane River in the 1990's Wrecker Johnson was alarmed when he noticed the mast bend on a fresh run. He asked skipper Len Heffernan what they could do about it, and Len typically replied "Don't look up!"

Plot your hollow sections out on paper as in drawing 13.5 and work out a series of cuts (with a circular saw with a fence) that will remove at least half the timber from the area to be hollowed. Remember that all spars have some taper, and the saw cuts cannot be constant for the whole spar. Plot out each section where there is taper every few feet, keeping the same incremental fence settings, but adjusting the depth. Double-check that your planned cuts will not exceed the depth of the hollow. **The plotted cuts at each section should go from that section to the next larger section.** The resulting 'steps' will be planed out when you fair in the hollow. If you are building your spar out of four or more parts in section, plot out the smaller hollows you need as seen in drawing 13.1. Bird's-mouth spars with eight parts generally do not need further hollowing. Chip and chisel out the waste, but be careful not to tear out strips in a manner that will tear up fibres from the parts intended to be part of the wall thickness. Once down close you can repeat the staggered cut system with a fenced router and the largest cove bit you can find. Plot this out on paper first. Or you can go straight to your hollowing plane, as illustrated in photo 13B. A core box plane if you can find one does a great job of knocking off the high spots in a semicircular hollow. Finish with very coarse sanding with the paper held on a round block with a

Photo 13B Saw cuts in mast.

Photo 13C Hollow in mast.

Photo 13D Core box plane.

Photo 13E Hollowing plane.

Photo 13F Two part mast clamped together.

Photo 13G Brit mast glue-up.

diameter a bit smaller than that of the hollow. Originally most builders would apply several coats of varnish to the hollows. In the 21st Century I can see no reason not to apply a couple of coats of epoxy resin.

Gluing Up

Round up all the clamps you own or can borrow. For a two section mast you will need a clamp about every 18", plus about 5 more for sideways alignment. For a four section mast you will need twice as many. Lay out gloves, wood pads to take clamp pressure and make sure the packers on your spar bench, or a closely-spaced series of firm trestles are in an <u>exact</u> straight line for the entire length of the mast. Clamp it up in a dry run to ensure all will go according to plan. Note any spots that seem to need more clamps and mark the clamp positions for when they are used during glue-up. Grab some 40 or 60 grit paper and hand sand the mating surfaces, preferably across the grain, then brush and vacuum the dust carefully.

It is better that epoxy cures at warm temperatures, but warm temperatures while spreading the glue reduce the open time before you need to clamp up, so find a friend or two. Or if it is cold, apply the glue in the cold shed, then warm the shed up for 24 hours after clamping up. Be very fire conscious. The epoxy needs to be of just brushable consistency, not too liquid. Apply to both mating surfaces aiming for an even 1/32" or so thickness.

Lift one section on top of the other and clamp them together, lining up some witness marks. For heaven's sake, take your gloves off when handling the clamps. If in two pieces, fit some clamps across horizontally to line the halves up, then fit the vertical clamps with pads to spread the load starting in the middle and working out, or at one end and continuing in the same direction. As discussed earlier, there is generally less work in cleaning off the glue squeezed out when wet than to leave it until after cure.

Using a Power Plane

As I used to tell clients at my boatbuilding classes, the greatest advantage of a power plane is that it removes a lot of wood in one pass. The greatest disadvantage of a power plane is that it removes a lot of wood in one pass. Plane conservatively clear of penciled reference lines and check often!

Tapering the Sides

After the clamps are removed and any remaining glue dags are cleaned off, you can mark out the taper for the remaining two sides, preferably on both sides measuring out from the central seam. Cut, power plane and finally hand plane to the line

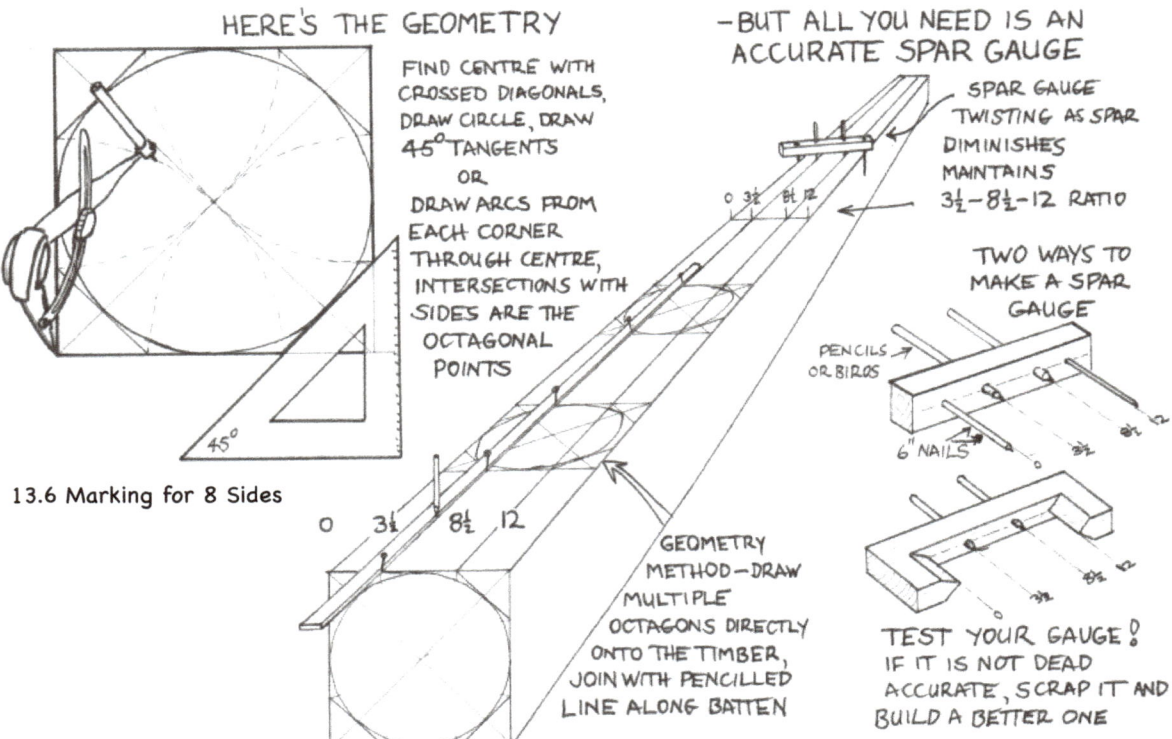

13.6 Marking for 8 Sides

ensuring a fair curve and also ensuring that the surface is dead square to the other sides. Check that the distance across the flats is the same at any point along the taper, that is, that it is a true square in section.

8-Siding

The path to roundness is to turn the square-sectioned mast into an octagonal section (8 sides), then knock off those corners to make it 16 sided, then 32-sided and then round. Drawing 13.6 shows a couple of methods for marking out for 8-siding,

Photo 13H Shading shows parts to come off for 8-siding.

one with a made-up gauge, one with geometry and nails and batten. With these masts having such straight sections it is quite easy to scribe the lines along most of the mast, but seeing there will be at least two masts of four sides each to mark out, the time spent to make up a gauge is probably worth it. The gauge should just fit over the largest diameter. It will still be accurate for the tapered head, but you will need to make up a smaller gauge for the boom and gaff. Masts this size require a bit of an effort to turn over, but not a big problem as long as you keep safety in mind, that is, making sure it can't fall off the bench or collapse the trestles, you could be injured.

A circular saw set at 45 degrees is the quickest way to remove the corners, just make sure you cut a bit outside the line, it usually doesn't pay to be too clever here. Power plane each new flat to just clear of the line with the mast set up with the new flat

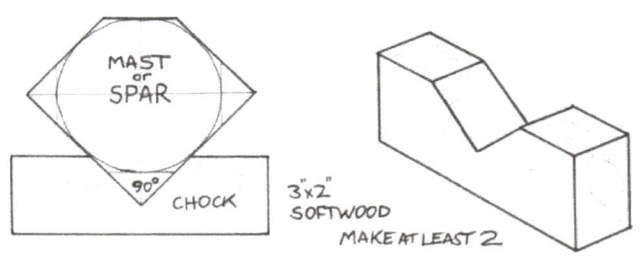

13.7 Mast/Spar Chocks

140

Photo 13I Spar Rollers.

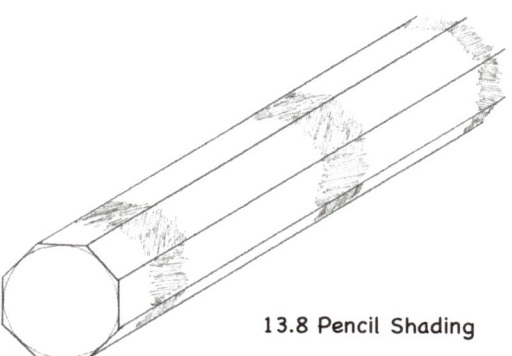

13.8 Pencil Shading

horizontal as in drawing 13.7. While you're making up the illustrated chocks, find the time to make up a couple of roller supports from hardware store wheels as in photo 13I. Start using them from this point as you will be regularly rolling the mast over. Chock the mast in the middle and at each end with horizontal blocking to keep it from rolling while planing.

Power plane all four new flats, and then hand plane them preferably with a No7, remembering four things:

1. The surface must be fair. Each ridge at the junction of two flats will be a fair line.
2. The new flat you are planing can't be wider than the old flat you are leaving, of course it must end up <u>exactly</u> the same width at the same point on the mast. Measure it! If your marking gauge was accurate, you can work exactly to your lines but be conservative until you are sure this is the case.
3. The surface will be 45 degrees to the adjacent surfaces.
4. The distance across each pair of opposite flats should end up at exactly the intended diameter of the spar at that point, and exactly the same as for each other pair of flats at the same point. Check with callipers. A variation of under 1/16" would hardly be noticeable, but try for closer.

16-Siding

You could make up a gauge to mark for 16 sides from details you will find in some textbooks on masts and spars, but I have found them of doubtful value on anything under a 6" mast. Any slight inaccuracy of the gauge or of the purity of the octagonal section will result in marked lines of doubtful value. The 16-siding can all be done by eye, with a few measurements to check. Colour-in each of the eight sides with pencil hatching every 18"-24" or so along the mast as in drawing 13.8. What happens is that when you plane the new flat it will have clean timber all the way along, and the residual hatching makes the alternate flats stand out. Don't try to get each new flat to its finished size, take a little off each before rolling the mast around and working on the next one. Keep rolling and planing until all flats are even in width. Check your progress with occasional measurements but your eye should be a good judge for most of it.

32-Siding

Colour in the new sides so the hatching is in complete bands, and repeat the process with a finer touch, planing the 16 ridges until the new flats are the same width as the old flats. Easy to say, takes a while to do.

Rounding

Several planing techniques can be used to remove the last flats. A careful pass with a very fine-set No7 plane can make the mast 64 sided, or you could try starting to spiral the cut as in drawing 13.9. Also illustrated in Photo 13J is a spar plane with body and blade hollowed. This is only useful of the curve of the blade is reasonably close to the curve of the mast. Bring out your metal tabernacle band and spreader band and the mast cap, and monitor your progress where those items are going to live so they will fit well.

A foam sanding block with a curve only slightly flatter than the mast curve is the next stage with the paper held by the two hands you are pushing the block with, in a slightly spiral direction. Try using the flat side first (still in a spiral motion), then shift to the hollow side. Each stroke will cover say 2', so slowly move along the mast overlapping your strokes. Penciled lines on the surface are a good guide to your progress as they will be sanded off the high spots but be left in the low spots and remaining flats. Start with 60 grit paper (or even 40 grit) and work down through the grades to finish at about 150 grit or whatever grit your varnish manufacturer suggests for preparation sanding. Spend plenty of time with each grade, it is tempting to hurry through the finer grades but the danger is that you will leave scratches from the coarser grades that you cannot see until you apply the first coat of varnish. Penciled lines applied and removed at each stage assist in even and sufficient sanding. You could even try curved cabinet scrapers if you have some experience with these. You can monitor your progress by running your fingers lightly over the surface. It is actually quite easy to feel small ridges that you cannot see. However, having said all this, plenty of original spars are quite uneven on the surfaces. This is partly from the fact that wood changes over time and often with the weather, so you can spend a lot of time getting your spars too perfect.

More than one power tool company now makes an in-line sander with foam blocks that you can shape to a required profile and attach sandpaper with Velcro. They are great if you can take the noise for the long periods necessary. They are slightly less tiring to use than hand-sanding but I have found that they do not save as much time as you would think. I generally change from one to the other for variety. <u>Do not</u> be tempted to use orbital or rotary sanders, they will inevitably sand the surface unfairly and the result will stand out like dog's balls under gloss varnish.

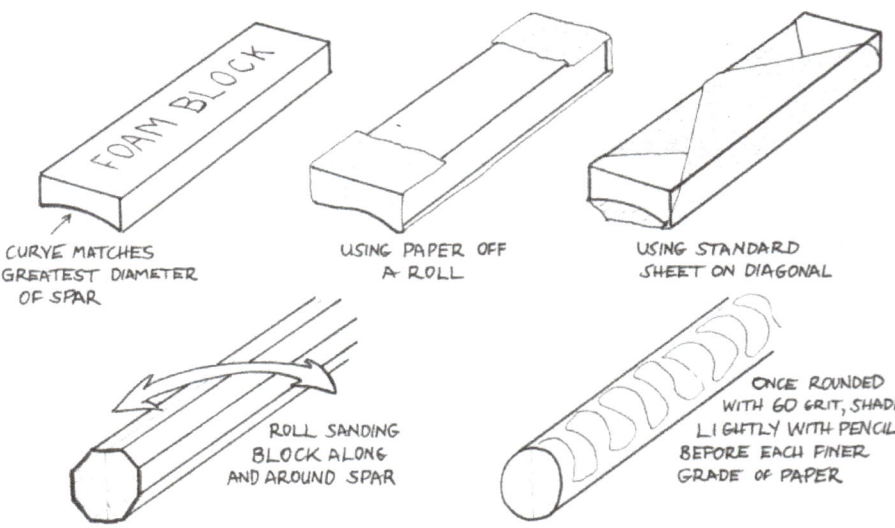

13.9 Sanding Spars

You could try a system recommended in some textbooks where you turn a sanding belt inside out and loop it over the mast, driving it with a drum on a power drill. I would advise against it. It is extremely easy to have an edge dig in which results in a groove around the circumference which will need a lot of planing and sanding to remove. Even if this does not happen, scratches around the circumference are across the grain, and the amount of longitudinal sanding to remove these scratches is just about equivalent to the amount of longitudinal sanding you would have done anyway.

Photo13J Spar planes.

Mast Cap

Australian Open Boats almost invariably had a metal mast cap, either cast bronze, or fabricated from steel and galvanised. This had to be fitted tightly to the masthead. Sometimes it sat on a shoulder so the shoulder had to be cut and the part above it shaped down to fit the inside of the mast cap. Otherwise it sat over the shaped masthead and it's inside diameter at the base was the diameter of the mast. The mast cap was generally drilled for a large-gauge screw driven in to prevent rotation.

Heel Tenon

The tenon to suit the slot in the mast step should now be cut, as in drawing 13.10. It requires a brass wear strip bent around the heel and screw-fastened.

Chocks

Upper shrouds were generally shackled to the mast cap, but lowers were generally spliced in served eyes looped over the mast. They need hardwood chocks screwed (and glued these days) and sometimes notched in to the mast to support them. Often the main throat halyard was run through a block on the mast cap, but sometimes it was on a spliced wire loop above the spreaders

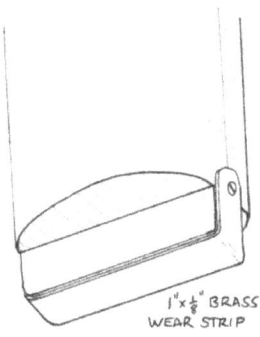

13.10 Mast Heel Tenon

which also needed a chock, on the forward side to keep it up, and a wide chock on the aft side to keep the turning block away from the mast. The spreader band was usually a metal band clamped on by one bolt through flanges on the forward side, so it had to be fitted before the chocks above it were fastened on. A timber cleat with an extra thumb cleat included was generally fitted to the front of the mast below the tabernacle band for the jib halyard.

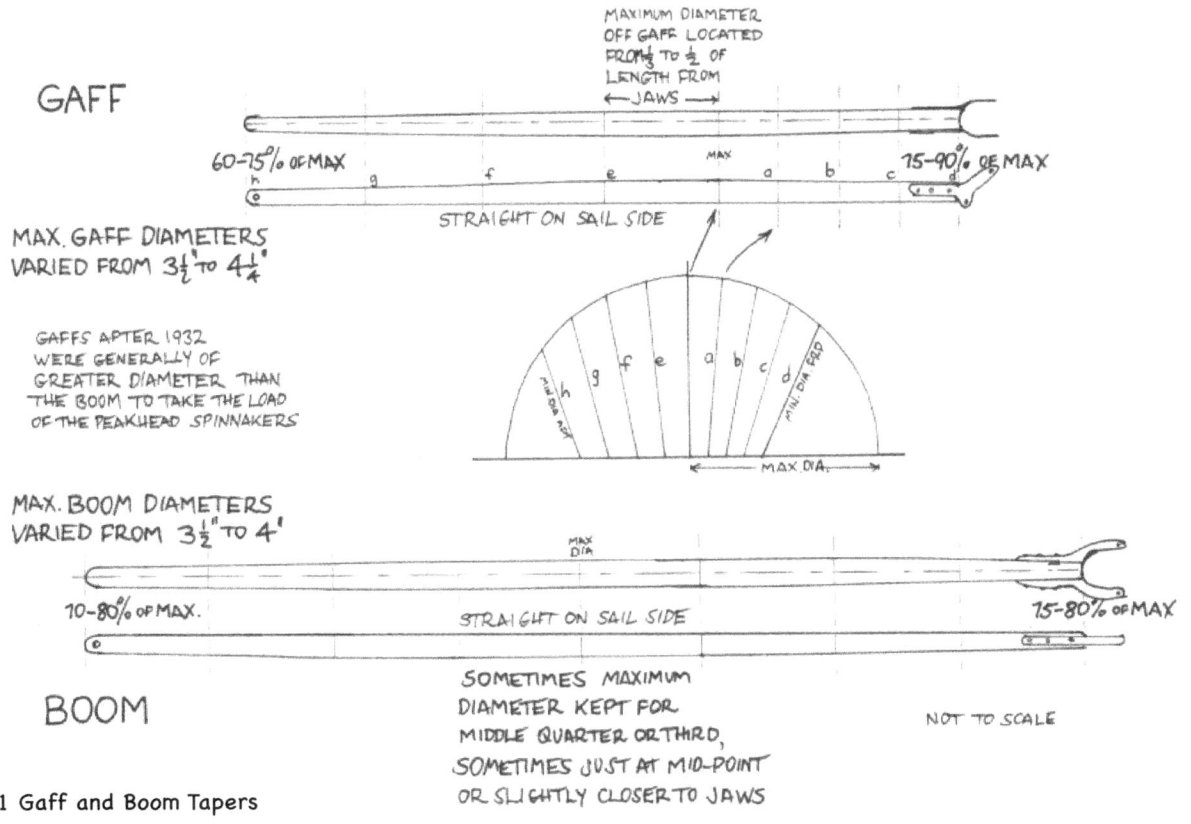

13.11 Gaff and Boom Tapers

The Boom

The boom is the next-biggest spar. The techniques for building a boom are exactly the same as for masts. The taper however is slightly different. Refer drawing 13.11. Booms were generally not tapered for the middle third of their length but were tapered towards both ends. Booms were hollow with wall thicknesses of 17 ½ to 20%. The smaller diameter means you will need new sanding blocks to match these. Many boats in the nineteenth and early twentieth centuries had a gooseneck fitting between mast and boom, but quite a few, plus nearly all later boats had Spotted Gum jaws fitted at the forward end of the boom to go around the mast. The sides of the boom were planed flat where the jaws land on each side and the jaws were riveted right through the boom with three copper rods. An eyebolt was fitted above and below (or some similar arrangement) at the base of the jaws to which the tack of the sail and the tackle for a boom downhaul were shackled. See drawing 12.4. Sometimes 3/8" brass pins were fitted vertically through the aft parts of the jaw to which halyards would be cleated. The aft end had a hole from side to side of about 1" diameter with edges eased through which the clew of the sail was lashed. The only other additions were a few low profile timber thumb cleats to locate the mainsheet blocks, and one or two wooden cleats each side towards the forward end to take the peakhead spinnaker halyards and the ringtail outhaul.

The Gaff

Pronounced "garf" by many of the older blokes, the gaff is also built in the same manner as the mast and boom. The maximum diameter was one third to halfway up the spar and they were tapered to each end as in Drawing 13.11. Wall thicknesses were 17 ½ to 20%. Don't be tempted to go thinner than this just because it is a gaff. Enormous spinnakers are set from the end of the gaff with the halyard taken aft and bending and compression forces on the gaff are considerably more than most yachts would have to take. Metal jaws were the norm, either cast bronze or fabricated galvanised steel, and after the mid-1930's aluminium, riveted through the gaff. A hole in the top end was drilled for lashing the head of the sail and lashing two blocks for the peakhead spinnaker halyards (one each side) and usually another single block for the ringtail halyard. Prior to 1932, the vast majority of Open Boats had a 3:1 tackle on the gaff in rope as illustrated in the colour drawing of *Britannia* but the sixteen-footers began to use a single halyard on a wire span on the gaff, sometimes doubled, and after 1932 this was adopted by eighteen-footers as well, as on the colour drawing of *Top Weight*. Wooden thumb cleats retained the strops or bridles to which the peak halyard was attached (see rigging details later).

Spinnaker Poles

Spinnaker poles became standardised by the 1930's to three poles of about 9' plus a "stub" of about 5'. This gave at least three different possibilities of length when assembled for at least

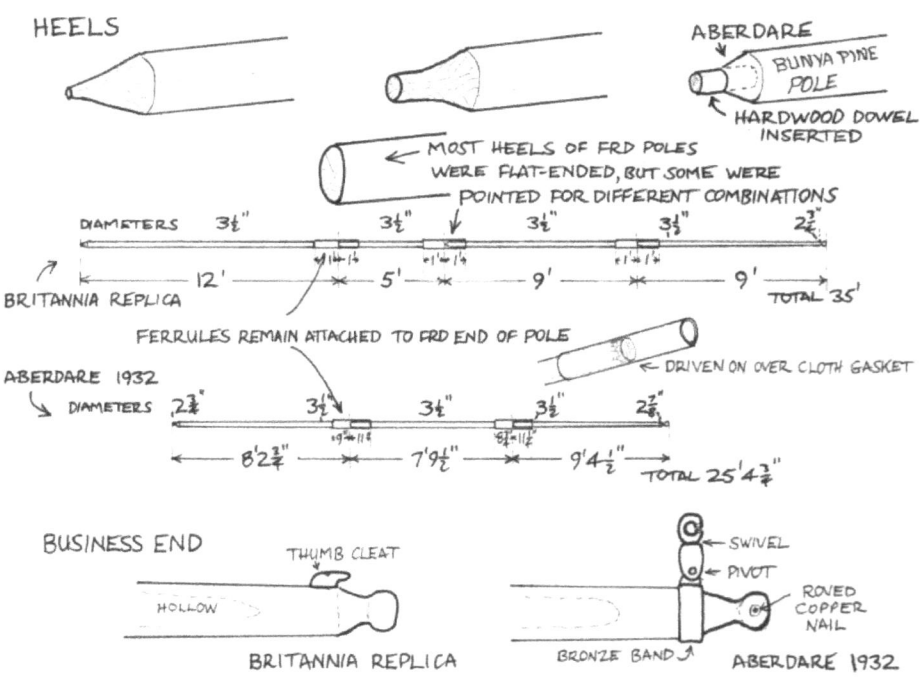

13.12 Spinnaker Poles

three different-sized spinnakers. Metal ferrules about 2' long were fixed to the forward end of all but the first, outermost pole, with about half the ferrule on the pole and the other half hollow to house the pole forward of it. *Britannia* and most earlier boats had at least one of the four poles longer (*Brit's* biggest pole is 13' including ferrule) to get reaches of up to 35'. Refer drawing 13.12.

Spinnaker poles at least after the 1920's were generally hollow (except the stub was usually solid) starting from at least 6" from the ferrule at one end and where the next ferrule would go at the other end, so about 18" from each end. All but the forward most pole and occasionally the innermost pole were generally 3 ½" to 3 5/8" in diameter and not tapered. The aft end of two poles (especially if they were of different length, giving a choice of which pole to use at the mast end) was sharpened like a pencil to fit into the rope snotter which would hold them to the mast. The aft end of the stub was left flat, as was the aft end of the forwardmost pole which was usually tapered from the maximum diameter aft to about 2 ¼" forward. The forward end was shaped into a knob over which a loop in the kicker would just fit with a thumb cleat close up to prevent the rope loop sliding aft, or the end was sometimes fitted with a metal band with an eye to which clips could be fastened.

The Bumpkin

This is the long spar that sticks out the front of all Open Boats, sometimes almost as long as the hull itself, to support the jib and the kicker to the spinnaker pole end. Lots of people are going to want to spell this **bumkin,** and they have every right to do so. Even more people are going to want to call this a **bowsprit**, and they have every right to do so. They just don't have the right to tell us to stop calling it a bumpkin. The term occurs in square-rigged ship terminology where a bumkin, bumpkin or boomkin, a spar extending from the hull either forward or aft, even from either side of the vessel. In Open Boats, the bumpkin was originally a small unstayed straight spar onto which the tack of the jib was fastened in small open boats, like that in illustration 1.5 and Brierly's painting 1.2. I believe that as Open Boats gradually developed bigger rigs, including staying the bumpkin and bending it down, they continually referred to it as the bumpkin. The oldest Open Boat sailors I knew always referred to it as the bumpkin. If you've got a yacht, you may have a bowsprit. If you've got an Open Boat, you've got a bumpkin. Judge's decision is final, no pedantic chat room correspondence will be entered into. Are we clear?

Britannia's was, I believe, one of the biggest on an 18-footer at 17' from the stem to the end cap and just under 20' overall. It was 5 ½" x 2 ½" at the stem, and tapered to 3 ½" x 2" at the cap. The taper is drawn out in the same manner as for all other spars. But the bumpkin was never round. Drawing 13.13 shows the shape that was most common, with a flat-ish but rounded upper side and beveled underside. The bevel fades out so the spar swells at the stemhead, remembering it is morticed underneath for the stemhead tenon. As boats got lighter and rigs reduced in the 1930's bumpkins were down to about 12' off the stem and 15' overall, and about 5" x 2" in maximum section.

It is important to select your timber so that the growth rings are close to parallel to either the long dimension or the short dimension. If the growth rings run diagonally the spar will want to bend more one way than the other, not that it should bend much while sailing, but it will do so while raising the mast onshore (see below).

Cut and plane the taper on the sides and the top and bottom keeping the edges at right angles, then cut the bevel under and finish off with rounding over the top. Trim the end down to fit the cap, cut the mortice to fit the stemhead, then offer it up to the boat and very carefully check that it is all exactly on the centreline before drilling for the aft bolt.

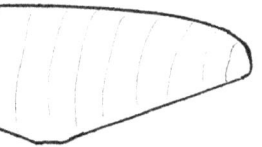

THE MAJORITY OF EIGHTEEN-FOOTER BUMPKINS (AND OTHER CLASSES) WERE IN A NARROW RANGE OF SECTIONAL SHAPES BASED ON THE ABOVE

BRITANNIA WAS A-TYPICAL IN HAVING HER BUMPKIN SECTION SHAPED AS ABOVE, WITH A HOLLOW UNDERNEATH. ANOTHER TO THE SAME SHAPE RECENTLY TURNED UP IN A SHED, SO THE BRIT WAS NOT THE ONLY ONE

13.13 Bumpkin Sections

Ringtail Spars

For details of ringtails, see the section on sails below. The two spars that fit the ringtail are not hollow. The lower spar is round and 2 to 2 ¼" diameter and tapered a little or not at all. The upper spar is always egg-shaped in section, about 2 ½'x 7/8" as in drawing 13.14. This helped the well hand to rapidly work out which was the upper spar to which he would clip the halyard. Some older spars appear not to have ever been varnished.

Jockey Pole

Before the 1930's spinnakers were rarely carried more than ¾ square, balloon jibs were used for shy runs and reaches. From sometime in the 1930's boats began to carry spinnakers on runs more shy than ¾, until the point where the brace could not hold the pole from hitting the forestay or jib and the compression bending the poles dangerously. A jockey pole came into use which had a slot and sheave in one end to hook over the brace, and a point at the other end which fitted to a rope snotter on the mast. The jockey pole was about ten feet long and acted as a spreader on the brace to enlarge the angle of the brace to the spinnaker pole end. It was about 3" in diameter, solid timber, and often not tapered at all.

Tops'l Spars

Tops'ls will be described later, but their spars consisted of a yard about 2 1/4" diameter along the greater part of the luff, and a short jackyard or club slightly narrower, solid and often not tapered, to which the sheet is attached.

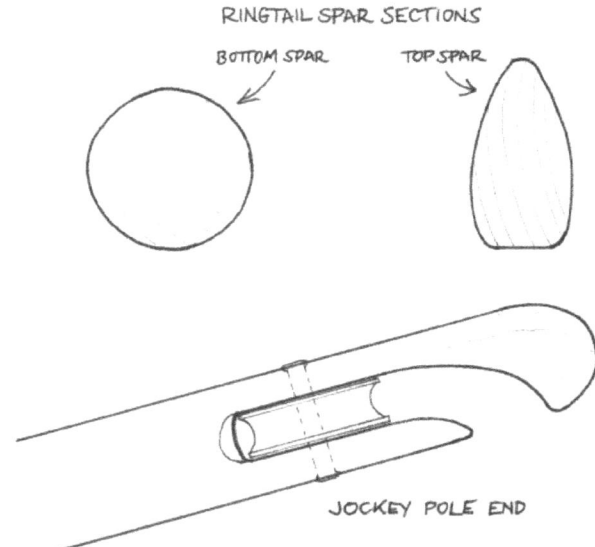

13.14 Ringtail spars and Jockey Pole

Aberdare's Spinnaker Poles

George McGoogan kept what he claimed to be Aberdare's spinnaker poles, and I ended up with them. There are three poles, all of Bunya Pine, the heel pole of 8' 2 3/4" timber length, the middle pole of 7' 9 1/2" and the outer pole of 9' 4 1/2". All were 3 1/2" in diameter, but the heel pole tapered to 2 3/4" at the heel, and the outer pole tapered to 2 7/8" at the end. Ferrules were of chromed brass 20" long, with about 9" of timber in the fixed end, jammed on over a cloth gasket.

The outer pole was seriously delaminating, so I considered that a bit of investigative surgery was warranted. With judicious use of wooden wedges I began to prise it apart from both ends. Despite more than half the length being delaminated, there was considerable resistance to separating in the areas where the glue still held on. It was clear from residues that it was an animal-type glue, but where it did hold on it did so very well, to the point where the grain split in a number of places before the glue joint let go. The splines helped strengthen it considerably. The hollow was irregular, and was cut with a spindle moulder, of two different diameters to allow for the taper, but with no hand-finishing to fair in the different sizes. The wall thickness varied from 7/8" to 1" (25-28%). The grain is oriented like a tree, outside of tree to outside of spar. The hollow is not varnished.

CHAPTER 14

Rigs and Sails

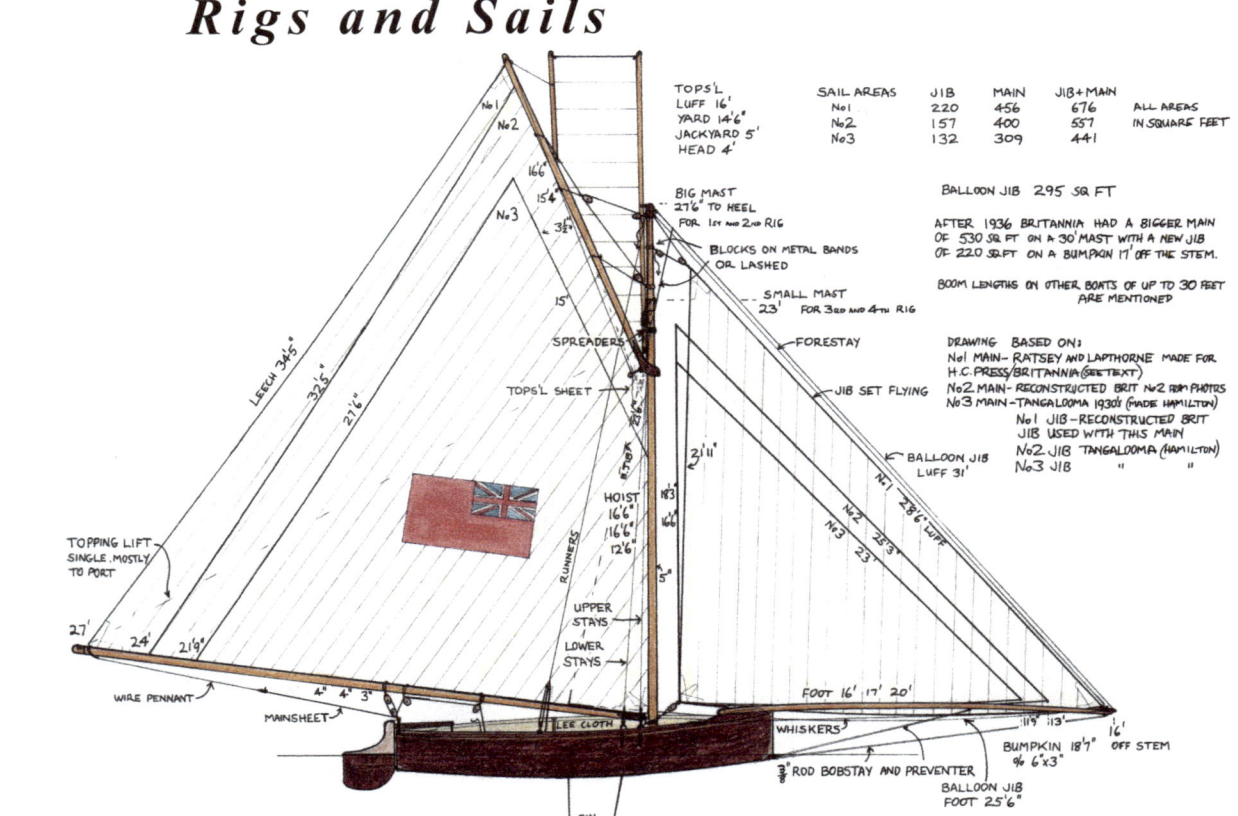

14.1 1900 - 1932 Upwind Rigs (Britannia)

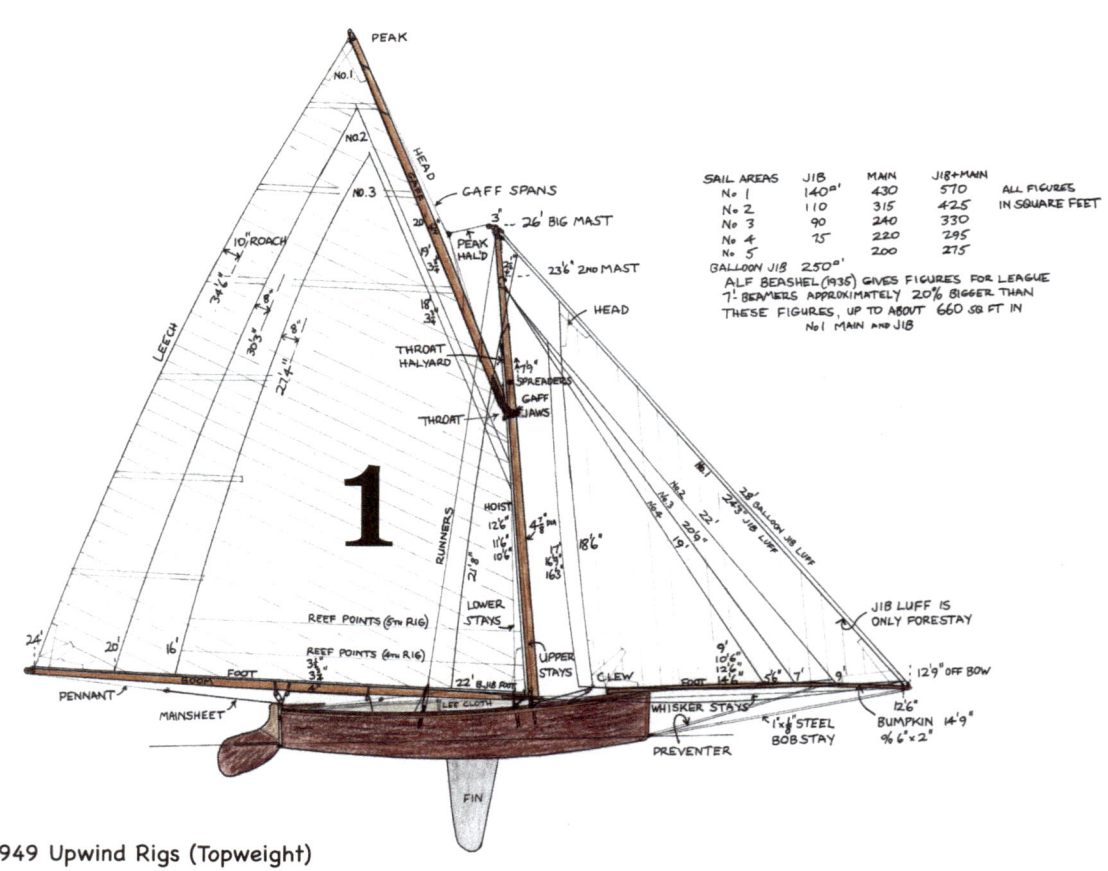

14.2 1932 - 1949 Upwind Rigs (Topweight)

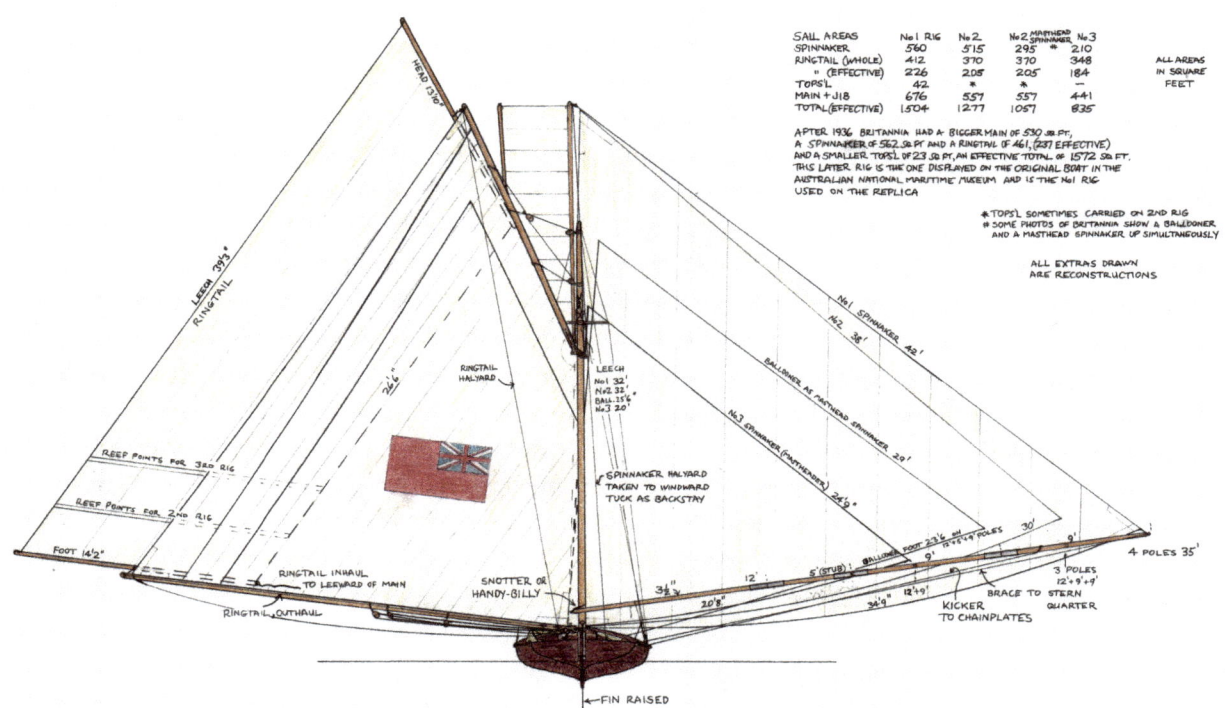

14.3 1900 –1932 Downwind Rigs (Britannia)

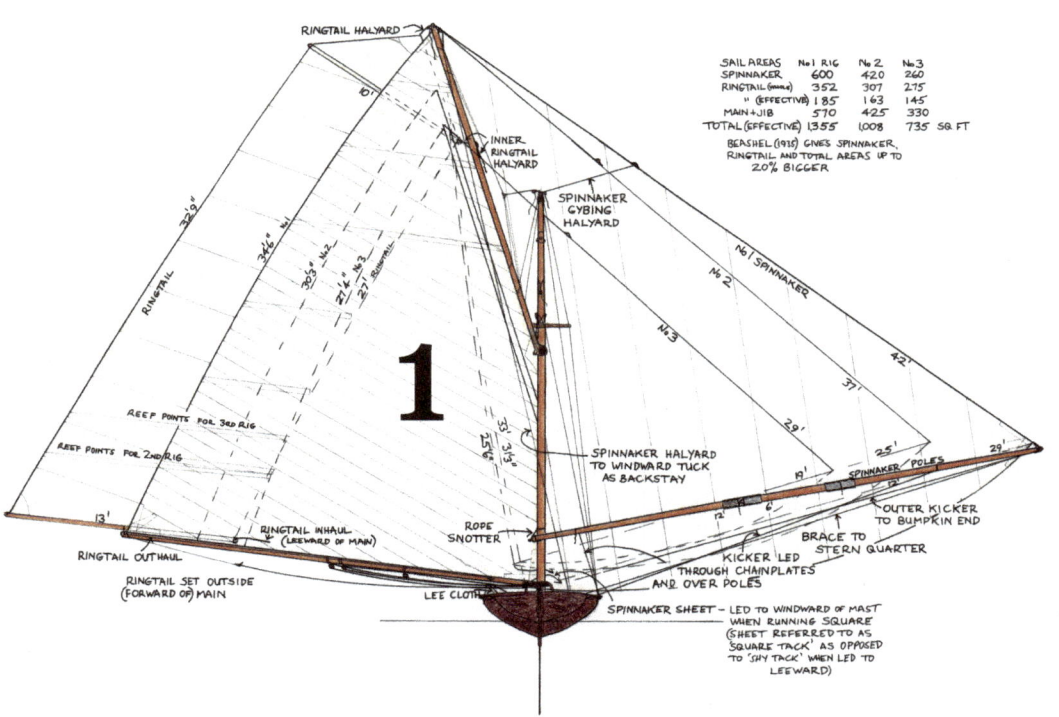

14.4 1932–1949 Downwind Rigs (Topweight)

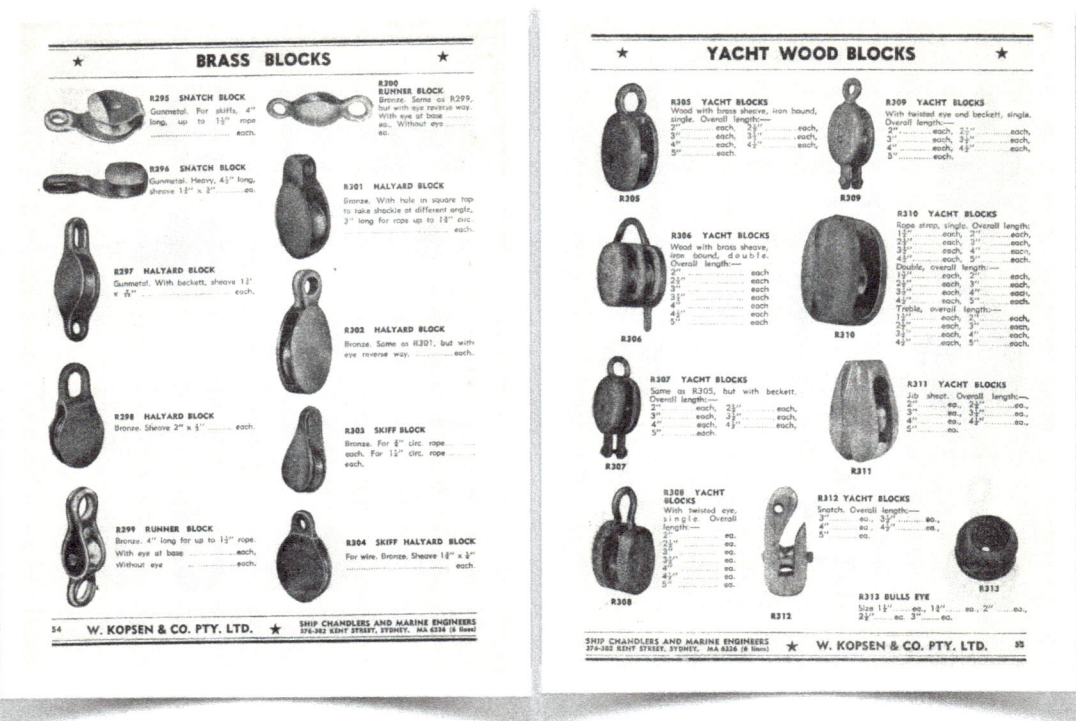

Photos 14A & 14B Pages from Kopsen Catalogue of 1948. These were typical of those used on open boats but often builders would make their own.

Splicing and Serving

Hand-splicing is a whole new field and for details I will direct you to the experts. There is plenty of information available and you will discover quite a bit of variation in methods. I hand-spliced all stays and wire halyards for the same reason I planked the boat: because that's the way it was done. It also is strong enough. New machine swages test out marginally stronger than splices but are far more susceptible to fatigue. I also spliced because I could. And I enjoy it. I learned from Neville Leishman, once Head Rigger at Garden Island Naval Dockyard, and from Brian Gale who in the 1930's used to splice for Nock and Kirby's customers. Sydney rigger Joe Henderson provided more recent tips and criticism. In fact Joe who makes occasional guest appearances on *Britannia* is as critical of my rigging work as I am of his woodwork. I still had to consult the manuals for many years, and the best one is Brion Toss's book *The Complete Rigger's Apprentice*. Brion explains the process better than I ever could. Brion came sailing on *Britannia* when in Sydney and appeared not to be too worried about the rig coming down and was too nice a bloke to criticise. All stays are best done with Liverpool splices (right-hand splices, where each strand is tucked away to the right and spirals up the same strand), but all wire halyards are safer with left-handed splices (where each strand is tucked away to the left and continues over and under each adjacent strand to the left just like in basic rope splicing) to ensure against any tendency to unwind. Left-hand splices are a little more difficult to do but the more flexible wire helps. They also finish a little shorter for the same number of tucks (at least mine do) which means a splice can be pulled closer to a turning block. All splices should be tapered, then greased with lanolin, parcelled (sports tape is best, ripped into 1" wide strips) and served. Tarred marlin is still available, but in another compromise I use a modern equivalent, tarred seine twine, about size 30, just under 2 millimetres, is best in eighteen-footer rigs, slightly smaller in smaller boats. The drawings show 6 x 7 and 6 x 19 wire lay. Using stainless wire you will have a wire instead of fibre core to contend with. Brion Toss's description of right-handed splicing has a very neat way of tucking in the core, but I have been unable to work out how to do it in left-handed splices. The simplest way is to divide up the strands of the core and add one of those little bundles to each of the six main strands when tucking. No wait, the simplest way is to cut off the core, but be aware that this weakens the splice by at least one seventh.

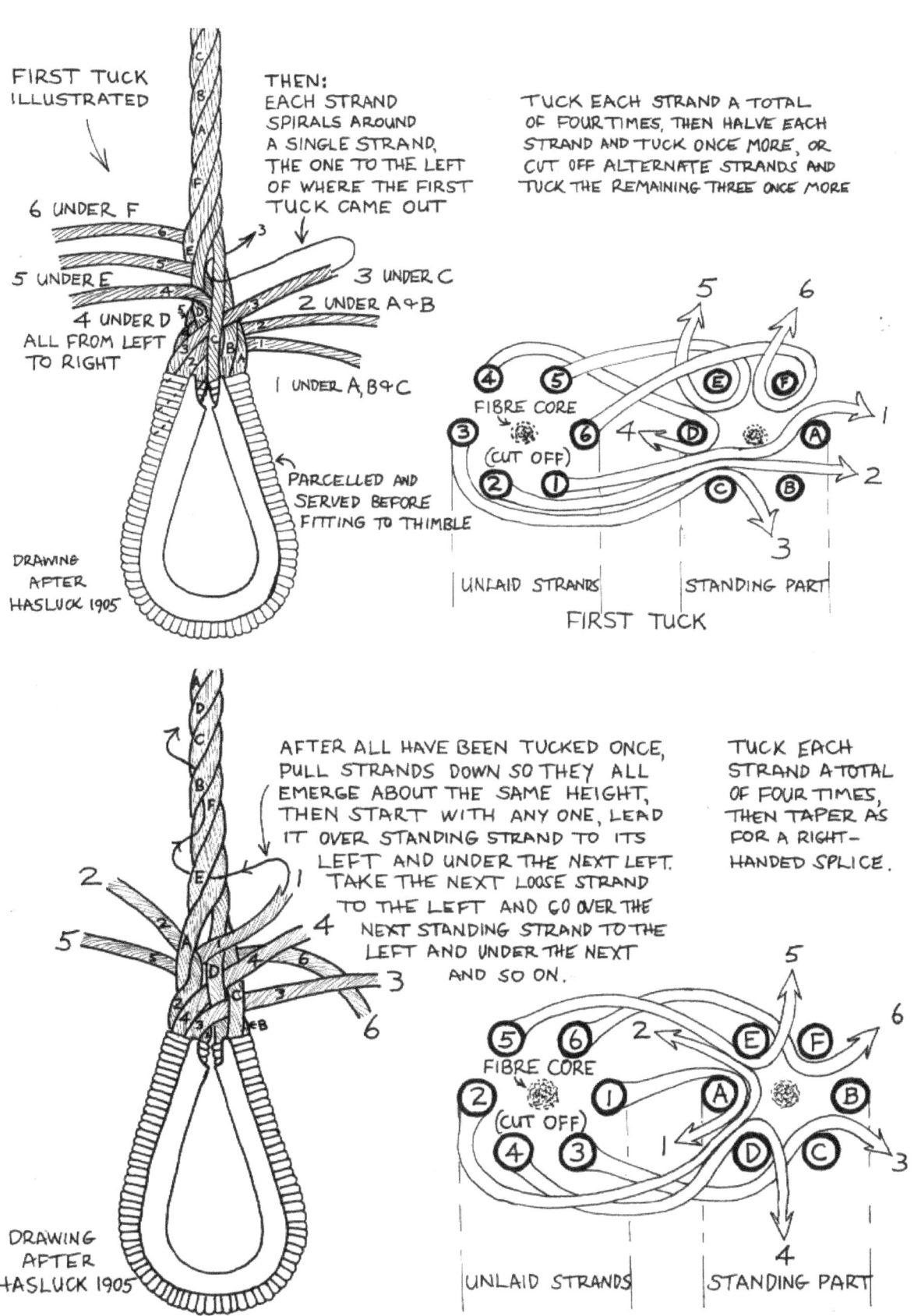

14.5 Right (top) and Left Handed (bottom) Wire Splices

Mast Stays

Masts were stayed with galvanised wire 6 x 7 with a fibre core of 5/8" to ¾" circumference, which translates today to just over 3/16" to ¼". The best available was called plough steel. As far as I am aware it is no longer available and the only galvanised wire available is not of good enough quality. The replica fleet all use stainless steel, including *Britannia*. Metric sizes are the norm in Australia today, and 4 and 5 mm wire is used in the replica fleet, but unfortunately most boats use 1 x 19 lay for stays and swage the ends which just looks wrong. *Britannia* has 5 mm stays of 7 x 7 lay, hand-spliced and served. The **upper stays** were spliced around a thimble and shackled to the mast cap in most 18 footers. Some smaller boats used spliced eyes looped over the masthead and supported with thumb cleats. The lower ends were always spliced around a thimble which was lashed to the open eyes of the chainplates with lanyards of ¼" diameter as in drawing 14.6.

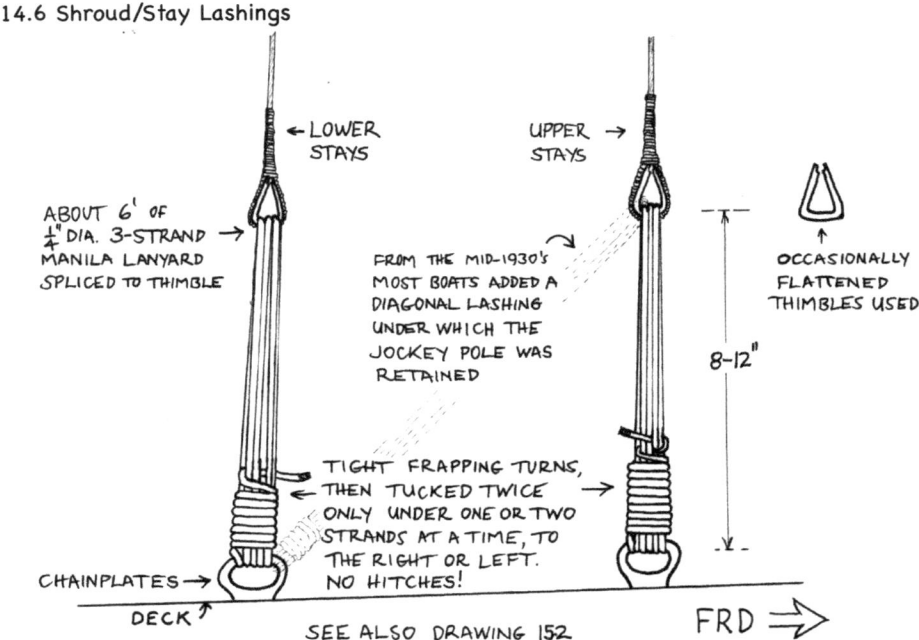

14.6 Shroud/Stay Lashings

The stay is parcelled and served before being spliced around an oversized thimble- oversized so there is plenty of room for multiple turns of the lanyard. Occasionally special lanyard thimbles were available with flattened bottoms which meant the lanyards were less likely to bind on each other when hauling taut. The uppers lead to the forwardmost of two chainplates each side, either dead in line with the mast or just aft of it, always over spreaders in 18-footers (but occasionally spreaders are not seen in some other classes such as the 22's and the 10-footers). The **lower stays** were generally fitted over the mast in spliced eyes, and supported with chocks or large thumb cleats just above the spreaders such that the spreaders fitted through the loops as in drawing 14.7, and lashed to the aftermost of the two chainplates.

Uppers aft or forward?

Traditionally on gaff rigs the upper stays go to chainplates in line with the mast athwartships or close behind, and the lowers go to chainplates

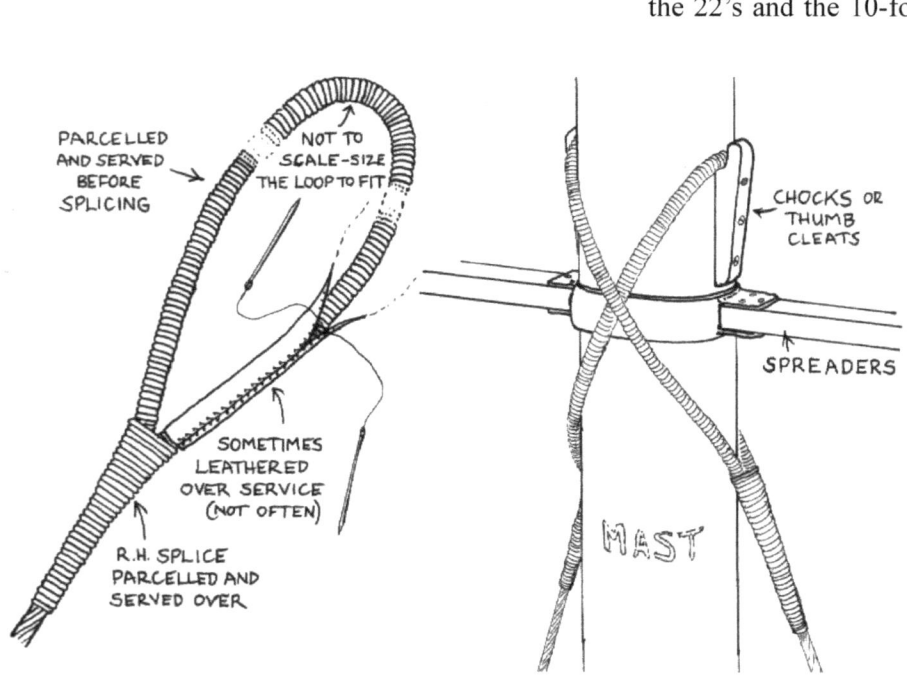

14.7 Eye Splices for Lower Stays

14.8 Mast Caps

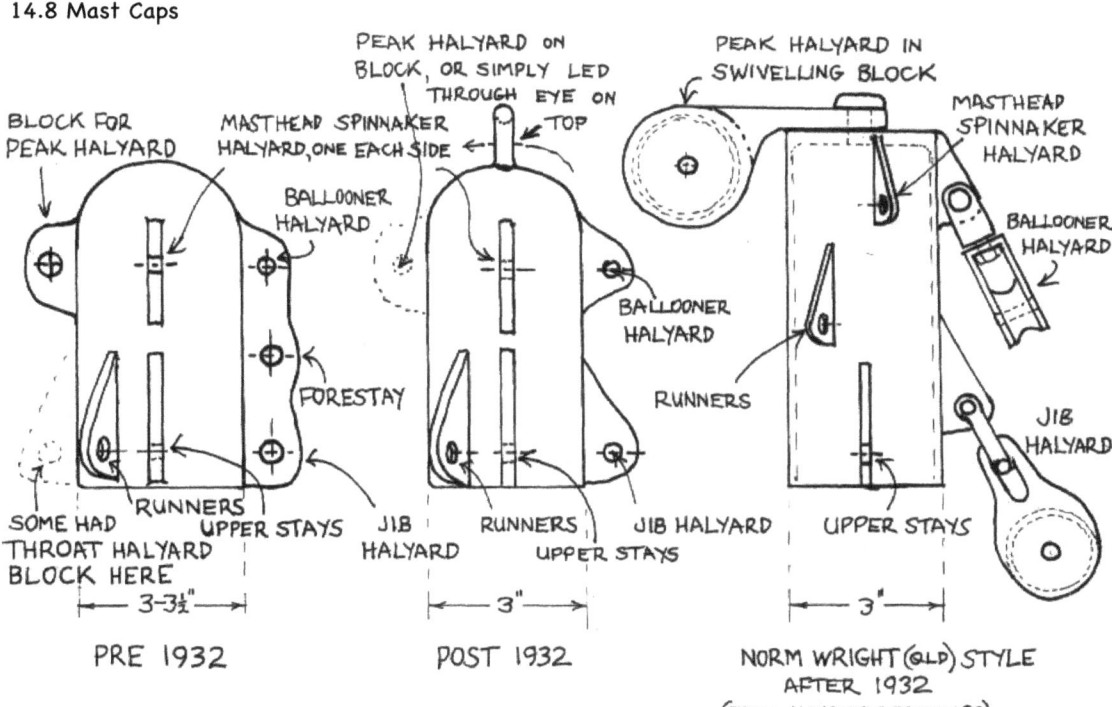

set a little further aft. Riggers familiar with gaff rig still advise this. In fact those with a mathematical bent tell us that the loads on the lowers are greater and recommend increasing the wire size, which seems counter-intuitive. There is huge load from the gaff jaws pushing the mast forward and the lowers led to the aft chainplates resist this. However, some of the older sailors in the replica fleet remember the uppers being led to the aft chainplates and the lowers forward. I am not sure that this is not a case of modified memory (see box) and I would rate this as **doubtful.** I am still studying photographs and the determining factor is that if the spreaders are in line athwartships, the uppers must be forward (alongside the mast) and so far all of the spreaders on pre-1950 boats appear to be in line. Most of the replica fleet rig with uppers aft reasoning that they can get better jib luff tension when setting-up by hauling the mast aft with the runners and then tightening the uppers aft (their spreaders are swept back). Their masts do not appear to bend forward at the gaff jaws. There have been a number of mast failures in the fleet over a decade and a half of regular racing, some in too-light wooden masts (not mine) but most in the aluminium sections that most of the fleet use, but any contribution to the failure by leading lowers forward has not been determined. So the jury is still out, but I would recommend that you stay on the side of authenticity and engineering theory if you want your mast to last longer.

The forestay has a thimble spliced at each end and is shackled to a tang on the lower part of the mast cap. The lower thimble is oversize and a lanyard is spliced to it for lashing to the bumpkin cap. From the early 1930's most boats deleted the forestay and the mast was only supported by the wire luff of the jib. The jib was dropped when gybing and the poles were swung across, then the jib was raised again.

Running backstays or simply runners are of similar wire and are also shackled to the mast cap (or looped), and terminate in an eye 2 to 3 feet above the deck. A 3 to 1 tackle (occasionally 4 to 1 tackles can be seen, but are rare) is shackled to the thimble, and shackled to an angled chainplate just aft of the mid thwart. Boats varied in the way the runner tackle was belayed when hauled on. Some had horn cleats on deck, some had belaying pins on the thwart close to the coamings, others led them through a hole in the deck across to a cleat (usually a jam cleat) on the middle of the thwart. Many of the replica boats use this system, but I can find no evidence that any boats before 1950 used it, nor any evidence that they did not. It is one of those areas I will label **doubtful.**

> **Are you sure they had those at that stage?**
>
> *As I noted earlier, there were quite a few guys still about in the 1990's when the Australian Historical Sailing Skiff Association got underway who had sailed in these boats in the 1930's and 1940's. There still are a few, though less of them. Many of them had very clear memories of how the boats were rigged and sailed. However, most of them continued to sail into the 1950's and 1960's in a period of relatively rapid change in the boats. I contend that many of their memories have been modified by these later experiences, in other words they can't be sure that certain things were used before or after 1950, which is the cutoff date for the AHSSA because after that gaff rigs began to be replaced by Bermudan, and for the purposes of this book, the last seam-batten boats were built in the early 1950's. The man who led me to this belief was Brian Gale. Rated by several people as the best for'd hand in the late 1930's, Brian continued to race 18's in the early war years as an Air Force officer at the Rose Bay flying boat base. After the war he moved to a farm on the Darling Downs in Queensland and commuted down to Brisbane every weekend to sail 18's on the Brisbane River for several years. The travelling became a bit onerous and in 1949 or 1950 he stopped sailing 18's (but kept sailing Sharpies and other boats on inland lakes). He had sailed on a lot of different boats, and had a terrific memory for details, and because he stopped sailing 18's just at our cut-off point, he was like a time capsule as his memory was not modified by later developments. I relied on him for judgments on many questions of gear and rigging and sailing. Leanne Gould recorded and transcribed a long interview with Brian about sailing 18's. Brian's information is one of the main sources for comments on particular aspects of 18 footer sailing to stack up against other opinions that I will refer to as **Doubtful,** or occasionally **Wrong***

Bumpkin Stays

Whisker stays are of the same wire as the mast stays or one size smaller (1/2" circumference, now 3/16" or 4mm diameter), are shackled to the bumpkin cap and have oversized thimbles at the aft end with ¼' 3-strand lanyards attached to lash them to chainplates on top of the sponsons forward of the mast, about 4' aft of the stem. The **bobstay** which connects the bumpkin cap to the stem heel fitting, and the **preventer** which connects the bumpkin just over halfway out from the stem to the stem heel were generally also made from wire. However the original *Britannia* and some other boats from evidence in photos used 3/8" rod here, with forged fork ends. By the 1930's most boats were using steel flat bar of 1" x 1/8" for both these stays. The preventer was fastened to a fitting bolted under the bumpkin, or if of wire, often looped over in a spliced and served eye supported by a thumb cleat.

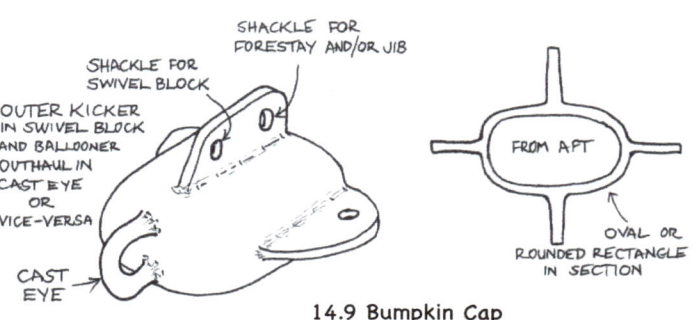

14.9 Bumpkin Cap

Halyards

Most Open Boat halyards were made from flexible wire by at least the 1920's, but the exact period when wire came into use has not yet been discovered.

Main: the **peak** halyard pulled the gaff in towards the mast. Before about 1930 most eighteens had a multi-part tackle as drawn in Drawing 14.1 and this was always of 3-strand manila of about 1 ½" circumference (1/2" diameter). The fall led down the Port side of the mast and was belayed usually to the closest belaying pin to the mast on the thwart. Because the

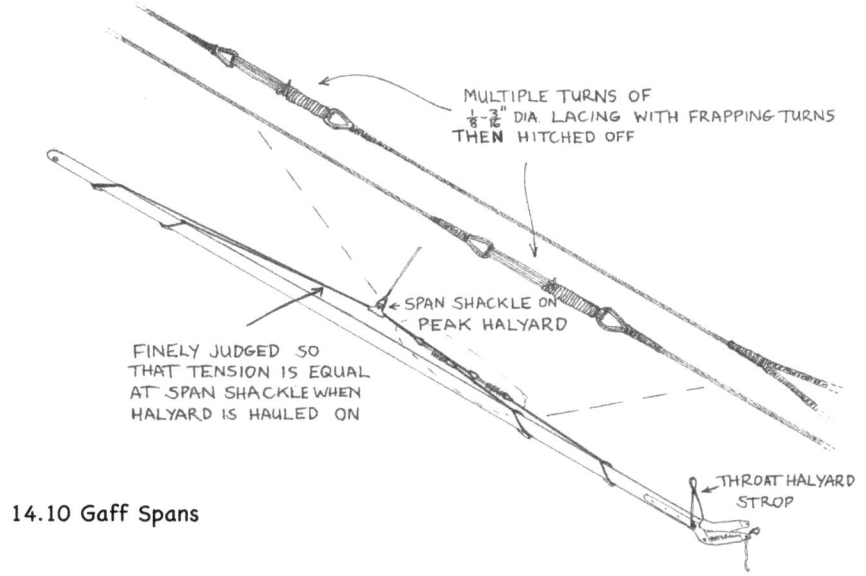

14.10 Gaff Spans

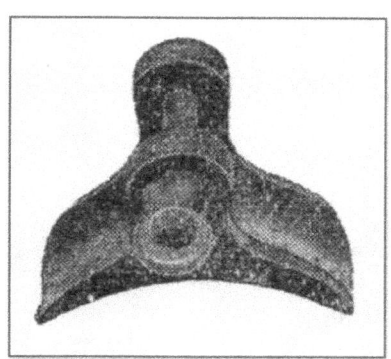

Photo 14C Span Shackle or Bridle Traveller, from Kopsen Catalogue 1948.

masthead was usually only level with about halfway out on the gaff, or even less, this tackle featured a heap of downward force which could only be resisted by a strong throat halyard tackle. From an early stage, before the First World War in fact 16-footers had carried higher peaked rigs, and they used taut wire gaff spans, usually two, attached to a wire halyard via a span shackle (see drawing 14.10 and photo 14C). This first appeared on an 18-footer about 1922 in a photograph of *Desdemona* but remained rare in the 1920's but was the general rule by 1933. This wire, usually 5/8" circumference (now 5mm diameter) of 6 x 19 lay (now 7 x 19) for flexibility was shackled to a block with a becket, with the rope led through the throat of the block and hauled on one to one at first. When more power was need a loop was pulled out of the throat between the becket and the throat, the loop being passed under a belaying pin, and the resulting purchase was 3 to 1, as illustrated in drawing 14.11. The length of the wire has to be judged finely as the spar must be able to come down close to the deck but is limited by the rope block hitting the wire block aloft, but it cannot be too long as there needs to be room to use the rope tackle when the halyard is hauled tight. The **throat** halyard was of the same construction, from an earlier but indeterminate date. Use of wire here would have been a great boon as the downward force of the old-style gaff halyard tackle would have put a lot of stretch and strain on a rope halyard. The throat halyard was usually belayed to the Starboard inner belaying pin.

14.11 Halyard Tackle

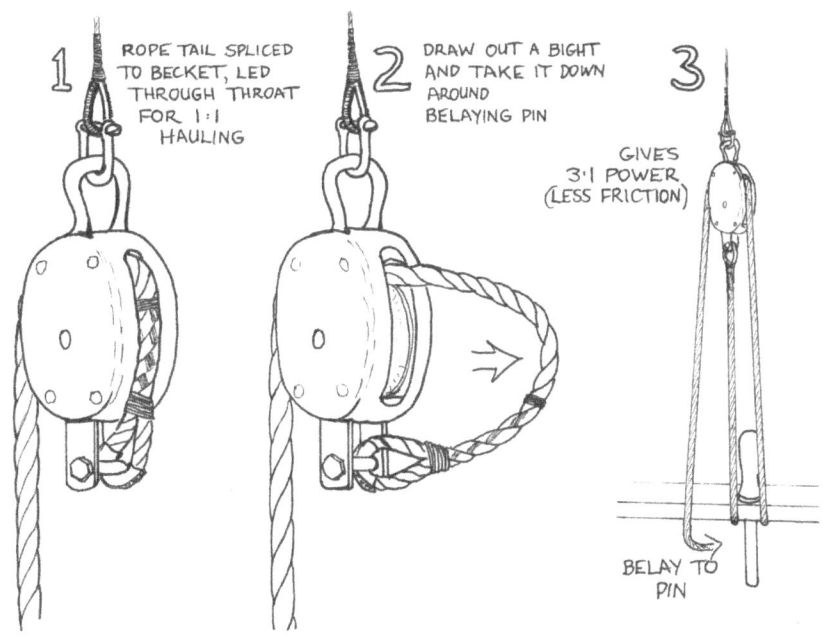

The **jib halyard** was almost always a 2 to 1 tackle as in Drawing 14.1 early on, of 1¼" or 1½" circumference 3-strand manila rope, but most boats after about 1932 went to single part wire of 5/8" circumference 6 x 19 wire, with a rope tail in a similar configuration to the throat and peak halyard tackles.

Spinnaker halyards were provided at the masthead and

the peak of the gaff. In both cases there was a halyard each side, shackled either side of the masthead and lashed either side of the gaff peak. The spinnaker was always attached to the windward halyard and the hauling part was belayed at the tuck as a backstay (not always with the masthead spinnaker, the runners take the main load of the masthead; some boats rigged their masthead halyard with a single part down each side). Spinnaker halyards were almost always of cotton three-strand rope of 1" circumference (now 5/16" or 8 mm diameter). I found, and you may find, some 3-strand matt white polyester that looks exactly like cotton but my suppliers have recently discontinued this.

The **Ballooner halyard** is double-ended, shackled centrally uppermost on the mast cap with a fall coming down each side, of the same size as the spinnaker halyards or one size bigger.

The **Brace** was a three strand manila rope of 1¼" or 1½" circumference (10 or 12mm diameter, 7/16" or ½") which had a spliced eye in one end which the for'd hand looped over the knob at the end of the first pole. It led back to a turning block or large metal or wood thumb cleat on the stern quarter and was belayed to a cleat usually on the swinging-out rail, or sometimes taken forward to the mid thwart.

The **Kicker** or **Kicking Strap** was a rope designed to keep the pole from skying. Before the 1930's it was generally attached with a served and/or leathered eye near the aft end of the first (outermost) pole and led into the boat through the eye of the forward chainplate to be belayed on the forward thwart, and later sometimes led through the whisker stay eye, back over the pole and down to the belaying pin on the thwart. As boats began to carry their spinnakers more shy, a forward kicker was attached to the end of the pole and led through either a block on top of the bumpkin cap forward of the forestay and jib or through a metal eye on the front of the cap, back to the forward thwart. The original inner kicker still shows up in photographs right up until 1949. Kickers were originally manila, usually of 1 ½" circumference (1/2" or 12mm diameter). Most of the replica fleet (including *Britannia*) use 12mm pre-stretched braided polyester, and use only a bumpkin-end kicker.

A boom **topping lift** appears in all photos before about the mid 1930's, attached to the boom end, leading through a block just under the spreaders and down to the base of the mast, usually to Port. It was used mostly to cant up the boom to de-power the mainsail when waiting at Clark Island for the race to start. It seems to have been discontinued at some time in the 1930's. The boom could still be canted up by attaching a masthead spinnaker halyard to the ringtail outhaul.

There was no **spinnaker topping lift used** on Open Boats, the wire luff of the asymmetric spinnaker was the only support for the spinnaker poles.

The ringtail was sometimes hauled up by the leeward spinnaker halyard, especially on the ten-footers. But more often on the eighteen-footers a separate **ringtail halyard** of similar construction to the spinnaker halyards ran through a block lashed to the front of the peak of the gaff and down each side of the main. Once ringtails were made with triangular heads, a second halyard attached to the forward end of the upper ringtail spar and led through a block on the gaff in a position to draw the set sail in close to the gaff was sometimes used. I say sometimes because Alf Beashel has them in his drawings, Cliff Monkhouse insisted that they all used a second halyard, while Brian Gale was sure that he never did. I'd say some boats did and some boats didn't! Most of the replica fleet that use triangular-headed ringtails find that they make setting the ringtail easier. A manila **ringtail outhaul** of ¾" circumference (1/4 ", 6mm diameter) was led through the lashing hole in the end of the boom, or sometimes through the mainsail clew cringle, along each side of the boom, belayed to a wooden cleat on the windward side of the boom well forward. An inhaul of similar size was attached to the inboard end of the lower ringtail spar and belayed to the leeward cleat on the boom.

On boats with boom jaws rather than a gooseneck, which is most of them, a small-block **boom downhaul** tackle tautened the mainsail luff by hauling the boom down toward the thwart.

The ballooner was hauled out to the bumpkin end by a **ballooner outhaul** which led either through a block shackled to the bumpkin cap or through a metal eye on the front of the cap (the forward kicker would be through one of these, the ballooner outhaul through the other). Both ends were attached to each other so that the line was endless and the ballooner tack could be brought back into the boat. It was belayed when in use to the forward thwart.

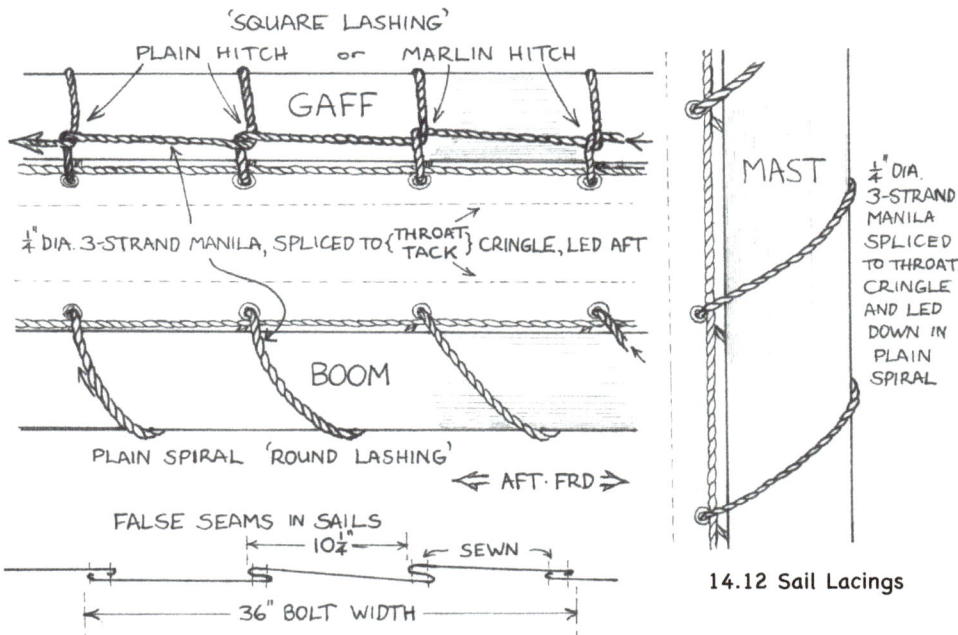

14.12 Sail Lacings

Mainsails

Mainsails were always cut from japara cotton with a weight of about 9 ounces per square yard. The best cotton was imported from Egypt. Before the 1930's mainsails were always cut with vertical panels, the cloths parallel to the leech and roped along the head, luff (or hoist- the part against the mast) and the foot. The cloth generally came in bolts 36" wide, and the sails were sewn with two false seams so that each panel ended up 10¼" wide. This fact has proven very useful in estimating sail sizes from photographs. Corners had brass cringles attached by hemp rope spliced into the bolt rope or fitted through strong reinforcing patches. Mains were laced to the gaff with hitched loops, either plain hitching or marlin hitching (see drawing 14.12), starting at the throat end (the starting end was generally spliced into the throat cringle). They were laced to the boom with simple spiral loops, starting at the jaws. The luff (hoist section) was laced in simple spiral fashion also starting from the throat cringle to which it was spliced. The lacing was usually ¾"circumference 3-strand manila (1/4" diameter, 6 mm).

Battens were rare in vertical-cut sails. They are occasionally seen in photos of 24 and 22-footers, but are rare in photos of 18-footers. Battens begin to appear in general at the same time as sails began to be cut with the cloths square to the leech, sometimes referred to as horizontal cut. Such sails had been used on 16-footers since the early 1900's. Battens were made from either 2" x ¼" wood (Silver Ash was the first choice) or 1¼" x 3/8" cane. Early battens were short, but by the mid thirties generally the top three battens were full,

Photos 14D & 14E Details of Cotton Sail Corners.

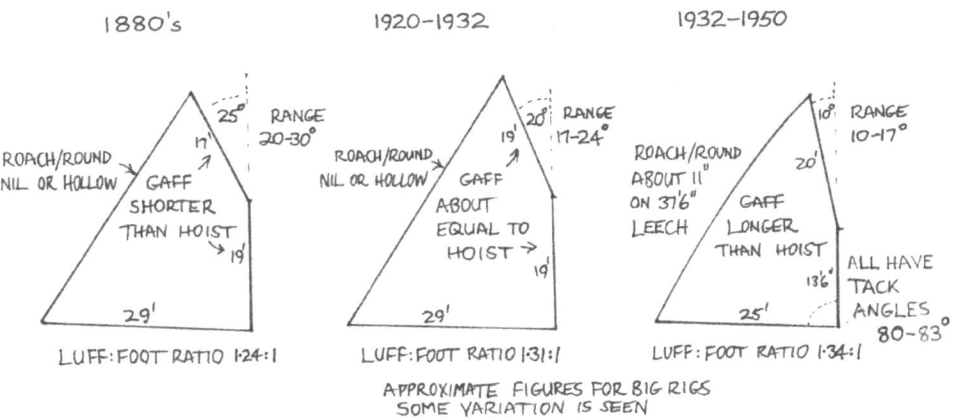

14.13 Changing gaff lengths, angles and aspect ratios.

that is, carried through from the leech to the boltrope against the gaff. The sixteen-footers used vertical-cut sails and full battens from before the First World War, and even had a full batten right across to the throat of the gaff, but there is no clear picture of any eighteen having this batten until at least 1949. Sailmakers differed on the best angle for the battens, photographs show battens between horizontal and square with the leech (in line with the seams). Battens allowed leeches to have a bit of round built in. The amount is up to about 10" in 34'6" of a mid-1930's sail to about 1' in 29'4" in a 1950 six-foot beamer sail.

Gaffs steadily peaked higher from the 1880's to the 1950's. Some of the 24's appear to have gaff angles (between the gaff and the mast) of about 25 degrees (180-25= 155 degree angle of sail at throat), which is still probably a smaller angle than most yachts of the time. By the boom period of the 1920's, gaff angles were about 15 to 17 degrees, and by the 1930's were down to a minimum of about 10 degrees, and the six-foot beam boats of 1950 were down to 7½ degrees. Along with the gaffs peaking, they also got longer relative to the hoist. In the nineteenth century, the hoist was always longer than the gaff. Between 1900 and 1932 they were just either side of even, but from 1932 on gaffs began to lengthen and were always longer than the hoist. Also over the same period the sails developed a higher aspect ratio, that is the luff height (hoist plus gaff) to foot ratio went from about 1.24 to 1 (foot c.80% of height) before 1932 to about 1.31 (76%) during the 1930's and early 1940's to about 1.34 (c.75%) by 1950. Reef points are often seen on 19th century mainsails, but during the period 1900 to 1932 they are rare. I assume this is because the racing had become so competitive that most boats had several separate rigs, a reefed sail is not as efficient as one designed to the size, and hard sailing with a reefed sail could distort the sail cloth.

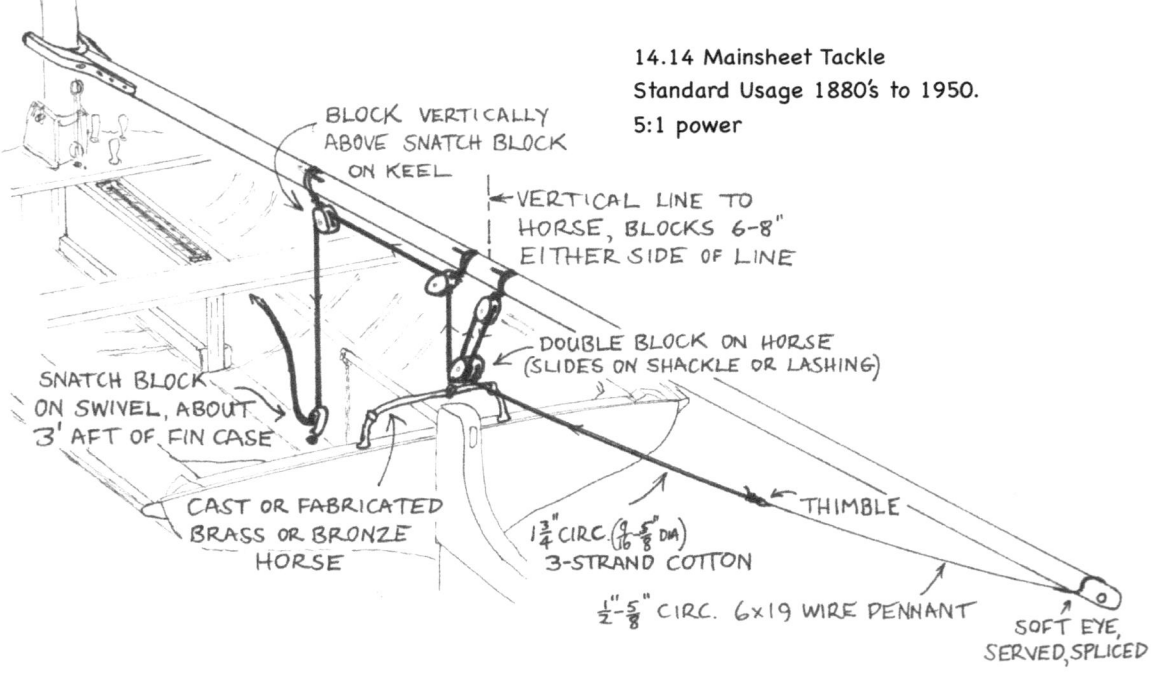

14.14 Mainsheet Tackle
Standard Usage 1880's to 1950.
5:1 power

Jibs

Jibs were wire-luffed and set flying, shackled to the back of the bumpkin cap and hauled up with a halyard to the masthead or occasionally just below it. After about 1932 the forestay was abandoned and the jib luff took the entire load. They were cut from japara cotton about the same weight as the main, with the cloths parallel to the leech, with false seams sewn in so the panel widths were again 10¼", and were roped along the foot. An occasional mitre-cut jib is seen, the earliest photo I have seen was *Desdemona* in 1922, but they were rare. Except for some later reaching jibs, the leech was entirely forward of the mast and usually close to parallel to it.

All the different jibs for the boat were rigged so that the clew ended up in the same fore and aft position and height, about a foot forward of the mast (some in-and-out adjustment was allowed for). Most boats didn't have as many bumpkins as jibs, so smaller jibs were often lashed to the bumpkin the right distance out to balance the main, with a few turns taken to the bumpkin cap to stop the jib from sliding back towards the stem. Generally this lashing is also taken around the bobstay though the contribution in engineering terms is disputable.

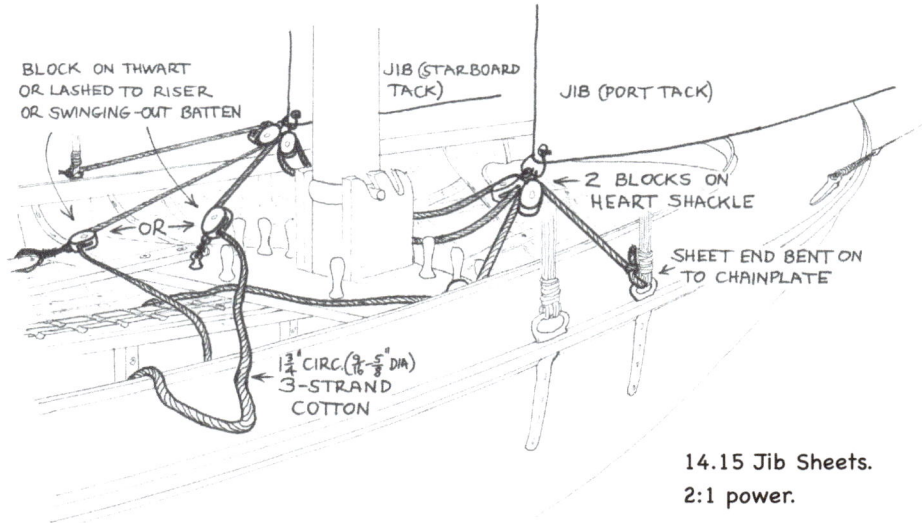

14.15 Jib Sheets. 2:1 power.

Jibs were invariably sheeted in two parts, generally starting at the forward chainplate, leading through one of a pair of blocks shackled (usually with a heart shackle) to the clew and back through a block which was either lashed to the chainplates if needed outboard on big rigs or shackled to an eye in the forward thwart when needed inboard on smaller rigs. The sheets were the same cotton as the mainsheet.

All other sails were referred to as Extras:

Spinnaker

As outlined below, before spinnakers were invented the 24 and 22-footers and the early 18-footers carried squaresails downwind. The first photograph of a spinnaker on an eighteen-footer dates to 1890, but squaresails were still used for a few more years but are not seen after 1899. Some skippers (and/or sailmakers) were reluctant to get rid of the yard, so during the 1890's there are numerous photos of spinnakers with yards at the top which vary from the biggest at about 10' to the more common curved yard of about 3 to 4'. The last known photo is from 1913. Most photos show the early spinnakers set from the masthead, but there is a photo of the Brisbane *Britannia*

Photo 14F Bronze spinnaker clips.

(not the same boat) carrying a spinnaker from the peak of the tops'l in 1896 (Elliott 2012 p26) and they appear regularly after 1899, some with yards, some without.

Whether set from the tops'l peak, the gaff peak or the masthead, there is a halyard through a block on each side. The spinnaker is hauled up with the halyard on the windward side, the forward part being led forward of the spreaders before clipping on, and the aft part taken back to the tuck and pinned to the tuck rail on the windward side as a backstay. Setting sequence is described in the Sailing section. Spinnaker halyards and sheets were originally tied on with bowlines, but at some indeterminate but early stage cast bronze flag halyard clips began to be used. Brian Gale was still tying them on in the late 1930's but I believe he was the exception. In the 1930's boats began to gybe their spinnakers (previously they would have to drop the spinnaker at the gybe mark, usually Shark Island and after gybing the main would haul up another spinnaker, or more usually a ballooner for the next leg). This meant dropping the jib (as mentioned before there was no separate forestay by this time) and swinging the poles across. Some spinnakers of this period were fitted with a cringle on the luff just lower than the masthead with a halyard attached from the masthead to take the weight of the poles off the gaff while gybing. None of the replica boats have this feature, their gaffs still take the weight of the poles while gybing.

Spinnakers were cut from light japara cotton in wide panels parallel to the luff which was roped, or occasionally wired (especially in the 16 footers). They were cut flat and were asymmetrical. Jack Hamilton, one of the last sailmakers trained in making cotton sails told me that some shape was cut into spinnakers by tapering the panels, but by no more than a few inches in the 36" cloth.

Balloon Jibs

Generally referred to as ballooners, these were the original asymmetric spinnakers, set from the masthead to the end of the bumpkin and sheeted back to the stern quarter. Cut from slightly lighter cloth than the main and jib, in wider panels of just under 18" running parallel with the leech (36" cloth with one false seam), ballooners were cut fairly full (we have no original figures) and had a rope luff. They were used when the wind was between ¾ and just ahead of abeam and the working jib was hauled down. In lighter conditions the ballooner also often replaced the jib downwind when a spinnaker was carried in an attempt to use every puff, but Alf Beashel admitted that a ballooner hardly ever filled when too square. In the mid-1930's some League boats began to carry a reaching jib which was flatter than a ballooner and a bit shorter on leech and foot and was used when the breeze was on the beam or forward of it. By this time boats were carrying their spinnakers even when the wind was on the beam, utilising a jockey pole. In the late nineteenth century there are reports of balloon jibs being poled out, and others that they set one to windward and sheeted it free of the bumpkin just like a more modern spinnaker.

The Ringtail

The ringtail is a light weather downwind sail which came from square rigged sailing ship technology. In light weather square riggers would send out studding-sails or stuns'ls on the ends of the square yards, and a ringtail on the fore and aft mizzen. These were still in common use in the last decades of the 19th century and were a natural sail to use in the unrestricted Open Boats and were also used on yachts on occasions. They were rigged as in the drawings, hauled up with a halyard at the peak of the gaff (with a fall each side of the main or sometimes with the leeward spinnaker halyard (which means they have to be hauled up from the leeward side), attached to the centre of the top spar (or the head of the triangle in later ringtails), and hauled out along the boom with an outhaul led through the hole in the end of the boom or the clew cringle, attached to the middle of the lower spar, and tautened back with an inhaul attached to the forward end of the lower spar. Most boats had a ringtail with reef points so it could set on at least their two biggest rigs, but some boats had two ringtails for their three rigs. They were cut from light weight japara of similar weight to the spinnakers, with wide cloths run vertically (later some were cut horizontally) and cut quite flat.

The ringtail provides a lot of extra power downwind, and also serves to balance the helm which with a big spinnaker as the only extra sometimes gives strong lee helm. It can be carried to ¾ or a bit further. When the breeze becomes shy enough to have airflow from forward to aft on the

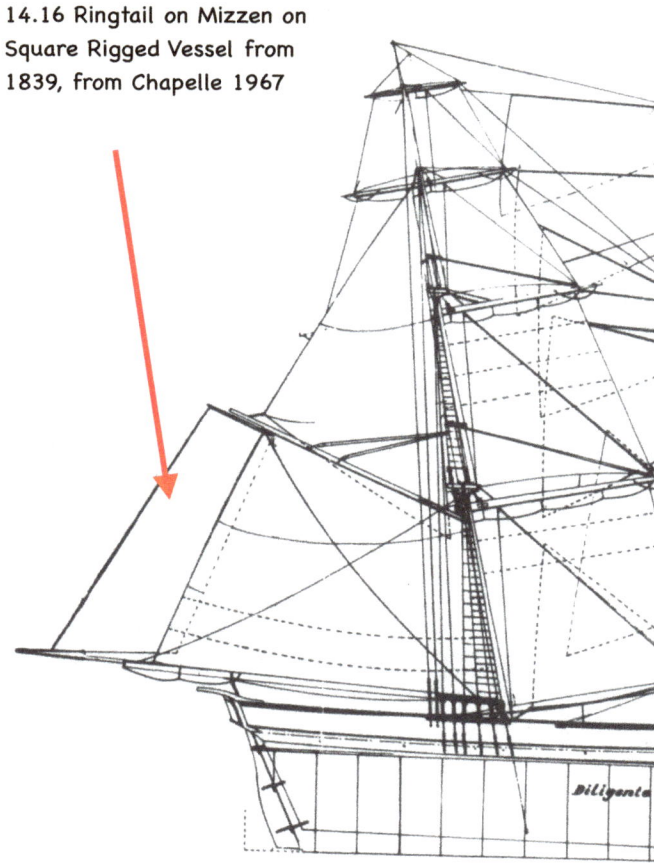

14.16 Ringtail on Mizzen on Square Rigged Vessel from 1839, from Chapelle 1967

lee side of the sail it cannot fill and provides only drag.

From the early 1930's ringtail heads changed shape to a triangle as in the drawings (oldest known photo is from the 1930-31 season). As I mentioned earlier, Cliff Monkhouse claimed that they were always rigged with a second halyard attached to the forward end of the upper spar and all boats in the replica fleet that use triangular-headed ringtails use this, but Brian Gale insisted that he used only a central halyard, so there must have been different systems in different boats.

Some late 1940's ringtails were fitted with 2 or 3 horizontal battens, and were sometimes cut with the cloths horizontal from the late 1930's. Ringtails lasted well into the 1950's, carried on Bermudan rigs, until mainsail roaches got so large the ringtail was blanketed.

Tops'l

Up until the 1920's most eighteens carried a tops'l with their number one rig. The 24-footers and 22-footers had always carried them, and although their gaffs were peaked higher than most yachts of the time there was still plenty of sail area in the tops'l to provide plenty of drive in light breezes. Even the ten foot and fourteen foot dinghies and the sixteen foot skiffs carried them during the nineteenth century. Eighteen-footer gaffs were peaked quite high from early on so there was no room for the magnificent large tops'ls carried on yachts of the time, or even the size of those on the 24's and 22's. The yard extends almost the full luff of the sail which was about the same length as the gaff, with a halyard from the masthead attached roughly halfway up the yard or a little lower. A short jackyard takes the sheet which turns through a block lashed towards the peak of the gaff and down through a lizard attached to the gaff jaws and down to the main thwart. The jackyard is parallel or near parallel to the yard. A downhaul is attached to the foot and is bowsed down as soon as the halyard is taut. The cloths are cut square to the luff and therefore the head is square. With luff lengths of 13-16', leech lengths (along the jackyard) of not much more than 4', and a depth between yards of 3 to 4' the total sail area was a mere 40 square feet or less. Not a great deal of help upwind. The main reason for carrying a tops'l was to have a spot from which to hang the biggest spinnaker (before spinnakers came into use in the 1890's, the head of the tops'l yard would carry the raffee downwind, see below).Two blocks lashed to the top of the yard each have a halyard, each pair leading down either side of the mainsail, and the spinnaker would be hauled up with the Starboard side halyard when the boom was out to Port (and vice-versa), led forward

The Ringtail Awards

The replica fleet at the Sydney Flying Squadron has instituted the ringtail awards to encourage their use. Every boat that sets one in a race is awarded a jug of rum and cola at the post-race results presentation. Most boats have one, but not every boat sets it in every race. The awards used to be introduced by the late local legend Graeme "Fergie" Ferguson where he explained what a ringtail is (though there was only occasionally anyone present who hadn't heard it before) always finishing with the statement that the only racing fleet in the world to carry ringtails are the Historical Skiffs of the Sydney Flying Squadron which is received with load applause. Yay us! All part of the ritual.

Photo 14G Ten-footer Commonwealth built in 1906, sailing off Balls Head in the 1920's with tops'l.
HALL COLLECTION ANMM

of the spreaders, and the tail was taken to the tuck to be cleated to the pin on the windward side as a backstay.

When the Australian Historical Sailing Skiff Association began in the early 1990's there were a number of members and others who had sailed in eighteen-footers in the 1930's and 1940's, so the way they were rigged and sailed has been communicated to us revivalists in a continuous line. But even in the 1990's there was no-one alive that had set a tops'l on an eighteen-footer. There were, and still are, plenty of people who have set, and still continue to set tops'ls on gaff-rigged yachts (including myself), but when we set a tops'l on the *Britannia* replica we had great difficulty in getting it to stand up when the weight of the poles came on when setting the big spinnaker, and this was only in 4-5 knots of breeze. Upwind the tops'l was difficult to get drawing and overall was providing more drag than lift. Seeing all our sailing on *Britannia* is in racing conditions, we haven't yet found the time to set aside to work out how it was done, but we will try again at some stage. We did regularly set a topsail on the ten-footer replica *Republic* as seen in the Photo 14H. We found we had to rig a wire

Photo 14H Replica ten-footer Republic with tops'l 1997.
TRICIA SMITH

leader, a taut wire looped over the mast at the lowers and bowsed down tight to the mast at thwart level with a rope tail. The heel of the yard was

Photo 14I Eighteen footer Aztec 1892 with tops'l, squares'l and raffee. ROBIN ELLIOTT COLLECTION

shackled to this wire and traveled up it when the topsail was hauled up, and the heel was then held close to the mast. This system is used on some yachts. Alternately a horizontal round thimble can be lashed to the heel of the yard through which the downhaul of the tops'l halyard is run to serve the same purpose. I have no evidence that it was used on eighteen-footers but it is the only traditional way I have come across that would hold the heel in against the pull of the spinnaker. There is at least one photograph that clearly shows the lower leech on a tops'l laced to the gaff which would help hold in the foot, but would mean that the tops'l would have to go up with the gaff and could not be hauled down individually. Other photos clearly show an unlaced gap between tops'l lower leech and gaff. Many do seem to be suffering from the effects of the pull of the spinnaker.

Tops'ls appear to have been made from the same weight of sail cloth as the jib and main or slightly lighter, probably because of the strain involved in linking spinnaker and gaff. Some had additional false seams and some were in wider panels. They dropped out of use by the early 1930's when crews began setting spinnakers from the peak of the gaff.

Watersails

There are a few photos of 24 and 22-footers carrying watersails, but not many on 18-footers. They are a light weather narrow sail that is hauled out under the boom, cut either like a narrow jib and rigged with the head of the jib outboard, or with a vertical batten (or two) in the middle to which the sheet was attached. We tried it once on the replica *Britannia* slinging a thin blade jib under the boom on a very light day. We found out why they were called watersails. It spent more time in the water than out of it. I would only consider it again in almost drifting conditions.

Photo 14J Underneath this main, jib, tops'l, ringtail, squaresail, raffee and watersails is the twenty-two footer *Secret*. HALL COLLECTION ANMM

Squaresails and Raffees

No original squaresails off Open Boats have survived to my knowledge, so we have only photographs to go on. Squaresails were laced to a yard of a length that would have to fit into the boat when not hauled up, so they would have to be say 17' or less in an 18 footer and 21' or less in a 22-footer and so on. They were hauled up through a block at the masthead under the jib and forestay, but nothing other than the halyard held the yard to the mast, unlike ship practice. The windward clew was attached to the end of the exact same type of multi-part poles that became used for spinnakers a little later on, used in exactly the same manner with the heel in a snotter low on the mast and a pole-end brace back to the stern quarter. The other clew was pulled down into the boat, which cocked up the windward end above horizontal, often quite a bit. There appear to be no braces attached to the ends of the yard. There are reports and one photograph *(Bulletin,* 22', Photo 3.20 p.37) of some boats lacing a bonnet, an addition to the lower edge of a squaresail.

In light conditions a raffee which was a smaller squaresail would be hauled up to the head of the tops'l and sheeted on one side to the windward end of the squaresail yard, and on the other side to the middle of the squaresail yard. There is no-one alive who has ever set one on an Open Boat, so details are a bit vague. I'd like to experiment but it all takes time and money.

Squaresails and raffees were both cut from light cloth running vertically in wide panels with no false seaming.

Above: Photo 14K Even the 10-footers carried ringtails and waters'ls   AUTHOR'S COLLECTION

Right: Photo 14L Ariel, Donnelly's first 18-footer carrying a squares'l in 1894. A raffee is slung in stops from the windward squares'l yard.
HALL COLLECTION ANMM

CHAPTER 15

Sailing

Rigging would start with the mainsail being lashed to the boom and gaff, usually set up on trestles. Often more than one size mainsail would be prepared, delaying the choice of which to use. The tack is shackled or lashed to an eye or fork at the boom jaws or gooseneck, pulled out tight along the boom, and the clew is lashed to the hole in the end of the boom as in drawing 15.1. The lashing, of ¾" circumference (1/4" diameter) 3-strand manila, is permanently spliced into the clew cringle, and led two or three times through the hole in the spar and back through the cringle. It is then hauled taut and hitched twice around both sets, pulling them together and tying it off. The tail is then led around

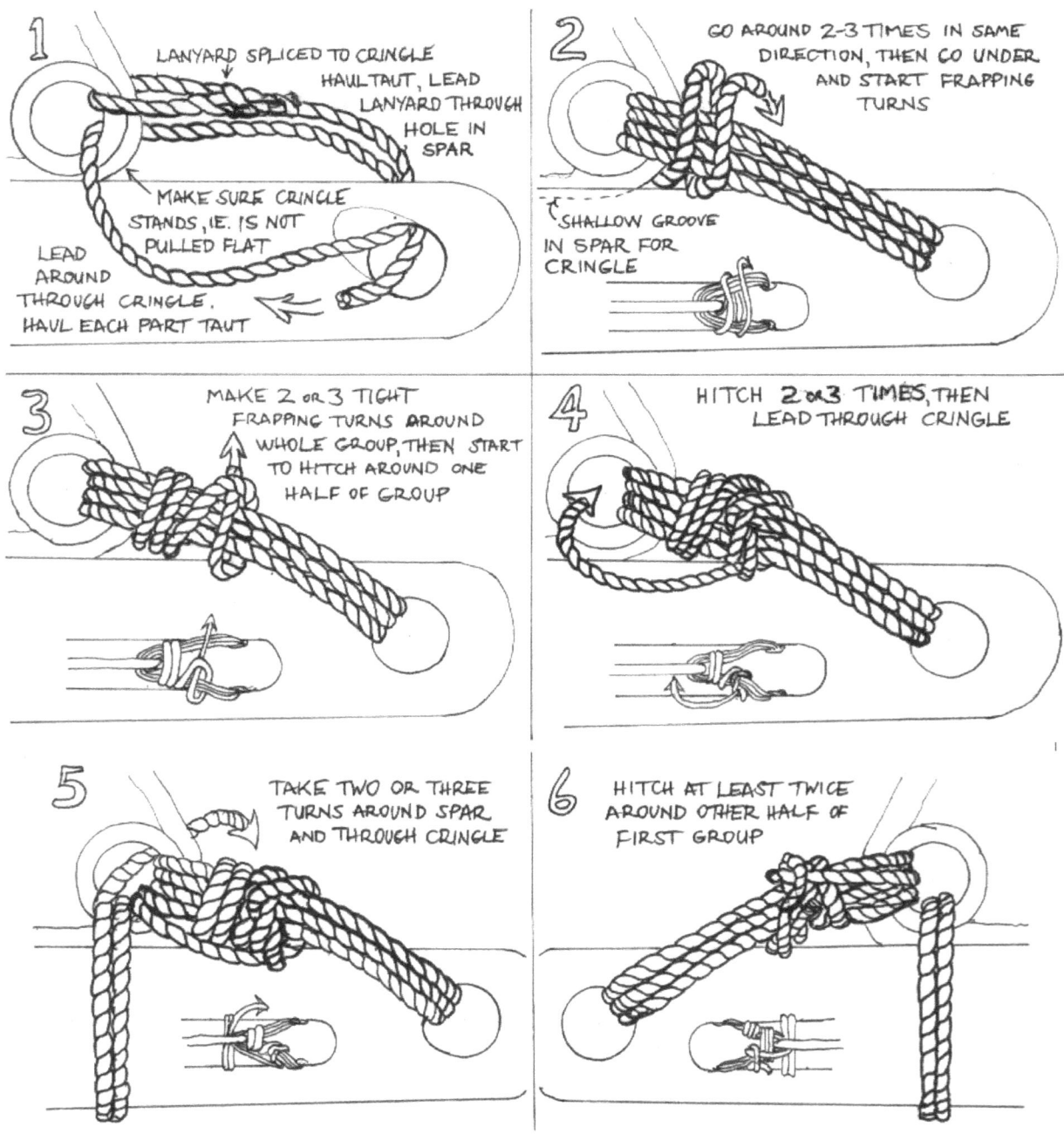

15.1 Boom and Gaff End Lashing

15.2 Shroud Lashings

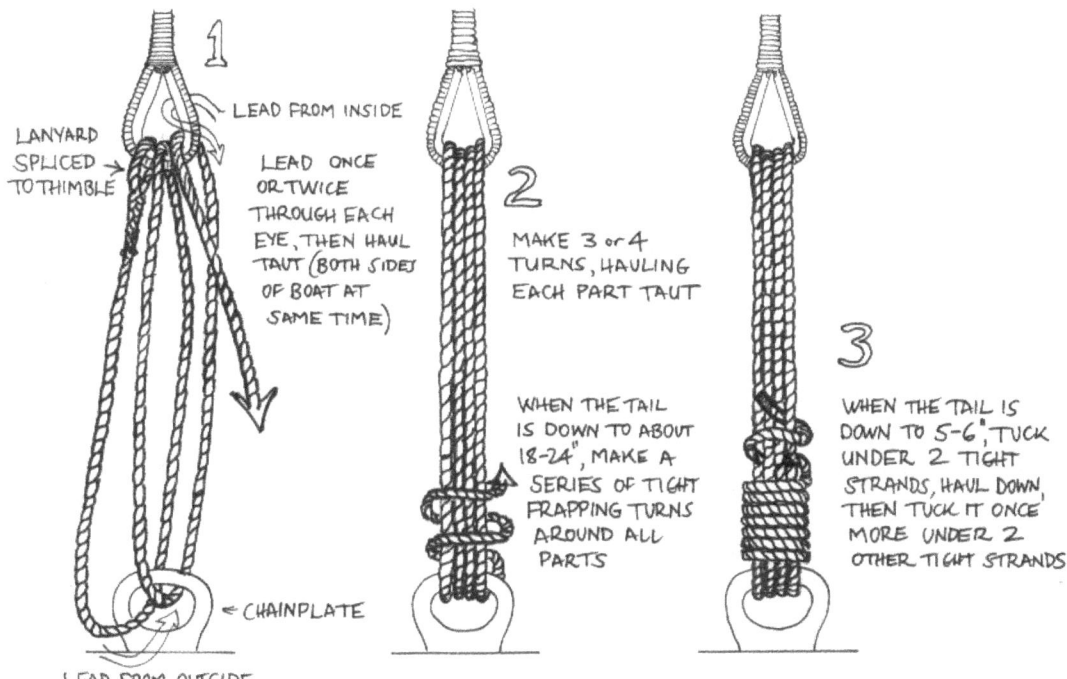

the spar and through the cringle at least twice, just tight enough to allow the cringle to stand but not to separate from the timber. It is then hitched off at least twice and any remaining tail buried so as not to be flapping loose and likely to get caught in any working block. Sometimes the tail is long enough to be used to tie to the served and/or leathered eye of the mainsheet pennant to stop it slipping aft off the end of the boom. The long lacing attached to the tack is then spiraled around the boom through the eyelets as illustrated in drawing 14.12, tautened so that the sail will stay close to the boom under wind pressure, but without flattening the eyelets onto the boom, and tied off outboard so that there is no loose tail. The sail is attached to the gaff in a similar manner, with the important difference that the lacing is hitched rather than spiraled, as in drawing 14.12.

Rigging the Bumpkin

The bumpkin selected is fitted over the stemhead tenon and bolted through the main deck beam or blocking attached to that. It may be necessary to force a slight bend down in order to attach the bobstay and preventer to the fitting at the stem heel (they are always fixed in length). Larger bumpkins may sag close enough of their own weight, smaller bumpkins on 16's 12's and 10 footers might need a fair bit of force. The whisker stay lanyards are then put through the whisker plate eyes and back through the stay thimbles just twice and hauled taut by two people simultaneously while a third person sights from aft to check that the bumpkin is central. Sometimes a fourth person pushing down on the bumpkin to slacken the whiskers while the haulers are hauling ensures the whiskers will be tight when the bumpkin is allowed to spring back. The lanyards are about or 6' or 7' long and are led down through the whisker plate eyes and up through the stay thimbles multiple times until there are 3 or 4 parts on each side of the eyes, hauling each pass taut, and when there is a tail of about 18" to 2' left, tight frapping turns are taken around the standing part until there is about 5 or 6" left, and this tail is then tucked twice only, under two different pairs of strands. This is illustrated in drawing 15.2. It is very secure. I would not suggest you sail around the Horn with stays lashed like this but it is more than adequate for three hard hours out on the water. In 14 hard seasons we have never had one come loose. With grass ropes it would have been nigh impossible to undo them if hitched, so this is why it is done with a couple of tucks and <u>not</u> hitched.

15.3 Raising the Mast

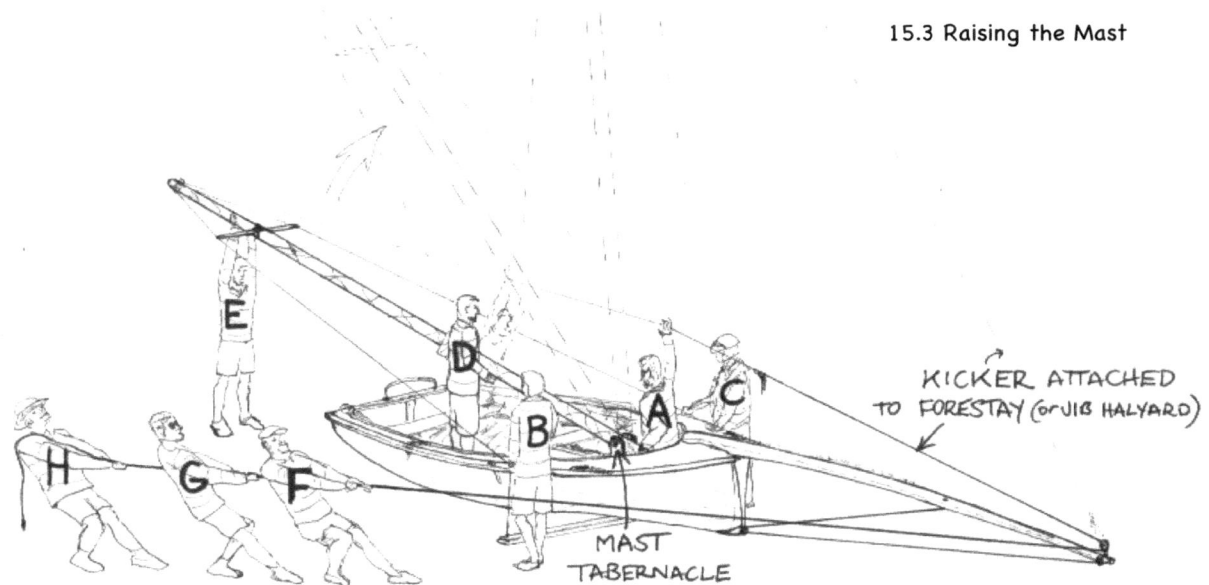

A CALLS IT, HUMAN SPREADER UNTIL FORESTAY IS OUT OF REACH, FITS MAST CHOCK WHEN UPRIGHT
B AND C HOLD UPPERS (LANYARDS LOOSELY THROUGH CHAINPLATES) AND PULL TO CENTRE MAST ON A'S CALL
D STRONGEST CREW PUSHES UP MAST WHILE STANDING ON KEEL
E STARTS LIFTING MAST OFF TUCK, JOINS F, G & H ON KICKER WHEN MAST OUT OF REACH
F, G AND H HAUL ON KICKER

Raising the Mast

With a 27'6" mast weighing about 150 kg (330 pounds) three or more people are needed to bring it to the boat and lay it so the tabernacle band lugs are located in the tabernacle and the mast is laid centrally back over the horse. The two upper stays (which should have been tied to the mast last when packing up previously), are undone from the mast first and the lanyards led twice through the forward chainplates, outside the boat to inside the chainplates and from inside to out through the stay thimbles. One person holds the wire part of the stay on each side. Their role is to watch the masthead as it is raised and prevent it from moving to Port or Starboard, they are not pulling the mast up. The forestay is next untied from low on the mast and held high so that it can be seen to be clear of everything. One end of the bumpkin-end kicker is tied to the forestay thimble (bowline on a bight is easy and strong), and the other end leads aft fairly close to the boat where at least two people will be ready to haul on it. Your strongest crew member should be in the well of the boat and reminded to walk only on the keel when supporting mast weight. Another strong person starts to lift the mast from the masthead and the kicker people start to haul. Someone should be in the boat forward of the tabernacle to call the shots, and it helps if he stands on the mast heel as it starts and holds the forestay above his head as a human spreader. Once the mast is high enough for the man in the well to get under, he does so and lifts, and the man on the ground aft moves to join those on the kicker as soon as the mast is out of his reach. It gets easier the higher it goes. The two people on the upper stays must also lean against the boat in case the cradle moves (even better if you chock it!). The forward person inside ensures the heel is guided into the trench in the mast step, and places the chock or bolt or whatever holds the mast into the tabernacle in place. Everybody can then relax. See drawing 15.3.

The uppers are then hauled taut together, with somebody checking that the mast is central. The lanyards are then finished off in the same manner as described for the whisker stays and illustrated in drawing 15.2.

The other stays and halyards lashed and/or twisted around the mast are then freed, but it is better to ensure that as each rope is freed it has somewhere to go. A real mess can ensue if several stays and halyards are adrift and blowing in the wind. The lowers are attached by their lanyards to the aft chain plates, the runners to their tackles which are usually left attached to the chainplates.

The main throat and peak halyards are loosely cleated to the innermost belaying pins, the jib halyard can stay attached to the cleat on the front of the mast until it is needed, and the masthead spinnaker and ballooner halyards are cleated off to wherever the for'd hand likes them to go. The kicker and ballooner outhaul are tied into the boat wherever the for'd hand wants them. Usually the kicker goes to a belaying pin on the aft edge of the for'd thwart on each side, and the ballooner outhaul is tucked out of the way under the foredeck. The braces, usually one each side are flaked down into the stern quarters, and the ballooner sheet tackle is attached to the eye on the stern quarter thumb cleat on the side of the boat it is most likely to be used, and flaked into the boat. If a spinnaker pole outhaul tackle is used it can be put loosely into the well.

The jib is set first. The halyard is hauled taut and cleated on the front of the mast. The mast needs to be bent forward so that the jib luff will really tension up when the weight of the main straightens the mast back up. It is better not to attach the jib sheets yet. The **shy tack** (a double-ended spinnaker sheet) is led around the forestay (and/or jib luff) and tied out of the way, often to the whisker plates or the attached lanyards on each side.

The Shy Tack

This is another language anomaly that drives pedantic yachtsmen crazy. Open Boat sailors always referred to the spinnaker sheet as the **tack or tack line.** This is another term that comes from square-rig practice. Before you get carried away, I know that the tack line on a square sail is attached to the leading lower corner of the sail, and a square course will have a sheet attached at both lower corners. I contend that when square sails were used on Open Boats in the 19th century, with a pole attached to the windward clew (yes a square sail has two clews), the line attached to the other clew appeared to be more like a tack line than a sheet as it was pulled down into the boat more than it was pulled aft. So when spinnakers took over, it was still referred to as the tack line. The spinnaker was always sheeted on the windward side of the mast (with the tack line) when running square-ish. When carrying the spinnaker more than about ¾ shy, the spinnaker clew would be pulled around the bow by the **shy tack.**

The main (with gaff and boom attached) is then lifted into the boat (this will take several people) and the throat and peak halyards attached. Make sure the peakhead spinnaker halyards are attached to the gaff end with one pair falling each side of the main and any ringtail halyards have a fall each side of the main. The main goes up easiest at about a 45 degree angle. One person outside the boat takes the peak halyard and pulls the gaff to that angle, and then he works together with the person on the throat halyard so it goes up at that angle all the way. It is done about 3 feet at a time with somebody spirally lacing the hoist during each pause. The throat halyard gets heavier the higher it goes, and it is easier with two people. Once the block on the lower end of the wire halyard is within reach, the rope is pulled out of the throat of the block (see Drawing 14.11) and taken in a loop under the innermost belaying pin. The resulting 3 to 1 tackle is used to haul the last bit as the boom is now being lifted too. It is lifted a bit higher than necessary as the luff of the sail will stretch down when the downhaul is attached and hauled taut (after the peak is up). The peak halyard tackle is now put onto the belaying pin, and the peak hauled high enough so that creases begin to appear in line with the luff and hoist as in drawing 15.4. The amount is a matter of fine judgment through experience. The weight of wind in a gaff main will always pull the gaff aft and without hauling it higher at first the gaff will sag under load and creases will appear from the throat to the clew. I usually stand on the boom jaws to reach as high as I can to tauten the spiral lacing on the mast while someone else hauls on the boom downhaul. The lacing is hitched off at the boom jaws (around the mast and hitched around itself).

The jib sheets can be attached to the clew and the extras loaded into the boat. The fin is lifted carefully into the boat and laid flat across the case and thwart. The replica fleet launches down a ramp to a beach and the boat is held bow to the wind while the rudder is fitted and the fin started in the case. We sail off and the fin is lowered as soon as depth of water allows. When launched at boatsheds, the original boats would be pulled alongside a wharf to fit the rudder, and often the heavy steel fin would be lowered in with a derrick.

Windward Work

The most important thing in trying to go to windward is that the sheet hand (mainsheet) and jib hand have to work together. The lever arm of the pressure in either sail is so far from the centre of the boat that uncoordinated sheeting can overwhelm the steering. Neither sheet is ever cleated off. Sheets must be spilled in any strong gust. The jib hand should spill first, even in moderate puffs and the main will drive the boat up to windward. But the sheet hand must be on the ball and get the feel for the strength of the puffs as he must spill wind when he judges any puff will put the rail under. He will need a hand to get the main back on after spilling in any pressure. It really helps to have someone on the rail calling the puffs well. Crew movement is vital, they are the only ballast. I tell new crew that if they are ever sitting still they are probably doing something

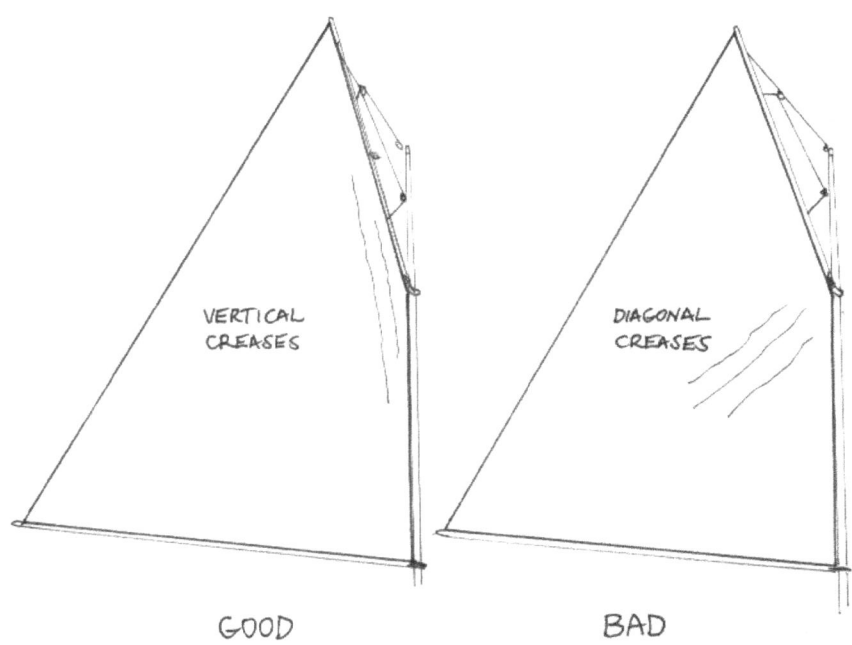

15.4 Correct Setting of Peak Halyard Before Wind Pressure Comes On

Photo 15A Tangalooma working down the Brisbane River in the 1930's. WRIGHT COLLECTION

Photo 15B Britannia replica working to the windward mark 2012. BRUCE KERRIDGE

wrong. Every movement of the boat requires a movement from all crew. Boats have capsized from not having enough weight on the rail, but they have also capsized from having too much weight on the rail if the breeze suddenly shuts off! Fore and aft weight is also important. Crew should be watching the attitude of the boat at all times.

The runners can be left on while tacking to windward and the leeward one only needs to be eased when not hard on. When tacking, a nimble person needs to cross the boat first to knock down the lee cloth prop, and the last person to leave props up the new leeward lee cloth.

The boats of the replica fleet vary in their windward ability but none can point as high as a modern racing yacht.

Running

Crew weight is vital when rounding the top mark. Weight needs to come into the boat and aft, otherwise an inglorious nose dive will result. The for'd hand may already have the halyard attached to the head of the spinnaker (he definitely will have attached the square sheet and usually the shy sheet (shy tack, remember?)) and if it is the peakheader he must be certain that the halyard is forward of the spreaders and masthead. All spinnakers are wooled onshore, about every 5 feet or so and they are raised this way in a tight bundle. The well hand hauls on the halyard until it is all the way up and passes it back to the sheet hand who belays it to the windward pin on the tuck. The crew in the meantime has been assembling the poles, the first two connected in line and usually extending back over the tuck, with the other(s) ready to add. The for'd hand attaches the windward brace to the pole end, as well as the kicker and the tack of the spinnaker. The poles are then pushed out, adding the desired number of poles, and as soon as the innermost heel is in the well of the boat it is attached to the outhaul tackle which pulls it up to the mast, or it is physically manhandled into the snotter. It is then braced back to the required angle, the kicker is hauled taut and the sheet or tack line is pulled to break it out of the wool stops. Then the fin is pulled up and held with a pin through one of a series of holes drilled in it. If the run is squarer than ¾, the spinnaker is sheeted on the windward side of the mast, usually through a snatch block near the for'd thwart on the swinging-out bar. If the wind is, or goes shy, the shy tack pulls the clew of the spinnaker around the bow. If so shy that the poles

Photo 15C Jenny III or IV Brisbane River with a bit on downwind, late 1940's. HALL COLLECTION ANMM

Photo 15D Aberdare replica on a dangerous fresh square run 2016. BRUCE KERRIDGE

Photo 15E Britannia replica with peak head spinnaker and ringtail 2006. DAVID TETLEY

are nearly on the forestay or jib luff, the jockey pole pushes the brace out to act as a spreader, with its heel put into a snotter low on the mast. Distribution of crew weight is vital the whole time.

Dropping the spinnaker is the same in reverse: the sheet is thrown, the poles are brought in and dismantled. Someone needs to haul on the brace as the poles come in to prevent it hooking around the bumpkin. The foot of the spinnaker is then detached from the pole, gathered by the for'd hand and lowered into the boat.

Setting a Ringtail

The ringtail is laid across all three thwarts along the swinging-out batten on one side, which should have been chosen on setting out as the likely side to require the ringtail. The well hand attaches the leeward ringtail halyard end to the centre of the upper spar or the cringle in the triangular head, and sometimes the forward ringtail halyard to the forward end of the upper spar. The leeward side of the outhaul is attached to the centre of the lower spar in a direct line from the end of the boom to the centre of the spar. The halyard(s) are then hauled on until the ringtail is all the way up to the peak of the gaff and cleated off on the boom. The outhaul then pulls the lower spar out to the end of the boom and is cleated on the windward side of the boom. The inhaul attached to the forward end of the lower spar is then hauled taut and cleated on the leeward side of the boom and the ringtail is set. It is easier if the boom is brought in a bit when hauling up so the ringtail more easily clears the slack runners. Dropping it is the same in reverse, the foot must come in first, and then the cloth is gathered as the sail is lowered with the halyard.

There are stories of how the spinnaker would be broken out as soon as the boat has rounded the top mark, and occasional photographs show wooled spinnakers hauled up before the mark, but only a few of the replica fleet ever do this. Alf Beashel even suggests that the well hand would have the ringtail halyards attached before the mark and the ringtail would be hauled up immediately after rounding the mark, but I don't believe any of the replica fleet has done this.

Gybing

Before 1932 boats rarely gybed with their spinnakers up. A permanent forestay made this impossible. We are still searching newspaper reports for the first mention of an eighteen footer gybing a spinnaker. On *Britannia* the spinnaker must be dropped before the gybe mark (usually

Photo 15F Avalon about to go under, 1920's. HALL COLLECTION ANMM

Photo 15G There was usually a launch for towing ashore.
HALL COLLECTION ANMM

the boom and of the turn are not combined and result in capsize. If there is too much wind pressure for the boom to start it is safer to abort the gybe and "granny" around, that is turning away from your intended destination, coming up on the wind, tacking, then bearing away onto the new course. This obviously takes longer than gybing so is costly in a race, so is only used when survival is at stake. With more than half the boom beyond the tuck in the bigger rigs, there is a considerable weight swinging over in a gybe.

Capsizing

In the 1920's and '30's the same course was used in all breezes, turning at Shark Island. In a Nor'Easter which is generally the most common summer breeze it is a gybe mark, from square or a bit shy with Port pole to shy with Starboard pole. As you will gather from the description of the gybing process, it is a dangerous manoeuvre which often ends in capsize. Spectators would gather on the Island for the almost guaranteed thrills and spills. Capsizing an historical eighteen-footer means the end of your race as the boats cannot be righted afloat. You get towed to a beach where you right the boat and bail it out and either sail or be towed back to the clubhouse. The closest beach to the Shark Island mark is on Point Piper and is the home of the Royal Prince Edward Yacht Club. A tradition developed in the early years of the twentieth century that a member of staff or a club member would bring a tray with glasses and a

Shark Island). The fin is lowered to allow crew to cross over, the boat begins to turn and the sheet hand grabs multiple parts of the mainsheet and pulls it in towards the boat. Crew weight is used to lean the boat away from the boom as the turn begins, and as soon as the boom starts to move over their weight is thrown back the other way, and the boat is steered in a slight 'S', ie turning downwind again so that the heeling force of the swinging of

Photo 15H Capsizes still happen in the replica fleet. BRUCE KERRIDGE

bottle of rum down to any distressed Open Boat sailors, and I am happy to say that the good folk at the Edwards value tradition and keep it up for the replica fleet.

In the replica fleet, no boat has totally avoided capsizing. Many boats will race a whole season without capsizing, but occasionally several boats will capsize on the same day. The "Atlantis Trophy" is awarded annually to the boat with the most capsizes and in recent years the winner has capsized between 3 and 6 times during the season, out of 26-30 races. Several rubber duckies follow the replica fleet with trained volunteers, so help is usually close at hand. This was not always the case in the old days. There are many stories of capsized sailors being left on Shark or Clark Island overnight, and others of capsized boats being taken out by the tide towards Sydney Heads and not being found until after dark, but generally there were enough private launches around to tow boats to a beach.

The original *Britannia* would always set a ballooner for the shy run to the next mark, but all of the replica fleet set a spinnaker. Most gybe their spinnaker.

Gybing with Peakhead Spinnaker

Alf Beashel described how he did it (Beashel 1935):

"The working Jib or Ballooner (if carried) is hauled down. The Halyard from the cringle on the spinnaker to the Mast Head is pulled into the Mast which then takes the full weight of the Spinnaker. The Brace is slacked up and the Poles pulled down and around by means of the for'ard kicking strap. The Brace is passed over the Poles and around the Mast and shrouds as the Mainsail is thrown across the Boat. The Poles are then pulled aft by the Brace. The Mast Head Halyard let go and both kicking straps strapped down. The wind in the Spinnaker must be spilled by easing the tack before Gybing, otherwise it is an almost impossible task to Gybe."

Brian Gale described his technique in a conversation with Leanne Gould (Gale and Gould 2004) in more detail. Brian remembered the spinnaker pole being sent out with two braces attached, one slack one leading back into the boat well for'd. *"The idle brace is thrown around the jib and picked up by the well hand and led outside everything to the cleat"* (on the stern quarter). *"Pass the spinnaker sheet over the spinnaker pole and back to the snatch block. Drop the jib. The well hand takes the idle brace and takes in the slack ready to gybe. Ease the spinnaker sheet to get pressure out of the sail. Gybing successfully takes 6 people with separate jobs, knowing exactly what their job is and working as a team:*

Person 1) Steers
Person 2) Main sheet
Person 3) Runners and leecloths in the gybe, and grabs spinnaker sheet.
Person 4) Brace- controlled ease of brace as pole goes forward. After gybe old brace is let go as the new brace is pulled on.
Person 5) For'd hand- kicker is pulled down hard before the gybe. Also takes charge of spinnaker sheet and takes it around the mast if necessary.
Person 6) A strong bloke takes the spinnaker halyard backstay forward (while keeping weight on it). He belays it onto the mast. As the gybe happens he goes under the boom, takes the other peak halyard and belays it aft.

When the jib is down it must be brought as much as possible into the well and strapped down to the bumpkin near the stemhead to prevent it going into the water. It is hauled up again as soon as possible after the gybe is completed."

Replica Fleet Gybing

Those boats in the replica fleet that do gybe do it a bit differently with regards to the backstay. Sometime in the 1950's eighteen footers began to use light wire backstays attached to the peak, belayed on the boom in near the mast when not needed. The weather stay is taken back to the tuck beam when the spinnaker is hauled up, so there is no need for the halyard to be taken aft. When gybing, the leeward stay can be taken back and hauled tight just as the boom crosses over, making it a little faster to get the spinnaker drawing again. I can find no evidence that wire backstays were ever used on 18 footers before 1950, and plenty of evidence that they were not used. Brian Gale says they didn't, and photos show halyards taken aft right up to at least 1949.

Why We Sail These Boats

Every Summer Saturday scores of people gather at the Sydney Flying Squadron on Careening Cove and rig their historical eighteen-footers. As of 2016, there are 8 boats regularly racing and three others that are less regular. There is great camaraderie, some sailors have sailed eighteen-footers since they were young, some are relatively new to these boats or even to sailing in general. Some are ex-champions, some (like me) are also-rans, but it is a team sport. It is a type of sailing that not many other classes can provide, especially in dinghies because everybody in an eighteen-footer has a small part in a big team. Newcomers can come as moveable ballast and if they have any aptitude there will be a long-term role for them. We use no instruments, there is only you and your team and the wind. The fun of sailing a difficult boat with a bunch of good people, on one of the best harbours in the world, with a few beers after packing the boats away and a presentation to the placegetters is the best way I can think of to spend a Summer Saturday.

We have a lot of fun sailing on the replica historical eighteen-footers, but we also feel we are doing something significant in keeping this aspect of our maritime heritage alive. We pay our respects to the builders who built them, and the sailors that sailed them. We are all getting older, so if this book helps younger generations to appreciate what the earlier boatbuilders and sailors achieved, I will be content.

I'll leave the last word to Brian Gale (Gale and Gould 2004):

"Sailing an old 18 footer isn't hard. It's just having the right attitude. Attention to detail is important, the boat must be set up properly. You get a team, you work out who does what, and you do the same thing over and over again every week".

Top: A close finish in the early 1920's. From right Britannia, Mascotte and Mississippi.
AUTHOR"S COLLECTION

Centre: Australia IV and Scot replicas 2010.
BRUCE KERRIDGE

Right: Britannia and Tangalooma replicas 2016.
BRUCE KERRIDGE

Bibliography

Ansell, Willits D. *The Whaleboat,* Mystic CT, Mystic Seaport 2014.

Beashel, Alf. *Plans and Specifications of the Modern Type Eighteen-Footer,* Sydney, NSW Sailing League 1935.

Black, J.F. *Australian Aquatic Annual,* 1937.

Bonnitcha, F. *The History of Drummoyne Sailing Club,* 1994.

Cheater, Christine & Debenham, Jennifer. *The Australia Day Regatta,* Sydney, UNSW Press 2014.

Chapelle, Howard. *The Search for Speed Under Sail,* New York, W.W.Norton & Co, Inc 1967.

Dakin, W.J. *Whalemen Adventurers,* Sydney, Sirius Books 1938/1963.

Dunbabin, T. "Whalers, Sealers and Buccaneers" Royal Australian Historical Society: *Journal and Proceedings,* vol. xi, 1925.

Elliott, Robin. *Galloping Ghosts,* Auckland, David Ling Publishing Ltd 2012.

Gale and Gould, transcript of an interview with Brian Gale by Leanne Gould 2004 in the collection of the AHSSA.

Hardie, Daniel. *Forgotten Fleets,* Sydney, D.Hardie 1990.

Hasluck, P.N. *Knotting and Splicing Ropes and Cordage,* London, Cassell and Co 1904.

Kunhardt, C.P. *Small Yachts, Their Design And Construction,* New York, 1895.

Molloy, Margaret. *Sydney's Flying Sailors,* Sydney, Sydney Flying Squadron Ltd 1991.

Mudie, Colin. *Sailing Ships,* Adlard Coles, 2001.

Stannard, Bruce. *Bluewater Bushmen,* Sydney, Angus & Robertson, 1981. Second edition by Heritage Press 2004.

Stephensen, P.R. *Sydney Sails,* Sydney, Angus &Robertson 1962.

Newspapers: from www.trove.nla.gov.au

Australian Town and Country Journal (Sydney, NSW: 1870-1907).
Balmain Observer and Western Suburbs Advertiser (NSW: 1884-1907).
Bell's Life in Sydney and Sporting Chronicle (NSW: 1860-1870).
Bird o'Freedom (Sydney, NSW: 1891-1896).
Evening News (Sydney, NSW: 1869-1931).
Illustrated Sydney News (NSW: 1853-1894).
Newcastle Morning Herald and Miners' Advocate (NSW:1876-1954).
Shipping Gazette and Sydney General Trade List (NSW: 1844-1860).
Sydney Mail and NSW Advertiser (NSW: 1871-1912).
Sydney Morning Herald (NSW: 1842-1954).
Telegraph (Brisbane, Qld: 1872-1947).

Magazines

*Seacraft (*Sydney, NSW: January 1948).

Glossary

ANMM: Australian National Maritime Museum

Athwartships: in a direction at right angles to the centreline of the ship, as opposed to **fore and aft** which is in line with the centreline of the ship.

BSC: Balmain Sailing Club, 1886-1892. Re-established as the Balmain Amateur Sailing Club in the early 1900's but did not survive the First World War. Re-establishing again in the 1990's.

Ballast: heavy materiel such as rocks, iron or lead stored low in a boat to resist the pressure of wind in the sails trying to heel the boat over.

Ballooner or **Balloon Jib:** a full-bodied jib with a long foot, set flying (not on a stay) and used as a reaching or shy-running sail. In the late 19th century they were often poled out and set like a spinnaker, in fact they were re-invented in the late twentieth century as the asymmetric spinnaker.

Batten-seam carvel: planking method where the planks butt up together in section and the seam is backed up on the inside by a batten to which the planks are fastened. It originated in whaleboats.

Belayed: A sheet or halyard is belayed when it is tied off to a cleat or a belaying pin.

Bobstay: a rod or wire from the bumpkin cap to the stem heel fitting to prevent the bumpkin from lifting.

Bowsed down: A sheet or line is bowser down when it is hauled very tight and belayed.

Breasthook: a bracing knee or gusset joining the two sides of the boat at the sheer to the stem, usually cut from a crook where the grain follows the required curve. See pp 93, 114.

Brace: a line attached to the outer end of the spinnaker pole bracing it back around a thumb cleat or through a block on the stern quarter of the boat to a cleat inside the boat preventing the poles from going forward.

Bridle: a wire strop attached to a spar on which a block can be slung. See also **gaff span.**

Built-heel: a boat where the planking in section takes a reverse curve down onto the keel at the stern.

Bumpkin: what others might call a bowsprit. See p 146 for explanation.

Buttock: in three dimensions a buttock is a plane vertical surface parallel with the centreline of the boat at a set distance from that centreline. Where it intersects with the hull will therefore be a straight line in plan view, a straight line in end elevation (body plan) and a curved line in elevation (profile).

Carlins: part of the deck structure, the fore-and-aft perimeter of a hatch or other deck opening and member housing the inboard end of the side-deck beams.

Carvel planking: planking method where the planks are butted together in section. If the seams are not backed up with a batten (see **batten-seam carvel**) the seam is caulked with cotton or oakum.

Caulked seams: carvel planking has its seams caulked with cotton or oakum and payed (filled flush) with pitch or putty.

Clinker planking: planking method where the planks overlap and are fastened to each other.

Coaming: wooden member covering the inboard ends of the deck beams at a deck opening, generally standing proud above the deck to deflect water trying to enter the opening.

Cringle: metal ring providing an eye in each corner of a sail.

Crooks: grown timber, that is timber with curved grain to give strength to a knee or gusset, generally cut from trees where breaches or roots join the trunk.

Deadrise: the angle of deadrise is the angle between the planking in section out from the keel and horizontal. A large angle means the hull has steep deadrise.

Diagonal: in lofting, a diagonal is a line or in three dimension a plane surface from the centreline of the boat which crosses the hull surface approximately at a right angle. When plotted out two-dimensionally is is the best indicator of whether the planking will lie in a fair curve, ie one without bumps and hollows.

Double-ender: a boat with a pointy stern as well as bow. Boats with a snub or pram bow as well as a square transom, locally **tuck**, were known as **double-tuckers.**

Fishplate: a piece of wood reinforcing the connection of the thwarts to the risers fitted under the thwart and along the riser, see p 120.

Floors: Large knees or crooks fastened to the keel and the first few bottom planks, tying both sides of the boat together as well as spreading the load of the mast step, see pp 106-107.

Gaff: a spar on the head of a four-sided gaff sail, the lower end of which pivots on the mast.

Gaff cutter: a boat with a gaff-rigged mains'l and more than one headsail.

Gaff span: a wire bridle generally hauled tight against the spar to which the peak halyard is attached, see p 155.

Garboard: the plank closest to, and fastened to the keel.

Gunl's: gunwales, in open boats this generally referred to the sponson or rub rail added at the sheer line outside the planking, also referred to sometimes as the moulding, which is technically just the outermost part, see pp120-121

Half-decker: a boat with a foredeck, usually not as far back as the mast, mostly a side deck, and occasionally a narrow back deck. Boating clubs in Sydney argued for decades but failed to define them. Many of what were referred to as Open Boats had some decking.

Horse: a bent rod fixed to the top of the tuck beam on which travelled a (usually) double block as part of the mainsheet tackle, in fact a primitive mainsheet traveller.

Inwales: a fore and aft timber fastened through the frame heads, see pp 120-121.

JBSC: Johnstone's Bay Sailing Club, 1890's.

Jackyard: A short yard to support one side of a tops'l, see p 161.

Jockey pole: a short pole with one end held in a spotter low on the mast and protruding beyond the deck at the side with the other end trapping the spinnaker brace, in effect a spreads for the brace to improve the angle of approach of the brace to the pole end.

Kicker: a rope attached to the inboard end of the furthest-out pole section, led down through the chai plates, back over the poles above the chainplates and belayed down to the main thwart, to prevent the poles from skying (lifting up). After the early 1930's boats began to carry their poles more forward on shy runs and an outer kicker was attached to the pole end and led down to the bumpkin cap and then back into the boat, providing much greater control over the pole height but also more compressive strength.

Knees: timber crooks, cut with the grain curved, usually from where branches or roots joined the main trunk.

Kopsen catalogue: Kopsens were a family-owned marine supplies store and ship chandlers in Sydney, practically one-stop shopping for boat owners, see p 150.

Lapstrake: synonym for **clinker** planking.

Lee cloths: canvas cloth strung between each side deck and a timber batten held forward and aft in a pivoting joint propped up about 12-14" high on the lee side to prevent water entry. The windward side had to be down to allow the crew to sit on the deck. Came in about 1898-99, see p 44.

Lizard: A wooden ring on a rope strop used as a fairlead.

Lofting: the process of drawing out the lines plan of the boat full size to get the full and fair shapes of the moulds around which the planking would be bent.

Lug rig: a lugs'l is a four-sided sail where the yard to which the head side is attached crosses the mast so that a small portion of it is ahead of the mast. A **standing lugs'l** remains on one side of the mast when tacking, a **dipping lugs'l** is pulled around to the leeward side of the mast on each tack.

Moulding: hardwood (generally Spotted Gum) shaped piece outermost of generally more than one piece sponson or rub rail. Sometimes used to refer to the whole set.

Offsets: measurements from a base line, waterline or centreline to a position on the hull for lofting purposes.

PJSSC: Port Jackson Sailing Skiff Club, est. 1901 for 16 foot skiffs.

Peening: the process of riveting, spreading the end of a metal rod or nail to prevent it from being pulled through a whole you don't want it to be pulled through, see pp 82-83.

Preventer: a rod or wire attached to the middle of the bumpkin and a fitting at the stem heel to prevent that part of the bumpkin from lifting, see p 154.

RSYS: Royal Sydney Yacht Squadron, est. 1859. Still extant.

Rabbet: the rebate in the stem, keel and stern knee to house the planking.

Raffee: a small squares'l slung from a halyard at the peak of the tops'l yard with the windward tack or clew hauled to the windward end of the larger squares'l yard and the leeward end hauled to the middle of the squares'l yard, see p 164.

Reeling: Staggering nail positions alternately.

Ringtail: a sail that extends the leech of the main for downwind sailing. The halyard is attached to the middle of an upper spar or after the early 1930's to a cringe in a triangle of cloth above the upper spar and is hauled up to the peak of the gaff. The middle of the bottom spar which is parallel with the boom is hauled out to the end of the boom and an inhaul on the forward end of the bottom spar pulls it into parallel with the boom. Half the sail therefore extends beyond the mains'l leech. See pp 160-61.

Riser: a fore and aft timber fastened though the ribs and planking at the correct height to support the thwarts, p 118.

Runners (Running Backstays): attached to the masthead or whichever band supports the jib halyard, and hauled on with a tackle on the gun'l outboard of the middle thwart. The windward runner must always be hauled tight. When tacking upwind both runners can usually be on tight.

SASC: Sydney Amateur Sailing Club, est. 1872, still extant.

SFS: Sydney Flying Squadron, est. 1891, now the home of the historical 18' replica fleet.

SSC: Sydney Sailing Club, 1899-1925.

Saxboard or Sackboard: a light timber on the inside upper edge of the **sheer plank** made to the same thickness as the seam battens, acting as a continuous packer under the rib heads, see pp 104-105.

Scarfing: joining two pieces of timber with matching angled cuts called **scarfs**. See pp 95, 135-136.

Scribing: drawing a line exactly parallel to an edge, generally using a set of compasses or a block of wood of the correct size, see pp 102, 114.

Sheer plank: the uppermost plank.

Sheerline: the top of the outermost edge of the deck as seen from the side.

Shy tack: A spinnaker sheet led to leeward of the mast, or "around the bow". Discussed p 169.

Sliding Gunter: a rig popular in the 1840's and 1850's where the vertical yard was set in a **gunter** fitting at its heel which allowed the yard to run vertically up and down the mast but not to pivot aft like a gaff, a sort of telescopic extension to the mast. The triangular sail could not be lowered, it had to be braided up against the mast, see illustration p 5.

Snotter: a short length of rope with an eye spliced in each end. One end is past around a spar, usually a mast, and led through the other eye, which in effect attaches a rope eye to a spar.

Sole boards: boards fastened on top of the ribs to protect the planking from boofy feet, usually only fitted in the well either side of the centreboard case, see p 128.

Spiling A technique for establishing the exact shape of a plank. See pp 94-96.

Spring in the keel: vertical curve in the keel, otherwise known as rocker. See pp 26 and 38.

Sprits'l: a four-sided sail with the leading edge (luff) laced to the mast and the peak held up by a sprit running diagonally across the sail, crossing the mast low down on the sail luff.

Sprit yawl: a boat with two sprits'ls on two masts, the aft mast (mizzen) being much the smaller.

Square tack. A spinnaker sheet led to windward of the mast.

Squaresail or Squares'l: a four-sided symmetrical sail attached to a yard all the way across the top. On Open Boats, hauled up to masthead by single halyard attached to the centre of the yard, the windward tack/clew is poled out, the leeward tack/clew is sheeted down and belayed somewhere near the base of the mast. Discussed p 164 and p 169.

Stemhead: the top of the stem at deck level. Generally had a tenon to go into a mortice under the bumpkin.

Stopwaters: small dowels of softwood rammed into hole through joints in the backbone structure of a boat to stop water migrating along the joint, see p 85.

Stringers: longitudinal members fastened to the ribs and planking to reinforce flatter areas of the hull, see p 117.

Swarf: the waste produced by drilling, like sawdust from a saw.

Tabernacle: timber structure to support the mast, containing slots into which lugs on a metal **tabernacle band** will fit, on which the mast will pivot when raising, see p 124.

Thwart: a plank fitted across the hull, fastened on top of the **riser.** Most open boats had three thwarts, the main thwart supporting the mast **tabernacle,** the middle thwart supporting the aft end of the fin case, and an aft thwart as a seat for the skipper, see p 119.

Tops'l: in open boats this always referred to the gaff tops'l, the sail filling the triangle between the mast and the gaff above the mains'l, see p162.

Tuck: local term for the transom.

Turn of the bilge: the area of hull planking between the bottom, more horizontal planks in section, and the topsides or upper, more vertical planks. A boat with a sharp turn here is referred to as **hard-bilged,** one with a more gradual transition has **easy bilges.**

WAMM: Western Australian Maritime Museum

Waterline: a plane horizontal surface parallel with the floating waterline of a boat. In **lofting,** a waterline represents the intersection of this plane with the hull surface, so will therefore be a straight line in the body plan (end elevation) and profile, and a curved line in plan view.

Whisker stays: wire stays from the bumpkin cap to chainplates on the deck outboard and forward of the mast, see p 154.

Worked frames: frames for ships and small craft that are built up out of smaller sections of generally curved, but sometimes straight-grained timber.

Yard: a spar attached to a sail. A squares'l has a yard at the top, open boat tops'ls had a yard on the luff (leading edge).

Yard tops'l: a tops'l with a yard on the luff. Open boat tops'ls were always of this type

Appendix I: Restorations

The Restoration of Yendys

Yendys was built by Charlie Hayes in 1925 for Norm Blackman who had already established himself as a skipper with two previous boats both called Sydney. All three boats carried the red anchor sail insignia. With a snub nose, the boat was considered a rule-cheater by some and was only accepted into the SFS after some heated debate. She was always one of the low-handicap boats and often the scratch boat, winning several championships over a long career which finished in 1942 when Norm Blackman became involved in War work at Garden Island Naval Base. *Yendys* was stored at Norm's home until he sold it to Jack Lloyd for conversion to a launch in the 1950's. After a series of owners the boat sank at her moorings in Balmain in 1977. George Williams, a relative of the then owner raised her with the assistance of Alan Bardsley a Sydney Maritime Museum member, and had his friend George McGoogan look at her. George had been a builder and sailor of 18-footers, and was by then the Dock Superintendent at Vickers Cockatoo Island Dockyard. George formed a committee with senior Vickers executives Capt Richard Humbly and John Jeremy and they decided to restore her.

Apprentice Garry Swindale, (now a leading Sydney boatbuilder), in foreground prepares forward back rabbet for planking. SYDNEY HERITAGE FLEET

Supervised by George, the hull was restored by several successive groups of Cockatoo Island apprentices. The launch's cabin and deck were stripped off and four braced moulds were fitted into the hull to retain its shape. The hull was replanked on the same plank lines, removing only a few planks at a time, then the ribs were replaced with new ones. Only the keel and the tuck from the original boat were kept. A new centreboard case, thwarts and deck were added. New hollow spars were built to fit the original second rig canvas sails which had been kept, though they needed some restoration by George's son Dennis McGoogan who had trained in canvas work at the loft of Harry West who had made the sails originally.

George McGoogan inspects apprentices beginning restoration of Yendys.
SYDNEY HERITAGE FLEET

Four moulds retain the shape of the hull. SYDNEY HERITAGE FLEET

The rebuilt *Yendys* was relaunched on 4 December 1982 with George McGoogan at the tiller and a crew made up of the apprentices who had worked on her. They sailed in several events that Summer but the boat was put into the shed at the Balmain 12 ft Sailing Club and did not go into the water again. In the 1990's it was moved into storage with the Sydney Heritage Fleet (a simple name change from the Sydney Maritime Museum) to whom it had been donated, and since the establishment of the Wharf 7 centre in the late 1990's in Darling Harbour which the Heritage Fleet shares with the Australian National Maritime Museum it has been on display in the foyer. Unfortunately it has never been sailed again. However a replica was built in 2006-7 by boatbuilder and champion 18-footer sailor the late Ian Perdriau, and Col Bailey who was one of the apprentices who had rebuilt the original boat at Cockatoo, so the Red Anchor flies again with the replica fleet. The hull was laminated and resembles the original only in shape.

George McGoogan stands proudly in front of the fully restored Yendys, 1982.
DAVID LIDDLE

The Restoration of Britannia

Britannia was built in 1919 by Wee Georgie Robinson and sailed every season except one until 1944, mostly in close competition with *Yendys* (who generally had the edge). Wee Georgie turned her into a launch, and when he retired from racing other people's boats in 1949 he made her into a launch and used her as the starter boat for the Sydney Flying Squadron until the mid-1960's when he replaced her with a clinker launch he built named *Brit*. She was also the starter boat for the Snail's Bay Sabot Club in the early 1960's.

In the early 1980's Wee Georgie began to restore her to the way she was in her racing heyday with the intention of donating her to the then Sydney Maritime Museum, but died before completion and left the boat to his old mate and frd hand Bob Lundie.

When the Australian National Maritime Museum was being planned in the late 1980's, Bruce Stannard the author of Bluewater Bushmen, the pioneering work of 18 footer research, convinced the Museum of the significance of *Britannia* and they purchased her from Bob Lundie. Curator and shipwright Michael Staples and shipwrights Rick Wood and Nigel Shannon were engaged to restore *Britannia* to display condition, removing as little of the original fabric as possible, and she went on permanent display at the Museum from its opening in 1990 until 2016, and should be on display again after current building renovations. During the restoration naval architect Alan Payne and David Payne (now Curator of the Australian Heritage Vessels Register) measured the boat, took the lines off and drew up a thorough lines, sail and construction plan. It was these plans that I used in building the replica in 2001-02.

Britannia on its way to the Museum for restoration. ANMM

Curator and Shipwright Michael Staples begins restoration. ANMM

Britannia on display at the ANMM. ANMM

Wee Georgie in his pride and joy, early 1980's.   DAVID LIDDLE

The Restoration of Mele Bilo II

Champion West Australian skipper Chris Garland purchased a set of moulds from Sydney builder Charlie Dunn and had Perth builder James Hall build *Mele Bilo* (I) in 1921. Some modifications to the moulds were apparently made. The boat won the Mark Foy Challenge Cup, effectively the Australian Championship, in Perth in January 1922. The boat was lost in a fire that destroyed the significant Barrack St boatsheds with a number of other boats in February 1922. Garland commissioned Hall to build another boat off another set of moulds purchased from Charlie Dunn (the first set had been destroyed as part of the deal), and there are no reports that these moulds were altered. This became *Mele Bilo II,* launched in November 1922, but Garland could not compete as effectively with the interstate boats as he had with *MB I*, being unplaced in Brisbane in 1922/23, Perth in 1924/25 and Sydney 1926/27. Garland commented that the second boat was never as good as the first.

After a successful local racing career (WA 18's stopped racing in the late 1920's and the boat's last race was the 1926-27 Championship in Sydney) the boat was retired and became a daysailer and then a launch. It was donated to the Western Australian Maritime Museum by Chris' son Harry Garland in 1982, but the Museum was only in formative stages at that time, and the boat was restored almost completely by the Fremantle Shipwrighting Company and displayed with other boats in temporary accommodation . In the late 1990's it was restored to display condition by a team led by Bill Leonard and moved to the new WAMM.

Having the lines plan, drawn up from the boat by Bill Leonard is invaluable. It is the only lines plan we have of a Charlie Dunn design, and Charlie was one of the most prolific boatbuilders and

Mele Bilo II on the Swan River in the 1920's. ANDREW WHITE COLLECTION

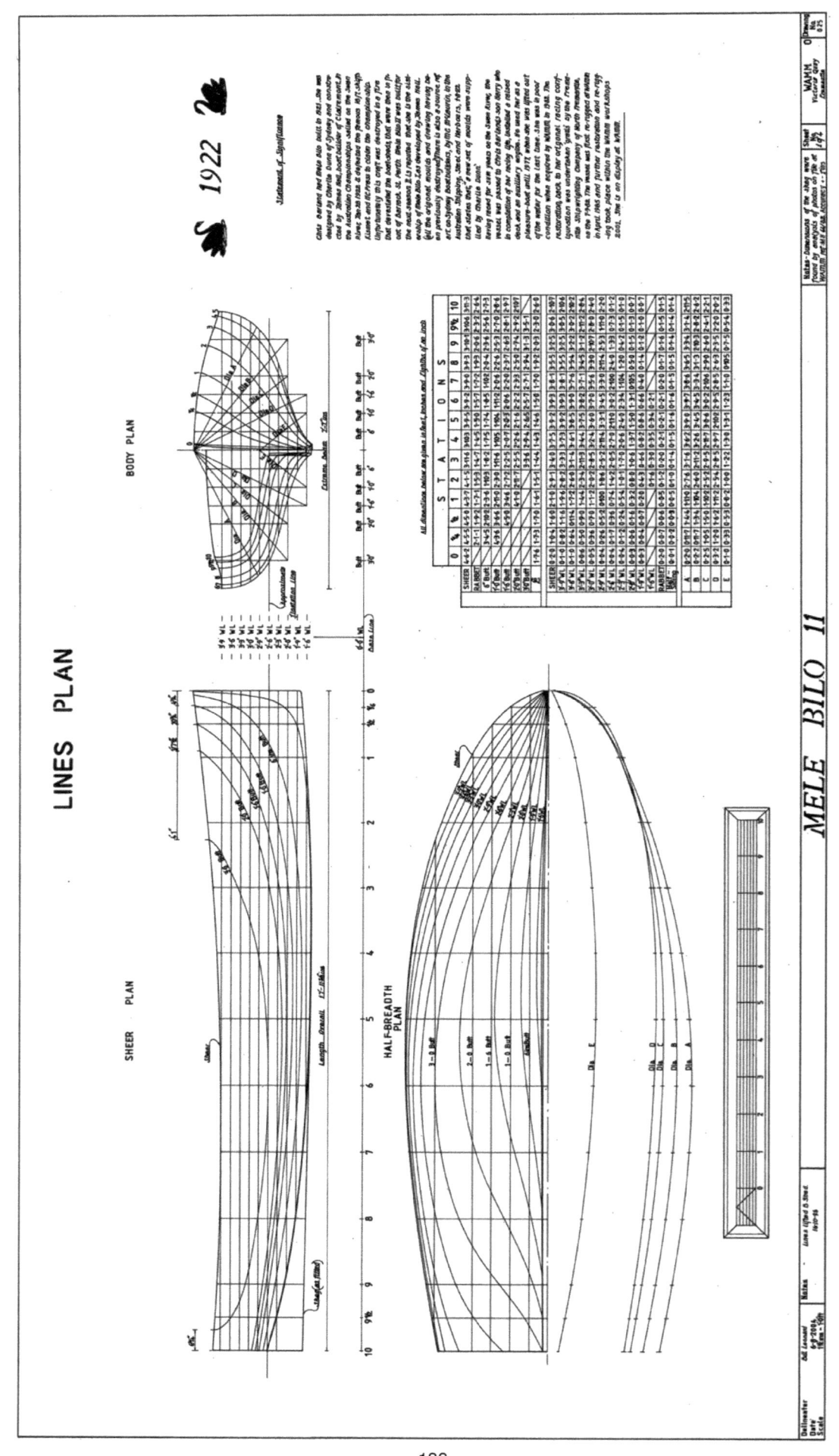

Lines Plan, Mele Bilo II lifted and drawn by Bill Leonard. WESTERN AUSTRALIAN MARITIME MUSEUM

designers of open boats in the early part of the twentieth century. Known as an innovator, Charlie's boats were often narrower than *Mele Bilo II*, and the skeg heel was uncommon on eighteen footers of the time, most boats had a built heel.

Mele Bilo II looks magnificent on permanent display with sails up at the WA Maritime Museum in Fremantle in the sailing gallery.

Mele Bilo II as a launch in the 1970's. JACK WHITE

Mele Bilo II on display at WAMM in Fremantle. MIKE LEFROY

Appendix II: The Boatbuilders

This list is not exhaustive, the active period of each builder is determined by the earliest and latest boats I have found recorded. It is highly likely that most of them built other boats including some of types other than listed here. Locations in Sydney are listed just by suburb. Dates after the name are known dates of birth and death.

There is much continuity during the period covered, with many multi-generational boatbuilding families. There are also other continuities, for example Sam Williams had been Joe Donnelly's apprentice, Joe had been Andrew Reynolds' apprentice, and Andrew had been apprenticed to George Green. Green was apprenticed to Thomas Day. The information on the 18-footers was originally researched by Robin Elliott and appears in list of boats as an Appendix in *Galloping Ghosts,* 2012.

NAME	LOCATION	ACTIVE PERIOD	BOATS BUILT
Anderson, Hugh	Brisbane	1894-98	1894 *Victoria* 18', 1895 *Britannia I* 18', 1898 *Imperial* 18'
Allen, T	Balmain		1890 *Grace Darling* 20'
Arcus, Larry	Perth	1902-08	1902 *Scallywag* 18', 1906 *Swan* 18', 1908 *Crescent* 18'
Arcus, A & R	Perth	1901	1901 *Spray* 18'
Balkwell, Horrie	Sydney	1951	1951 *Progress* 18' to a Bill Barnett design. Horrie was a leading skipper of 18-footers from the late 1930's to the early 1950's, also a champion of the ten footer class in the 1930's, and a sailmaker. He also built a number of laminated boats in the mid-1950's.
Balkwell, Ron (Son of Horrie)	Sydney	1948-1980's	12's, 16's,18's clinker Launches, yachts. His 1950 *Unique* 18' was a snub. Ron was also a leading 18-footer skipper in the 1950's and 1960's. As a boatbuilder he was apprenticed to the Minter brothers. He built many laminated boats in the 1950';s, 1960's and 1970's. Ron was consulted for this work.
Barbour, Bob (Barber some sources)	Sydney	1913-1941	1913 *Eagle* 18', 1925 *Alert* 18', 1927 *Rene* 18', 1929 *Arakoon* 18', 1932 *Waratah I* 18', 1937 *Pandora* 18', 1941 *Zephyr* 18'
Barnett, Charles	Millers Point	Before 1847 to ?	Unknown
Barnett, George (relation and apprentice of Charles Barnett)	Millers Point, then Lavender Bay side of Blues Point after c 1870	c1860-1889	Skiffs, 16's including *Julia* and *Novice* ,24's including *Sea Breeze* (1870's), yachts, steam vessels
Barnett, William (Bill) b.1915	Berry's Bay side of Blues Point	1940's-1980's	Canvas 12's, eleven batten-seam 18's: 1948 *Hy Flyer* and *Myra*, 1949 *Aloma*, 1950 *Myra II (Too)*, 1951 *Myra III* and *Apex* and *Nymph*, 1953 *Can Can* and *Chris Webb III* and *Jan*, 1954 *M.G.* Bill is a legendary boatbuilder and skipper, a pioneer of laminated boats from 1954. He also built surfboats, Dragons, 5.5's and the 12-Metre *Gretel II*. Bill was one of the boatbuilders consulted for this work.
Beashel, Alf	Sydney	1935-52	Four 18's for himself, 1935 *Alruth*, 1943 *Alruth II*, 19947 *Alruth III*, 1952 *Alruth IV*. Alf was a stalwart of the NSW 18 Footers League.
Beattie, W	Balmain	1900-1911	1900 *Elsie* 18', 1904 *Vision* 18', 1911 *Hero* 18'

NAME	LOCATION	ACTIVE PERIOD	BOATS BUILT
Bell	Balmain	1850'-60's	General boatbuilding
Bennett Bros	Perth	1900	1910 *Eurus* 18'
Blackford, C	Sydney	1922	1922 *Caledonia* 18', reported to be designed in Scotland
Blake, Laurie	Sydney	1943-45	1943 *Desdemona III* 18' (with Tommy Doyle), 1945 *Defiant*
Carneby, Fred	Perth	1908	1908 *Cygnus* 18'
Christensen, Fred	Brisbane	1921-28	1921 *Vione* 18' (4'10" beam!), 1928 *Vagrant* 18'
Clark, Colin	Brisbane	1915	1915 *Britannia II* 18'; also designed *Vision* 1919 and *Tangalooma* 1930
Cole, Alan	Sydney	1949-52	1949 *Almae* 18', 1952 *C.A.P* 18'
Coleman, Frank	Brisbane	1909-19	1909 *Ariell* 18', 1910 *Pastime* 18'
Collins, Roly	Sydney	1922-1942	1922 *Florrie II* 18', 1942 *Eileen III* 18'
Court, E	Sydney	1937-43	1937 *Invicta* (with Donoghue) 18', 1943 *Irene I*
Cowie, Peter	Sydney	1934-38	1936 *Jean* 18', 1938 *Jean II* 18'. 12' *Jean* 1934 and other 12's for Greenwich sailors. Peter was a top skipper from a multi-generational sailing family. His father, also Peter Cowie, commissioned *Scot* from Joe Donnelly in 1906.
Cribb, Ben	Brisbane	1930	1930 *Tangalooma* 18' (to owner Colin Clark's design)
Crouch, Jim	Brisbane	1927	1927 *J.C.* 18' (6'6" beam, deadwood heel)
Crowley, Charlie	Brisbane	1936-38	1936 *Poinsettia* 18', 1937 *Malvina* 18', 1938 *Ardath* 18' and *St George* 18' (which is still afloat)
Cuthbert	Sussex St Sydney	1850's-1880's	Boats and ships. Cuthbert had the biggest yard in Sydney, building coasters and ships
Dawson	Sydney	1880's	Canvas 14's *Grand Flaneur*, *Olivette* and *Estelle*
Day, Thomas Snr	Darling Harbour prob. Sussex St as below	1816-1842	Whaleboats
Day, Thomas, Jnr	24 Sussex Street, Sydney	1842-1864	Whaleboats
Dearing, Edgar	Drummoyne, Sydney	1880-1914	10's including *Planet* 1895, 14's including *Jessie* 1904, 16's, 18's including *Stella* 1894, *Stella II* 1895, *Kyeewa* 1898, *Blanche* 1905, *Viking* 1906, *Boronia* 1914, 22's including *Uranus* 1880, *Wonga* 1896
Degan, George	Sydney	1947-48	1947 *Honora* 18', 1948 *Allison* 18'
Degan, Jack	Sydney	1937-53	1937 *Nereid* 18', 1938 *Nereid II* 18', 1953 *Victor* 18'
Degan	Leichhardt		1905 *Aspirant* 18'

NAME	LOCATION	ACTIVE PERIOD	BOATS BUILT
Donnelly, Joe	Glebe, then Woolloomooloo Bay, then Glebe again	1875-1911	Rowing skiffs, 1875 *Florrie* 19' skiff and *Ettie* 22' skiff, 1870's *Effie* 19' skiff, *Desdemona* 19' skiff, *King of the Ring* 24', *Big Berry* 24', 1876 *Lottie* 24', 1877 *Carlotta* 24',1878 *Anthea* 19' skiff, 1879 *Victor* 24', 1880 *Rosetta* 22', 1880s 16 footers *Daisy, Violet, Regina, Nereid, Our Boys, Thistle*, 20-footers *Angela, Clytie, Petrel*, 14' canvas dingies *Chance, Bessie*, 1881 *St Crispin* 22', 1883 *Asteroid* 36' half-decker,1888 *Irex* 22', 1891 *Susie* 24', early 1890's hero 14' wood dingy, *Olga* 10', *Ida* 24', 1894 *Ariel* 18', 1896 *Wanda* 14' and *Effie* 22', 1898 *Donnelly* 18' and *Plover* 22', 1905 *Zena* 18', 1906 *Scot* 18', 1907 *Oweenee* 18', 1911 *Donnelly II* 18' Donnelly was one of the most prolific and innovative of open boat builders. Many of the developmental changes in open boats are down to Joe. He was a champion rower in his youth, but was in bad health in 1910 when a benefit event was held for him, and he retired in 1914.
Douglass, Willis	Narrabeen	Before 1935-1949	Leading 16'skiff builder, 13 known 18's: 1935 *Dee Why*,1936 *Collaroy* and *Lightning*, 1937 *Aries* and *Gloria*, 1939 *Narrabeen Lakes*, 1940 *Ada A, City Tatts II* and *Dee Why II*, 1941 *Top Weight*, 1942 *Trade Wind*, 1949 *Chris Webb II* (still exists in storage with Sydney Heritage Fleet). Jimmy O'Rourke worked for him in the late 1940's.
Doyle, Tommy	Sydney	1943-1949	1943 *Desdemona III* 18' (with L.Blake), 1945 *Othello* 18', 1949 *Desdemona V* 18'
Dunn, Charlie	Berry's Bay	1901-1927	10's (*Planet* 1895 plus several named *Crescent*), 14's (including *Clio* 1897? which brother Billy sailed with success and 1905 *Air Motor* which sailed at St George), 16's, 18's, power boats, small coastal ships, ferries. From an old boatbuilding family (a W.Dunn is listed as a boatbuilder on the North Shore in 1864), Charlie and his brother Billy (1880-1973) were leading builders and skippers of the early part of the 20th century. Eighteen-footers : 1901 *Mascotte*, 1903 *Qui Vive*, 1905 *Crescent IV* and *Crescent V*, 1906 *Crescent VI* and *Acme*, 1908 *Crescent VII*, 1912 *Desdemona* and *Kismet*, 1913 *Swastika*,1916 *Onda*, 1919 *Mischief* (for Cairns FNQ), 1921 *Crescent VIII, Endeavour* and moulds sent to Perth for *Mele Bilo I*, 1922 *Avalon* and moulds to Perth for *Mele Bilo II*, 1927 *Pastime II*
George Dunn (Brother of William?)	Berry's Bay	1870's	Skiffs, open boats. yachts, launches. Had built 50 launches before 1877, 15-30 men employed.
Dunn, William (father of Billy and Charlie)	Berry's Bay	1860's-1890's	Carried on family business. May have built 14-footer *Clio* for son Billy.
Ellis, George	Balmain	1873-1902	8'-25'open boats, Yachts. 1873 *Aileen* 24', 1876 *La Belle* (6t. yacht),1878 *Deronda* 24', *Naiad* and *Lisel* 18'skiffs,1879 *Lucia* 19' skiff and *Harpy* 39'7" yacht, 1880 *Ouida* 16' and *Dreamland* 24', 1880's *Aileen 2*'and *Elaine* 24', 1881 *Velox* 22' and *Tethys* 25' half-decker, 1884 *Wanganella* 20',1886 *Genesta* 20', 1887 *Genesta* 8'canvas dingy, 1889 *Thelma* 53' yacht, 1893 *Kelpie* 2 1/2 rater yacht at Thompson and Co Drummoyne (*Kelpie* was restored in 1988 and still sails on Sydney Harbour). As well as a prolific builder, employing up to 15 hands at times, George was a leading skipper of his own and other people's boats from the 1870's to when he left for Vancouver, Canada in 1907 and died there in 1924.

NAME	LOCATION	ACTIVE PERIOD	BOATS BUILT
Charles Fisher (C.A.M. Fisher)	Berry's Bay later La Perouse	1890's-1930's	Yachts, launches, 1 known 18' *Doreen* 1901
Fisher, Billy (son of Charles)	Berry's Bay, later La Perouse	1921-1946	Yachts, launches, 10 known 18's: 1921 *Australia*, 1935 *All British*, 1936 *Australia II*, 1937 *Miranda* and *J.L.Glick*, 1938 *Australia III*, 1944 *Amy* and *Spindrift*, 1946 *Clovelly* and *Shamrock III*
Fisher, Jack (brother of Billy)	La Perouse	1925	1925 *Cutty Sark* 18'
Fisher, Tom (son of Billy)	La Perouse	1943-1954	Eighteen-footers: 1943 *Australia IV*, 1949 *Top Dog IV*, 1952 *Balmoral*, 1954 *Toogara II*, plus later moulded boats
W.M.(Watty) Ford	Berry's Bay	Late 1800's	Dinghies, power boats, ferries, island traders, small ships. Also built 10 ton yacht *Sirocco* 1880, later owned and wrecked by Errol Flynn
W.M.Ford (Jnr)	Berry's Bay	Early 20th C	Dinghies to ships, continuing father's business, especially links with Pacific Islands. Built one known 18', *Gladwyn* 1906. Owned *Australian II* and *III* skippered by Chris Webb and was Webb's mainsheet hand.
Gardiner, H	Balmain	1850's-1880's	Yachts, boats, Several 24' fishing boats including *Kingfisher* and *Sylvia*
Gardiner, W (probably son of H. Gardiner)	Balmain	1880's-1905	At least one 24' in 1889, 1905 *Merlin* 18'
Golding, William 1855?-19?	Figtree Point Balmain	1872-1913	1872 *Alpha* 16' (when aged 17 just out of articles of apprenticeship) and *XLCR* 16', 1880 *Nereus* 20', 1880's *Nereus II* 20' *Our Own* 16', *Itonia* 20', *Vacuna* 20', *Leonie* 22', *Rosalind* 23', *Lizzie M* 23', *Pandora* 24', *Aeolus* 24', *Edith* 18', 1886 *Nyoola* 22' for Brisbane, 1887 unknown 24', 1889 *Gymea* 18', 1893 *Olinda* 18' and *Caneebie* 22' for Brisbane, 1894 *Nereid* 18', 1895 *Yvonne* 18', 1896 *Vigilant* 22', 1897 *Thalia* 18', 1898 *Federal* 18' 1899 *Question* 18', 1903 *Arline* 18' (became *Australian* 1905), 1907 *Eileen* 18' (became *Arline* 1910), 1909 *Nimrod* 18' (became *Mascotte* 1918), 1910 *Golding* 18' (became *Life Saver* 1923), 1912 *Australian III* 18' Billy Golding was a prolific builder who seems to have been the only builder other than Joe Donnelly whose business was completely taken up by racing boats. He sailed his own and occasionally other boats with great success. Golding boats were always at or near the top of their fleet. His *Gymea* of 1889 was probably the first recognisable eighteen-footer and though he retired in 1913 some of his later boats raced up until the early 1930's, meaning his boats are represented for almost the whole period we are looking at.
Gooud, S (Goond?)	Balmain	1870's	3 known 24's, *Young Jim, Young Sam, Young Charlie*
Grove, Fred	St George district	1930's	16' skiffs including champion *Jessie* and several boats named *Neptune*
Green, George	North Sydney, chiefly Greenwich, Gore Cove side	Early-mid 19th century	George built many types of boats including whaleboats and yachts such as *Eclipse*. Also competition rowing skiffs.
Green, Harry (son of George)	Sydney, Lavender Bay	1889-1902	24' for Press, yachts including *Ku-Kuburra* 1901, *Scotia* 1902. Famous for innovative designs in competition rowing skiffs.

NAME	LOCATION	ACTIVE PERIOD	BOATS BUILT
Greenhalgh, George	WA	1904-1912	1904 *The West* 18', 1909 *Westana* 18' and 1912 *Eileen* 18'
Griffin, Harold "Darkie"	The Spit, Middle Harbour	1920's-1940's	"Darkie" ran a boatshed at the Spit and built many types of boats including 16' skiffs and yachts.
Hall, James	WA	1921-1922	1921 *Mele Bilo* I-burnt in shed 1922. 1922 *Mele Bilo II*, both to a Charlie Dunn design
Hall, John	Botany Bay	1922-1930	3 known 18's, 1922 *Hallmark*, 1924 *Eileen*, 1930 *Mascotte II*
Hayes, James	Woolloomooloo Balmain	1867-1890's	14' canvas dinghies including *Maggie*, *Fedora*, *Estrella* and *Pearlie*, 19's including *Maggie* 1875, 1884 *Maritana* 20', 1880's *Cynthia* 20', *Esmerelda* 22', *Lilian* 22', yachts. First mentioned building a schooner in partnership with Dan Sheehy, Woolloomooloo. Then Paul St Balmain after 1879.
Hayes, Charlie	Balmain, Careening Cove	1907-1935	1907 *Maritana* 18', 1925 *Yendys* 18', 1927 *Arawatta* 18', 1935 *Minnawatta* 18', yachts
Hayes, Frank	Sydney	1952	1952 *Minnawatta II* 18'
Heron, Tom	N.Qld	1902?	1902? *Fearless* 18'
Hill	WA	1903-1907	1903 *Phryne* 18', 1907 *Robin* 18'
Holdsworth	Pyrmont	1850's	Fishing boats, yachts
Holmes, W	Sydney	1898-1903	1898 *Ira* 18', 1902 *Arawa* 18', 1903 *Wandeen* 14'
Howard	Balmain	1840's-1850's	Fishing boats
Hubbard, James E.	Glebe Point	1889-1905	1889 a 22' plus 2 x 24's *Volunteer* and *Mantura*,1892 *Aztec* 18', 1890's *OK* 18', 1893 *Ethel* 18' and an unnamed 22', 1894, *Ruby* 18' plus another 18', 1897 *Muriel* 18', 1904 an oil launch, 1905 40' fishing boat for Ulladulla
Hudson, A &G	WA	1907	1907 *My Lady Dainty* 18'
Hurst, Gus	Sydney	1941	1941 *Fern* 18'
Imber, Alec	Sydney	1945-1948	1945 *Crusader* 18', 1948 *Irene* 18' and *Midstream* 18'
Irvine, Captain	Pyrmont	1840's-50's	Whaleboats
Langford, William and Thomas	Millers Point	1859-1881	1859 *Fawn*, a ballasted open boat, 1866 *Nereid*, yacht, 1868 a 4-oared gig for Lyttleton NZ, 1870's *Alice* 15' deep keel, *Clio* 22' deep keel, *Coryphene* and *Mulgoa* (later *Adelphi*) 24' CB Fishing boats, *Myra* 16', *Tocal* 16', 1875 *Ripple* 24' and *Torment* 19' skiff, 1876 *Lizzie* 24' (one of the first 24' designed just for racing), 1877 *Snowdrop* 24' and a 22' waterman's skiff as a prize for the Sydney Mail newspaper, 1878 *Guinevere* 42' yacht,1879 *Oithona*, 43'9" yacht designed by Watson (UK), 1879 *Syren* 22' "one of the first of the modern racing models") and *Rosetta* 22'. Langford brothers were prolific and respected builders of all types of boats from 15-footers to yachts. Thomas died in 1877, William moved to Blues Point. William was killed in an industrial accident in 1881 aged 48.
Langford, Harry (son of Thomas)	Millers Point	1881-1903	1881 *Walter* 18' skiff, 1884 unknown 22', 1893? *Secret* 22', 1902 *Wallami* 18', 1903 *Alert* 18'

NAME	LOCATION	ACTIVE PERIOD	BOATS BUILT
Lomax	Balmain	1870's	Skiffs, sailing boats (15' and 22' deep keelers), whaleboats
Luke (Looke)	Balmain	1880's	Skiffs, whaleboats
Macbeth	Sussex St	1860's, 70's	Skiffs, whaleboats
McCleer, J	Brisbane	1880's	1881 *Eugene* 18' half-decker, 1889 *Bulletin* 22' (assisted by Jack Whereat, skipper)
McCleer, J (Jnr)	Brisbane	1930's	Prominent Brisbane 16'skiff builder, including a series of boats called *Dove*
McGoogan, George	Balmain	1940's, 1950's	1949 *Diane* 18', 1953 *Toogara* 18', restoration of *Yendys* 1983 at Cockatoo Is Dockyard
MacRitchie, Bob	Sydney	1905	1905 *Mona* (Donnelly design)
Mercer, Joe	Sydney	1953	1953 *Ajax* 18'
Messenger	Double Bay	1890's	The Messenger family ran a boat hire shed. 1893 *Willia* 24' (shortened to 22' late 1890's, 1890's *Flying Fish* 24' catamaran for Mark Foy (also shortened to 22' late 1890's)
Miller, Bill	Sydney	1946-53	1946 *Donnelly I* 18', 1949 *Donnelly II* (Too) 18', 1953 *Donnelly III* 18'
Minter, Ken	Sydney	1940's-60's	Ken was a prolific builder of 16-footers for himself (a series of boats called *Joan* after his wife) and others from the batten-seam era until well into the moulded boats era. He was one of the builders consulted for this work
Monteith	Kangaroo Point Brisbane	1880's-90's	22's
Morrow, F W	Sydney	1935	1935 *Lois* 18'
Morrow, Ken	Sydney	1949	1949 *Kangaroo* 18'
Munce, Wally	Sydney	1936	1936 *Burrawang* 18'
Newton, Fred (Podge)	Sydney	1913-15	1913 *Admiral* 18' (became *Mississippi* 1914), 1915 *Rosetta* 18'
Nimmo, W	Queensland	1896	1896 *Trilby* 18'
O'Rourke, Jimmy	Sydney	1940's-1960's	Jim worked for Willis Douglass after returning from the Second World War, and built and sailed many sixteen ft skiffs at Middle Harbour into the 1980's. Jim was one of the boatbuilders consulted for this work.
Parcell, Billy	Sydney	1906-09	1906 *Pheasant* 18', 1909 *Sunny South* 18'
Parkin, G?	Sydney	1933	1933 *Chance* 18'
Pearce, W	Sydney	1935-37	1935 *Pastime III* 18', 1937 *J.N.* 18'
Perry, George	Sydney	1908-1921	1908 *Eunice* 18' for Perth (Billy Golding design), 1913 *Eunice II* 18', 1921 *Sydney* 18' for Norm Blackman
Phillips, C	Balmain	1898	1 known 14'
Phillips, Tom	Balmain	1913-1944	Numerous 16' skiffs after 1913, 1924 *Furious* 18' (heel-less), 1937 *Hope* 18', 1938 *Novice* 18', 1944 *Aberdare II* 18'

NAME	LOCATION	ACTIVE PERIOD	BOATS BUILT
Phillips, Roy	Balmain	1946-1950	1946 *Sylvia Chase* 18', 1947 *Nerang II* 18', 1947 *The Tiger* 18' (with Horrie Balkwell), 1950 *Sylvia Too* 18'
Pontey, A	Sydney	1891	1891 *Cygnet*, one of the first recognisable 18-footers
Press, HC	Woolloomooloo	1880's - 1920's	1912? *Intrepid* 18', *H.C.Press* 18'. H.C.Press ran a boatshed and hire business in Woolloomooloo Bay as well as the shed at Audley in the Royal National Park, continued by George Press
Press, George	Woolloomooloo Double Bay	1921-53	George Press built a series of 18's for himself. He had Chris Webb steer them in the 1920's and took the mainsheet himself. After the late 1920's he steered the boats himself. 1921 *H.C.Press II*, 1925 *H.C.Press III* (snub), 1933 *H.C.Press IV*, 1935 *H.C.Press V* (7'-beamer for League, 1941 *H.C.Press VI* (back at the SFS), 1944 *H.C.Press VII* (6'3" beam), 1948 *H.C.Press VIII*, 1950 *H.C.Press IX*, 1953 *H.C.Press X*
Pritchard, HC	Leichhardt	1889-1904	Rowing skiffs, motor launches, 1889 24' half-decker, 1898 *Zephyr* 8' x 8', 1899 *Procella* 10'x 10', 1900 *Canaris* 28' Catboat! 1903 3 motor launches.
Pritchard, Harry and brother, sons of HC.	Careening Cove	1904-1936	Harry and his brother trained and worked with their father in Leichhardt and helped build, and sailed *Zephyr* and *Procella* (their sister Irene often steered) but when they set up in Careening Cove in 1904 they concentrated on motor launches, included racing them, and were involved in early high speed propellor design.
Rann, Tommy	North Qld	1924	1924 *Goodrod* 18' (Billy Spring design)
Read	Glebe Point	1885	1885 *Aeolus* 22'
Reynolds, Andrew	Balmain	1850-1877	Rowing skiffs, sailing boats. 1850-1860's numerous 15', 16' and 22' open keelers, 1875 *Ettie* 19'CB skiff, 1877 *Bronte* 24' ("last boat" of Reynolds) Reynolds was the mid-19th centuries leading builder of racing boats both sail and oar. Joe Donnelly was his star apprentice.
Robinson, Jack	Balmain	1906-08	1906 *Young Jack* 18', 1907 *Zanita* 18', 1908 *Livonia* 18' Jack was a noted skipper, and father of George.
Robinson, George	Balmain	1919-1947	1915 *Britannia* 6', 1919 *Britannia* 18', 1922 *Waitangi* 30 yacht, 1930 *Jean* 10', 1947 *Scamp* 18' (with son Ron), 1964 *Brit* 20' clinker launch (still afloat). Wee Georgie was the builder and skipper of *Britannia*, featured in this work.
Robinson, Ken	Balmain	1949	1949 *Brooklyn* 18' Ken is believed to be George's cousin.
Robinson, Ron	Balmain	1947	1947 *Scamp* 18' (with father George) Ron was a successful skipper in the 1950's and built his own laminated 18's. Ron was consulted in the process of building the replica *Britannia*.
Roddam	Sydney	1875	1875 *Surprise* 19' skiff
Rodrick (Roderick)	Sydney	1880's	14' dingies, including *Violet* and *Thomas Punch*
Sheather, CH	Sydney	1937	1937 *Strike* 18'

NAME	LOCATION	ACTIVE PERIOD	BOATS BUILT
Sheehy, Dan	Woolloomooloo	1858-1879	Yachts and open boats. 1858 *Australian* 30' yacht, 1864 *Xarifa* large yacht. 1860's open keelers *Blink Bonnie, Sybil* and *Thought*. Sheehy was Sydney's leading pioneer yacht and boat builder. In 1865 he employed 5 men, in 1867 he partnered with James Hayes, insolvent in 1879.
Speers, A	Sydney	1909	1909 *Sonia* 18'
Spring, Bill	Brisbane	1913	1913 *Recovery* 18'
Spring, Harold	Brisbane	1940-48	1940 *Reform* 18' (chine hull-banned), 1948 *Janet* 18'
Stannard, William	Double Bay	1888-9	Stannard ran a boatshed and hire business in Double Bay and built a range of vessels. He built the 24' *Our Jack* in 1888 and another in 1889
Stephens, William	Pyrmont	1860's-80's	General boat builder
Stephens, Bob	Pyrmont	1888-96	1880's *Ettie* 16', 1888 *Idothea* 24' for H.C.Press and another in 1889. Other 24's were *Enterprise* and *Isadore*. He built two 22 footers, *Violet,* and in 1896 *Figtree*. Bob Stephens was a prolific boatbuilder, probably son of William.
Stevens, E	Perth	1912	1912 *Kangaroo* 18'
Tait, Tom	Sydney	1915-1934	1915 *Tom Tait* 18'(became *Rocket* in 1916), 1922 *Eclipse* 18', Tom was a skipper who built his own boats and rebuilt Sam Williams' *Mavis* into *Eclipse II* in 1929, and rebuilt his his own 1922 *Eclipse* into *Springbok* in 1934
Thomas, F and Perry, G	Perth	1904	1904 *Aeolus* 18' to Billy Golding design
Tomlinson, Ted	Perth	1920	1920 *Parole* 18'
Townes	Newcastle	1898	1898 *Myee* 18' Townes was a leading general boatbuilder in the Newcastle area.
Underwood	Sydney Cove	1820's-40's	Whaleboats, ships Underwood was a former convict who became Sydney's first leading boatbuilder and shipbuilder and successful merchant including a fleet of whalers.
Ward, C and Allen and Ward	Dawes Point and Balmain	1880's	General boatbuilding
Ware, Chick	Sydney	1935-36	1935 *Betty I* 18', 1936 *Victor I* 18'
Ware, Ernie	Brisbane	1933	1933 *Marjorie Too* 18'
Watts and Wright	Brisbane	1937-1950	Nine eighteens: 1937 *Marjorie (III)*, 1946 *Culex*, 1947 *Culex II* and *Alstar*, 1948 *Marjorie (IV)* (known as *Marjorie Too*), 1949 *Culex III*, 1950 *Alstar II* and *Buccaneer I* and *J.M.H*
Watts, Lance	Brisbane	1949	1949 *Flying Fish II* 18'
Watts, Lance and Harold	Brisbane	1952	*Frolic,* first moulded 18

NAME	LOCATION	ACTIVE PERIOD	BOATS BUILT
Whereat, JH (Jack)	Brisbane	1893-1935	1893 *Vera* 18', 1896 *Ibex* 18', 1899 *Nellie* 18', 1915 *M.J.B* 18', 1922 *Ou-La-Lah II* 18', 1925 *Defiance* 18', 1929 *Kiwi* 18', 1933 *The Mistake* 18' (with Lance Watts), 1934 *Fourex* 18', 1935 *Valora* 18'
Whereat, AJ (Toby)	Brisbane	1920's-1933	Toby was a 5-time Australian Champion in 16' skiffs, and built his own boats. He is credited with doing away with the heel on the 16's in the early 1920's, and built *Aberdare* 18' on skiff principles in 1932 which revolutionised the sport. He died in 1933 of pneumonia but lived long enough to see just how fast *Aberdare* was.
Whitehouse and Spring	Brisbane	1950	1950 *Helen* 18'
Williams, Sam	Pyrmont	1896-1922	1896 *Australian (I)*, 1898 *Keriki* 22', 1904 *Mavis* 18', 1909 *Advance* 18', 1912 *Quibree* 18', 1922 *N.S.W* 18' Williams apprenticed with Donnelly
Williams, Cyrus	Brisbane	1891	1891 *Truant* 18'
Winspear & Smith	Sydney	1933	1933 *Yarranabbe* 18'
Wood, R (Woodhead?)	Brisbane	1897	1897 *Wilo* 22' (designed by F.Cowell)
Woodforth, Lester	Sydney	1942-47	1942 *Swansea* 18', 1945 *Top Dog III* 18', 1946 *Planet* 18', 1947 *No Mistake* 18'
Wright, Norm Snr	Bulimba, Brisbane	1912-1947	Founder of Norman Wright and Sons. Many ten-footers, 14-footers, ten known 18's: 1912 *Vanity*, 1915 *Langham*, 1916 *Thelma*, 1918 *Thelma II*, 1919 *Thelma III* (became *Keriki* 1920), 1937 *Joyce III*, 1938 *Joyce IV* and *Taree*, 1946 *Iris*, 1947 *Top Weight II*
Wright, Norm Jnr	Bulimba, Brisbane	1946-52	6 known 18's: 1946 *Sea Witch*, and *Australia* and *Jenny II (Too)*, 1947 *Jenny III*, 1950 *Jenny IV*, 1952 *Jenny V* Norman Wright and Sons were Brisbane's leading builders of everything from dinghies to large yachts and motor craft. They were also leading skippers.
Yarrow, Fred	Brisbane	1899	1899 Aeolus 18'
Yates	Woolloomooloo	1860's to 1885	Yates was an early builder of centreboard fishing boats, having built two in 1865 and 1866; built *Sea Spray* and *Wyvern* 24' gentlemen's fishing boats in the early 1870's.
			This list will be added to as information comes to hand, and will eventually find its way onto the Boatbuilders page on www.openboat.com.au if I live long enough.

Appendix III: Towards a Study of the Recording of Heritage Skills

When the process that led to this book began over a decade ago, I enrolled in a course at UTS in Public History to learn oral history techniques. I told the lecturer about my intention to document the construction of a batten-seam boat, and asked was there any guidance from the academic world over the recording of heritage skills. Her answer was no, no-one had ever thought of it.

There are certainly many individual efforts. In the boatbuilding field, Howard Chapelle was a pioneer in documenting not only the boats but the construction methods. John Gardiner continued the tradition and was better at recording the processes as he spent much of his time teaching those processes. In other fields a number of books exist on the subject of cooperage, and you can find out about bronze casting, plumbing with lead, metal spinning and even a little about cotton sailmaking, though I suspect that at least in the latter case many of the finer details have not been recorded. Video recording of heritage skills is a new field, but the pioneers are making it up as they go along and there are as yet no standards, though some work along these lines has been done in Sweden.

Why do we need it? Well many of the processes have been mechanised, but <u>somebody</u> needs to know the basic skills in order to design, build and maintain the machines. Lost skills may be found to be useful again in unknown ways as technology advances, but is of no use unless recorded. Mankind has invented lots of techniques for all sorts of things, and although we may not need to actually train someone in a process that is no longer used, it is important to <u>record</u> it. Archaeologists had to re-invent flint-knapping, and there is a whole fascinating subject of Experimental Archaeology where extinct processes are re-created, but how good would it be to find that the ancients had written down all they knew. It has happened, Greek and Roman building methods were well-documented, and it has been invaluable for those involved in restoration.

Standards and guidelines are needed, the body of knowledge of documenting of skills needs to be examined to see if best practice principles could benefit newcomers to the field. Areas with inadequate documentation could be identified. There's a whole exciting new discipline to be established, anyone? Anyone?

Ian Hugh Smith December 2016

Final word:
The author's research and his fascination with these boats will continue in the website
www.openboat.com.au
A 15 minute video "Building Britannia" with footage from 2001-2002 is on the website Videos page and YouTube at https://youtu.be/kMaClFVOf30 (or type Building Britannia into YouTube search).

 Ian Hugh Smith has had a forty-plus year career in boatbuilding and boatbuilding education, during which he built upwards of 80 wooden boats from dinghies to yachts. He set up the Sydney Wooden Boat School in 1990 and has taught hundreds of first-timers to build their own boats. With a long-standing interest in maritime heritage he joined the emerging Australian Historical Sailing Skiff Association which builds, sails and displays traditional Aussie Open Boats and built a six-footer *Balmain Bug* and ten-footer *Republic* to join the growing replica fleet. In 2001-2 he built the 18-footer replica *Britannia,* and still sails it every Summer Saturday with the replica fleet at the Sydney Flying Squadron.

www.ingramcontent.com/pod-product-compliance
Lightning Source LLC
Chambersburg PA
CBHW041714290426
44110CB00025B/2834